DISEMB●DIED

POETICS

AMERICAN POETRY SERIES

LEE BARTLETT
General Editor

NATHANIEL TARN
Views from the Weaving Mountain
Selected Essays in Poetics & Anthropology

WILLIAM EVERSON
Naked Heart
Talking on Poetry, Mysticism, & the Erotic

MICHAEL MCCLURE
Lighting the Corners
On Art, Nature, and the Visionary
Essays and Interviews

ANNE WALDMAN AND ANDREW SCHELLING, EDITORS
Disembodied Poetics
Annals of the Jack Kerouac School

D I S E M

EDITED BY

ANNE
WALDMAN

&

ANDREW
SCHELLING

POETICS

ANNALS
OF THE
JACK KEROUAC
SCHOOL

B O DIED

UNIVERSITY OF NEW MEXICO PRESS
ALBUQUERQUE

C © N

Library of Congress Cataloging-in-Publication Data
Disembodied poetics : annals of the Jack Kerouac School /
edited by Anne Waldman & Andrew Schelling.—1st ed.
p.   cm.
Includes bibliographical references.
Contents: The activist front—Talking poetics—Gnosis—Film—
Ancestral presences—Documents from the Jack Kerouac School.
ISBN 0-8263-1517-8 (cl) ISBN 0-8263-1518-6 (pbk.)
1. Poetics.   I. Waldman, Anne, 1945–   .   II. Schelling, Andrew.
III. Jack Kerouac School of Disembodied Poetics.
PN1042.D57   1994
801'.951—dc20   94-3206
CIP

Designed by Linda Mae Tratechaud

TENTS

CONTENTS

CKNOWLEDGMENTS

Many people have helped with this book—searching out tapes, transcribing lectures, corresponding with contributors, offering encouragement and advice. We want to thank Bil Brown, Bruce Burrows, Rebecca Bush, David Cope (for his work on "A Declaration of Interdependence"), Danika Dinsmore, Christopher Funkhauser, James Grauerholtz, Anselm Hollo, Robert Masterson, Chuck Pirtle, Randy Roark, Eleni Sikelianos, Kimi Sugioka, and Katie Yates.

Several of these talks and essays have already appeared in magazine, journal, or book form:

- Amiri Baraka's "Cultural Revolution" in *Callaloo*.
- Bernadette Mayer's "From: A Lecture at Naropa" and Leslie Scalapino's "Thinking Serially" in *Poetics Journal*.
- William S. Burroughs' "Screenwriting and the Potentials of Cinema" in *Writing in a Film Age*, Keith Cohen, ed. (University Press of Colorado, 1991). Thanks to Keith Cohen for providing footnote information.
- Portions of Clark Coolidge's "Kerouac" appeared in *Talisman*. Portions of the "Philip Whalen Zen Interview" have appeared in *Gas, The Shambhala Sun*, and *Mountain Record*.
- Susan Howe's "The Captivity and Restoration of Mary Rowlandson" in *Birthmark: Unsettling the Wilderness in American Literary History* (Wesleyan University Press, 1993).
- Andrew Schelling's "Mounting the Poetry Vehicle" in the *Denver Quarterly*.
- Anne Waldman's "Rocky Flats: Warring God Charnel Ground" and Allen Ginsberg's "Negative Capability: Kerouac's Buddhist Ethic" in *Tricycle: The Buddhist Review*.

We also thank The Fund for Poetry and The Rex Foundation for generous support of the Jack Kerouac School, which assisted us in the editorial costs of this book.

ANDREW SCHELLING AND ANNE WALDMAN

INTRODUCTION

In an older, more civilized day than ours—a day at least when subtle thinkers and skilled practitioners of the experimental arts seemed less at variance with the ruling powers—a range of schools opened their doors to wandering writers. There were halls of training in China where poetry comprised the standard curriculum for scholars and civil servants. On the island of Lesbos, it is conjectured by scholars and poets, Sappho's *moisopholon domos* or "house of the muses" enjoyed a lively reputation, one of several such houses. In diverse *akademis* or oak groves throughout the Hellenic world, philosophers and rhapsodists met to talk, debate, swap poems and songs, or test out theories. The annals of these "schools" comprise one of our precious heritages.

In probably the largest, most visionary experiment yet attempted on our planet to house this sort of education, a string of *viharas* sprang up across North India between the fifth and eleventh centuries. Part monastery, part college, part convention hall or alchemist's lab, these massive universities welcomed not just contemplatives, wizards, hermits, and yogins of the Buddhist world, but all manner of artists. Wandering the sandstone courtyards and cool hallways, writers, sculptors, dancers, actors, editors, logicians, and linguists encountered one another. Pilgrims from T'ang Dynasty China visited, as did *gymnasts* from Greece. Of these centers, best known was Nalanda University—in present-day Bihar State you can see ruins of the buildings that housed as many as 10,000 scholars at a time. The renowned teacher and Tantric adept Naropa served as abbot of Nalanda for a spell, before setting out from its symposium halls and shrine rooms to pursue further studies elsewhere.

When sophistry grows, however, or information comes under rigid control, schools that can accommodate an activist, engaged gathering of scholars and artists come under siege. The siege may be explicit or subtle, but in response an adversary or "outrider" tradition develops. Scour history and you'll find heretical schools which were persecuted, some swiftly and cruelly destroyed—the Cathar Troubadours of southern France come to mind. Other schools never dared make themselves public—only whispered accounts remain—like the School of Night to which Chapman and Marlowe may have belonged, if such a school in fact existed. More commonly, the schools simply slip out of sight, away from the public eye. But like monasteries of the European Dark Ages which survived along the wild Irish coastlines, they keep lit some flame.

This continent has seen countless experiments—socialist, utopian, antinomian, countercultural, Fourierist, buccaneer, radical, dissident, heretical, underground. The Jack Kerouac School of Disembodied Poetics resembles these "outrider" experiments more than it does an ordinary college, not least because it sets up shop on the grounds of The Naropa Institute, first Buddhist college in North America, direct descendant of the *viharas* of India, and the only college this side of the Bering Straits to found itself upon a tradition of contemplative practice.

The Kerouac School is an *akademi* of writing and poetics at which a peripatetic faculty gathers, disperses, and gathers again— a faculty that is out in the world—active, doing things, engaged. The flavor of their teaching is as various as their jobs, their lives, their travels and love affairs, their studies—it is informal, inflammatory, activist—a socratic rap or rhapsody that takes up issues as various as militant naturalism, race, feminism, ethnology, and of course Language. Yes, we invite them here to transmit their secret hard-won knowledge, to address the fronts on which they're active, to magnetize and instruct apprentice writers and like-minded seekers. These high-altitude grounds in Boulder, Colorado are grounds which incite acts of poetic license. Grounds on which students move toward acts that in contemporary America seem profoundly subversive—clear seeing, trust in the wisdom of one's own mind, compassionate action, and the development of a tough-minded language.

Crafted language. Hence *poetics*—which is the theory and technique of *making* something out of words. Tough work, this making— fragile as the breath it stirs upon, delicate as books, delivering messages and maps for the apprentice traveler. Is the intention of poetry so important then, this concern with how one makes it? Of course. It is likely that since humans began to speak they have

ANDREW SCHELLING AND ANNE WALDMAN

noticed how swiftly accurate language dispels confusion—lively language, free language, language that crosses conceptual boundaries to return with reports of what lies beyond. Poetics is not about rhetoric, not about the old verse-against-prose contest. A poetics by nature harbors contradictions. It takes in the vagabond phrase, the unarticulated desire, the thought that has nowhere else to sleep. Not consistency, but "what works"; what survives and lets others survive—poetics is a bag of tricks like Krazy Kat's, and newcomers, interlopers, mavericks embellish it at each turn.

This book locates not *a* poetics but many poetics, variegated and outspoken as the writers involved. Each essay printed here is a *disembodied poetics*—a spoken poetics revisited. Our faculty air their ideas orally, their voices come alive for a second time—this time on the printed page. Some speak spontaneously, others spit upon and polish a well-cadenced phrase; a few request some other voice to animate their own, thus the interview. Some write manifestos, others mythologies; some investigate history and revise the past; others examine the flickering of celluloid, or the flickering out of biological species. What rises from the page is of interest, of passionate interest. A community exists to listen, and to challenge the thoughts as they come forth. We offer the same to you.

Andrew Schelling and Anne Waldman
12 October 1993
Boulder, Colorado

PART ONE

THE
ACTIVIST
FRONT

PART ONE

1

THE
ACTIVIST
FRONT

CULTURAL REVOLUTION AND THE LITERARY CANON

The reactionary trend of the 1950s which produced McCarthyism and the Hollywood and academic purges, the Korean War, and Eisenhower was reflected in American literature by its domination by a punishingly dry, highly mannered magazine verse equipped with hot and cold running Latin and Greek phrases mit footnotes and the emotional significance of a *New York Times* crossword puzzle.

This kind of literature was trumpeted and proselytized by the so-called New Criticism, which sought to remove all social relationship from poetry, from literature generally, making it a completely solipsistic and elitist artifact that jingled stiffly about its not not self.

As it turned out the New Critics were hardly that. Their leaders like Allen Tate, John Crowe Ransom, Cleanth Brooks, and Robert Penn Warren were identified with the Southern Agrarian Movement. (Allen Tate's book *Reactionary Essays* says most of it!) The Southern Agrarians preached a national chauvinist and metaphysical sentimentalization of the Chattel Slave Empire, claiming that industrialization was destroying the South and a culture that ranked with the Greek Attic.

But the raised level of U.S. productive forces after WWII and the Korean War expanded advanced industrial labor and educational access to a much broader segment of the U.S. population, particularly to the second-generation immigrants and new generations of blacks. There were ideas set in motion that disrupted the basic disposition of class forces in post-Korean War U.S., that challenged the basic social relations of the society, particularly to class privilege in the U.S. and white supremacy, the fundamental social organization of imperialist U.S. society.

On one hand there was the group of largely petty bourgeois white youth who were called the Beat Generation, who claimed to rebel against the complacent mediocre hypocrisy of American life. This middle-class rebellion appeared in literature heralded by Allen Ginsberg's poem *Howl*. The so-called Beats, along with other young

American poets (e.g., the New York School of Frank O'Hara, Koch and Ashbery, the Black Mountain poets identified with Charles Olson and Robert Creeley) challenged the polished ready-made academic poetry as lifeless and socially irrelevant. They also challenged the American petty bourgeois lifestyle with their varied versions of mid-twentieth-century American bohemia.

But an even larger and even more sharply anti-imperialist development in the 1950s was the rise of the Civil Rights Movement and the most recent major upsurge in the continuing African American National Democratic Movement, the 1960s Black Liberation Movement, from the 1954 Supreme Court decision to desegregate public schools "with all deliberate speed" which apparently is extremely slow. (But that's just 35 years ago!) The movement took on momentum with the MLK-led Montgomery bus boycott of 1957, the formation of SCLC and SNCC and the student movement, the sit-ins, freedom rides, countless demonstrations as the MLK-led "nonviolent" civil rights phase peaked by 1963 and the March on Washington, and Malcolm X emerged as the new maximum leader of the movement, ushering in a more militant period, with Stokely Carmichael, Rap Brown, Huey Newton, the Black Panthers, "US," RNA, and CAP rising to make revolutionary challenges to imperialism and white supremacy.

The largely white anti-war movement that rose at the same time took shape as part of the general resistance to Vietnam era U.S. imperialism but influenced in great part by the African-American movement.

Any period of sharp social upsurge produces a corresponding arts and cultural movement reflecting the social motion in the arts and culture. In the nineteenth century, the antislavery movement gave rise to the slave narratives, a whole genre of powerful American writing revealing the material, ideological, and psychological basis for continuing U.S. racism.

At the same time a more original (i.e., less imitative of Europe) native U.S. literature arose from other sectors of the society as well. The work of Melville, Whitman, Dickinson, and Twain revealed this development, but such work was attacked or ignored by the still

Tory-dominated academic and official culture which was, and still is, English and European. The works' very "Americanness" made them untraditional in form and content. Part of the backwardness of official U.S. culture is its continued domination by Europe, and America never has been Europe.

In the early twentieth century, as whole cities of African-American people moved from the south to north and were transformed from rural dwellers to urban, from farmers to industrial workers, an anti-colonial, anti-imperialist movement came into sharp relief throughout the world, particularly throughout the black world. The frenzied industrialization of and preparation for World War I itself raised the level of productive forces so that the newly developed world-girdling form of capitalism, imperialism, also gave rise to ideas in its superstructure advanced enough to counter it.

Du Bois founded the Niagara Movement (1907) and the Pan Africanist Movement (1901). One was the first major integrated domestic organization of the twentieth century to fight for democracy and equality for the African-American people. The other was the beginning of the effort to unite African peoples worldwide to resist their common enemy, imperialism, in the form of colonialism and white supremacy.

The African-American people had been betrayed by the U.S. government and the destruction of Reconstruction after the Civil War. Instead of reaping the fruits of emancipation (1863) called for by the Thirteenth, Fourteenth, Fifteenth Amendments and forty acres and a mule, black people had been reattacked by the newly formed Ku Klux Klan and gradually forced back into a neo-slavery, disenfranchised and legally segregated by the end of the nineteenth century. The so-called Black Codes imposed on the black population in the South instead of full U.S. citizenship proved to be the model for Hitler's racial laws. This is understandable since fascism is fundamentally about slave labor. But under fascism even white people can be slaves!

The black arts and cultural movement in this early part of the twentieth century was called the Harlem Renaissance, but of course it was not limited to Harlem. Harlem had become the largest black city in the world. And that was where the unifying force of the newly rejuvenated black thrust for democracy, in its domestic and international forms, was focused.

This literary, arts, and cultural movement produced great writers like James Weldon Johnson, Langston Hughes, Zora Neale Hurston, Jean Toomer, and Claude McKay (not to mention Duke Ellington, Louis Armstrong, Bessie Smith, Aaron Douglass, among so many others). It was an art that reflected the social movement of the Pan-African peoples as it expressed itself through every aspect of their lives.

Hughes's *Negro Artist and the Racial Mountain* was even a formal challenge to the social and aesthetic values of the segregated white supremacist U.S. and called for an attention by black artists to the lives and culture of the black masses as the inspirational muse that would create a great African-American Art.

The more genuine American theater that O'Neill helped create during the same period saw black characters on the stage in something approaching realism for the first time, as well as an American working class. In fact the so-called age of Modernism, one general reaction to the breakdown of the nineteenth-century formalism, metaphysics, and idealism of the Western world, its passage from competitive capitalism to monopoly, cannot be fully explained by telling us about the O'Neills, Steins, Pounds, Eliots, WCWs, Stravinskys, Picassos unless we also hear about the Harlem Renaissance and with that the Negritude, Negrismo, Indigisme movements in Europe, West Indies, Africa, and Latin America which it catalyzed.

The outbreak of the 1960s, the third major political upsurge by the African-American people in a history of continued struggle for equality and self-determination, also gave rise to an arts and cultural movement. The Black Arts Movement and, with that the Black Theater Movement, wanted to create a poetry, a literature, which directly reflected the civil rights and black liberation movements. We wanted an art that was recognizably African-American (like Duke Ellington or Billie Holiday or Charlie Parker), that was mass-oriented, a poetry for instance that could come out of the libraries into the streets where the people were. Not a poetry whose very profundity was measured by who it didn't reach, by who it was not relevant to. A poetry that was direct, understandable, moving, and political. And lastly an art that was revolutionary, poetry that would help transform society, not merely lament or mystify the status quo.

People like Larry Neal, Askia Toure, Henry Dumas, Amus Mor, Carolyn Rogers, Mari Evans, Sonia Sanchez, and Leroi Jones emerged along with thousands of others to raise a black art that was a continuation of the social uprising that fought to change society itself, as well as writers like James Baldwin and Lorraine Hansberry whose great writings began just before this period, and in some ways even set the tone for it.

The challenge to society brought with it a challenge to the philosophical, aesthetic, and institutional superstructure of the society as well, since it is not just the material base of the society that is imperialist but the ideas reflected in its superstructure as well.

The idea of Black Art was to challenge the "whiteness" of art as posited by a white supremacist society, as if somehow the society could be a slave society but the art not reflect that slave-owning and slave-being mentality.

The literary canon, for instance, that accreted self-aggrandizement and solipsistic conquerors' mentality that is referenced as the greatness and profundity of so-called Western Art, Western Philosophy, is simply that, a body of materials whose content supposedly is the aspired revelation and evolution of humankind, but is in reality nothing but a justification (not very convincing) for imperialism. When Bloom and the other mothers accuse anti-imperialist thinkers of relativism in opposition to his colonial absolutism he is correct but unenlightened.

The attempt to re-establish the power of the actually nineteenth-century imperialist retake on so-called classic Western values and their fragile but sweaty kitbag of "masterpieces" is part of the normative reaction to any progressive or revolutionary social period. That is, like the Sisyphus myth, the rock is pushed up the hill, but then it is rolled partially back down again.

After the 1960s attack on the social and aesthetic values of U.S. imperialism, the late 1970s saw reaction rising by the time of Jimmy Carter, with both Malcolm X and Martin Luther King shot to death, and both Kennedys shot to death, equally mysteriously. The 1960s had raised the questions of the multicultural and multinational character of society and had challenged the white supremacist origins of the so-called literary and artistic canon.

In education Black Studies was set up in many schools, though it has yet to reach the high school and elementary school level and is still shaky even on the university level. To show you how deeply and profoundly cultural revolution is necessary to continue any political advantage the insurgents make, understand the falsity of an English Department when this has never been England, and the strength of the English Departments in contrast to American Studies or Black Studies. After the U.S. Revolutionary War, the Tories continued their hold on the superstructure until this day. We still have a colonial relationship with England in our arts and culture. Broadway, for instance, is still the home of old British playwagons.

The social thrust of democracy and anti-imperialism carried with it ideas that attacked the Eurocentric bourgeois nature of American education and official arts and pushed for a multinational and multicultural American culture and art expression that reflected reality. Just as the society was attacked as an oppressive exploitative one, so the literature, the art, was attacked as merely reflecting that exploitation, and being equally exploitative.

Mao Zedong's prescription for Cultural Revolution was as a continuing political struggle in the sphere of arts and culture to maintain the dominance of the working class and revolutionary ideas in the superstructure. Mao said further that if the Chinese Communist Party could not mount and maintain such a cultural revolution then the party would "change colors" and become a bourgeois party, even a fascist party. We can see from events at Tiananmen Square the tragic accuracy of Mao's teaching.

In the U.S. since the revolutionary trends of the 1960s there has been a distinct counterrevolutionary and reactionary trend. On one hand assassinations, jailings, and exiles disrupted a great part of the movement, both black and white, according to the Cointelpro documents and papers received through the Freedom of Information Act.

This meant that not only were the basic gains of the progressive period called into question as surely as the Baake decision called into question affirmative action, but as the Carter years gave way to the Reagan years many of the things we had struggled for in the 1960s were openly agitated against. Witness, for instance, how the term "Liberal" by the late 1980s had become almost akin to how "Communist" was used in the 1950s. Opposition to affirmative action was made vague by opposing "quotas" instead, but the effect was the same.

By the same measure calls for a restoration of the Eurocentric and white supremacist so-called Greco-Roman, Judaeo-Christian standard of philosophical and aesthetic measure are really calls for a restoration of the social norms of the pre-rebellion 1950s. For instance the way subjects are understood and classified and taught in the university confirms the segregation and white supremacy of the foulest aspect of the material base.

Historical periods of American literature are routinely taught in a divided, nationally segregated fashion. Twentieth-century American literature is taught that does not connect Euro-American Modernism with the Harlem Renaissance, or the Beat Generation with the Black Arts Movement. Nineteenth-century literature removes Fred Douglass, Moses Roper, William Welles Brown, Nat Turner, Linda Brent, etc. from the literature and any aspect of the slave's life is made sociological. But to quote Bruce Franklin, "African-American culture is not peripheral to American culture but at its heart." So that by ascribing some metaphysical racial greatness to the role of works corresponding to the bourgeois American canon not only is the history of the world distorted for oppression's sake but the very psychological development of the American people, certainly that of its *soi disant* intellectuals on these campuses.

For one thing the African people had a different aesthetic basis before our transportation to the New World. It was based on the animist philosophy which sees everything in existence as "living" but to different degrees, an aesthetic whose ancient religion was characterized by priest and congregation in a call and response relationship, in which the spirit that was to be sought could only be brought into proximity by music, and whose highest aspiration was to become possessed by that *allest* spirit.

These multiregistrations of being were reflected by the polyrhythms of the music (speech and thought) and by the polychromatic registration of bright color. Art was always preeminently social, for all from all, a part of the very development of the total society.

The separateness of art from mass concern, the emphasis on the Apollonian attributes of form and restraint, the enslavement of women by the rising philosophy and society of the northern cradle of Greece and Co., the ultimate separation of thought from emotion as Nietzsche testified to in his *Birth of Tragedy* (Hamlet's disease of liberalism) are all social, philosophical, and aesthetic verifications of the culture manifest above the Mediterranean, after the ancient African-derived cultures were put in check politically and ultimately dominated. Women still carrying on the Dionysian ecstatic culture of the southern culture cradle were lynched by the Apollonian demagogues up into our own society at Salem witch burnings.

In addition to the traditional and historically developed differences of the African aesthetic, certainly the role of slave in relationship to slavemaster creates even larger distances of social and class perspective that must inform any black aesthetic. To impose the Apollonian, the formal, the academic above the creative, the womb man ness of art, is part of imperialism's continuing work which seeks not content but only form, not ecstasy but memoranda, and chauvinism and narrowness instead of the cosmopolitan, and the spontaneous or improvised, is imperialist superstructural work.

This is why the cultural revolution is so important today. We are in the midst of a deep reactionary period when revolution is once again held up as fantastic and only cynicism and betrayal and upholding the status quo qualify as realism. In the 1960s indeed, "Revolution Is the Main Trend in the World Today," that's what we used to say. "Countries want Independence, Nations want Liberation, People want Revolution." But that is when the principal contradiction in the world was Imperialism vs. the People and Nations. But soon after, the contradiction of Imperialism vs. Imperialism, which is the trend that leads to imperialist war, became principal, and the revolutionary movements were turned around by rising fascism.

We are at a crossroads in that struggle today. The attempt to restore the so-called literary canon to make political prisoners of world art and culture in the name of some self-aggrandizing superculture with neither origins nor relationship to the rest of the world is simply white supremacy returned. You cannot speak of Greek culture without relating it to the whole of the ancient world from which it sprang and which it continues to reflect.

In the Channel 13 bit of Goebbelsmania called *The Art of the Western World*, a statement was made that "Creativity began in Greece." Naturally I wrote letters to them and a number of other folks challenging this mindless protofascism. A white rock critic for the Star Ledger told me "Creativity did begin in Greece . . . for the Europeans." Any way you take this it's gas chamber logic, but then this was Boy speaking not Tarzan.

There is no life or culture, no art or philosophy separated from the whole expression of human life and being on the planet. It is the separation that is the first strand of barbed wire for the fences at Auschwitz, the more modern versions of southern plantations.

For those of us in the arts or the universities, those of us involved with the institutions and ideas of the U.S. superstructure, we must see that the only positive direction we can go, that is the direction of life supported over death, is cultural revolution. We must oppose the re-institution of the racist canon, like we resist Part 25 of *Friday the 13th* or *Rambo 11*.

For instance, we must join forces to socialize the university and all institutions that affect our lives. By socialize I mean to make the university deal with real life and the actual society in which it stands. If the university is the repository for higher learning, advanced philosophy, and innovative technology, why are the cities in which they stand so bereft of these resources? There is no other way to measure ideas' usefulness except in the crucible of real life.

The university professor is never made to measure his ideas in relationship to the real world, in relation to how much change (i.e., human advance) or how close to reality the world measures those ideas to be, but is valorized only by the abstract and frankly elitist interacademic dialogue. We publish for each other or to get tenure, we create and do research for the same reasons. While the great challenge, real life, real society, stands ailing and ill because our resources have been removed.

Why poor education, unemployment, no housing, drug panics in these cities and communities of our world if the universities are full of so many self-proclaimed geniuses and mountains of ominously profound conclusions? The university must be made to relate to these cities, to establish partnerships in developing real life to higher and higher levels of understanding and sophistication, not stand aside and praise itself for being so clean and so heavy and so outside everything, as is mostly now the case.

The cultural revolution at the university must see Black Studies, Latino Studies, Woman and Labor Studies as the missing links of progressive education and preparation for a new and more humanized world society. Ignorance and lack of education must be made extinct. It is dangerous to the whole world for uneducated masses to exist. The extent to which we raise the world educational level is the extent to which we raise our own consciousness and the level of human life on the planet.

Such studies must also be extended to the high schools and elementary schools, and used in psychological tests for public employees to make sure none of them suffers from the vicious illness of racism and male chauvinism or some other fascist malady which we will lament once we see another black youth stretched out on the ground with a bullet in his head, not for playing his radio too loud, but for being black or Latino, or raped, not for playing her radio too loud, but for being a woman.

Another critical aspect of Cultural Revolution is that we must support the presence of art and artists in the educational process from elementary through university. Art is the main force against Arent. It is the creative aspect through which Being is maintained. The development and destiny of humanity is contained more directly in essence in its art than any other dimension. The very devaluing of art is evident throughout society. There is no university without art. Art is the social life of humanity, its philosophical expression the ideological reflection of human life. To devalue it is to devalue creativity. Talk about creativity to the big money guys, and it's, ha ha, a joke, you know. Yet their big money comes from the control of people and society through the control of their art, from the most basic art, the creation of society itself, to the articles of its expression. Whether clothes, furniture, music, food, houses, it is all art. Let us be clear it is not academic life that is principal but creative life, the question of human development and evolution. The critical, the academic, are secondary aspects, absolutely necessary, but not to be confused with the making of what is, the continuing of life in opposition to death.

o o o

BARAKA: I guess I'm supposed to take some questions now. If there are questions I'd be glad to answer them.

BOBBIE LOUISE HAWKINS: I don't have a question so much as something you brought up earlier in the panel. It went by really fast and I'd like to see it brought back. When you said "representative democracy"—I think there are probably people in here who don't understand the functioning of representative democracy as opposed to a party system.

BARAKA: Let me say this: this is a republic, actually. This is not a democracy, which is the great jammed toilet of the age . . . this is a republic, which means indirect representation, see. When they say "democracy" they actually mean the old Greek model in the first place, they mean two hundred guys living off the backs of a hundred thousand slaves, is what they mean. And that is why you can see in the Southern culture a continuance of the old Greek Attic philosophy. What I meant, when I said "direct democracy," I meant that there should be no electors in our way. For instance, I mean you don't vote for the president, the whole thing is a joke, a canard from the beginning. And that democracy should be in the schools, in the factories, it should be direct, and at the place of it, it should not just be "Uh, you vote for Jojo & then Jojo goes right on ya," you know what I mean? I mean, it should be definitely *direct democracy*. The whole Constitution needs to be grappled with by those of us who think we've gone beyond the Constitution. Because we haven't gone beyond it, we haven't even got up to it. That is, bourgeois democracy has not been sufficiently flushed out of its corner. In other words, we can't take people to socialism because we can't get them past the limits of bourgeois democracy, because we haven't taken bourgeois democracy to the hoop. We have to take bourgeois democracy to the hoop and dunk it. And then we can be talking about socialism. That's what I was saying.

HAWKINS: I was thinking of the Danish system, which is a representative system. For instance, in a representative system you would not have such a thing as an appointed vice president. In a representative system, if you had these offices going begging, a presidential office, a vice presidential office, what would happen is every one in the country would vote, and the one who got the most votes would be president, and the one who got the second most votes would be vice president.

BARAKA: Absolutely. See, you're saying "Denmark," but that's the U.S. Constitution. Party politics have obscured the Constitution. If you read the U.S. Constitution, you'll find out that that's the way it's supposed to be. It's still whoever gets the most votes is president, but in the U.S. Constitution, it's whoever gets the second most votes is vice president. But they're two separate elections. You know, I tried to mash that on Jesse Jackson in 1988 in Atlanta, to tell him that this was the time to do that. They were stalled on the floor. I told him, "Now, if you were to move for vice president, the sentiment is such that you could get it. You could go back to the Constitution to justify it, and you could push it over." But his addiction to the Democratic Party is what stifled that. You see, if you go back through the Constitution, you'll find out that there's more democracy in it than we know. But what they do is wave their hands at the Constitution, knowing that the radicals will never even look at it. "It's a corny document, I don't even want to see it." The radicals go past it, then wonder why they can't get people to go beyond it. It's because they haven't got up to it yet. That's really the question. You know, direct democracy, we have to begin to talk about that. All of these so-called intelligent people . . . it amazes me that we're always putting down these policies. We're talking bad about "Reagan is an actor," "Bush is this," and so on—but if they're running our lives, then what does that make us? If all these people are chumps, then what does that make us? That's my question, you know. A chump's chump's chump's chump.

HAWKINS: I just want to say two things and then I'll sit down. One is, get rape off t.v.!

BARAKA: Yeah. Get rape off t.v.! Get t.v. off t.v.!

HAWKINS: And one is tax the robots.

BARAKA: Say what?

HAWKINS: *Tax* the robots. The reason they're running out of money is because they're financing factories to robotize, and all those people are out of jobs, and there isn't that tax income, so we have to tax the robots.

BARAKA: Now let me pose this to you all. In 1945, when we "won" the Second World War, our enemies were Germany and Japan. Remember that? Since then, we have trashed our allies, who were Russia and China—those were our allies in the fight against fascism. The two fascists have become the masters of the world economy—check it out—and you should check that the transfer of capital from the United States to Germany and Japan, since 1945 to now, is where your jobs are. All the manufacturing jobs—look in the back of your clothes—you want to know where all the jobs are? Look in the back of your clothes.

Before the Second World War, the corporate powers effected an alliance between Standard Oil, Krupps, the people who made the cyclon-B gas that they used to gas the Jews—what's the name of that company?

ANSELM HOLLO: I. G. Farben.

BARAKA: Farben, right. Krupp, Farben, Standard Oil, Matsushita, and Mitsubishi. And they said this: no matter who wins the war, that all these corporations will not pass into the public coffers. You remember that the spoils go to the victors? Well those corporations never passed into the public coffers. They were held in blind trust so that whoever won the war, private enterprise would come out with the same prices. That's why there's no money here. All that money has been invested in Germany and Japan, who now control the world economically. But the United States, since it has to trash its own economy to do that, can only rule through military might. So now it becomes the international Samurai of the Germans, who're going to rule through what they call the European Common Market which is going to be a German control power block. The French and the English are dragging their feet. I think the Danish refused to sign the accords. And of course the Japanese are going to use Southeast Asia and the Far East as their block. The United States has no economic base at all, just a sword to run around and threaten people. No jobs internally, except they can threaten people. And the United States can only threaten people here since it can't keep up. So there is the question of the transfer of funds. This country is run by imperialists. These people are not even capitalists anymore, you know what I mean? I mean, they don't even want to make a profit here any more. They want to take the money and invest it other places, make jobs other places. That's the problem. There ain't no jobs here. That's essential.

The only way we can get that away from them is another party, is a third party. And I understand what the brother said there, "It's never gonna happen, it's never been done." Well, in the United States there's been a history of third parties that've come and gone, come and gone, come and gone. The question is, How can the independent, intellectual and radical, revolutionary sector of American society create an institution for once that will not be destroyed by opportunism? You understand what I mean? That will not be destroyed by sell-outs and co-optation? And that organization, that institution has to be more than just "take people to vote." It has to publish books. It has to create television programs. It has to open art galleries, it has to open hot dog stands and bars. It has to create an alternative life to these people, while fighting them.

You understand what I'm saying? You learn more in a bar or sitting there looking at stuff on a wall or listening to music than you do from some lecture. I teach music for instance simply by putting a record player in the hallway in my department with the music playing. And it plays all the time. And people come by there, you know, they're going some place else, they're not going there. And they say "Professor, what is that?" I say, "That's Duke Ellington." "Oh yeah, who's that?" What I'm saying is that even the most minute aspect of our lives has to be an area in which we struggle to create an alternative to this. But what we usually do—and I myself have been as guilty as many people, although at the same time I can say maybe less guilty than others—we denounce imperialism twenty-four hours a day, yet wait to be discovered by it. We wait to be made successful by it. We're lamenting the fact that so-and-so won't publish our books, when our books are saying death to so-and-so. Why should so-and-so publish a book that says death to them? Why should they produce plays that lay out that they need to be iced? There's no reason at all—if you want that done, you have to create that yourself. And I'm saying all these cities that you're going back to, in those communities where there is nothing—you can tell there's nothing—just go look at it—there's nothing! You can't get in where there's something, 'cause that space is already taken. Where there's nothing, where there's vacant lots, where there's empty playgrounds, where there's abandoned buildings—where there's nothing. That's where you have to take up that space. And fight that space for influence, you know.

PETER LAMBORN WILSON: Well, I wish you'd been around all month. There's a lot of other issues that've come up around here I would've appreciated your comments on. There's one I could briefly describe, and I'd love to hear what you have to say about it. And that is this question of the Language project, the Language poets, and the revolutionary potential of Language Poetry, as expressed in certain theoretical writings by members of that school. Are you willing to put your foot in this one?

BARAKA: Sure. Absolutely. Why not? It's always about content to me. Content is always principal. So if you're talking about another way that you want to fiddle with the language, it's perfectly all right. But at the same time the content has to be dealt with. And if you're talking about language qua language, what's different about that from the New Critics? What's the difference between that and the Deconstructionist folk? It's the same thing. Finally, to remove expression from its social context—I don't know. If you're not talking about the question of content, what are you saying? Now, obviously as writers, particularly as poets, we're in love with language, we want to use language, you know, to express life, to express the need for change. But finally, what is it that you're saying? And that to me always remains important. And if you arrive at a new-fangled theory of boring people, if you can find out a new way, you know—I mean avant-garde boredom—well, I guess every era has to have its own boredom, so that it knows it's alive, you know what I mean? But the question always is how do you raise the level? And what makes me happy about what's going on generally, you know some of us older folk—I see Allen here, and Victor Cruz, I don't know if he'd call himself old or not, maybe middle-old—what is important to me is that when I heard the rappers some years ago I knew what we had been doing was not in vain, that no matter what these bullshit academics had told us—no matter how they waved their hands at us—I knew that the living word—that the word was alive—that after they got through putting us down—like I said in a poem, "Oh, you thought it was over, huh? You thought it was over"—that then the young people come around—and just like they want to attack Souljah, just like they want to attack Ice Cube— it's the same way we were attacked. I mean, do you remember how we were attacked? "*Howl* is the worst thing in the world! Who ever heard of that language? Get him outta here!" The same thing that we suffered. "Whoa, he's anti-this, he's anti-that, get him outta here!" Why? Because we dared to make language live. We dared to make poetry that people could actually remember and go down the street saying "bebupebupbebupbedadup." That's right.

When I went to jail in 1967, the judge actually read my poem in the court. And he kept saying, when he came to the words, he would say, "blank," and I would supply the word, "That's 'motherfucker,' judge." The newness of the language has to do with how you take the content that is most relevant to the time that you're in. How you take that content and shape it, so that it actually becomes a conscious part of the psyche of the people, you know. And that's why, finally, poetry's so dangerous. And these people are trying to tell us, "Well, your children don't know anything about the finer things in life." Our children walk up and down reciting poetry twenty-four hours a day. In my house, that's all I hear twenty-four hours a day is poetry. I'm talking about POETRY badapadapda—yeah. But that's the way it is. You're surrounded by eight, nine poets, little teeny poets that're getting to be big poets. And that shows you the kind of violence that they see in your work. Because you're trying to do violence to the status quo. You know, like I said, Set. The Egyptians called it Set. If you try to fix anything—you can't fix anything—that's death. You can't fix anything—the thing's in motion—everything's in motion. So you *Set* it—that's a death grip. So they're trying to Set this thing, this status quo.

But it's up to us, as poets of truth, if that's what we want to be—and obviously that's why we have class struggle because some of us are not—we have to face that, we have to be willing to struggle. I've never been afraid to struggle. But some people say "Well, you struggle too hard." I think as long as you're principled, as long as you're not trying to wipe anybody out, kill anybody—I'm talking about the world of literature and art—that you have to struggle above board and forthrightly to try to get a higher level of unity. That's what I've always wanted. And I think if we can't pass out of this world without leaving something of value, some kind of institution like a political party—'cause when I say political party, all people think you mean is voting—political party has to do anything it has to do—you know, lead demonstrations, open museums, fight economically—it has to do anything it has to do, you know. Where are our revolutionary filmmakers, for instance? We've already seen that the camcorder is a revolutionary object. Every time we look up, we see another camcorder film—"The Rodney King Story"—we see another camcorder epic. But where are our camcorder films? We can't make eighty-million-dollar films about Batman, nor do we want to, but where are the two-hundred-dollar films? Where are the thousand-dollar films that we circulate ourselves? You know what I'm saying? Where are the little art galleries that only fit ten people at a time where they sell the painting for a dollar and a half or ten dollars? Where is that? Where is that little mimeograph stuff that we sell for two dollars or a dollar? Where is that? We're not fighting these people. All we're trying to do is get in it. You have to fight these people, you have to fight 'em even when you're locked up, you know, bite 'em, you know, I mean, but DO SOMETHING. Don't just stand there lamenting, you know what I'm saying? I get so tired of lamenting. Just *fight them.* I believe there's enough resources right here, in this tent, to set up at least one theater somewhere, one film studio somewhere, a network of nightclubs, a network of poetry readings, I mean something, but don't just wait to be accepted by the NEA. I mean, we have to fight Jesse Helms. Don't wait for them. That's what I'm saying. Are there other questions?

Q: This is kind of a broad topic, but it's from the previous lecture. I was wondering what your take was on the genesis of the crack/cocaine epidemic? I know that all my dopehead friends and I when it first came out in the eighties and they were publishing the formula for it in the *Miami Herald*—nobody'd ever heard of it before—it was like, what are they talking about, free base? Where did this stuff come from?

BARAKA: Well, the same place most bad stuff comes from: the state. I think the Iran Contragate thing and then the whole Noriega scam revealed very clearly the connection between international dope pushing and the state. That's why I kept saying you need the legalization, the decriminalization of drugs. Same way that you had with prohibition. All of the murders and violence and craziness during prohibition—that's why they got rid of it. And this whole so-called moralistic—I mean more people die from cigarettes—it's an old cliché—I never heard about anyone dying from lung cancer smoking bush. Maybe because we haven't smoked Bush, and he's still in Washington, maybe that's the problem. All of those things definitely are the state. We got Freedom of Information Act papers—I've still got about a thousand of 'em to get, but they cost a dime a piece, and I'm reluctant to pay that money to them. When you look at them, it's clear they spare nothing—they sit in audiences like this with tape recorders, when they could just buy the book. See, the poem's in the book, they could just go buy the book.

STEFAN IELPI: I just want to add to your feelings about Rap music in general. Some people wonder why I'm even here. I'm kind of a punk rock singer. And there's some teachers here who believe that this is a valid form of music as well as a valid form of expression. I'm here nosing around academia, kind of checking out what's worth seeing and stuff, and I think, I guess I'm trying to use your impetus and strength to say that the non-academic poet, the non-academic music and word is still a valid, live, in-your-face form, and that I want you to read all the books you can possibly read, but if you can, take your poetry and just calmly put it in front of someone's face and say "check this out." 'Cause when I started, the only poetry reading I ever got was by standing up in the middle of Washington Park and acting like—I put a garbage pail over my head, threw out the contents, and started screaming at the top of my lungs.

I think the best poetry readings are downtown like at Life of Brian, Monty Python's. Just go out there and scream and yell, and don't worry if you can't quote somebody in your work, some dead person four billion years ago. I think that's what we're going to hear—I hope that's what we're going to hear when we hear you perform. I've seen you perform many times, and it's always like, I can walk away singing this man's words! Emma Goldman said you've got to dance to the revolution, well, you've got to be able to sing to the music! I think a lot of people have to loosen up a little bit, maybe put the book down for a moment and jump on a table and get in people's faces. People walk away remembering that. If they're not scared they get some kind of reaction instead of confusion. That's what I mean, the Language Poetry—there were some great Language poets here, I mean Harryette Mullen—she had this content inside her work—about advertising, manipulation, politicians, and then the word play went out from that point. It wasn't a bunch of straight arrows shooting at one elusive target. I'm encouraging craziness right here. And never mind male-female, it's all just crazy children under the Muse now.

BARAKA: Well. I certainly agree about rap—I mean, that's the oldest form of poetry that I know of—rap. That's the way it always was. It comes from the whole African rap, to beat on the wood. That's the way you communicated. You beat on the wood, on the drum, you know. That's what it always meant—rap—to communicate, to speak. What they disagree with is the content. The form's the same. I mean whether you listen to John Henry or The Signifyin' Monkey or back to the ancient chants beating on the wood, you know (drums on table) "Meet . . . me . . . tomorrow night . . . 7 o'clock . . . down by the water . . . bring your knife . . . don't be late." It's the same thing. That's what rap means, essentially. Beating on the wood, the rapping. And Rap Brown from the sixties, who was a revolutionary leader of SNCC—we called him Rap Brown because he could speak, because he spoke, he could talk, he could verbalize. You know, every nation has two cultures—the culture of the oppressed, and the culture of the oppressors. And ours does too. And it depends on what you identify with, the culture of the oppressed, or the culture of the oppressors. Rap is about speaking, talking. But they trying to co-opt that, as you well know. There're serious rappers, but at the same time we're getting a whole kind of bourgeoisified rap that wants to sound like soap operas. You know, Jazzy Jeff, and the dude that was on television—what's his name?—Fresh Prince and all that kind of stuff. I mean, there's a lot of gar-bage. Vanilla Ice, MC Hammer, "We should pray"—probably he means p-r-e-y. All these kind of people who come up who really are representing less than nothing in terms of intellectual and political confrontation. But it's like everything else—they always co-opt you. They always buy and sell.

(Inaudible comment from the audience)

Right. That always works. That's why they have to keep the music segregated. That's why in America you always have what they call "covers" because you have to keep the music lovers segregated. Because if the music lovers ever come together and hear what's in the music together, and what they need to do together, then they will change this together. So you have to keep them segregated. Like what Columbus did—he discovered America. He dis-covered it. Discovered is to be dissed and covered, if you understand what I mean. You get covered which means that the content which is the truest content gets covered up with b.s., you understand? And the dis of course is to be disrespected, dis-whatever. Which is interesting, because the biggest capital of hell, of Hades, was Dis. But what they can always put on you is to make you dis-appear. Which is always the final dis.

E COPOETICS AND THE STATE OF NATURE

I want to start by recalling that this is the five hundredth year anniversary of Columbus' entry into North America. There's a belief that the conquest is over but in fact it continues. It's important for us to understand the nature of this conquest, almost everybody in this tent being part of it. In 1492 when the conquest began, there existed about 320 languages in just North America. These are now down, in terms of Native American languages, to about 100. For the conquest to proceed, a massive genocide had to occur.

Similarly, there are about 100 species a day dying on the planet. Most of those species have no recorded names. It's not like losing a buffalo, an eagle, a cockroach, species we are familiar with. Most of the animals and plants live in parts of the planet we've never even known about. Before we even get to know them well enough to give them names we're killing them off.

You are the last generation to know what a community of the earth or the planet looks like, one that has no major influences from human beings. I'm not talking about minor influences like those we see in the Amazon among remote peoples—I'm talking about complete renovations of the landscape such that when your children are born they will not know what the post-Pleistocene period of the earth ever looked like, and will have no reference to it. Because of that we are in a state of linguistic chaos. In the 1800s, people like Thoreau and the Transcendentalists looked at nature as a reflection. They reflected on nature as a support for their own thought. When I was first in Africa in the 1960s, Disney Studios was there making a movie on baboons. The first thing they did was to go out and capture some baboons and drug them, so that when they made the great scene of the leopard attacking the baboon, they'd be sure the baboon couldn't run away. When everyone saw this movie of the leopard hunting and the defense by a drugged baboon, few understood that this was a change in the way that everyone would view reality. Nature was now masked—

PETER WARSHALL

in fact it was perverted—and our main understandings of nature since then are through films, which means at least second hand.

Recently we've gone even further. We no longer need to mask or pervert nature, we simply have to pretend that it doesn't exist. Thus a mouse has more to do with what you move around on a Macintosh computer then it does with the actual rodent. We have gone so far that there is in fact no need to have a cockroach in order for the cockroach to be part of our mythology. There is no need to have any animal—we only need a simulation of it. The world itself has become a simulation of what we used to think was some kind of basic reality, or at least an appearance of reality. This is the effect of conquest.

I have just come back from visiting the Vatican with four Apache people, trying to save a sacred mountain in Arizona. Ultimately, as we found out, what people believe is not even important because all of nature has been transformed—especially in the Vatican and in Italy—into a kind of humanoid social life. Nature is simply another source of gossip. And the issue regarding language is, What language retains any meaning? Even if you are a scholar and you have information, when does that information have power, and how does one give information power?

Now I rediscovered, along with a friend named Barry Spicer, the Mount Graham red squirrel. The mountain where the Mt. Graham red squirrel lives, by the way, is what's called a "sky island." Mt. Graham has one of the highest rates of biodiversity in North America, the fastest ascent between desert and the equivalent of Alaska spruce/fir forest in North America. The illustration I give is, bear eats cactus fruit in the morning and when you find the bear shit in the afternoon on the top of the mountain it's filled with cactus fruit, so there you are in Alaska, tracking bear by cactus fruit. A unique place. The Mt. Graham red squirrel is a kind of sub-species. Manuel Lujan, our Secretary of the Interior, simply made fun of it, the way you call something sub-normal, sub-human—this was a sub-species. So what was its importance? His authoritative question was, Do we have to save every *sub-species*? Do we have to keep an endangered species alive in every place that it lives?

When you live in a world that approaches language this way, how do you think about poetics, how do you think about truth? How do you give your sense of a "subspecies" more power than Lujan's? President Bush is an "environmentalist." He told you that. Everybody is an environmentalist.

I have a friend, Tom Clark, who wrote a beautiful poem about nature without going outside of his house. He simply read *Scientific American* and a few books on marshes. So even a poetics can become an artifice. You no longer have to have experience in almost anything, and it leads me to wonder, what are we going to do in this kind of a world? Let me clarify this. The original word *ecology* comes from *oikos logos*—the Greek word *oikos* meaning "home," *logos* meaning "the governing principles of, or the governing principles by." When we first used this term, the earth was considered your household, you treated it like your household—friend Gary Snyder called his book of essays *Earth House Hold*. Economics was *oikos nomos* meaning the accounting of time, space, and money within your household. Accordingly, in the sixties we all said, "Think globally, act locally." Well, what we've been hearing from various people on the panel today is that this no longer makes sense—the way the earth has become our household today, we can just as well say: "Act globally, think locally." We don't even have a language appropriate to our circumstances.

Certain people, those who are kind of soft on the planet, use words like "planetary" or "Gaian" in respect to the Earth Goddess. If you're more interested in economics you use words like "global" or "multinational," and one of the challenges I give when I work with multinational corporations is to say, "Don't use the word 'global' today, try to use the word 'planetary' instead." Just try to change your language. And I do that with everyone. When I meet people who are kind of mushy on the planet, who would make it into this little Disney World filled with cute little animals, I try to say, use the word "multinational" today, or use the phrase "global economy." Bend your brain a little, because the language has been co-opted everywhere. Nobody knows if there is even anything to define.

Anyway, we went to talk to the Vatican. As soon as the Apaches in my group went to the Vatican to present information on the sacred nature of *dzil nchaa sian* (Mt. Graham), the University of Arizona and the Vatican invented another group of Apaches. It was headed by a former tribal council chairman who had been charged with embezzlement of tribal funds and needed a way out of his predicament, so the university promised to help him. "We know all the judges in Arizona. The judge is a part of the big boy's circuit—now you just say that the mountain isn't sacred to the Apaches." So we see the ultimate form of conquest, which is to set a people against one another. Then the conquerors just sit back and watch the divided people fight it out.

So this other Apache went to the Vatican (actually, a judge forbade him to leave the U.S. so he sent his group), and given that they were a part of the power play, they of course got to see the Pope. They explained to the Pope that the other group was just a bunch of poor Apaches whose minds had been completely brainwashed by environmentalists, who were being used by white people. The language reversed itself! The people who were being the *Apples*, red on the outside, white on the inside, became the conquerors by turning the language in on itself.

So the *fin de siècle*, the end of this century, is not only the end of the Great Dying. *This is the Great Dying.* It is the beginning of our recognition that we have lived in the Dark Age, and the Dark Age was a lack of respect for life and for sustainable life and for the diversity of life.

I have a certain form of Buddhism of my own, but we must understand that even Buddhism is an imported religion, imported into the United States, trying hard but as yet not connected to the land, just as Christianity has never connected itself to North America. If you are a true Christian, your sacred mountains are in the Mediterranean. If you are a true Buddhist, or a certain kind, then most of your sacred mountains are still in the Himalayas. How do you become localized then? How do you set roots in a place, how do people who have no lineage set down roots? This is the second thing I'd like to talk about. What has really happened is the destruction of lineages.

The first time I ever taught Native American history, this was back in the sixties, almost all the people who signed up were Native Americans and I got very nervous. "What can I say?" I started like a typical anthropologist and said, "Let's talk about kinship and family, let's talk about the extended family." And a Shoshone friend of mine turned to me and said, "Peter, we have no extended families, we have families. What *you* have is a *contracted* family. " And that was the end of my whole course. There was nothing I thought I knew that wasn't actually the opposite of what it was.

Here we are, living in these contracted families that are practically and literally down to single kids living alone without parents— living alone on the streets of New York or the streets of Sao Paolo— kids whose sense of community has no sense of lineage whatsoever. And we are trying to say, "Protect the earth for seven generations." Remember it's only the Australian Aborigines who could even hold in their minds seven generations of kinship. They knew their own and they knew seven other generations, and they projected into the generations behind them. When they made any decision, it was a decision for seven generations. Whenever we make a decision, no matter how good we are, we have no lineage to connect it to. I think the positive thing I am saying today is that here you can listen to someone like Ed Sanders telling you to make up a lineage that *continues*. It is not something here for the year.

I'll make it clear with an example. In the seventies we discovered marijuana, we thought it was a great plant, we learned a great deal from it, we still learn a lot from it, especially about timing and senses of timing. The dope smokers weren't just involved in politics, they were also determining how you hand down the lineage of plant powers. Yet the further generalization was never made. Marijuana deteriorated into a recreational drug—it never led to a philosophy which recognizes all plants on the planet to have powers, and that those powers can be used or abused. You can eat too many carrots. You can eat too much brown rice. You can use or abuse any plant. The question became for me, Where was the lineage that was going to teach children the proper use of marijuana? Where was the lineage that created a tradition of the proper use of plants? As we all know, the Christians try to use wine that way, as a substitute for cannibalism—as a substitute for drinking Christ's blood—or the wafer as a substitute for flesh. Christianity has maintained its lineage by passing down simulations of cannibalism.

In *The Practice of the Wild*, Gary Snyder tried to do a very human thing—simply to create a prayer over food that people could recite before they ate, so you could stop, take a step back and say, "Where did this food on my plate come from?" I don't think there's a person in the United States, maybe there are a handful, who could look at something on their plate and say what the nature of the soil was in which that food grew. And this is unsettling because since about 5,000 B.C. the nature of human life was to understand soils.

I would say the ultimate nature of conquest, and the ultimate danger to the earth itself, has to do with soil types. No one has classified which soils are being lost from the planet. There is a great deal of hope about restoring the earth, but as soon as people truly try to get back into it they are going to come face to face with the problem of soil restoration. Here's an example. The sacred groves of Greece, the oak groves, the last groves of Greece, were cut, and when they were cut it led to the topsoil known as the A Horizon washing into the ocean. This meant that Greece could no longer plant A Horizon crops, such as grains. They were stuck with the subsoil, with B Horizon crops which include those wonderful things like grapes and olives for which Greece is known today. But because they had no A soil, no topsoil—except for Sparta, which was in the valleys—they had to go out and make a trade, an economy of that ecology. That economy included making pots and urns for olive oil and wine and selling it to the whole Tigris/Euphrates/Nile valley areas which because they still had their rivers at that time, had a topsoil that renewed itself and grew all the grains.

The Phoenicians finally defeated this trade network—they realized they could make extra-fast boats and pirate the Greeks. And so from a dependence on subsoil economy came the end of the Athenian empire. But history is not written that way—history is not written from the point of view of the soil. So an important message is the message being written all over the earth right now—what has happened to the soils? Not to some abstract earth at large, but to its intimate detail? What happened to the soils and can they be restored? Sometimes the soils were made under completely different conditions of global warming or global cooling. All the soils of the Midwest were made under great glacial pressures. Unless we have glaciers, we're not going to get those soils back. We're talking about ten to twenty thousand years of restoration if we're going to use nature, which is nothing—I mean ten to twenty thousand years is nothing from the point of view of the earth.

One thing we should know about Europe is that Europe lives entirely on artificial soils. They have absolutely no conception of a virgin soil. They have no conception of what a virgin soil might even look like. That loss of understanding, that something took this length of time and was so fragile that it could be lost in a century or two and will take hundreds of years or thousands of years to restore—that is the nature of the fragility. This is not a nostalgia for nature. Rather, it is the start of an understanding of where you live. You not only ask the question Ed Sanders put to you, Where does your water come from and where does it go? but you ask the question, What are the soils that I'm standing on? What are the soils that produce my food? What is my responsibility? All of this comes down, at this point, to what is your circle of responsibility. That is the question that can help you get out of the chaos into which the language has fallen.

Each individual person has to make their own decisions. A person who drives a car has harvested eighteen different elements from the earth. Take the aluminum in any car you drive—it was usually harvested on the backs of workers in Jamaica, or in strip mines in Africa. Is the car company responsible for the living conditions of those people? How far does Volvo have to extend this sense of responsibility to be a responsible car company? If you don't buy a car does that mean you're outside the circle of responsibility to the earth? Ultimately, then, what I'm talking about is a sense of song and prayer because that is the only way that I have seen to reconnect to the earth. That is why I'm pushing today for a poetics of song and prayer. Here's a slave ditty from South Carolina and it's usually sung with tap dancing:

It rains on the just and the unjust fella
but mainly on the just
cause the unjust's got the just's umbrella

When I was in the Niger Delta, I worked as a kind of thirteenth-hour man. When no one can figure out what the hell to do they say, well there's this guy over in Tucson who knows a lot about working where there is no water, let's go get that guy. So they sent me over to Africa during the sixteen years of drought. As you can see, California is going through chaos in five years of drought. Africa went through sixteen years of it and they say, Okay, now go out there and do a rain dance or something. In the middle of the Niger Delta, there were arguments among the Bozo people about whether there should be a sanctuary for fish, just to keep the fish alive—to sustain the people through the drought—and should that sanctuary be an off grounds for fishing.

So all the old men and all the young men of the village got together. I was invited to sit in on this meeting and observed them argue. One man will say, "I've lived here for sixty years and we've been through many droughts. In those droughts we've always been able to cut back on our fishing but we've never needed a place for just fish to live." A young man will say, "This is a different time. This is a time when we have more people eating fish, a time when we have city people coming in and fishing. This is a time when the drought has lasted longer. We need a sanctuary so the fish will survive." When someone got to the right phrase for "this is a time that's different from the old times," everyone would burst out and say that phrase over and over again like a chant. The chant would echo through the whole group until everyone had memorized it. After the chant had been memorized, "this is a new time, this is a different time," everyone would burst into laughter and they'd go on with the argument. This is how a ceremony was combined with conflict resolution.

That's what we gringos call it—"conflict resolution" or "consensus building" is the new psychobabble from California—you know, "let's all build consensus." What we don't have any more is that sense of how to combine it with fun. I mean, there's nothing more boring than a town meeting, but we all go through them. We sit through them because we want to reconnect, in some responsible way, our own body, which is sixty to eighty percent water, with the waters of the earth. But how do we get a language back in there which can make these town meetings no longer boring?

I would like to end by saying that we really need to look at how we're going to cut through this simulation of language, these layers and layers of meaningless language. I didn't go to Brazil for the international Environmentalism Conference for one good reason—I would have thrown up hearing the word "sustainable" every fifteen minutes. Sustainable this, sustainable that, sustainable life and sustainable economy. Frankly, all economies must exploit the earth. The idea is, How do you do it in a way that reduces the speed in which you kill the earth itself? How at the same time do you create an artificial human environment that can substitute for what's lost?

So an eco-poetics ultimately winds up with three economic values. The first is *option values,* which is that we preserve animals and plants and water so that they remain options for our future. As you may know, there's a little Madagascar periwinkle that saved many kids from leukemia. There are plants that have had such a long evolution on the planet that they've created molecules which are impossible for human beings to invent. That process—of creating molecules—has been one of the great healers. It's also why we like *tetrahydrocannibinol.*

The next value, *transformation value,* has to do with consumer production—the kind of value we cannot in fact get out of. But we must learn to change the language we use here. In reality we are not "consumers." Things do not end with us. We are not "producers." Things do not stop producing without us. We are *transformers of energy.* We are transformers of mass. Do we want to take responsibility for that web that we are part of?

Finally, the one that is really just based on the human spirit, the one economists now call *existence values.* What price can you put on the Mt. Graham red squirrel? What price can you put on a sequoia tree, ultimately? What price can you put on a mountain for prayer? How do you make people feel the emotions, the awe that has to do with existence value? That something should exist simply because it exists? Would the earth really be different if no one spoke Navajo? Would the earth really be different if there were no elephants left? We can only answer these questions through that one absolutely unique characteristic that human beings have—the ability of the species to speak to itself in complex ways.

STEVE ABBOTT: Many groups use their power to silence other viewpoints, such as the Vatican getting the overpopulation question taken off the Rio de Janeiro Conference this Spring. There is an indisputable link between overpopulation and the current ecological crisis, yet no one could address this because of the Vatican's move.

PETER WARSHALL: The question of access to power is a major one at this point. Let's back up a little bit—I'll explain what I was doing in the Vatican and what I found out.

In 1632, Galileo sold the first telescope to Venice as military equipment. Ever since then astronomy and the military have been combined. The astro-military complex has a long history. The Vatican persecuted Copernicus and persecuted Galileo. They were essentially caught, when the new scientific discoveries came in, with their pants down and their frocks open. They then said, well, we better have our own observatory because there, beyond, in outer space, we might see the Great Patriarch with his flowing beard and we want to be the first persons to see it before the astronomers do because it will be embarrassing if they see him first. The Vatican founded an observatory, and one of the places they wanted to put a telescope was on the sacred mountain of the Apache. This telescope is an optical/infrared telescope—its prototype mirror was first used in Los Alamos to track satellites that aim laser cannons. It is a major part of the Star Wars equipment. The Vatican of course claims that they're doing "pure research," but their research can be used to make the telescope better for Star Wars, and better for laser cannons.

Suddenly the Vatican was then found in this embarrassing situation, accused of conspiring against the environment, and indirectly supporting global armament. After the Pope had declared his respect for all Native Americans, he was now caught wrecking the top of Mt. Graham. That's how this all started. We were trying to get the Vatican's telescope off the mountain. That's why the Apaches went to Rome to talk to the Roman curiae—in particular the Apostolic Council for Peace and Justice. What we found—and this is a wonderful word—is that everyone in the Roman curiae has their "competence." They don't work outside their competence. If you go talk to the man in peace and justice, his competence is not astronomy. If you talk to the astronomer, his competence is not peace and justice. You wander the halls, everyone telling you that what you're concerned with is outside their competence, feeling these icy chill winds of the 1600s when I'm sure some Sioux Indian or some Iroquois stood there in front of the Vatican asking for something equivalent. Finally, you ask—well, you have something (telescopes) for outer space where God used to be—but do you have a biologist? Do you have an ecologist? Do you have anything for the earth? You find out that the Vatican has no department for the earth or the planet itself because God is out there, not back here.

29 June 1992

▼OW TO POETRY: ANNE WALDMAN INTERVIEW

RANDY ROARK

RANDY ROARK: Can you remember deciding to be a poet? Was it a decision?

ANNE WALDMAN: I loved hearing poetry read out loud, I loved reading poetry, and I wrote poetry from an early age. It was a tacit human occasion. Understood as a natural mode of communication. Poetry was a way certainly to express my "secret" emotions and I felt comfortable, happy inside the making of it. Later it was necessary to assert the position. It became my course of life—marginal, subterranean at first—maybe there was a decision there—that I'd never "sell out." Poetry then *defined* my life. Habit and manner took over. Then I never could go back. I took a vow at the famous controversial Charles Olson reading at Berkeley in 1965 to never give up on poetry or on the poetic community—to serve as a votary to this high and rebellious art.

ROARK: What was your scholastic preparation for becoming a poet? Did your parents encourage you? Did your teachers, contemporaries? Anyone in particular as a mentor? Anyone discourage you? Who were the first poets you met and their influence on you?

WALDMAN: My parents were extraordinarily encouraging from a young age. My mother Frances LeFevre was tendentious about poetry. Both parents: readers and writers. I grew up among books, many of them poetry. So my first teachers were books. My father John Waldman preferred fiction. It's not surprising my brother Carl is also a writer (of atlases, screenplays, novels). I had some inspiring English teachers—Jon Beck Shank in particular in junior high—a poet himself who was an aficionado of Wallace Stevens's work and used to read him to us *out loud*. With *passion*. I remember the sensation of hearing certain lines from "Sunday Morning"—"She dreams a little, and she feels the dark/Encroachment of that old catastrophe". Key lines of "The Snowman"—"Nothing that is not there and the nothing that is" and of "The Idea of Order at Key West"—"And when she sang, the sea,/Whatever self it had, became the self/That was her song, for she was the maker," which acted on me like a religious conversion experience. Tremendous support from my best friend in high school—Jonathan Cott, the critic, poet, essayist—who shared my desire "to be a poet"—who read my early work—who turned me on to Rilke and others. "Letters To A Young Poet", "Duino Elegies"; these poetries became fires smoldering in my skull. At Bennington both Howard Nemerov and novelist Bernard Malamud took me seriously. They were professional, practicing writers. I learned something about discipline from Nemerov, a love of Blake and Yeats and something about crazy mind, the poetic leaps imagination can take. He didn't have a lot of pretense—was very direct in fact. He loved classical poetry and conveyed his passion with an inspiring fierceness and heartbreak. But as a female I always felt I could only absorb some of the story and transmission. I was reading women writers but not meeting them at this point. Elders Sappho, Gertrude Stein were somewhat familiar. And I had been reading novels by women for years: the Brontës, Austen, Virginia Woolf. I knew Edith Sitwell's recording of *Façade,* an eccentric rhythmic excursion. Allen Ginsberg, Gary Snyder, Kenneth Koch, Ted Berrigan, other contemporaries, mainly men were important allies. Allen in particular gave me tremendous encouragement by his example—his expansiveness and compassion. Barbara Guest was later supportive. When I first saw Charles Olson in Berkeley in 1965 I was overwhelmed. He was dancing—his feet were literally off the ground and dangling in the air as he rested his massive body on the on the podium—and obviously *suffering* at the same time. Meeting the poets always drove me deeper into their work. I first met Diane di Prima when I was fresh out of high school—at the Albert Hotel in Manhattan. I was impressed that she could manage a household—an exotic one at that—with babies! It was helpful to see her commitment as an artist. She was also extremely political and at the same time considered herself an alchemist. She breathed a fierce passion for poetry, which is always the case with authentic poets. They've got it bad. One trembles with it. After Berkeley, I was constantly meeting others who felt the way I was feeling myself to feel. Or knowing what I felt I already knew. Because there's all that wisdom and energy in poetry. Poetry has been the teacher in all aspects of my life. Meeting Frank O'Hara before he died in 1966 provoked a strong commitment. I loved the exuberance in his work. The consciousness of his poetic persona was alive, infectious, multidimensional. He was so matter-of-fact about my wanting to be a poet: Welcome to the club, he said. He invited me to come work at the Museum of Modern Art as a volunteer, this was something a poet should do. But I needed money, I protested! There's interesting history in those "mentor" friendships. But I always felt equal to their challenge.

ROARK: Can you remember much of your first readings?

WALDMAN: I remember an early (second?) reading at the St. Mark's Church In-the-Bowery parish hall circa 1966/1967. I was nervous. I was seated at a wooden table. I wore a yellow and blue striped dress and my head was bent over my "works," hair probably in my face. I remember hearing my young woman—more like a girl—voice and thinking "This isn't the *real* voice." The real voice was deep inside in my *hara*—and it was a deeper, more seasoned and musical voice—an *ageless* voice. I realized I would eventually have to find the words to match it—the words would have to grow up to the voice and the wisdom of that voice. The poet's path. It's not that I have to "find my voice"—it's already there waiting for me. I've just begun to recognize it. It's always been there trying to wake me up.

ROARK: That reminds me of Allen Ginsberg's story about hearing what he thought was Blake's voice and decades later realizing it was actually his own mature reading voice.

WALDMAN: I became confident as I continued to read and "perform" more and more. And I felt in a way once I was speaking the words and making these sounds they no longer were mine. My body was a receptacle. My voice was everywoman's *cri de coeur.* I've always been on the track of the wizened hag's voice, the tough tongue of the crone free of vanity and conditioning. She's terrifying, liberating at the same instant. She's exhausted her hope and fear.

ROARK: I imagine that in 1967 there wasn't much of a context for the kind of poetry this voice of yours needed in order to express itself.

WALDMAN: It was a smaller, more sedate scene in the beginning, not that poets weren't outrageous in how they presented themselves at times, but there's always been the "boring" stigma attached to the poetry reading as event. The self-absorbed poet who dully mumbles obscure musings way beyond the appropriate time frame . . . much of that's changed for the better. I always liked the monotony of a John Ashbery reading, but he's a brilliant poet, after all. He doesn't need to strain. When I read at a festival in India—in Bhopal in fact, 1985—I was the only woman and one of two Americans—the Indian poets all asked, Is this the fashion? Is this what poets are doing in America? Is this acceptable? They had never seen a woman so "out there." I summoned the Hindu tantric deities as I sang the chant poem "Skin Meat, Bones." ("The jackals came/ this was in India/to collect the meat of my father's forefingers.") I sounded the hag. I felt on "home" soil. India is a frequent ground for dreams, musings, the "other" landscape in my life and work. An old scarecrow mumbling mantras over desiccated corpses is one past-life image that comes up. Very glamorous.

ROARK: Charles Bukowski said he was glad he began publishing late, that poets who receive too much recognition early in their life are encouraged to become "writers" rather than real people. How did early recognition affect your life?

WALDMAN: In a positive way. I was encouraged, inspired by the early response. Old work feels distant now, insubstantial, naive, yet I learned a great deal publishing young and the subsequent work has become more interesting to me at least, has moved consistently, gathering momentum, since the ambition, the flame, intensity was in my "blood" then and now. And the other aspect of what I do is the poetics "community" work—the political, ambassador of

the potential enlightened society kind of work which is really a practice, practice in the best sense. As I've said I took a vow to work with
anyone, any situation through the "vehicle" of poetry. And key here
is the bigger vision of an enlightened community or society based
on compassion and generosity, generosity which is the "transcendent friend." I put my life to this. There's a wonderful text Buddhist
practitioners read during oriyoki meals, the Zen monk's style of eating with chop sticks, lacquer bowls, napkins, and other implements—
which you clean yourself and wrap up with an elegant flourish at
the end. It goes something like this: "By this generosity one is free
from enemies. Generosity is the transcendent friend. Therefore generosity is said to be essential. Generosity is the ornament of the
world. Through generosity one turns back from the lower realms.
Generosity is the virtue that produces peace." There's perhaps the
poet's Boddhisattva Vow at play here which is the same as anyone's Mahayana vow: to be a bridge, a boat, a fountain pen, a
typewriter, a publisher, a school to anyone who has need of these
"vehicles"—not personally, mind you, that it's *my* particular style
bridge, made in my image, my brand of typewriter or poetry. Who
I am as any kind of identity which does in the world any good is
merely my *skillful* means. In any case, there was always support in
that aspect of my life as well. The St. Mark's Church was there at
an auspicious time to house the Poetry Project. The arising of The
Naropa Institute which would house the Jack Kerouac School of
Disembodied Poetics is a miracle. Making a strong connection with
Allen Ginsberg and founding our school was no accident. The people who've found their way to Naropa have a so-called "karmic"
connection to the vision: Bobbie Hawkins, Anselm Hollo, Joanne
Kyger, Andrew Schelling, you Randy, others. They certainly haven't
come for the salaries they get. I've seen the meddling hand of "purpose" throughout my life and the projects I've been engaged with.
The making of poetry is double-edged, painful. The making of community is difficult, a life's work. But participation of others is a great
boon and their poetry and their struggle too is an inspiration. I'm
grateful. There are so many people I love and bow down and pay
homage to. So many who have contributed luminosity through their

work, who have been generous in the world. I think it was harder for women getting started when I did, but I had a lot of confidence to meet my male muses upon the battlefield of Mars, which is the ground of love and war and poetry.

ROARK: Can you list and discuss the history of your work with various artists and contemporaries? Is there any idea of you co-creating in a community of artists? Is this something new? Can you co-create as well with artists who are long dead? Do you feel yourself as part of a long tradition of artists who are in a sense co-existent despite their deaths?

WALDMAN: There have been many important collaborations with other poets, visual artists, dancers. I've completed a long poem with Susan Noel (an early summer student of mine at Naropa) entitled "Speak Gently In Her Bardo," in memoriam to a friend of ours who died in 1987. The friend, Judy Gallion, is very much a part of the poem as well. *Triptych: Madonnas and Poets,* a collaboration with artist Red Grooms, includes portraits of Kerouac and his mother, W. C. Williams and his mother, and Marianne Moore and hers in Italian Madonna-and-babe styles, as Bellini, Raphael. So in a sense it's a collaboration with those dead artists as well. I wrote the "Legends" which appear in Gothic gold lettering. It's hilarious, and quite beautiful as well as exquisitely carved. I enjoy Red's work—the *wit* of it—it was certainly an honor to work with him. "Her Story," a lavishly boxed item with lithographs by Elizabeth Murray was recently published by Universal Artists Editions Ltd. Over the years I've worked with artists Joe Brainard, George Schneeman, Yvonne Jacquette, Susan Hall, and with writers Ted Berrigan, Reed Bye, Eileen Myles, Denyse King, Bernadette Mayer. The work at St. Mark's Poetry Project was community-based and inspired. I've co-edited publications with Lewis Warsh, Reed Bye, Ron Padgett and am now working on a new poetics anthology from The Naropa Institute with Andrew Schelling. This interview we're doing is a collaboration, no?

I've worked with dancers Barbara Dilley, Douglas Dunn, Yoshiko Chuma, Lisa Kraus, Helen Pelton, Marni Grant. I've worked with composer/musician Peter Garland, Gretchen Langheld, Steven

Taylor, Elliot Greenspan. I feel that Allen Ginsberg and I have an on-going administrative collaboration beyond our lifetimes. He called me his "spiritual wife" in front of three thousand people in Czecho-slovakia. It felt like my wedding night. I am inspired by Sappho's ex-istence as a writer. Dante (I steal some of his lines), others. Translation is a kind of collaboration. I'm working with nun's songs from the Pali Canon, circa 80 B.C.E. I just worked on a translation of the "Caillech Na Beara," a Gaelic hag's song with Naropa graduate student John Wright who knows Gaelic.

ROARK: Directing the Poetics Naropa must be a strenuous job. T. S. Eliot thought that having to work for a living—and I imagine a sched-ule like yours—forced him to concentrate harder during the time he had to write. He found that being otherwise occupied didn't stop his thinking about what he wanted to say and that the increased ratio of thought to writing prevented him from writing too much or thinking too much on paper.

WALDMAN: I believe W. C. Williams felt similarly. He spoke of the "tense state" in which the best work occurs, and he said it might be when you're most fatigued—presumably after a hard day's work—in his case visiting sick folk and delivering babies. I know that ten-sion—it's really an altered state—very exhilarating. I was inspired to write "First Baby Poems" after having given birth to my son Ambrose and I was exhausted. Fatigued, elated, and full of energy simulta-neously. I remember once when Allen Ginsberg and I were walking uphill at Rocky Mountain Dharma Center in Feather Lakes, Colo-rado, I expressed concern about his blood pressure and the lateness of the hour (we were climbing to join fellow seminarians at a large bonfire) and he said "This gives me energy, it restores me," and it wasn't only the climbing he meant. The goal—getting to the camp-fire and socializing with friends and singing and reading poetry—was an important part of the seductive energy of the occasion. And it doesn't, it's true, have a lot to do with "thinking," as T. S. Eliot notices. It's the direct connection to the poem, whatever that may be—it's the whole process of making it, that's obvious. How does that parallel thinking? How is it separate? How does thinking interfere?

These are stimulating questions. There are different levels of "thinking" in Buddhist psychology. Spontaneous mind is perhaps the closest to poetic expression. But there's a refinement that occurs as well.

ROARK: Pound felt that an epic was no longer possible because distractions had intensified, outside stimulation had intensified and our powers of concentration had weakened from a kind of fatigue. Are our abilities to concentrate approaching the vanishing point? Is that a negative thing?

WALDMAN: Perhaps we have to work harder to concentrate. I have been working on an "epic" for five years which I am completely committed to as a kind of ongoing practice. Therefore I disagree from a personal standpoint. But, yes, there are many distractions—particularly, I would say, those manifesting and promoting materialism, which is disheartening, even when you don't buy into them. Television is a good example, when it's particularly insidious, idiotic. It leaves one feeling dis-empowered, fatigued. Charles Olson, a poet who worked in epic mode most of his life, ranted against t.v. Insight grows dimmer in our world. Living becomes degraded through the lack of compassion toward other sentient beings—not just humans, but animals, rain forests, tundras, the ocean, and the fabulous and mysterious creatures in that ocean. We are motivated by passion, ignorance, aggression. Ignoring, playing it safe—although this doesn't mean you have to be a political activist in the literal sense, for poets may be activists by the work they do. They are activating sound-consciousness, speech, language. Transmitting a heavenly music. Passion: seduction, magnetizing for one's own gain. Aggression: territoriality, violence towards others. The epic is a way to parallel the instability and potent energy of our world. My epic takes on both the nightmare and the nirvana of male energy. Isn't that a paradigm for the Kali Yuga?

ROARK: Well, it seems that times of certainty, such as the European Middle Ages, seem to produce great works of art, like cathedrals and epics, because they believed they'd had "Truth" revealed to them. In other times, the search and bickering over "Truth" consumes a great deal of energy. If these times are truly getting darker, how does this affect you as an artist?

WALDMAN: Truth is available even in an uncertain age. Truth is unconditional. But we, as a world culture, don't seem to be urgent about it at present. It's not in our interest, or so we think. Of course there are still great visionaries everywhere as well, who will probably teach in secret and work conscientiously to preserve the wisdom traditions which are in danger of disappearing from our civilization. Civilization is a curious notion these days. There is an inordinate amount of deception in our own American so-called "democracy," founded on the suffering of so many people. And this way of life promises to infect the whole world with its military power and dominance in the name of peace. It's a myth, in fact, the American "new world order." It's international cartels and unseemly cutting of endless deals. The root of so much suffering is "ego" which manifests as a lack of compassion. Our government feels cruel, hubristic, ruled by greed. Yet I find consolation, delight, insight, humor in the generosity of the work and the camaraderie of many contemporary writers and younger writers. Also the community we're developing at Naropa is already very strong and continues as webwork extending into the planet at large. Maybe these are not great "monuments" like those of the Middle Ages, but they are sustaining. I feel I write against the darkness, "straining against particles of light against a great darkness," Keats wrote. Also I frequently return to great texts of the recent and not so recent past—Sappho, Dante. They're still relevant. Olson, Duncan, O'Hara, Schuyler, Gertrude Stein, Pound, Stevens, Williams, Berrigan's sonnets. I go to the work of my comradesses: Bernadette Mayer, Alice Notley, Joanne Kyger.

ROARK: There's a speech in *The Third Man* where the character played by Orson Welles recalls the turbulent history of Renaissance Italy—war, plague and the Borgias—producing Leonardo Da Vinci and Michelangelo, and compares it with Switzerland's hundred years of peace, wealth and brotherhood which produced the cuckoo clock. What about this implied correlation of strife with the creation of great works of art, and of complacency with the reverse?

WALDMAN: Classic vintage Welles; he has a point. It has some substance. I always felt like a rebel. These are I say *dark times*. I strive to make sense of them in my work. It's not an easy time, fighting the lords of materialism. I don't know many complacent poets—it seems a contradiction.

ROARK: I've spent an incredible amount of time trying to determine where words come from—the words of our thoughts, the words that appear in our mouths during conversation. Do you know what I'm looking for?

WALDMAN: You're looking for the point—synapse?—perhaps where the magic occurs and how it gets translated. Even after analysis, speech remains a mystery. Words are sacred from some point of view. They emerge—when they aren't purely discursive—out of luminosity I believe. They are particles of light. They also come out of silence, if there is such a thing. We are communicating through our whole body as well, like illusory angels. Burroughs calls the word a "killer virus." It has that power as well. Language is also a net of desire and illusion. It mirrors every complexity. It is angular, muscular. It doesn't give up to meaning readily. Let it be difficult, dangerous. Look at the language used in weaponry. "Mantra" means "mind protection."

ROARK: Do you think in words? Do you think in associations or chains of concepts? Do you think in musical phrases?

WALDMAN: Yes, I think in words, associations and musical phrases. All of the above. In "Fast Speaking Woman" there are obvious sound and associational moves. "Iovis" is full of sound out of all those instances as well as structures within structures. And hidden agendas. And others' voices. "Hopes and Fears" is a chain of concepts with a musical phrase as constant refrain. But sometimes there's little meaning or message in what's construed. It's more rune-like sometimes, oblique.

ROARK: So where do these words come from as you're writing—from the scene, from the music (form) of the poem, from your mind, from looking at the outside world, outer space, god, etc.?

WALDMAN: All of the above! Every experience is a cypher waiting to be unearthed, unlocked, revealed to its attendant music of language. Objects suggest words—quotidian reality provides language all the time—along with the visions of hag-deities wrapped in tigerskins.

ROARK: The Greeks thought that poetry came from the muses—in fact, that one must empty one's head before the muses could appear. Bob Dylan said that the songs he's written were "in the air" and came through him, perhaps, but always existed and he just happened to be the one who wrote them down. Do you write your poems?

WALDMAN: My "you" is just a conglomeration of tendencies. Some of those tendencies manifest in an articulate and refined poetic language, if you will. But I also feel the distinct meeting of my consciousness with a confirmation from the sun, the moon, stars who are my allies all. Muse is an energy. It is the reciprocation of the phenomenal world, as well as the body of light or enjoyment—the *Sambhogakaya* we say in Buddhism—that responds to the energy we put forth. My poems invite participation of that larger energy or connection. The Muse plugs you in. It's that direct. Electricity. It's always available, batteries not needed, but you have you see, magic keys or access to the illusory batteries which are needed and available. When you are genuinely ready and alert. Who's to say how or when or why this occurs. It's the reciprocity with "bigger mind." And it can involve other people. I get that hit—don't you too? in the poetry one loves.

ROARK: Actually, I kind of distrust poetry as a medium for truth. When Allen Ginsberg writes about politics or Buddhism I never confuse that with "The Truth." It's pretty clear he's telling me what he thinks about politics or Buddhism, and his understanding changes as he does. I think everything unconsciously becomes our mirror. I tend to sift poems for the person there. The philosophy or otherworldliness I skip over. It was Catullus, who thought the poet was responsible for the poem and that everything which occurred to the poet—even the most mundane facts of the poet's life—what he had for breakfast, his petty spites, disagreements and quarrels, the weather—was transformed by the poet into art, the way Midas turned common objects into gold. Ted Berrigan comes to mind as a modern example. Are these two ideas—the inspired and the created—oppositional?

WALDMAN: No, these ideas are not opposing one another. Of course I'm responsible for what I put down. I'm not simply a "channel." Those facts—the donuts, Pepsi Colas, pet peeves—are deities, muses, as well—they speak to me. Things are "symbols of themselves." "No ideas but in things," etc. And they are words in relation to other words. Art belongs, needs to be part of ordinary, quotidian, daily life, "close to the nose" as Williams says. It's got to reflect the truth of the relative reality as well as its vision, desire, aspiration. Art is ugly from some point of view when it's shocking, uncompromising. It's also beautiful for these same reasons. Thank goodness. You want it all.

ROARK: In the Walt Whitman program of the PBS series "Voices and Visions" they talked about the difference between "blind" poets and "visionary" poets. Blind poets would be those who, like Poe, created out of their imagination or their unconscious. Whitman would be a "visionary" poet because he wrote poems of a particular time and a place which depended so heavily on the eye. Do you see yourself as a "blind poet" or a "visionary" poet?

WALDMAN: My work probably fits into the "visionary" category, although much of the writing arises out of an oral yearning and attraction. I hear words before I "see" them, if you know what I mean. I "mouth" them before I see the letters. But imagination—the words appearing out of dreams, out of fantasy, and out of imagined hells—also plays a part. Cut-up and certain experimental methods are interesting in light of this question. You can get a "phantasmic" construction butchering text, re-arranging phrases. Is this "blind" work?

ROARK: Well, John Ruskin, the great late nineteenth-century art critic, was disgusted by the state of art in his age because paintings were done in the studio, not in real light, and used as models contemplative notions of "the beautiful" as opposed to actual models. He thought that Gothic churches were the last great works of art because they were made by hand, by a craftsman who was seeking to express, to personalize, his faith. Of course, there were rules you couldn't break except when you were carving gargoyles and such. You had to carve the Madonna within the tradition, for example. But Ruskin thought even these radiated the personality of the artist and his or her contact with the vibrancy of the real world. It was an individual vision. Pound, too, found it in San Zeno in Verona, with the signed capital where the artist carved in pride "I made this." Even in prehistory, it's always the handprint, whether in the Neanderthal caves of France or the Canyon de Chelly, where the artist seems to assert his or her existence. Yet in postmodern art the intention seems towards an effort at erasing all traces of the individual through cut-ups, chance operations, or the hunting down of the "folly of intention."

WALDMAN: When Reed Bye and I saw the cave paintings at Font de Gaum in Le Eyzies we both felt the "hand" of the poet. And yet there was no meeting that individual who is erased, muted in time. So only the product of his/her exquisite muscle and heart and eye survives. It's sublime, authentic, unquestionably so, and in the cleanest sense. This "viewing" was a religious experience you might say, I felt something vibrating there—hand in motion, scoring lines which delineate the untamed beast in motion. We name it Cro-Magnon. Great art is "nowness" for lack of a better way to say it. This experience brought up an imagined reality of that past—hundreds of thousands of years ago. The paintings carry high talk and text and image with them which exists in fact because we have imagination. If we didn't see them what are they? They are secret teaching. They wait for us. And we were ready, or are we? It depends. We don't know what to do with our inheritances sometimes. Which is why ongoing wisdom traditions understand how to interpret and receive and preserve teaching. The images from the caves are like the Tibetan buddhist "terma," or found treasures. They are hieroglyphs, seed-syllables that unlock insight. Ruskin had a point of course,

Pound too. You want the real thing, not the artifice, although arti-fice is an interesting style when combined with intellect and humor. Not by rote, endless stock similes. The real thing is a "luminous de-tail", like the rune or seed-syllable.

ROARK: What is the relationship of dreams and unconsciousness to your life and work?

WALDMAN: The relationship is active, useful, continually interesting. Like watching film. I pay attention to the messages from the phenom-enal world (which is somewhat illusory itself: "regard all dharmas as dreams"), dream images such as my shoulder being opened like a lid and having molten iron poured inside my body which is a caul-dron of fire anyway, to synchronicity—how I may be thinking the same thing, the same "word" as a close friend—auspicious coinci-dence, conjuries emanating from the unconscious, resonances, bizarre associations all the time. I had a dream recently entitled "Uncle Vanya" in which Allen Ginsberg and I were leaders of a large touring company that had settled into a western movie set. The Chekhov play, which is about one woman stealing another wom-an's lover, disinheritance, and the disillusionment of the character Uncle Vanya, seemingly had nothing to do with the play we were performing. But Allen and I had travelled together to Czechoslo-vakia (so there was the obvious "translation" of the word Chehkov) as part of a tour with Nanao Sakaki and a band of Japanese rock musicians. Allen is a kind of "uncle" figure. "Vanya"? Vanity? We were about to perform "it", whatever it was, but decided to have a political rally instead. Something about a rally in support of the Modees, a political party—obviosly "poet maudits". But I must have had the rap singer my son likes—Kool Moe Dee—in mind too. The idea of a play with singing and dancing, a musical version of Uncle Vanya if you can imagine that, was perhaps a pretext. The visuals were strong. We put on our makeup in a makeshift tent backstage. I could see every pore in our faces. An obvious interpretation is that I'm dreaming about the Jack Kerouac School of Disembodied Po-etics at Naropa and my relationship to Allen, and our mission in life together. I later re-read the Chekhov and realized there were a lot of interesting male figures in the play that shed light on my relation-ship to Allen from several points of view. This is not without humor. "Uncle Vanya," the play, is by contrast, bleak, lugubrious. I'll try to write about it. "Interstices of waves" came into a recent dream—I used it in the poem "Speak Gently In Her Bardo." I have quite a few armageddon dreams, with William Burroughs as frequent Wizard of Oz figure, *behind the scenes.* Also dreams involving masses of peo-ple I've known, large street and battle scenes on papier mâché sets. These feed the work. I've incorporated some of this kind of ma-terial in the web of "Iovis" which is a long collage anyway. "Ma-triarchly" has a series of dreams at the end including the notation "Dream 'Wolverine' comes before 'Woman' in the dictionary / per-functory and true/giddyup giddyup." "When The World Was Steady" weaves in a lot of dream material as well. The roots for "dream" in-clude joy and music. The Indo-European "dher" is "echoic of a hum-ming." That dreams—these sensations, thoughts, images—come to articulate soundings is a fascinating process for the poet.

ROARK: Would you disagree with Jacob Bronowski, the mathemati-cian and scientist, who believed the most significant step for hu-manity happened in the Enlightenment, when science once and for all separated from "magical beliefs"—that the distinguishing ele-ment of a scientific statement is that it rests on the question "Does it work?", whereas magical beliefs exist in a non-world beyond proof—where everything's a matter of assertion or belief only.

WALDMAN: I don't disagree with Bronowski but appreciate the shift he acknowledges at the Enlightenment. Going for the proof can be fun. On the other hand, much is occluded. I follow my instinct, pas-sion, dreams, imagination. I know certain things to be true I can't prove. I love the yearning exactitude of science. Or the rules of a ballgame. Marianne Moore had an interesting dichotomy in her poet self—an intense attention to creating form, a passion for exac-titude yet a non-linear imagination and a way of putting disparate "things" together unscientifically. Naturalistic expression versus scien-tific accuracy perhaps. A poet's logic. Structures. Indeed, does it *work*? Yet, how can you *prove* a poem works? There's absolute truth and relative truth. There is so much we still don't understand about our own universe. Niels Bohr's idea things become real when we focus on them, turn our attention to them is a captivating one. Think of the Elizabethan view of the act of seeing. It was believed that the eye darted forth a stream of very fine particles which pierced or fastened upon the beheld object then relayed impulses back to the sender. The arrow was the appropriate image for such an eye-glance ("But no more deep will/I endart mine eye"). And was a useful metaphor for the poet. Not necessarily accurate science, but psychologically true perhaps. I find "neutrinos" very poetic. Here's something—what is it?—coming out of radioactive decay with no mass, no weight, passing through matter and traveling at the speed of light. They connect to *nothing*! It sounds like enlightened consciousness and actually parallels what's called the Dharmakaya in Buddhism, a state of mind needing no reference points. Burroughs thinks science and art will merge in the future. He speaks of how science can tell us how association blocks form in the mind, for example.

ROARK: Is there a difference in your work between common speech and poetic language?

WALDMAN: Often. I like to play with both. "Dialogue At Nine Thousand Feet" works in an elevated language, inspired, in part, by the altitude I was living at at the time. I'm working common speech into the many sections of "Iovis"—overheard conversations and the like. I'm attuned to how—not merely what—people say—my ten-year-old and his friends talking about video games and basketball is just one example. One boy says at one point in the poem: "You cuss at the game because it cheated & a guy killed you or a bad snake or a mushroom or a snail or a fish killed you." And the other responds: "They waste yr butt on Megaman II." What appeals here is the young male's sense of the dangers, the obstacles, the primal (female/Nature) threats that challenge him. And the response of getting "wasted" by the Superpower—Megaman—the machine, the game. "Cuss" and "butt" carry the adolescent edge. But archness, artifice in speech excites me as well. Poetic language, perhaps. "Dialogue

Between the Self and the Soul" carries an elegant double-speak. I don't work so much with the meaning or message but the tone and carriage of the words. Say it "slant," advised Emily Dickinson. What goes into the writing is often heard in slant, oblique ways.

ROARK: What is your primary method of composition—typewriter/notepad (handwrit/typewrit)?

WALDMAN: All of the above—handwritten in notebooks of all sizes, on yellow lined pads, on manual typewriters, now on computer.

ROARK: Do you find a difference in the finished work depending on its compositional situation/form? Where does editing/rewriting fit into your compositions?

WALDMAN: Yes, there's a difference in shape with the different size notepads and notebooks. Lately I'm training myself with the long poem to work on the computer. I edit on a print-out.

ROARK: Do you vary your method when you write prose or poetry?

WALDMAN: Prose is more streamlined on the computer. But I'm working with both. The computer is a *performance*—all your works are appearing lit up and dancing on a screen! It's a shrine as well, with all the precious, totemic, sacred icons there waiting to be worshiped. I miss the simple white-page-in-machine at times however. At the computer I feel I'm on the verge of evolution, about to mutate, sitting at the dawn of a new civilization, staring at the brink of the void which is an image box of my own mind. And it's more organized than my mind. Will I even need a mind again?

ROARK: Will and Ariel Durant in their epic *History of Civilization* claim that poetry evolved out of the religious need for chants and hymns and that prose arose from the needs of merchants—i.e., that poetry derived from the imaginative faculties of the human psyche and prose from the need for a more or less factual representation. As someone who's written in both prose and poetry, do you see any difference in the way each is used?

WALDMAN: Yes, I see this to some extent. Poetry operates frequently along a spiritual trajectory—a need to join heaven and earth—to "connect." But prose is telling stories—hagiographies—epics of creation and who begat whom begat who. Some native peoples see stories in the flames of a campfire—fantastic images of birth and death. Factual representation, of course, and the need for accounting come into this. This is also a human endeavor and very necessary. Those wonderful chapters on whaling data in *Moby Dick* are an example of investigative poetics, a tabulating poetics.

ROARK: The Durants follow the above line of thought to the point where they see poetry as coming from the beginnings of civilization where the imaginative powers and needs overcame (or arose from) an inability to understand the world cognitively (or factually). For them it follows that prose is the mark of a fully developed culture whereas poetry comes more from the beginnings of a civilization.

WALDMAN: One is always writing the "first poem." Each time is regenerative. We are perhaps at the end of a civilization, and yet I'm always writing the first poem. How do you explain this? A fully developed culture needs to record itself—it's an intelligent survivalist move. I still don't "get" the world "factually" in spite of the magnificent data, and so I'm stuck with poetry. They need to exist simultaneously. We are now never more "fully developed," yet coming apart drastically and dramatically at this very instant.

ROARK: Lew Welch described the New York poetry scene in the fifties and sixties as "fierce" and the San Francisco scene as "cool jazz." As you travel around the country do you get a geographical sense of the various poetry scenes? Do you think that there's a geographical influence on poets—for example, city versus rural, West Coast versus East Coast, etc.?

WALDMAN: Poets are more peripatetic these days, many have lived on both coasts and in both city and rural settings. And are more commonly found by magazines, correspondence, tape cassettes, videos, fax, plus the more important community gatherings at Naropa, the St. Mark's Poetry Project in New York, reading events in the Bay Area. But friends in Bolinas and Kitkitdizze (Gary Snyder's area), Cherry Valley, New York seem in some respects more cognizant of basics—where their energy comes from, and so on. They are more ecology-minded than their city cousins who are frequently careless, negligent, impatient, not as frugal. This comes in thematically into some of the writing. New York City is still "fierce" but for different reasons than Welch intended back then. It's extremely dangerous, desperate now. The poor have gotten poorer, more crack babies born all the time, the suffering amongst the homeless, the minorities . . . is endemic. It's quite a tangle when you look at the urban scene. Where to place the blame? The priorities are skewed. A lot of poets ignore these realities. You can excuse some for their brilliant work. Some escape to safer waters. Every city and town I've traveled to has an interesting subtext of some kind. An alternative. It's hard to put a cohesive poetic imprint on the different scenes, based purely on geography, states of mind, experience and method. I'm no longer writing a city poetry the way I was when I lived in the Lower East Side in New York City in the sixties and seventies, but I'm not writing a small-town poetry just because I live in Boulder. I travel a lot, all those places come into my own work, what I hear or dream in those places enters as well, what I read comes in. The work is all over the place prismed through my cones and rods of attention. Yet in terms of requiring a poetic "zone of control" we are developing a community here that has a distinct flavor, compared to New York or San Francisco. What influences it? Something magnetizes people here. Geography is part of it.

ROARK: Are there any poems you've written that you won't read in public, which you'd rather people would read in private, alone?

WALDMAN: "Both Other Self Neither." Parts of "Iovis."

ROARK: Do you ever utilize tone of voice to suggest ironies in your writings? How does this translate on the written page?

WALDMAN: In a piece entitled "Coup de Grace" I seem to be working with a distinctly ironic tone. It's an accusatory tone, and yet the language travels in myriad directions. I think this piece is most successful on the page. It's steady and doesn't strain. With other pieces my reading style may color or change the words. Perhaps the oral pieces are not as fixed. More fluid.

ROARK: Some of your poems, "Battery" for example, read softer than they're performed. Do you think you may be trapped into a certain performing style which subverts the poems themselves?

WALDMAN: Sometimes that's true. I'm pushing too hard, not letting the poem breathe. Perhaps it comes from frequent readings to larger audiences where I wonder can they hear me in the back?

ROARK: Sometimes your poems don't seem to progress forward as much as circle an idea or concept. But as you're writing do you feel the poem moves forward? Do you discover things as you write the poem which you didn't know before?

WALDMAN: I usually feel I'm propelling forward, and yet aspects of the poem spiral back in and continue around. Discovery is the reward of the curiosity. I never know where I'm going, but I'm not interested particularly that the poem climax to a revelation at the end. The making of it, existing inside the poem as it occurs (and as it re-occurs) is the point.

ROARK: Aristotle, Robert Frost, and Marianne Moore said that the ability to make associations was the hallmark of a poet. Pound, George Grosz (the artist), and Marianne Moore suggested endless curiosity. What do you think are the abilities which create a great poet?

WALDMAN: Both a resonating mind plus vast curiosity I agree. Also quick and clear eyes, a good ear. Imagination. I would not be a very good poet, I think, without passion. Others might suffer with their passion. It's not always a personal self-motivated passion, more transcendent when it's working. I get passionate about the words.

ROARK: Yet sometimes it seems the energy in your poems moves from thought as opposed to feeling.

WALDMAN: Yes. "I Digress . . ." is a good example. Most of my so-called meditative poems work that way, and yet it is an emotional thinking. There's passion in it.

ROARK: How much of your work is "first thought"?

WALDMAN: The root, the initial and sustaining "hit" is the first thought. What got me into it in the first place. The tinkering or refinement that comes later never *feels* major, although the whole poem could be radically different. Ed Sanders says it could be "First thought, worst thought," a funny twist. Often that first thing is ugly. I love to work with cut-up and other people's words at times. Is my first thought someone else's in that case? And what about arrangement? Time shifts, narration isn't stable in the usual way. So a lot of my work if we're being strict about it is not "first thought," although the impulse is unconditionally "best" or genuine.

ROARK: Nabokov said that "Writing is rewriting." Raymond Carver said "Writing is revising." The argument against "First thought, best thought" could conceivably run like this: When the writing is initiated there is the primary experience of the poem or language. The writer at a later date rereads the poem from a fresh, more detached, distant perspective. This fresh mind is the mind of a new person, essentially, NOT the person who wrote the original "work." And rewriting is, or can be, Re-writing—as intuitive, inspired and fresh as the original writing. As Corso reportedly told Kerouac, "I don't want to ignore any part of my mind—including the part which cringes when I reread something I've written and knows how to improve it."

WALDMAN: I don't hold to "first thought best thought" as "never revise" or "don't improve the poem if you can." But the inital rush, blast, spontaneous explosion is the way into the poem. There's a radiance, a limitless energy at times. One is king or queen of the world. Isn't this every artist's experience? Sometimes it's when you finish the difficult thing. These slogans are only useful up to a point. The notion of "first thought" is to inspire confidence not contrivance.

ROARK: I've been reading the mathematician L. E. J. Brouwer lately, who wrote a book in 1905 called *Life, Art and Mysticism.* He talks about that limitlessness, that radiance as well. It's kind of difficult to summarize but he said that we began in isolation amongst nature without any concept of future. But when we began thinking, the rational mind created a seemingly continuous world different from our actual experience of it—which is actually more like discrete moments interspersed with emptiness. One begins to dismantle this "world of causality." The phenomena succeed each other in time, bound by causality because your colored view wants this regularity, but right through the walls of causality "miracles" glide and flow continually, visible only to the free, the enlightened. "Only he who recognizes that he has nothing, that he cannot possess anything, that absolute certainty is unattainable, who completely resigns himself and sacrifices all, who does not know anything, does not want anything and does not want to know anything, who abandons and neglects everything, he will receive all; to him the world of freedom opens, the world of painless contemplation and of—nothing."

WALDMAN: Brouwer sounds very Buddhist in what you just quoted. There is no goal. We are all "gonna die." The practices and "concepts" in Buddhism are just stepping stones toward nothing. "Nothing" means that you don't need to be grasping and territorial and self-perpetuating. There is no "self," which is a very heretical notion. When you go to look for a solid self, a soul, something made of DNA, recognizable, this big "me" that will carry your identity for ever and ever, you can't find it. And yet you are colorful, individual, only you will write that particular poem, only you manifest a very wonderful and particular vivid energy. Or you can be dark and wrathful, a terrorist. Only you suffer what you suffer. But you are still going to die and you can't take anything with you. Your consciousness might return, some people experience that possibility, but you won't ever be Randy Roark again. And I won't be Anne Waldman. I find this "view" a tremendous relief. And it makes you feel more compassion towards other lifeforms as well. So perhaps a bit of your art remains that might encourage someone else. Great. You want to live to experience your own immortality? You want to imagine that? Is that the point of it all? I doubt it.

ROARK: The Moslem philosopher Avicenna claimed that the highest understanding, say spiritual love of God, is unavailable to all but the highest minds, so parables, such as stories of a physical paradise and bodily immortality, are to be used for the masses while the other purer knowledge is to be used with only the most advanced students. Do you ever code in language what you are afraid may be misunderstood?

WALDMAN: I'm working around many aspects, the public poetry being an important one. At one level I want to be accessible. I don't want to depend on "interpretation." But I'm curiously writing explanatory notes to poems now. Probably writing them to myself. I wanted to examine what the notion of "Lokapala" or a local deity is so I wrote a prose meditation on this to accompany the poem. It's more interesting, in fact, than the poem. Notes may be fascinating and take the experience of the poem in one possible direction. "Coding" can be like a game. Poetry is always a kind of code. My Tantric studies come into the work constantly, and wouldn't be obvious to everyone. Some more attentive readers and listeners will naturally absorb more subtleties and connect the resemblances. Gary Snyder heard "Om Ah Hum" right away in "Skin Meat Bones." No one else noticed that. There are hidden references, puns, associations that are highly personal. "Helping The Dreamer" was in part a vision I had on the top of Bald Mountain in Boulder. So when I talk about the town "below" I'm being literal. And the bars and joints opening up with "names of initials" are a kind of code. "J.R." = "just right." Kenneth Koch got that I was thinking of myself as an opera singer during one reading. My love poems are often coded. But I don't think there's a danger of the material being too esoteric too handle. Avicenna is talking about spiritual teachings. But the great wisdom traditions in any case are self-secret. If you are an initiate in spiritual practices you are for the most part moving along a progressive path. So it's inappropriate to receive certain teachings if you have not accomplished the preliminaries. They can backfire if you haven't experienced the "ground." You might be thrown into chaos, confusion, further ego-projection. You might start hallucinating the deities and thinking you're creator of the universe. Maybe you are! But can you handle that?

ROARK: Since I first heard of Keats's idea of "negative capability" I've collected some notes on it. For instance, a diagnostic symptom of mental illness is "all-or-nothing" thinking where a person can't contain contradictory ideas about a person, incident, or object— "I hate my mother and I love my mother"—instead it always has to be either "My mother is the devil" or "My mother is an angel." This seems a corollary to Keats's idea—"the ability to keep in mind contradictory ideas without an irritable searching after facts." One also thinks of F. Scott Fitzgerald ("The test of a first-rate intelligence is the ability to hold two opposed ideas in the mind at the same time and still retain the ability to function."). Both Aristotle's and Einstein's definition of genius was "the ability to contain contradiction." Whitman, of course: "Do I contradict myself? Very well! I am large, I contain multitudes." But how precisely does this affect any concept of poetry or the poetic act?

WALDMAN: Andrew Schelling states it well: "A poem is a mind that holds contraries."

ROARK: Is esoteric Buddhism a key in deciphering some of your more intellectually complex poems? For example in the Vajradhatu Sun, a Buddhist publication, the reviewer writes of "Romance" that "'She' is wisdom abandoned and therefore found." I don't get it.

WALDMAN: I guess the reviewer means once you (she) give up hope of wisdom it's staring you in the face. Something like that. It's important to guard against buzzwords or buzz-concepts. But, for example, to appreciate a poem, such as "I Digress . . ." it would be useful to know something about the Abhidharma in Buddhist philosophy. Yet the poem is just like hearing someone ramble on, literally digressing off a point and coming back. It's a speech really. As for "Romance," the "she" is part of a play/dialogue with the "lover". It's this notion that once you give then it's all there I think the reviewer was referring to. The "she" is constantly shifting positions but in a very romantic, seductive way, not "owning" her power. Once you let go you're wiser. And she does it through words!

ROARK: Yet when I first heard you read "I Digress . . ." I didn't have the slightest idea it had anything to do with Abhidharma. I still don't know what Abhidharma means. But I think it's one of the most rigorous, uncompromisingly intelligent poems I've ever heard. Are you telling me any affection I have for the poem is mistaken?

WALDMAN. Not at all. But you might get interested in Abhidharma and that could further your appreciation of the poem. Abhidharma notices how the mind moves through "heaps" of experience which are at some point illusory. It's a very precise description. It's a footnote to the poem. You are an ideal, attentive reader. You "get" as much as you need and more. You love poetry, you love to crack the code. You are a serious student of Pound. How do you read the *Cantos*? Do you want the notes? Do they enhance the poem for you?

ROARK: It's funny but I think of them as totally different activities. Reading Kenner on Pound makes me realize I don't know what I don't know. I assume I have all the information needed to read a poem. If it's in English and I don't understand it I think it doesn't make sense rather than that I can't make sense of it. But in the *Cantos* and in some of your work I bump up against Greek or Tibetan or Chinese and I KNOW I'm missing something—there's a big skip in the poem, I lose the continuity. Pound said that when you come across something you don't understand in the Cantos, something in a foreign language for instance, don't worry because it'll be repeated in a form you do understand nearby. I think he's wrong about that, but it doesn't matter. What's interesting is if a poem interests you enough you find out about it. With the *Cantos* or with Joyce or Pynchon or Eliot there's plenty of secondary texts to expose the underpinnings of the work. Your situation is a little different in two ways: One is that you share your vocabulary with a select group of Buddhist practitioners and there isn't any significant secondary material. But what I like about poems I don't totally understand is that you don't have to believe it or argue with it because you're interested in how the poet's mind is working. You see the connections made in the poet's head and you also begin to see the movement of electricity through the poet's mind, even though you might arrange the energy in a different pattern. It's Pound's "rose in the steel dust." And so I find in my scholarship a freedom, a loosening of my sense of self into a concept of time where I'm an insignificant speck totally circumscribed by my times. I know you as a scholar as well and wonder if you find inspiration in your studies. What exactly do you find yourself drawn to in your studies?

WALDMAN: I am drawn to the passion that manifests in other cultures' ritual and oral traditions, to a study of how mind articulates its states of ecstasy and exploration. How art stretches the boundaries of logic. I'm interested in Sandhyabhasha, "ulatbamsi"—the "upside-down language" you find in Kabir, Sanskrit poeties and in Tantric Buddhism. A close ethnologist friend turned me toward certain hearings of gamelan when I was in Bali which relate to cosmological time cycles. I am interested in how and where the synapse occurs that transmits through juxtaposition of semantics and sound. I listen to a lot of ethnic music which carries those messages. I am also a student of my own time and place which is circumscribed by poetry, and I work to forge a poetics which is close to my mind-grammar and body-mind vibration.

ROARK: The poet Basil Bunting, friend of Pound, wrote "Pens are too light/take a chisel to write." Pound himself said the most important tool for a writer was an enormous garbage can. Allen Ginsberg tells the story of his reading "Howl" and "Kaddish" to an audience including Bunting in the sixties and Bunting's response: "Too many words." The inclinations towrads compression or expansiveness in writing and editing seems at odds. Who do you sympathize with— writers who chisel at words or those who open a vein?

WALDMAN: Both. Both. I appreciate "condensare." I return to Dickinson, Niedecker, Creeley with awe and inspiration. I love the succinct angular tension of Chinese and Japanese poetries. Sappho survives through her fragments, chiseled by time. I myself tend to be more verbose, probably on the side of "too many words." *Not A Male Pseudonym* is somewhere between the two. I need the lyricism extra syllables provide. I work with song, and need to manifest and explicate contradictory psychological states. Olson "opens a vein," Robert Duncan, too. Lorine Niedecker, Dickinson chisel. Williams is somewhere between the two. Does there have to be a choice? Obviously there are preferences. There's an interesting preference among poet-readers I know for a more self-less, chiseled yet hieratic (by this I mean there's a priest's voice or knowledgeable voice coming through) poetry—exemplified by some of the work of Susan Howe, for example, who I admire tremendously, Bunting, Zukofsky, Jonathan Williams are chiselers. Both, both as far as my personal "taste" and praxis is concerned. Both paths are energetic.

ROARK: How can you tell the difference between an acceptance of "both" which is a weakness, an inability to choose or an inability to take a stand, and some genuine insight? Kerouac said "Until you assert yourself nothing ever happens to you." In my own life it seems the real breakthroughs have happened when someone's pushed me uncompromisingly until some raw primal energy came out screaming "I am!"

WALDMAN: I recognize that push too. But I'm talking about negative capability. I don't feel compromised by my personal range. Heaven forbid I ever "find my own voice." I'm not really *searching,* you know. Embarrassing. Creeley and Ginsberg can co-exist. I've always been excessive. I assert myself all the time. There's no particular problem with that.

ROARK: One of the things I've learned about you through this interview is you don't intimidate easily. When you're challenged you rise to the challenge. In fact, you even seek out the challenge. I think that may be a contributing factor to explain why you've been so successful.

WALDMAN: Thank you for the compliment. It's enjoyable to talk about poetry. I'm always amazed that people aren't more inquisitive, aren't asking specific questions about particular poems. Poetry works out of ordinary mind as well as sacred speech and sound. It can be *discussed.* As a reader of poetry one wants the company of other readers as well. That's one of the reasons we started a poetics school.

ROARK: Why have you chosen to incorporate nonverbal aspects such as video, music, dance, etc. into the performance of your poetry?

WALDMAN: I am interested in the contrast the non-verbal aspects provide in relation to the words—to the poetry. I enjoy collaboration. I learn a lot about color, body, nonsyntactical form.

ROARK: Your poetry is very direct to the subject matter—whether it be a "take" on a political subject or an interior experience. Is this a conscious choice away from subtlety? Is there any sense of the personal, the private, in your work, as opposed to "the public"?

WALDMAN: Yes, certainly. I seem to be working in both directions, always, simultaneously. The "takes" feel necessary on current issues. It's a way to understand where my mind is, relative to outside challenge, insanity (the war in the Middle East), and how to empower myself in the miasma where one could otherwise dissolve into total chaos and despair. I can create a spell that says "I'll make your semen dry up/Your genitalia will wither in the wind!" addressed to the "men of war," the arbiters of our industrial-military-mafialike complex, and actually feel its potential efficacy. Other works such as "Science Times," "Both Self Either Neither" are subtler, for the page primarily. "Pseudonym" is more private.

ROARK: There seems to be no negative capability in your political stand. You seem to feel a need for eternal vigilance because you see the government as a Machiavellian and almost demonic force, especially the U.S. government, which is out to destroy you and everything you believe in. But it seems to me your shrillness and inability to draw political distinctions makes you, politically at least, marginal and ineffectual. What is your feeling about political poems in general? For instance, I can't imagine an overtly political Frank O'Hara poem.

WALDMAN: What, no capability in my political stand? How provocative of you! I disagree. True, I find the government—and most governments, not just ours—demonic. They are so rarely motivated, it would seem, by compassion, but rather by greed. The Scandinavian governments are perhaps an exception, and more humane, more involved with the welfare—the health—of their citizens. They seem wiser in matters concerning the environment, for example.

What are the distinctions? Keep a sense of humor, see the inanity of some of our political figures, but don't be naive about how their decisions are affecting our reality and survival. The war in the Middle East was cruel, misguided. In spite of what a monster Saddam Hussein is, there's a lot of blood on "our" hands. I can't help being shrill at times, although the song I wrote, "Tormento del Desierto," about Operation Desert Storm is slow, sedate, almost dirge-like. I often appreciate the sentiments, the passion of a political poem but it has to move in other directions as well—Amiri Baraka's political poems shine in their vocal power, in their complex and engaged rhythms. You might not even agree with him on the semantic level. Frank O'Hara's poems are *humanly* political. The consciousness of the persona he conjures is awake. He's a good citizen.

ROARK: Many have said that an author's works are their autobiography. I'm familiar with most of your work but very little of it is self-revealing, although this doesn't mean that it's non-autobiographical. But am I wrong in thinking that there is more of the artist creating a work in your poetry as opposed to the artist leading the reader into an experience?

WALDMAN: Perhaps. Perhaps there is no "self" ultimately to be revealed. The "I" exists insomuch as "other" and vivid phenomena exist. I don't think you mean "confessional," do you?

ROARK: I don't know.

WALDMAN: I write to make up the world, it's true. I live inside that "world" or universe. You're welcome to come in as well. But it's not all artifice either. I want you to get inside my eyes and heart.

ROARK: Do you have a conscious, underlying reason that you write, a purpose to your writing? Is it only to make up a world?

WALDMAN: "I'm here to disappear," I've said. So why leave words and tapes behind? The writing confirms the fragility and unbearable beauty of our existence. Its purpose isn't immortality. It's more complex and interesting than that. It's discovering life at the edge of death, all the time.

ROARK: In ancient Greece the four arts (lyric poetry, song, instrumental music, and dance) were one art. It wasn't until later that they became separate. It seems as if you're trying to put the pieces back together.

WALDMAN: Yes, often I want to bring the pieces back into a comprehensive whole again so the efficacy, or whatever "good" or insight or energy comes through the work, can travel further into human psycho-physical streams so that the poetry has more of a "pulse." I find music expands my own mental capacity. It triggers associations and imprints on me in a visceral way. Dance gesture is necessary to any ingesting of any knowledge or wisdom. And its rituals are exonerating. My inspiration comes out of a natural inclination to push boundaries which I deem artificial in the first place. The directions continue to be interesting. Sometimes in writing workshops I've encouraged a collaborative choral form, where everyone is contributing words, music, song, gesture, movement. Many directions. At the moment of performance, all arts are the same.

ROARK: Plato's Academy was more or less a religious fraternity dedicated to the muses. Is there any feeling at Naropa of a religious or spiritual foundation, a concept of fraternity, or a dedication to something "other"?

WALDMAN: Naropa Institute was named for the Indian Buddhist pandit/scholar yogin who was the abbot of the Nalanda Institute which flourished from the fifth to the twelfth centuries c.e. He left the halls of academe, however, after seven years, for the wilds of charnel grounds and caves and passed some extraordinary endurance tests over a twelve-year period. "Intellect and Intuition" is the Naropa slogan. Well, the "other" is not an external "other." We honor our own innate wisdom and poetry at Naropa. That's the purpose of bowing together to one another's best effort, aspiration. There is a wonderful sense of camaraderie based on the underlying understanding of letting go of ego—that it ultimately "doesn't work." So there's a lot of chaos and groundlessness as we say, but there's also a great deal of an abundance, generosity, commitment. Naropa definitely presents an alternative to most educational institutions. The school really falls much more within the Shambhala tradition, which is a wisdom tradition based on the idea of an enlightened society. Although it has the accommodation of Buddhist background it is a secular school interested in other traditions and points of view. It certainly acknowledges the outrageous "outrider" tradition in American poetry and poetics.

ROARK: One of my primary experiences in meditation is a state of mind which is virtually wordless. This experience must somewhat resemble a child's experience when s/he has not yet begun to place names on objects, to literalize their experience and then experience this literalization as their primary "experience." Does your experience of meditation affect not only your relationship to your mind (as preword) and its reaction with your "experience" but also your reentry in the land of words in your writing?

WALDMAN: I would say the experience you describe is sometimes accurate. And that's the point, to exhaust the mind-stuff. But often when I meditate I am not in that "wordless" state at all. My projecting mind is racing with all kinds of thoughts that also are labeled "words." I've learned about "gap" through meditation and also directly experienced "negative capability." Sometimes the oral work develops as sound first, before word, concept, then the latter kicks in. But meditation makes you *stop what you are doing.* This is an interesting contrast to the rest of my daily life. "I" is not so reliable. Who is thinking, watching, etc? These are always provocative questions.

ROARK: St. Francis of Assisi said, "Who we are looking for is who is looking."

WALDMAN: That's the first step. Finding the "watcher." But you can get beyond that. The watcher isn't always so interesting.

ROARK: Actually I think it's very interesting. I think if you begin to examine "the watcher," as you call him, there's an interesting moment when you realize that if you're observing the watcher then who's doing that? And if you can observe yourself observing the observer it begins to get very interesting. From that point it was clear that reality seemed to change as my perception of it changed, and my perceptions were disturbed by these weird filters. I keep trying to get out from behind these filters. So the question is, Who is this "I" I'm trying to get out from these filters? I see similarities to Pound's point of the vortex or the point connecting Yeats's two gyres where the maximum energy is. It's the point of pure energy without manifestation. And I think it's the point where words come through although I don't know where they come from because that point has no depth, it doesn't contain anything as far as I can tell. I don't know what it is, really, because it's not a thing. I can never really back it up against a wall. In fact, isn't that where you observe your thoughts in meditation? Isn't there a total identification with emptiness at that moment, the moment you, say, witness an attachment or observe your thoughts from the point of view of the "who" who is looking?

WALDMAN: That's the point in meditation, and the watcher dissolves. It's just experience at that point. No reference point back to the solid "I." As a writer that can be exciting because of the groundlessness. You are free to explore other states of mind, states of being. You can get inside the language. Down with the narrative, the autobiography, the "self," the dull ownership of experience, tired emotion, semantics. Cut-up eliminates the "watcher" to some extent or it gets fractured, multi-headed, a more curious beast. But the organizer is still on the job.

ROARK: In many ways, words themselves continue to exist when the object they refer to no longer does. For example, William Carlos Williams's red wheelbarrow probably no longer exists outside the poem itself. Plato suggests that words (ideas, abstractions) are the only eternals—that all the wheelbarrows in the world will cease to exist whereas the word "wheelbarrow" will continue to connote an idea even after all the wheelbarrows eventually disappear. This seems in contrast to William Carlos Williams statement "No ideas but in things."

WALDMAN: Do you know Jack Spicer's letter to García Lorca where he says "I would like to make poems out of real objects" and "the imagination pictures the real"? He speaks of how the lemon he shellacs to the canvas will decay, develop a mold, become garbage. "Yes, but the garbage of the real still reaches out into the current world making *its* objects, in turn, visible—lemon calls to lemon, newspaper to newspaper, boy to boy. As things decay they bring their equivalents into being." "Things do not connect: they correspond," he says. "No ideas but in things" does not say "no ideas," so there's a philosophical argument here. Words are things, however, as Gertrude Stein reminds us. The dialogue is always shifting in my head. My poetics is open, expansive. Words are very much things to me, personally, whatever they evoke semantically. But they carry communication, if you will, on many levels. I am not interested in a fixed position vis-à-vis words. Never.

ROARK: There seems to be a very definite line between poets who conceive of poetry as *primarily* language—the sound, the juxtaposition of words, the visual impact of the letters themselves where the meaning is secondary or contained in those qualities of sound, etc. or even nonexistent—and those who think of poetry as primarily communication. Where do you fit in this dialogue?

WALDMAN: Probably with the former, in these sense of how I practice the art. Message poetry can be most tedious. You might communicate better by telephone, by an embrace, by sending your money to a worthy cause. But poetry will always communicate something however it's "done." It might be more complex than some people are used to. My poetry communicates my mind, my nervous system which rages with passion whatever the words "say."

ROARK: The idea of relativity of experience came into disfavor as early as mid-period Greece. The position taken was that if all experience was relative then a sleeper's, a drunken person's or a maniac's vision of reality would be as true as anyone else's. They came to believe there must be an objective truth and so the question became, Is there a road or path to it?

WALDMAN: The relative and the absolute, sure. But the absolute, in a way, is beyond anyone's version and description. In a way it is our own mind using the simile of the mirror, which simply reflects things as they come up with no attitude.

ROARK: In their *History of Civilization,* Will and Ariel Durant point out that the earliest dated printed book is the Diamond Sutra. In Sumer, the oldest western civilization which has left a record, archeologists have uncovered "shattered tablets (which) contain dirges of no mean power, and of significant literary form. Here at the outset appears the characteristic Near-Eastern trick of chanting repetition—many lines beginning in the same way, many clauses reiterating or illustrating the meaning of the clause before. Through these salvaged relics we see the religious origin of literature in the songs and lamentations of the priests. The first poems were not madrigals, but prayers."

WALDMAN: This feels right. Sutras are sayings of the Buddha. Prayers are a yearning for confirmation. Their efficacy makes the world keep spinning, from some point of view.

ROARK: It has been said that during the Golden Age, arguably the height of Roman culture (circa 30 A.D.), poets ceased to mingle with people and or even speak their language. (One thinks of a statement from Patricia Hampl's review of *Makeup on Empty Space:* "The famous 'difficulty' of contemporary poetry is here, the surface angularity that confines poetry to a skimpy audience.") Artificial (Greek) forms had become the model for poetry. Horace's "profane crowd" preferred satires and "lower forms" of art, such as bar songs. This atmosphere co-existed with (or perhaps created) a ribald underculture which included, before his eventual banishment, Ovid. Ovid and his crowd (the *poètes maudits*) set themselves up explictly in opposition to what they saw as the "piety" of Virgil and his imitators. Petrified versus lively; polite versus profane. Is this a continual flux? Do you find similar drives in your own "career"? Where do you fit in with "the profane crowd"?

WALDMAN: I take Virgil's line "Iovis Omnia Plena" (All is full of Jove) as a subtitle, and the joke is that it's Jove's sperm it's full of. I tell the senators their semen will dry up, I write love poems to women, I scream "Mega Mega Mega death bomb—enlighten" while demonstrating at Rocky Flats. But some of the longer more meditative pieces sound more "polite," and contained, perhaps, although there's a radical thinking going on inside them. I'm a subversive at heart.

ROARK: What's the longest period of time you have gone without writing a poem? Do you get a feeling of restlessness when you're not producing?

WALDMAN: Five minutes? I'm crazy when I'm not writing. I'm sick. I have no purpose in life. Something devastating like that.

Winter/Spring 1991, Boulder, Colorado.

PART TWO

TALKING
POETICS

PART TWO

TALKING POETICS

C|ANTE MORO

This week's rubric being "The New American Poetry," what I have to say will relate to that. But I'd like to touch on it where it opens onto matters we wouldn't necessarily expect it to entail—not necessarily "new," not necessarily "American," not even necessarily "poetry." What I'd like to touch on is the New American Poetry's Spanish connection: García Lorca's meditation upon the "dark sounds" of *cante jondo,* deep song, the quality and condition known as *duende.* I'll be talking about that in relation to an array of "dark sounds" which bear upon a cross-cultural poetics intimated by the inclusion of Lorca's "Theory and Function of the *Duende*" in *The Poetics of the New American Poetry,* an espousal of not only cross-cultural but intermedia fertilization and provocation which I'll relate to the work of a number of writers.

The title "Cante Moro" goes back to a recording which came out twenty-five years ago, a recording by Manitas de Plata, probably the flamenco musician best known to listeners in the U.S. at that time. At one point during one of the pieces on the album, "Moritas Moras," after the opening run of singing by José Reyes, a member of the group says, "Eso es cante moro," which means "That's Moorish singing." Calling deep song *cante moro* summons the past rule and continuing cultural presence of the Moors in Spain; it acknowledges the hybrid, heterogeneous roots not only of *cante jondo* but of Spanish culture generally, of, in fact, culture, collective poesis, generally. A Gypsy doing so, as in this instance, allies outcast orders, acknowledging hybridity and heterogeneity to entwine the heterodox as well—heterodox Gypsy, heterodox Moor. *Cante moro* bespeaks the presence and persistence of the otherwise excluded, the otherwise expelled.

Let me begin by saying a bit about Lorca. Of the twenty-five writers in the anthology *The Poetics of the New American Poetry* Lorca is one of the anomalies, perhaps *the* anomaly—the only non-anglophone poet and one of only two non-Americans included. It's fitting he should give the volume its heaviest cross-cultural, cross-pollinating touch. He himself was drawn to the marginalized, the anomalous, to those relegated to the outskirts of sanctioned identity and culture. A large part of his importance to Spanish poetry is the respect he accorded the vernacular culture of southern Spain. He sought instruction in the mixed cultural inheritance of Andalusia, in the music of outcast Gypsies, in reminders of the expelled Moors. The book which made him famous is *Gypsy Ballads,* published in 1928. There's a correspondence between what Lorca was doing in Spain and what was going on in this country among black writers during the Harlem Renaissance of the twenties and thirties. The tapping of vernacular resources was a defining feature of the Harlem Renaissance and it's no accident that one of its most prominent poets, Langston Hughes, was one of the first translators of *Gypsy Ballads* into English. Lorca in fact had direct contact with Harlem and the Harlem Renaissance writers while studying at Columbia in 1929 and 1930. The work which came out of that stay, *Poet in New York,* contains a section called "The Blacks" which celebrates Harlem. The recently published translation of that work by Greg Simon and Steven F. White includes letters Lorca wrote his family from New York. In one of them he tells of meeting the Harlem Renaissance novelist Nella Larsen, author of *Quicksand* and *Passing,* and of the party she gave for him at her house at which "there were only blacks." Of the music they played and sang he writes: "Only the *cante jondo* is comparable."

In his essay on *duende* Lorca is working with the black aesthetic of Spain. One of the things he does early in the essay is quote the Gypsy singer Manuel Torre as having said, "All that has dark sounds has *duende.*" That, at least, is how it's translated by J. L. Gili in the version which appears in *The Poetics of the New American Poetry.* Christopher Maurer, in the more recent translation which appears in *Deep Song and Other Prose,* renders it: "All that has black sounds has *duende.*" Maurer also points out, in a footnote, that when Lorca met Torre in 1927, Torre, evoking the Gypsies' fabled origins in Egypt, said to him, "What you must search for, and find, is the black torso of the Pharaoh." He meant that you have to root your voice in fabulous origins, find your voice in the dark, among the dead. But that's a side conversation we can't go into right now. Anyway, the word *duende* means spirit, a kind of gremlin, a gremlinlike, troubling spirit. One of the things that marks the arrival of *duende* in flamenco singing is a sound of trouble in the voice. The voice becomes troubled. Its eloquence becomes eloquence of another order, a broken, problematic, self-problematizing eloquence. Lorca also quotes Torre as having told a singer, "You have a voice, you know the styles, but you will never triumph, because you have no *duende*." So you see that *duende* is something beyond technical competence or even technical virtuosity. It is something troubling. It has to do with trouble, deep trouble. Deep song delves into troubled water, troubles the water. As a character in Leon Forrest's novel *Two Wings To Veil My Face* puts it: "Still waters don't run deep enough."

Lorca tells a story of the Andalusian singer Pastora Pavón, also known as La Niña de los Peines. He tells of her singing in a little tavern in Cádiz one night before a group of flamenco aficionados. He says that when she finished singing she was met with silence. Her voice, though technically perfect, and her virtuosity, though impressive, didn't move anyone. "When Pastora Pavón finished singing," Lorca writes, "there was total silence, until a tiny man, one of those dancing manikins that rise suddenly out of brandy bottles, sarcastically murmured 'Viva Paris!' as if to say: 'Here we care nothing about ability, technique, skill. Here we are after something else.'" Which is not to say that you get there by not having skill. You get there by not being satisfied with skill. It's the other side, the far side of skill, not the near side. Then Lorca goes on to say:

> As though crazy, torn like a medieval weeper, La Niña
> de los Peines got to her feet, tossed off a big glass of
> firewater and began to sing with a scorched throat,
> without voice, without breath or color, but with
> *duende*. She was able to kill all the scaffolding of the
> song and leave way for a furious, enslaving *duende*,
> friend of sand winds, who made the listeners rip their
> clothes with the same rhythm as do the blacks of the

Antilles when, in the "lucumí" rite, they huddle in heaps
before the statue of Santa Bárbara.

It's interesting that Lorca makes the Old World–New World connection, a black connection, a connection between *duende*, black
song in Spain, *cante moro*, and black song in Cuba, the music of
the Yoruba-Catholic mix known as *lucumí*. That's one of the reasons
Lorca is relevant to new American possibilities, to an American newness which is about mix, the meeting of different cultural styles and
predispositions. He was interested in Old World predecessor mixes
like those in Andalusia, whose further inflections in the Americas he
recognized and embraced.

Lorca doesn't so much define *duende* as grope after it, wrestle
with it, evoke it through strain, insist on struggle. He says, for example, that "one must awaken the *duende* in the remotest mansions
of the blood." He says that "the *duende* loves the rim of the wound"
and that it "draws near places where forms fuse together into a
yearning superior to their visible expression." He writes: "Each art has
a *duende* different in form and style but their roots all meet in the
place where the black sounds of Manuel Torre come from—the
essence, the uncontrollable, quivering, common base of wood,
sound, canvas, and word." One of the ongoing challenges of
Lorca's essay is how to bring *duende,* which he discusses mainly in
relation to music, over into writing, how to relate it to writing. So
what I'd like to do now is touch upon four American poets whose
work intersects with Lorca's and then play you some music I've put
on tape, weave back and forth between tape and talk. Three of
the four poets were included in the anthology *The New American
Poetry 1945–1960:* Jack Spicer, Robert Duncan and Amiri Baraka. The
fourth, Bob Kaufman, was not included, though he should have been.

First, Jack Spicer, who was based in the San Francisco Bay Area,
a San Francisco poet. Though he began writing in the forties he felt
that his real work began with *After Lorca,* which was published
in 1957. It's a book of poems and prose pieces, poems which are
presented as translations of poems by Lorca, translations in a very

loose sense, loose translations. Some of them are translations in an even looser sense, in that they're translations of Lorca poems which don't exist. Interspersed among these translations are the prose pieces, which are written as letters addressed to the dead García Lorca. Lorca was killed during the Spanish Civil War. He was executed by Franco's troops. Which is another reason he has attracted a lot of attention—as a symbol, a sign of the times, times we continue to live in. Here is this poet of cultural openness, cultural mix, cut down by the emergence of fascism. A lot of writers have identified with Lorca and the position, implicit and explicit, he took against fascism. Remember that the Gypsies he celebrated so were one of the targets of fascism, that a million Gypsies were killed in concentration camps.

Lorca was killed in 1936 near Granada. Spicer, a very playful writer, albeit a bit grim, begins *After Lorca* with an introduction attributed to "Federico García Lorca / Outside Granada, October 1957." The gremlin, the imp, is very active in what he's doing. Also, he's picking up on something that's very important in Lorca's discussion of *duende*, which is that, among other things, it's a conversation with the dead, intimacy with death and with the dead. "The *duende*," Lorca says, "does not come at all unless he sees that death is possible. The *duende* must know beforehand that he can serenade death's house and rock those branches we all wear, branches that do not have, will never have, any consolation." The disconsolate character and tone of Spicer's work agrees not only with this but with the fact that one of the phrases which recur a great deal in *cante jondo* is the phrase *sin remedio,* "without remedy." You'll also hear the assertion *no hay remedio,* "there is no remedy." Pepe de la Matrona, who has one of the darkest, gruffest voices you'll ever hear (more an extended, variegated growl than a voice), sings a song called "Remedio No Tengas," which means "You Would Have No Remedy." *Duende* often has to do with a kind of longing that has no remedy, not simply loss, unrequited love and so forth, but what Lorca calls "a longing without object." He talks about this in relation to *Gypsy Ballads,* to a poem which has to do with a woman named Soledad Montoya, who, he says, "embodies incurable pain":

> The Pain of Soledad Montoya is the root of the
> Andalusian people. It is not anguish, because in pain
> one can smile, nor does it blind, for it never produces
> weeping. It is a longing without object, a keen love for
> nothing, with the certainty that death (the eternal care
> of Andalusia) is breathing behind the door.

So Spicer opens *After Lorca* with an introduction written by Lorca, at that time some twenty years dead. In it Lorca says that several of the pieces in the book are translations of poems he has written since his death, though he doesn't say which. In the essay on *duende* he writes: "A dead man in Spain is more alive as a dead man than any place else in the world." Spicer seems to have taken him at his word. Impish play and disconsolate spirit—"The dead are notoriously hard to satisfy," we read—repeatedly embrace one another in an introduction whose antic humor gathers troubling undertones. The words *execution* and *executed,* used in reference to Spicer's technique, resonate with and are darkly inflected by the circumstances of Lorca's death. Likewise the joke with which the introduction ends:

> But I am strongly reminded as I survey this curious amal-
> gam of a cartoon published in an American magazine
> while I was visiting your country in New York. The car-
> toon showed a gravestone on which were inscribed
> the words: "HERE LIES AN OFFICER AND A GENTLEMAN."
> The caption below it read: "I wonder how they hap-
> pened to be buried in the same grave?"

Another poet who was engaged with Lorca's work, another San Francisco poet, is Robert Duncan, an associate of Spicer's. In his book *Caesar's Gate: Poems 1949-50* there's a preface Duncan wrote in 1972, the year the book was published, and in that preface there's a section called "Lorca." The book includes a poem called "What Have You Come to Tell Me, García Lorca?" and in the preface Duncan recalls the forties and fifties when he was reading

Lorca. He talks for several pages about Lorca's importance to his development and he mentions Spicer as well. He talks about a number of things. He talks about the historical predicament, the historical moment that was Lorca's fate, the Spanish Civil War and the rise of fascism. He talks about *duende*. He also talks about Lorca as a gay poet, a troubled, conflicted gay poet who was important to him and Spicer as gay poets. Not that he advanced a gay poetics but that they saw in him and his work some of the trouble, for him, of being gay—a certain depression and self-censure, a censuring of his own homosexuality. He writes this about *duende:*

> In his lecture "Theory and Function of the *Duende*," Lorca tells us: "The dark and quivering *duende* that I am talking about is a descendant of the merry demon of Socrates." The madness, then, however it may relate to the practice of deliberate alienation which Lorca's intimate friend from student days, Salvador Dalí, had brought into Surrealist circles of Paris from their Spanish conversations, and which led to the work of Breton and Eluard in *L'Immaculée Conception,* contemporary with Lorca's *Poeta en Nueva York,* with Breton's essay on the simulation of verbal deliriums from various categories of insanity—this madness is not ultimately a surrealist simulation drawn from a clinical model in a program of systematic alienation but, past that state, means to return to the divine madness of daemonic inspiration, the speaking more than one knew what, that Plato tells us his Master, Socrates, thought to be at once the power and the dementia of the poet in his art.

He speaks of *duende* as a "mode of poetic dissociation" and of "disturbed meanings." The poet speaks in tongues, multiply, troublingly: "Freed from reality, the trouble of an unbound reference invades the reader's sense of what is at issue."

So *duende,* for Duncan, is "the speaking more than one knew what," the taking on of another voice, and that's very much what *duende* is in *cante jondo*. It's a taking over of one's voice by another voice. I'll be playing some examples of this, not only from flamenco but from the African-American traditions that I'm interested in, jazz and blues musicians who seek another voice. This wooing of another voice, an alternate voice, that's so important to *duende* has as one of its aspects or analogues in poetry that state of entering the language in such a way that one is into an area of implication, resonance and connotation that is manifold, many-meaninged, polysemous. One has worked beyond oneself. It's as if the language itself takes over. Something beyond the will, the conscious design or desire of the poet, is active, something which goes beyond univocal, unequivocal control. That's what Duncan means by "the trouble of an unbound reference"—an inordinacy, a lack of adequation which is to language what *sin remedio* is to a longing without object. Bound reference, univocal meaning, is no solution to the riddle of language.

Let me move on to Amiri Baraka, who cites Lorca as an influence in his statement on poetics in *The New American Poetry*. There's an early poem of his called "Lines to García Lorca," which he prefaces with an epigraph taken from an African-American spiritual: "Climin up the mountain, chillun, / Didn't come here for to stay, / If I'm ever gonna see you agin / It'll be on the judgment day." By doing so he not only acknowledges Lorca's interest in African-American music and culture but furthers the analogy, the sense of rapport, between African-American spirituality and Andalusian spirituality. Gypsies, though they don't appear explicitly in this poem, come in elsewhere in Baraka's early work to embody a mobile, mercurial noninvestment in the status quo. One of the things going on in "Lines to García Lorca" is the implicit connection between that mercuriality, that nomadism, and the lines "Didn't come here for to stay," behind which lies a well-known, resonant history of African-American fugitivity and its well-known, resonant relationship to enslavement and persecution. Thus the resonant apposition of the poem's opening lines: "Send soldiers again to kill you, García. / Send them to quell my escape." At the end of the poem Lorca's voice, "away off," invested with fugitive spirit, laughs:

But, away off, quite close to the daylight,
I hear his voice, and he is laughing, laughing
Like a Spanish guitar.

The way in which fugitivity asserts itself on an aesthetic level, at the level of poetics, is important as well. The way in which Baraka's poems of this period move intimates fugitive spirit, as does much of the music that he was into. I recall him writing of a solo by saxophonist John Tchicai on an Archie Shepp album: "It slides away from the proposed." That gets into, again, the cultivation of another voice, a voice that is other than that proposed by one's intentions, tangential to one's intentions, angular, oblique—the obliquity of an unbound reference. That sliding away wants out. Musicians like Tchicai and Shepp were called "outside" players. Robin Blaser called Spicer's work "the practice of outside." Let me, though, let another poem of Baraka's, "History As Process," say it, show it. Lorca doesn't explicitly come in, but the Gypsies do and so does the guitar:

1

The evaluation of the mysteries by the sons of all
experience. All suffering, if we call the light a thing
all men should know. Or find. Where ever, in the dark folds
of the next second, there is some diminishing beauty we
    might one day
understand, and scream to, in some wild fit of acknowl-
    edged Godliness.

Reality, is what it is. This suffering truth
advertised in all men's loveliest histories.

The thing, There As Speed, is God, as mingling
possibility. The force. As simple future, what

the freaky gipsies rolled through Europe
on.

(The soul.)

2

What can I do to myself? Bones
and dusty skin. Heavy eyes twisted
between the adequate thighs of all
humanity (a little h), strumming my head
for a living. Bankrupt utopia sez tell me
no utopias. I will not listen. (Except the raw wind
makes the hero's eyes close, and the tears that come out
are real.)

You hear the pronouncements, the propositions. You also hear the slips, the slides, the shifting ratios—rhythmic, predicative, quick.

The last of the four poets I'll touch on is Bob Kaufman. His work was not included in *The New American Poetry,* even though it was very important to the Beat movement. He was very involved in the development of the Beat movement in San Francisco, in North Beach, and is said to have coined the term "beatnik." Some people consider him the prototypical Beat poet. Steve Abbott has called him "the hidden master of the Beats." Anyway, he was a poet of African-American and Jewish descent to whom Lorca's work was very important. He refers to Lorca in a number of poems, echoing lines from his work, sometimes quoting or paraphrasing them outright. In "Lorca," for example, you find the line "Give Harlem's king one spoon" harking back to *Poet in New York,* where "The King of Harlem" begins with the lines "With a wooden spoon / he dug out the crocodiles' eyes." What spoke most to Kaufman was Lorca's valorization of African-American presence. In his lecture on *Poet in New York* Lorca argued that "the blacks exercise great influence in North America," that "they are the most delicate, most spiritual element in that world." The "great sun of the center" he encourages black people to seek in "The King of Harlem," to continue seeking, is, among other things, the covert centrality of an otherwise marginalized people, a "sun" which cross-linguistically puns on "soul" ("el gran sol del centro").

Kaufman's apocalyptic, ironically patriotic prose-poem "The Ancient Rain" generously samples, as we would say nowadays, "The

King of Harlem" and "Standards and Paradise of the Blacks." Its embrace of Lorca's endorsement of new American possibilities, new American mixes, resounds in telling counterpoint not only with Kaufman's non-inclusion in *The New American Poetry* (only one non-white poet's work was included) but with the negligible attention accorded him and his work in the numerous writings on the Beat Generation as well:

> At once I am there at the great sun, feeling the great
> sun of the center. Hearing the Lorca music in the end-
> less solitude of crackling blueness. I could feel myself
> a little boy again in crackling blueness, wanting to do
> what Lorca says in crackling blueness to kiss out my
> frenzy on bicycle wheels and smash little squares in the
> flush of a soiled exultation. Federico García Lorca sky,
> immaculate scoured sky, equaling only itself contained
> all the distances that Lorca is, that he came from Spain
> of the Inquisition is no surprise. His poem of solitude
> walking around Columbia. My first day in crackling
> blueness, I walked off my ship and rode the subway
> to Manhattan to visit Grant's tomb and I thought be-
> cause Lorca said he would let his grow long someday
> crackling blueness would cause my hair to grow long.
> I decided to move deeper into crackling blueness.
> When Franco's civil guard killed, from that moment on,
> I would move deeper in crackling blueness. I kept my
> secrets. I observed those who read him who were not
> Negroes and listened to all their misinterpretation of
> him. I thought of those who had been around him,
> those that were not Negro and were not in crackling
> blueness, those that couldn't see his wooden south
> wind, a tiltin' black slime that tacked down all the boat
> wrecks, while Saturn delayed all the trains.

"Crackling blueness," out of "Standards and Paradise of the Blacks," is the sky cracked by lightning, the imminence of thunder and rain, wrath and redemption, "the bitter freshness of . . . millenary spit," as Lorca puts it. It's also the raspy, cracked voice of *duende,* the ominous, black vocality of the blues and of *cante jondo.*

Those, then, are four instances of American poets making use of the work of Lorca. They relate to the question of how one's writing can draw upon that of predecessors, the sense of tradition, a lineage one creates for oneself, that one seeks out in the work of others. Influence without anxiety call it. As a writer one has to find one's tradition, create one's tradition, and in doing that you're creating lines of affinity and kinship which can cut across national boundaries, ethnic boundaries and so forth. They also relate to the question of how one's writing can be informed and instructed by other artistic media, how one can create or pursue lines of kinship and conversation with nonliterary media. That's one of the useful senses the phrase "cultivation of another voice" I used earlier has. A different medium is a different voice, an alternate vocality. Lorca's sense of *duende* comes out of his engagement with music, the Andalusian music he was obviously moved and inspired by. Attentiveness to those other, alternate voices which speak to you—painting, sculpture, whatever—can make you susceptible, impinge upon you in ways which alter your own voice.

My work has a pronounced relationship to music. I was always struck by Louis Zukofsky's definition of poetry as a function whose lower limit is speech and whose upper limit is song. He uses the integral sign from calculus to suggest that we're integrating that lower limit, speech, and that upper limit, song. Poetry is an integral function. But even before I came across Zukofsky's formulation of it I heard poetry as a musical deployment of language, the music peculiar to language, language bordering on song, speech bordering on song. From doing a lot of listening I've gotten certain ideas about music, a thematics of music, but also an impulse towards a musicality in the writing. Years ago I wrote a poem for John Coltrane, "Ohnedaruth's Day Begun," in which there's this passage:

> I grope thru smoke to glimpse New
> York City, the Village Gate, late

'65. I sit at the bar drinking scotch between
sets, some kid comes up and says he'd
    like to hear *Equinox*.

            We play *Out of*
    This World instead, the riff hits
me like rain and like a leak in my
    throat it won't quit. No reins whoa
    this ghost I'm ridden by and again
                        I'm asking
myself what "climb" will Nut ask of
    me next? . . .

This has to do, among other things, with a surge, a runaway dilation,
a quantum rush you often hear in Trane's music, the sense that he's
driven, possessed—*ridden,* as it's put here, which recalls the African
possession religions in which worshippers are spoken of as horses
and the gods, the spirits, are spoken of as horsemen, riders. To be
possessed is to be mounted and ridden by a god. You find that im-
agery in *vodoun* in Haiti, in *candomblé* in Brazil, in *lucumí* or *santería*
in Cuba. Possession means that something beyond your grasp of it
grabs you, that something that gets away from you—another sense
in which fugitivity comes in—gives you a voice. Like Lorca, who, remember, refers to *lucumí,* I think of this as related to *duende.*

So that's one place in my work where ideas having to do with
duende come in. Another place is *Bedouin Hornbook,* which even
more extensively and graphically has to do with music. It's prose,
written mainly in the form of letters addressed to an angel by a mu-
sician/composer, N. *Duende* is a term which comes up a number of
times in these letters. One instance is this one, towards the end of a
letter which accompanies the tape of a composition which N. has
written:

The name of the piece is "Opposable Thumb at the
Water's Edge." Its basic theme I'd put this way:
Graspability is a self-incriminating thirst utterly native to

every hand, an indigenous court from which only the
drowned hope to win an acquittal. The piece makes
use of two triadic phrases which I call utility riffs: "whatever beginnings go back to" and "an exegetic refusal
to be done with desire." These generate a subtheme
which could be put as follows: Thirst is by its nature unquenchable, the blue lips of a muse whose refusals
roughen our throats with *duende*.

Unquenchable thirst is a longing without object. Blue, the color of its
ostensible object, plants a disconsolate kiss.

What I want to do now is play some music which relates to these
matters. First let me play a piece by the singer Lorca talks about in
his essay on *duende*, Pastora Pavón, La Niña de los Peines. It's a
piece called "Ay Pilato" and it's a type of song known as a *saeta*
("Ay Pilato," *La Niña de los Peines* (Le Chant du Monde LDX 74859)).
The *saeta* is a form of song which is heard in Andalusia during Holy
Week, the week before Easter. A procession takes place, a procession through the streets, a procession which includes musicians—
sometimes playing nothing but muffled drums but often including
horns, brass instruments. The procession carries an image, which is
either of the Virgin or of Christ, sometimes both. At each point where
the procession stops there is a singer on a balcony overlooking the
street, overlooking the procession. The procession stops right beneath the balcony and the singer sings to the image they carry.
Saeta means arrow. The song is piercing, heartrending. The singer
sings from a position of being pierced.

Next I'll play another *saeta,* the first one I ever heard. It's by Miles
Davis, taken from his album *Sketches of Spain* ("Saeta," *Sketches of
Spain* (Columbia CS 1480)). Miles was very attracted to flamenco
early on. On the *Kind of Blue* album there's a cut called "Flamenco
Sketches" and on a later album, the famous *Bitches Brew* that came
out in 1970, there's a cut called "Spanish Church." All of which lends
itself to the Andalusian/African-American rapport we've seen Lorca
and others get at. Anyway, in 1960 Miles teamed up with pianist/
composer/arranger Gil Evans and recorded *Sketches of Spain*. One

of the five pieces on the album is a *saeta*, with Miles, on trumpet, playing the role of the *cantaor*, the singer on the balcony. They even simulate the procession, opening and closing the cut with march music. You can hear that tremulous, piercing sound Miles gets out of the trumpet. There've been various attempts to describe it. One critic called it the sound of a man walking on eggshells and there's the story of a little girl who said he sounded like a little boy crying in a closet. Anyway, that was recorded in 1960. Like *Kind of Blue*, it was a very important album for a lot of people. Ezra Pound called poetry "news that stays news." That's what albums like those two are.

The next piece I'll play doesn't relate as explicitly to Andalusia but it still has to do with the things I've been talking about. It's John Coltrane with Miles Davis's group, from the last concert tour that Trane made as part of Miles's band. It was recorded in Stockholm in 1960 ("All Blues," *Miles Davis & John Coltrane Live in Stockholm 1960* (Dragon DRLP 90/91)). I want you to hear the solo he plays on Miles's composition "All Blues," because the quality of reaching for another voice, stretching the voice, passionately reaching, is very, very audible in Coltrane's playing, especially so in this particular solo. It has that quality of *duende* that Lorca talks about as a tearing of the voice, a crippling of the voice that paradoxically is also enabling. I've talked, in an essay called "Sound and Sentiment, Sound and Symbol," about the connection between limping and enablement in relation to the African god Legba, one of the gods of *vodoun, candomblé,* and *lucumí*. Legba is the god of doorways, gateways, entrances, thresholds, crossroads, intersections. Legba is crippled, the limping god who nonetheless dances. That conjunction of limping disability with the gracefulness of dance is one of the things I hear coming through in Trane's solo. I think you'll hear what I'm talking about. This also relates to a forking of the voice, so that you have the intersection of two lines of articulation—doubling the voice, splitting the voice, breaking the voice, tearing it. There's a dialogical aspect to African-American and African music that's very strong. It comes across in call and response, the antiphonal relationship between lead singer and chorus, preacher and congregation.

It comes across in the playing of musicians like John Coltrane who use the upper and lower registers of the instrument as though they were two different voices in dialogue with one another, in a sometimes quarrelsome conversation with one another, competition with one another. In this instance Trane gets into doing some things with overtones, multiphonics, that make it sound almost as if he's playing two different horns, trying to play in two different octaves at the same time. It makes for an unruly, agonistic sound in which it seems that the two lines of articulation are wrestling with one another, that they are somehow one another's contagion or contamination.

It's appropriate that that solo should come in a piece called "All Blues." This business of the pursuit of another voice, an alternate voice—in *Bedouin Hornbook* N. calls it the pursuit of a meta-voice—is very much a part of the African-American musical tradition, very much a part of the African musical tradition. The dialogical quality in music of this disposition can be heard in a number of different idioms and forms. The blues is certainly one of them. What I'm going to play next is something by a blues musician from the Mississippi delta. One of the striking things about the blues tradition is the way the instrument becomes that other, alternate voice. Everyone talks about the speechlike qualities of instruments as they're played in African-American music. Built into that is some kind of dissatisfaction with—if not critique of—the limits of conventionally articulate speech, verbal speech. One of the reasons the music so often goes over into nonspeech—moaning, humming, shouts, nonsense lyrics, scat—is to say, among other things, that the realm of conventionally articulate speech is not sufficient for saying what needs to be said. We're often making that same assertion in poetry. That's one of the reasons that in poetry we seek out that "trouble of an unbound reference" Duncan talks about. That's one of the reasons this music has been so attractive, so instructive, such an inspiration to poets.

Let me play a bit of music by Mississippi Fred McDowell ("Everybody's Down On Me," *I Do Not Play No Rock 'n' Roll* (Capitol ST-409)). Listen to the interaction between his voice and the guitar, a slide guitar, the way that the line between speech and song is very fluid, frequently blurred. That's very much a part of the tradition. There's an album called *Singing Preachers* which features preachers whose sermons would taper off into singing, speech into song, and vice-versa, back and forth. At any rate, notice that he starts off talking and that he works that talk into song, but notice also what he says, the mini-lecture, the sermonette he gives as to what this recourse to sound, a sound peculiar to the slide guitar, a raucous, unruly wail, is about, what it comes out of. He's talking about being betrayed and he's saying that you need an unruly, outrageous sound when you feel there's no other way you can get satisfaction. What you can say, what can be stated within the limits of conventionally articulate speech, isn't enough. What you need is this *sound.* Notice too how he starts stumbling, how he stumbles as he tries to talk about that sound, stumbles until the sound itself comes to his rescue. Notice how the sound itself rescues crippled speech—which, again, is the eloquence of Legba, the limping eloquence, the limping enablement of Legba.

I'll play another piece by Fred McDowell, but before I do that I want to give you another context in which to think about this recourse to an alternate voice, this movement into a voice beyond one's voice, into a meta-voice. That context is shamanism, the shamanic roots of music evoked by the Cuban writer Alejo Carpentier in his novel *The Lost Steps.* It was published in the fifties and it has to do with the journey of a composer/musician into the jungles of South America in search of the origins of music, something of an ethnomusicological expedition. Carpentier was, among other things, a musicologist. He did research, for example, into the African roots of Cuban music and culture, into *lucumí* and so forth, and his first novel, *Ecue-Yamba-O!,* has to do with that. Anyway, the recourse to another voice, the need for an alternate voice, is something he goes into in several passages in *The Lost Steps.* In the depths of a South American forest the narrator witnesses a shamanic rite performed over the body of a hunter who was killed by a rattlesnake bite. He takes this to be the origin of music, the shamanic confrontation with death to be the birth of music:

. . . the shaman began to shake a gourd full of pebbles—the only instrument these people know—trying to drive off the emissaries of Death. There was a ritual silence, setting the stage for the incantation, which raised the tension of the spectators to fever pitch.

And in the vast jungle filling with night terrors, there arose the Word. A word that was more than word. A word that imitated the voice of the speaker, and of that attributed to the spirit in possession of the corpse. One came from the throat of the shaman; the other from his belly. One was deep and confused like the bubbling of underground lava; the other, medium in pitch, was harsh and wrathful. They alternated. They answered each other. The one upbraided when the other groaned; the belly voice turned sarcastic when the throat voice seemed to plead. Sounds like guttural portamenti were heard, ending in howls; syllables repeated over and over, coming to create a kind of rhythm; there were trills suddenly interrupted by four notes that were the embryo of a melody. But then came the vibration of the tongue between the lips, the indrawn snoring, the panting contrapuntal to the rattle of the maraca. This was something far beyond language, and yet still far from song. Something that had not yet discovered vocalization, but was more than word.

He later speaks of this as his having seen "the word travel the road of song without reaching it," and later still of "its verbal exorcism turning into music when confronted with the need for more than one intonation."

Think about that, then, in relation to the music we've been listening to. Think about it in relation to La Niña de los Peines, whose voice breaks, seems intent on some higher octave, some higher voice. Think about it in relation to the John Coltrane solo, where, working with multiphonics, he sounds, voices, discontent with the given intonation, bent on going beyond it. Think about it in relation to antiphony, the call-and-response, dialogical impulse which can be heard even in music played by a lone performer, the interplay between voice and instrument especially within the blues tradition, in the music of someone like Fred McDowell. One of the reasons for the development of slide guitar was the need to get a more human (but not quite human) sound out of the guitar, out of the instrumental line—human-but-not-quite-human speech as well as human-but-not-quite-human cry.

You can hear that in the next thing I'm going to play, another piece by Fred McDowell. It's called "Jesus Is On The Mainline" and one of the striking things about it is the way he lets the guitar speak, actually lets it take parts of his lines ("Jesus Is On The Mainline," *I Do Not Play No Rock 'n' Roll* (Capitol ST-409)). He'll begin singing a line only to break off and let the guitar finish it, suggesting a continuum, a complementarity, between human voice and instrumental voice, an interchange between speech and song, verbal articulation and nonverbal articulation.

If you've read Ishmael Reed's novel *Mumbo Jumbo* you may remember the episode where he talks about an ancient musician named Jethro, an ancient Egyptian musician whose sound he describes as a kind of muddy, delta sound, blurring—muddying—the distinction between the Nile delta and the Mississippi delta. Fred McDowell's guitar has the kind of sound he's talking about.

Another example of multivocality I'd like you to hear is from an album with the shamanic title *I Talk With The Spirits*. It's by Rahsaan Roland Kirk and on it he plays flute throughout. It's the all-flute album he recorded in the sixties ("The Business Ain't Nothin' But The Blues," *I Talk With The Spirits* (Limelight LS82008)). I'll play a bit from a piece called "The Business Ain't Nothin' But The Blues." You'll notice that he hums while playing, which is something you'll sometimes hear other flute players do as well. Yusef Lateef is one of the first I ever heard do it. It's become something of a standard technique in the repertoire of jazz flutists. On the current scene, James Newton is a flutist you'll hear make use of it a lot. Interestingly, it wasn't something that Eric Dolphy, who was a great flutist, did that much with, but that's another conversation. Anyway, you'll hear Rahsaan humming and even speaking as he plays. Again, it's the play of voices, a move into multiple voices which is analogous to speaking in tongues. So you have a braiding of vocal and instrumental lines. I've even heard some saxophone players do it, hum while playing. Pharoah Sanders does it from time to time. I've heard Dewey Redman do it. It's a wild sound. It'll take your hair off. Anyway, there's a piece in Amiri Baraka's book *Tales* in which he writes: "The dialogue exists. Magic and ghosts are a dialogue, and the body bodies of material, invisible sound vibrations, humming in emptyness, and ideas less than humming, humming. . . ." It sounds like he'd been listening to *I Talk With The Spirits*.

One of the things I've been talking about is cross-culturality, sensing rapport across cultural lines, picking up on rhymes between cultures, dialogue between cultures. What I'm going to play next relates to that. It shows the multivocal technique we just heard from Rahsaan, humming while playing the flute, in another context. This is a piece from Iran, a love song from Luristan ("Love Song," *Folk Music of Iran* (Lyrichord LLST-7261)). It's performed by a singer accompanied by a flutist playing a reed flute known as a *nay*. The *nay* has quite a special place in the mystical traditions of that part of the world. Rumi, for example, writes of the *nay*: "Listen to the reed, its lament speaks to us of separation." He goes on to say that the reed was cut from rushes and that what we hear in the sound of the *nay* is the remembrance of that cutting, that the very sound calls to mind the cutting which brought it into being and which it laments. The sound subsists on that cutting. The *nay* not only mourns but embodies separation. Fittingly, the song I'm about to play contains the lines "I am burning, / I have the taste of separation." That's typical of the poetry and music of Iran. You'll hear the flutist humming while playing the *nay*. In Iran this technique is known as *zemzemeh*. In this piece the splitting of the voice, the cultivation of a multiple voice, seems to embody at the instrumental level the "taste of separation" that's being talked about in the lyrics. So there again you hear humming, the additional voice and vibration it brings in, the buzz it elicits.

Think about that buzz, that vibration, that multiply-aspected vocality, in relation to poetry, to the cultivation of multiple meaning in poems, the play of polysemous articulation. A poem's order of statement is what one critic called "the buzz of implication," something you can hear in even a very brief passage. Take, for example, these lines of Robert Kelly's in a book called *Songs I-XXX*:

> I was not a tree,
> I hung in my bones like a man in a tree,
> the tree talked. I said nothing

The play of assertion against a recanting of assertion amounts to a buzz. The changes it registers concerning the status of treeness, the status of the speaker and the status of speaking make the passage what Rahsaan took to calling his band: a vibration society. The words buzz, whisper among themselves, vibrate with such implicit assertions as that the tree which talks is a skeleton, the man is not his bones, bones are gallows and so forth. I think of this also in relation to the cultivation of resonance in African music. In Zimbabwe, for example, they not only place the mbira, the so-called "thumb-piano," inside a calabash gourd which they call a resonator, but they also attach cowrie shells to the outside of the gourd, shells which rub against the gourd and make a raspy, buzzing sound when the mbira is played. The African predilection for a burred, "dirty" sound, which the Camerounian musician/musicologist Francis Bebey, among others, has commented on, is reluctant to let a tone sit in some uncomplicated, isolate, supposedly pure sense of itself. Poems likewise buzz with meanings, implications and insinuations which complicate, contaminate, "dirty" one another.

Let me now come full-circle, back to Andalusian/African-American resonances, by playing you part of a piece by Sonny Rollins. It's a piece called "East Broadway Rundown," the last few minutes of which I'll play ("East Broadway Rundown," *East Broadway Rundown* (Impulse! A-9121)). What you'll hear is the bass player, Jimmy Garrison, soloing, playing the bass like a big guitar (which is what it is), playing it, more specifically, like a Spanish guitar, playing the flamenco riffs which came to be one of his trademarks. You'll hear

Sonny Rollins come in. What takes place is an interesting interchange which has remained a suggestive, poetic image for me over the years. Rollins removes the mouthpiece from his saxophone and plays it, sans horn. So, again, it's a kind of separation, breakage, amputation. *Bedouin Hornbook* opens with the idea of music as a phantom limb, a phantom reach with/after something you have but don't have. It's a kind of re-membering, a mended dismemberment. This is one of the pieces which put that idea, that figure, into my head. It's perfect—a bassist playing flamenco while a horn player makes a voice, a high, falsetto voice, out of breakage, an alternate voice out of separating the mouthpiece from the horn.

I'll finish by mentioning some of the music I hoped I might have time to play but don't, some further extensions and elaborations of *cante moro*. One of the interesting things which has been happening lately with flamenco in Spain is the assertion of its ties to the Moors, to some of the Arab musics of North Africa. This includes collaborations between flamenco musicians and North African performers of a type of music whose roots are in Muslim Spain, a type of music still known as Andalusian throughout the Maghreb. Two recorded instances are José Heredia Maya and the Andalusian Orchestra of Tetuan's *Macama Jonda* and Juan Peña Lebrijano and the Andalusian Orchestra of Tangier's *Encuentros*. In the seventies and eighties Lole Montoya, of the group Lole and Manuel, recorded a number of songs in Arabic, traveling to the Sono Cairo studios in Egypt in 1977 to record a song made famous by the legendary Om Kalsoum, "Anta Oumri." Also interesting are the connections some of the younger flamenco musicians have made with New World extensions of the African-Iberian mix. A group called Ketama blends flamenco with Cuban rumba, Brazilian samba and so forth. They've also collaborated with a kora player from Mali, Toumani Diabate. One of their influences is a musician named Manzanita, whose 1978 album *Poco Ruido y Mucho Duende* presented him accompanied by, as its liner-notes explain, "dos músicos de color en razón a su sentido improvisatorio y a su 'feeling,' muy próximo al gitano" ("two black musicians because of their improvisatory sense and their 'feeling,' very close to that of the Gypsy").

The two musicians are bassist David Thomas, from the United States, and percussionist Pepe Ebano, from Cuba. Another of Ketama's influences is singer Camarón, who in the late seventies expanded his instrumental accompaniment to include trap drums, keyboards and electric bass. Finally, I would also have liked to play you something by a group called Pata Negra, which a few years ago released an album called *Blues de la Frontera.* As is clear from the title, they play a flamenco-blues mix. It builds on the rapport which has long been noted between the two. I remember hearing a radio documentary on Jimi Hendrix. One segment was a tape from a recording session, maybe a jam, and Hendrix was talking to the other musicians and said, "What I want is a Muddy Waters/flamenco sound." The other musicians said, "Yeah!" Everyone knew exactly what he meant. No problem.

8 & 11 July 1991

BIBLIOGRAPHY

Donald M. Allen (ed.), *The New American Poetry 1945-1960* (New York: Grove Press, 1960).

Donald M. Allen and Warren Tallman (eds.), *The Poetics of the New American Poetry* (New York: Grove Press, 1973).

Amiri Baraka, "Four for Trane," *Black Music* (New York: Morrow, 1967), pp. 156–161.

———, "History As Process," *Black Magic: Poetry 1961–1967* (Indianapolis and New York: Bobbs-Merrill, 1969), p. 38.

———, "Lines to García Lorca," *New Negro Poets: USA,* ed. Langston Hughes (Bloomington and London: Indiana University Press, 1964), p. 55.

———, "Words," *Tales* (New York: Grove Press, 1967), pp. 89–91.

Alejo Carpentier, *The Lost Steps,* trans. Harriet de Onís (New York: Noonday Press, 1989).

Robert Duncan, *Caesar's Gate: Poems 1949–50* (Berkeley: Sand Dollar, 1972).

Bob Kaufman, *The Ancient Rain: Poems 1956–1978* (New York: New Directions, 1981).

Robert Kelly, "Song XVII," *Songs I–XXX* (Carnbridge, MA: Pym-Randall Press, 1968), pp. 52-53.

Federico García Lorca, *Deep Song and Other Prose,* trans. Christopher Maurer (New York: New Directions, 1980).

————, *Poet in New York,* trans. Greg Simon and Steven F. White (New York: Noonday Press, 1988).

Nathaniel Mackey, *Bedouin Hornbook* (Lexington: Callaloo Fiction Series, 1986).

————, "Ohnedaruth's Day Begun," *Eroding Witness* (Urbana and Chicago: University of Illinois Press, 1985), pp. 70–74.

————, "Sound and Sentiment, Sound and Symbol," *Callaloo,* Volume 10, Number 1 (Winter 1987), pp. 29–54.

Jack Spicer, *The Collected Books of Jack Spicer* (Los Angeles: Black Sparrow Press, 1975).

ADDITIONAL DISCOGRAPHY

Camarón, *Calle Real* (Phillips 814-466-1).

————, *La Leyenda del Tiempo* (Phillips 63-28-255).

Juan Peña Lebrijano and the Andalusian Orchestra of Tangier, *Encuentros* (Ariola I207240).

Lole and Manuel, *Casta* (CBS S-26027).

————, *Lole y Manuel* (CBS S-82276).

————, *Nuevo Día* (Movieplay 15.2320/3).

Ketama, *Ketama* (Hannibal HNBL-1336).

————, *Songhai* (Hannibal HNBL-1323).

————, *Y Es Ke Me Han Kambiao Los Tiempos* (Mango 539.879-1).

Manitas de Plata, *Manitas de Plata-Flamenco Guitar, Volume 2* (Connoisseur Society CS965).

Manzanita, *Poco Ruido y Mucho Duende* (CBS S-83188).

José Heredia Maya and the Andalusian Orchestra of Tetuan, *Macama Jonda* (Ariola I295400).

Pata Negra, *Blues de la Frontera* (Hannibal HNBL-1309).

Pepe de la Matrona, *Pepe de la Matrona, Volume 2* (Hispavox 150-055).

Singing Preachers (Blues Classics BC-I9).

ROM: A LECTURE AT THE NAROPA INSTITUTE, 1989

What I'm going to do is go through this motley assembly of my published books and explain to you what the structures of the books
are. I'm not going to talk about any other aspect of the book except the structure, the form of the work, which I'd prefer to call
structure since that's more architectural.

This is the first book I ever published. I published it myself. It's
called *Story*. It has no page numbers. It's about thirty pages. The
way it came into being was I wrote a story that was about falling
down, tripping and falling down. It was nicely written, experimentally so, but it seemed dull. So I tried to figure out what to do with it;
and being a twenty-year-old person at the time, I went overboard
and made a structure that is like a diamond shape where I accumulated other texts. I was very interested in American Indian myths
at that time so I included a Kwakiutl myth about hats and about
smoking; their description of a hoop and arrow game; and then
an Italian folk tale about fourteen men who went to hell; another
Italian tale about a man who sold cloth to a statue; then from Coos
myth texts, a story of the five world makers, and the man who became an owl. Then I accumulated some lists from the dictionary
of other words for beginning, middle, and end. There's a recipe for
true sponge cake, there's a 19th Century letter about etiquette, a
couple of quotes from Edgar Allan Poe, and an article by the biologist Louis Agassiz about coral reefs. Each of these things I thought
was relevant to the diamond shaped nature or accumulation of the
story. Smoking, and cooking. That's all I have in my notes.

As I was saying to Clark Coolidge, there is some aspect of this work
that I can't remember (as to how I did it). I took the longest work which
was the story I'd written about falling, and I made that begin at the
beginning and end at the end. Everything was going on in the exact
middle of the work, and at the beginning and end only one thing
was going on and it was gradually accumulating and decreasing.

To make things worse, I decided to interrupt the text at random moments with all the words I could think of that would mean story. Here's the list of those. There are fifty-one. (Reads from the list: anecdote, profile, life-story, scenario, love-story, lie, report, western, article, bedside reading, novel, thumbnail sketch, tale, description, real-life story, piece, light reading, confessions, dime novel, narrative poem, myth, thriller.)

It was interrupted at random. The confluences were amazing. All of a sudden it would say detective story, and the section that was randomly chosen to be a detective story really became one. Or could become one in the reader's mind. Probably more so than in my mind.

(Reads examples of the beginning, middle, and ending definitions.) They were interspersed in this text at the beginning, middle, and end.

The structure of the next book is simply the duplication of a journal that I was keeping when I was about seventeen, and it includes translations from Ovid, *The Golden Age,* sort of funny journalistic notes, poems, and things about my grandfather. All I did was print the journal itself, and the reason I did it (I didn't actually do it myself, but the reason I wanted to do it) was because the keeping of this journal was what had inspired me to really want to become a poet. So I thought it would be useful to other people. It's called *Ceremony Latin 1964,* which is the year it was written.

Next comes *Moving,* a book that relates to some people here. Anne Waldman (did you publish it by yourself?) published this book. She discovered me. I went to the country; I had received some inheritance, and I rented a house in Great Barrington, Massachusetts, someone's summer house that they wanted to rent for the winter. At that point, it was very cheap to do that. I set myself the task of not writing as much as possible. Only writing when I absolutely felt compelled. Never writing in the way most of us do: well I have to write; or I haven't written enough; or I should write every day. Not doing anything like that, but only that which seems to come from something other than the self. I tried very hard not to write. After a year, I produced this book which Anne discovered as a pile of pages on the top of my typewriter when she came to visit me. She decided to publish it.

The structure of *Moving* is hard to describe except in terms of *this* book. (Holds up *The How & Why Wonder Book of Our Earth*.) I always felt it was important if there are things you don't know about to read good children's books about them and get good explanations as to why the sky is blue. So you really know, instead of reading some abstruse text. So you could really tell somebody. *Moving* is based on the structure of this *How & Why Book*, the table of contents of which reads: The Beginning of the Earth; Upheavals in the Earth; Souvenirs of the Past (that included things about fossils and glaciers); Water, Water Everywhere; The Earth's Surface; Treasures In the Ground; The Underground Rooms (that's all about caves); and The Beginning of Man. That's how I ended *Moving*, with the beginning of man and all of man's talents or lack of them. That's exactly the structure, although the book looks funny. The other thing I should tell you about the structure is that Anne had this nice printer in Williamstown, and he was really very patient. (Anne Waldman says: "Saint.") I told him I didn't want a left hand margin in the book. I wanted it to be raggedy on the left side as well as on the right side. Since he was setting real type, it was almost impossible for him to do that. He said to me, "How do I do it, where do I start the line?" I said "At random," obviously not the right thing to say to a very careful craftsperson. But he did a beautiful job of it. So that's that structure.

Let's see what comes next. *Memory*. Well, this is a complex one too. Notes about *Moving* are in *Memory*. I forgot to tell you, in *Moving* I also incorporated, I solicited work from other poets and writers to include. I invited a lot of people to contribute to the book, whatever they wanted to and I would just intersperse it at random. *Moving* begins with a chance poem beginning with words from ten different kinds of books left in random order but repeatable. That's how the book begins, with this poem that was written in that manner. I used ten different kinds of books, chose random words, and left them in random order but gave myself the right to repeat them. Then I have this note on the back: "I put it all in together. I thought the poem should be information and also political, but not by me. That was an important part of this book, an important political part of the book that it not be written necessarily by me."

This is a book called *Memory*. It originally was a series of photographs. It's a diary of one month. I shot a roll of film, thirty-six pictures every day. I had a patron at the time, Holly Solomon. She paid for the film and the developing. I shot slides and she made them into prints. She put it up as a show. We did it along the wall; it was about forty feet long and four feet high from left to right as a book would read. I kept journals. We always painted our journals, at the time. I didn't have an automatic light meter, so I kept my list of exposures for the film in the backs of the journals. I wrote incessant notes and made drawings about everything that happened every day. I wrote down as much as I could without interrupting my life. It was the month of July, 1971. I had chosen the month at random without knowing what I would be doing during that month, because I didn't want to choose a time to do this experiment that would be particularly loaded, or particularly interesting or dull. At the show, all the journals were turned into reel-to-reel tapes. It opened up in this funny gallery, which was trying to do kind of new things at that point in time. Conceptual art I suppose, is what it's called. So we played the tapes; it was an eight hour show. If you wanted to hear the whole show, you could follow the whole month by walking along with the pictures, and spend eight hours in the gallery.

Praeger Publishers said that they wanted to publish it as a book with all the photographs in it. I thought this was amazing, what a great thing. This agent said, "Can I come and discuss this with you?" and I said, "Fine." He said if you'll make love with me, I'll get the book published. That's how it wound up in *this* form. So I only have a few photographs in the published book by North Atlantic Books.

Structurally speaking again, when I put the text together I took my journals and I projected the slides on the wall, very small, right next to my desk. When you project the slides very small the colors are very vivid. I wrote sort of around the pictures, around the text I already had, added to it from the pictures. This nearly drove me crazy. One of the reasons I did it was to be nasty to Gertrude Stein who always said you can't write remembering, so I wanted to say to her that maybe you could. I think she's right that you practically wind up in an insane asylum on a project like this. Stein has a lot of theories that while you're writing, you should be writing in the present moment or in the continuous present and not be saying things to yourself like, "What was I going to say next? Was the couch green or did I say it was green on the previous page?" That sort of thing. It's also a philosophical stance of hers, from her studies with William James. But in a spirit of fun, I was doing it *with* Gertrude Stein.

The next one is *Studying Hunger*. This book is actually two lectures culled from a series of journals. I don't know what to say they're about. What are they about? Hunger? My work with a psychoanalyst. Most of the books are the size of big drawing books. A lot of pictures in them, a lot of colored pens. I knew this was not a publishable work. It's almost masochistic in and of itself to do something like that. When I was invited to give two readings during the years I was keeping these books (there are about seven of them) I took things from the journals and made them into sort of lecture style or lecture length. That's what's in this book. It is a combination of prose and poetry, published by Big Sky.

I recently attempted to publish the *Studying Hunger* journals. The publisher balked because there's five hundred pages of text. I'm trying to think if there's anything else I should say about the structure of this book. The combination of poetry and prose and moving freely between both is something that's always been inspiring to me, and especially from reading Dante's *Vita Nuova*. Also, obviously, William Carlos Williams' *Paterson*. Can anyone think of other books that do that, that move between prose and poetry. Basho. (Students say: "*Desolation Angels*.") Sure. Those are my favorite kinds of books. I love that form. That to me seems like the ultimate freedom. And especially if you have the nerve to analyze your poems after you've put them in the text, as Dante did. He'd say, "And then I wrote this poem" and he gives you the sonnet. He'd analyze them in kind of a dumb way; he tells you what it means, the structure. (Anne Waldman: "What the occasion for it was.") I think it's a great exercise.

The next book, in chronological order, is a book called *Poetry*. I think it's my most boring book. It's divided exactly in half. It was the first time anyone wanted to publish a book of real poems of mine. So I was very excited about the prospect, and I tried to include everything. What I put in the beginning was all my old poems, and in the second section I put the poems I'd written in the last two weeks. That's another possible structure, but I resent the book in a way.

Here's a fascinating idea. This book is called *Eruditio Ex Memoria*, which basically means learning out of memory, or learning that is memory. I had thousands of high school and college notebooks that were sitting in a room in my ancestral home. I had to move everything out of that house. Everybody had died. I didn't have any place to put all the things I wanted to keep or save. I thought, regarding the notebooks, they're really all the same in a way. I decided to tear out random pages from each one so I had something from each. I threw the rest away. I took those pages and wrote this book, which is a book really about what you learn in school or how you learn it. The other structural question about this book was how to deal with commas. Because there was so much related material. How to pause, or how not to pause. Here the question was how to make a transition or how to choose not to have a transition.

It's getting easier. As it gets closer to the present, it gets easier. This is really the only real book of poetry I've published. It's called *The Golden Book of Words.* The only structural thing to mention about it is that I chose to keep it in chronological order, because I couldn't stand not having any structure at all. I'm not advising people to do that, just that it often works very nicely to do it.

Next is this book called *Mid-Winter Day,* published by Turtle Island Foundation, which is one long poem which also includes prose that was written about one day, December 22, 1978. Nobody ever believes me when I tell them that it was written in one day, but it almost was. I did rehearsals for the first section, which is dreams. I practiced for about two weeks before the December 22 date and tried to sort of fine-tune my dreaming so that when I had dreams on the 22nd I would be good at remembering them and they would be vivid and worth recording. Or worth sharing with people; or I would get better at writing them down. So that was an extension over that day. I also took photographs, and wrote about them later.

I divided the book into six parts. It was the six parts of the day, as I perceived the day to be. The last part was the time at night when

I would go to my desk and write. For the sixth part of the book, that's what I did. The rest is regular daily doings. I was mostly taking care of babies, and entertaining friends. I also made sure to keep copies of the newspapers for that day and whatever other written or visual material happened to pop up by accident. I'd keep track of it so that when I was putting the poem together later, I might want to intersperse some of that material. But the only real notes I have are those about the photos. Actually I have extensive notes about dreaming but it would be pointless to begin on that.

I wrote this list about the photos (it was one roll of film). I tried to describe what it was before I attempted to use it in the text. "1. Trying to see myself in the mirror over the typewriter as sea. 2. Breakfast at the bottle of milk, white light. Lewis in shirt jacket. Marie stripes putting oatmeal in mouth." I should say that in this instance and also the use of the photographs in *Memory* that I was never trying to take beautiful photographs necessarily. I was always trying to take as many as possible; to take photographs as what you're really seeing, not trying to isolate objects and put them in the center of the frame. But just take them to reflect what actual vision is, and not romanticize it. Certainly not the writing either, but not romanticize the visual.

(Reads other examples.) That's more than you could note in a moment if you were sitting with a notebook. The other thing is that you don't always see all these things when you're looking with your eyes.

It became more information. As I said in the workshop this morning, it would be interesting to write about what you know and leave out the self. I mean for an extended period of time, like a year or so.

Then I wrote *Utopia,* which is red and black. This is another book where I thought it was very important to include contributions by other writers, so there are footnotes and whole sections by other people. Surprisingly, a small number of people actually respond to those requests to be a part of a collaborative writing project. I've worked in workshops and magazines that are collaborative, and it's amazing to see how frightened people are of sharing their anonymity. Being anonymous and sharing knowledge with others.

I wanted to make *Utopia* tongue-in-cheek like a text book with a table of contents, a preface, and index. (Reads from the front matter, the essential idea of which is: any part of this book may be reproduced by anyone.) My love of indexes came from a time when I was apprenticing myself to poetry and I decided to write in every form that really couldn't be written. One of those things obviously is to write an index for a non-existent book. (Reads examples from *Utopia*.) Bob Holman created the index for *Utopia*.

Utopia is a form.

This is *Sonnets*, which is my most recent book. It is a book of about seventy sonnets. I was reading a transcript of a Ted Berrigan workshop on sonnets. He apologizes as I do for writing them. After all this work described as experimental and thousands of other manuscripts not even mentioned here, we wind up writing sonnets? Is that what becomes of us? None of the sonnets are really sonnets. A bunch of them that are in the book were originally published in this form called "Incident Reports Sonnets." A friend of mine works as a psychotheraist at The International Center for the Disabled. Even though it's a place that does wonderful things for human beings, it's very bureaucratic. They pass around memos between offices, such as reporting if a plant has been knocked on its side. My friend would (very much against the rules) give me the incident reports so that I could write poems based on them because they had all the nature of poetry in them. Surrealistically described surrealistic events and everyday things.

Story, 1968
Moving, 1971
Memory, 1975
Ceremony Latin, 1964, 1975
Studying Hunger, 1976
Poetry, 1976
Eruditio Ex Memoria, 1977
The Golden Book of Words, 1978
Mid-WinterDay, 1982
Utopia, 1983
Mutual Aid, 1985
Sonnets, 1989
The Formal Field of Kissing, 1990

E PIC & WOMEN POETS

Does a woman have a story? Or, real question, does anyone have a story? With regard to epic, a man who writes one need not have or know a story so much as have a feeling for what a hero does (he can set that character in motion), or for what level (that lofty level) an epic takes place on. Dante's "I," for example, does not really act: he walks & talks; on the other hand he converses with every man Dante can think of who presumably did act. A woman who would write an epic has two choices: she can try to make her heroine man-like in action (but what man has ever really done these things?), or man-like in experience & knowledge, or she can attempt to change epic to suit what a woman is like, or a person is like: make something lofty & grand in another way than a man's way. When I was just beginning to think about such a project a few years ago, I was continually asking myself, "What does a woman 'do'?" At the time, I was trying to tell the story of a mother of an ex-soldier whose actions in a war had rendered him guilt-laden, that guilt finally bringing on crisis & death. But *he* had obviously done everything: he had been to war, he was guilty; he was tragic, he would die, he was the natural focus. Her role was essentially passive: sufferer, survivor. That isn't the stuff of a story—her part—except a Jamesian sort of story; though it could be a poem of course. But if a very long poem (an epic), it would turn into his story again. I did write the poem, but it was only six pages long (long pages though), letting the focus shift between the two of them & also including myself.

Soon afterwards I found my solution to the problem of women & action in the area of myth & dream; I even found a partial model in an old, newly famous poem. What happens in dream, & myth— which is like a more formally organized thought-out dream—is unreal, illogical, symbolical. Yet it is action, it is story. Insomuch as women dream, they participate in stories every night of their lives. Profound stories which may involve sex, death, violence, journeys, quests, all the stuff of epic & much of narrative. A case can be made that in going back to myth for women's sake, I simply took epic back to its own origins—manifestly true—for a refresher course.

ALICE NOTLEY

At any rate, in dreams, what happens is *the equivalent* of what happens in a life, so much of which takes place in air as it were, in the interplay there of character, subtle conflict, personal sorrow, changes, that everyone goes through in ways that haven't apparently so much to do with vivid story shapes, vivid scenes. I let my heroine, whom I eventually named Alette (I dreamed the name), develop out of a dreamlike ground: I took clues from my dreams at night, but essentially daydreamed the poem through its length. During half of the poem, like Dante's hero, she does not really "act," she journeys & observes, she talks to others, etc. Later she receives magical powers & finally there is combat, she confronts & vanquishes the villain, but in a magical, mythological way—not with a sword or a gun. Every "action" is as in a dream, fluidly symbolical, according to dream logic, or the slightly more conscious logic of mythology. A woman whose head has been cut off speaks through her throat; my heroine is instructed as to how to put the woman's head back on. There is a subway system in which animals as well as humans live: my heroine converses there with a giant serpent; she observes a female beggar change into an eagle. Another woman becomes a geode, a woman & child are seen to be continually on fire, there is blood in a subway car which comes from wellsprings in people's legs, & so on.

As I've indicated, there was a partial inspiration for my poem: I got some of my permissions from the Sumerian myth of the descent of the goddess Inanna into the Underworld, her death, rebirth & ascent, & pursuit of her husband Dumuzi, whom she chooses to die in her place. One interesting thing about this story is that it is unclear to us (probably not so to the Sumerians) why Inanna presents herself at the door of the Underworld, why she risks this death at all. Some interpreters say she wanted to rule the Underworld, some that she wanted knowledge; perhaps she is simply meant to be, in a symbolical way, in a life-death crisis. The point, for me, is that her "action" consists of showing up, presenting herself at that door, & then dying. When she re-emerges above, her "action" consists of choosing, in a fury, her ungrieving husband to take her place, as the Underworld's laws require a surrogate if she will live again. His action consists of flight, & then being caught: he & his sister come to take perpetual alternate six-month terms in the Underworld. There is no war, there is no combat. There is minimal action, in the way of myth, not of epic. What there is is the poetry of the "unreal" setting & its meaning, & of the "illogical" or "irrational" mythological action. In the Underworld Inanna is stripped of her powers & garments & hung up on a meathook for dead. She is rescued by two magical creatures created from Father Enki's fingernail dirt; they obtain her rebirth from her sister Ereshkigal, monarch of Hell, because they soothe Ereshkigal in labor (Is she giving birth to the new Inanna perhaps? As in a dream, this is never explained). The loftiness, the grandness, which make people call this poem an epic, has greatly to do with the story's stark embodiment of life, death, rebirth, in the simplest most generic way possible. It is important that Inanna & Ereshkigal are goddesses, not because the story is then about grand figures, in the male way, but because, as goddesses, they are both women & principles. Inanna is life, Ereshkigal is death, they are sisters. The story is allegorical, & allegory is one way in for women. As well as for men who are tired of this century's lyric "I," or tired of fragmentation, disjunction, literary theory, & hipness.

Sometimes it seems that the worst consequence of the modern split between poetry & story has been the emergence of pure action, pure violence, as the major mass genre, as in movies, novels, TV. In a parallel world, poetry has become more & more intellectual & specialized, has become words. Somewhere in between are a lot of "real-life" novels, journalism, & poems of the quotidian. People speak of "modern myths": the stories in the violence genre involving cowboys & cops & drugdealers & vigilantes for example. But there is no real mythology here (I would say), because the necessary & precise connection to dreams (literal dreams at night) has been lost. These stories are end-of-the-line, rational, knights' tales: anti-women, or extra-woman (the new female private eyes are more men.) Rational in that everyone knows exactly how they work & what comes next. But somewhere in real dreams, dreams at night, you may find substantially both women & men, real men & real women. There we are equal; the old stories are mixed up & redone to the dreamer's perpetual surprise. Anything might happen in a dream, everything is potential. If we studied them we might find new myths, & out of new myths might come new forms.

Dream is the ocean into which all of twentieth century forms are being dumped, those forms being forms of dissolution, the dissolving of the old continuous narrative & lyric coherences & the reconstituting of them into fragments, collage-like entities, & disjunctive & often abstract pieces of language. To change by breaking & regluing is not exactly to change, is it? The final dissolution & rebirth is taking place in darkness; & what will be born probably hasn't been seen yet, because no one has walked straight into the dark & stayed awhile. To break & recombine language is nothing. To break & recombine reality, as Dream always does do, might be something. Dreams are not language; they are fleshly & vivid, they are "real." And they are "about" us & everything; both the source & paradigm of art. They are the bed of new beginnings, the place to turn to.

2

If Dream could be the source of story & action in an epic, what about its formal requirements, its exacting shape? Part of what interests me in continuous narrative is the skill required to write it, how difficult it feels to do it after a century gone counter to that, & therefore how worthwhile it feels. The old twentieth century forms are now becoming too easy; continuity at length is now hard. Continuity at length implies measure; by which I mean a somewhat consistent unimpeded measure. A new content, a new consciousness, implies the need for a new sound; form & measure are often the same.

What a poem says must arise together with how it sounds: they must somehow become the same thing. We have perhaps lost our sense for the unity of story & sound—I think we think of the two as necessarily separate, first there is a story & then the finding a form for it—which seems a phony process to us, it doesn't happen in the present. There are several replies. One is that a story properly entered by the author or reader is in the present any time it is told. Another is that the story may be invented, or partly invented, as it is told. No poet is ever quite sure what she's going to say next, if she's doing it right—in any poem. But how can a measure invent a story for you, as a story invents a measure for you, if measure is preordained? A measure, any measure, is very flexible—we've forgotten what measures really are, because we mistakenly assume that we don't use them. Since we think that we don't use them, we hardly ever consciously invent them: thus we are incapable of story poems. Stories, & measures, are dresses to slip into that give as you walk, at least as much as any poem bound by, say, restrictions of language & demeanor, whether the language of philosophical theory or some sort of plain speech, or by line length or prose-seemingness or marked surface variation.

But how can you invent a measure? Think for a moment about what poetry is as sound: it is a formalized distortion of the sound of speech. "Distortion" was the key notion for me as I invented the measure I used in *The Descent of Alette*. Think of the typical cadences of the various kinds of modern poetry—Language poetry, New York School, New Yorker–type poetry, etc.: most are rhythmically understated, though some are not (e.g. Robert Creeley's line). The modern trend is to sound very much (though there are many different versions of this) like a person speaking. Language poetry, on the other hand, often sounds like a mind or voice reading printed matter. But there is the possibility of pushing harder at cadence, of using something that sounds made, sounds arbitrary, sounds aggressively musical. You choose an artifice, you accentuate it as artifice, as music—as the Greeks did with dactylic hexameter. Your foot or line should be very flexible, & yet all your lines should be similar, so that the story will continue to unfold without your getting in its way. Yet your line can be as interesting as your story: we don't have to sound like prose any more, poetry's sound doesn't have to be unprepossessing, a story is not necessarily quietly told—it used to be sung. The effect of song or chant is possible without your literally chanting or singing, if your measure is interesting & you know how to ride it.

A measure comes out of the individual & the culture at the same time: but you the poet will perceive it to come out of your body, your head, the sounds that play there; you will not be able to analyze it into being. It will be indigenous, you will discover it; it will sound like poems & songs you liked when you were a child or a teenager, as much as any poetry you've read in adulthood. To devise it, to know what it is at least semi-consciously, you will have to concentrate on demarcation, on clarifying the boundaries of the measuring unit. Most specifically you may want to accentuate the end of the unit or line—something contrary to much of twentieth century practice, which is characterized by run-over lines with blurs of meanings at their ends, prose-like prosodies in which the sentence is more pronounced, aurally, than the line, & so on. You will start to hear what your measure is like, more & more, as you understand what story you are telling: as in good twentieth century poetry it will not be possible to attain to form & content separately. But narrative poetry tends to drone (not always) without a real rhythmic push—a good pushing long line alone is sometimes adequate, but if it pushes too hard, the story is over too fast, the sound of the long line of our century is a sound that pushes quickly towards resolution, some sort of closing speech. Unless the line is *very* long, as is James Schuyler's line in his long autobiographical poems. Or unless the long line is simultaneously a line & broken into pieces, as with Williams' variable-foot/line in *"Asphodel, That Greeny Flower."* Both these instances are still of a poem couched in the form of lengthy intimate first-person address; *Slinger,* by Ed Dorn, is not, & uses a shorter line that swings.

I was not consciously aware of any other poet's line as I invented my measure for *The Descent Of Alette*. It felt to me as if I were dragging everything up whole—story & measure—from the primal pool. I would say retrospectively that that wasn't exactly so but it seemed like it then. I felt very strongly at the time that I didn't want a "male" line—& that category seemed to include every line I knew about, those used by women as well. I wanted, as I always do, to try to begin as if at the beginning of the world, before things were male & female in the ways that they are now. I believed, & do, that measure may be found somewhere in the same depths where dreams originate, where worlds & new worlds are born. We don't need new words, new languages, new syntax, we need a whole new flesh, new beings to look at, literally, a new universe. The key is not in language; the key is in vision, in the most unrestricted sense of that word. Words are shallow & subject to selfish usages—but to see a new world is a first step towards changing an old one.

Here, in closing, is an example of the measure I used in *Alette*, the opening page of the poem:

> "One day, I awoke" "& found myself on" "a subway, endlessly"
> "I didn't know" "how I'd arrived there or" "who I was" "exactly"
> "But I knew the train" "knew riding it" "knew the look of"
> "those about me" "I gradually became aware—" "though it seemed
>
> as that happened" "that I'd always" "known it too—" "that there was"
> "a tyrant" "a man in charge of" "the fact" "that we were"
> "below the ground" "endlessly riding" "our trains, never surfacing"
> "A man who" "would make you pay" "so much" "to leave the subway"
>
> "that you don't" "ever ask" "how much it is" "It is, in effect,"
> "all of you, & more" "Most of which you already" "pay to live below" "But he would literally" "take your soul" Which is what you are" "below the ground" "Your soul" "your soul rides"
>
> "this subway" "I saw" "on the subway a" "world of souls"

O N, AT, AROUND ACTIVE ECO-LIT

A BIRDWALK IN TANGLEWOOD

> A raindrop falls.
> It falls on my nose—
> delicate, light, transparent.
> —"Lune" by Nebraska HS student

We must *throw* care into the future. Image fuels care. The central question seems at last to be: how image forth ecology?

Images haunt my life, haunt all lives, serve as mental icons for the religions of memory. At age ten, I was reading American Indian tales & remember the figure of "Old Man" in an illustration. It was the darkness of the light & the strangeness of the man that drew me. I wanted to go along that twisty path behind him, into the deep woods, into "the other." Magic, which is the familiar, scrambled: the scary sudden shapes of branches. The only newness, sense of light. The next Sunday at Congregational Church services when Reverend Stubbs asked us, reasonably, to bow our heads in prayer, I raised my face to Manitou—my grandmother, to my right, wriggled & reddened in distraction. I never went back. She was too large for me to turn red without feeling burdened, & I was small.

I raise a fog of images, speaking of that image. Let it be; necessary atmosphere. Point is, the image stuck.

All my life too I've remembered Hendrik Willem Van Loon's image, at the beginning of *The Story of Mankind,* for time—a bird coming every thousand years to sharpen its beak on a great, super-Gibraltar rock, & when the rock was worn altogether away by this sharpening, a "day of eternity" had passed.

o   o   o

Witches gather round a cauldron on a lonely crag, tossing in "eye of newt" & various bits of Earth's crust, reconstituting scattered reality to a little universe in a black pot, uttering prophecies as they stir.

JACK COLLOM

Long, full images or image pileups could be adduced from Dickens, Henry Miller, many others, as *analogs* of biodiversity. Any list compiled with cunning sensitivity, even if it's urban/human phenomena, shows the *type* of multiple accumulation of relationship—the structure, the chaotic but miscellaneously meaningful structure—that our surroundings are, that nature is, looked at with negative capability.

We all "know" now that knowing is not suited to the categorizations of denotative language, including the linear shape & reasonable tone of the essay. This is an essay try, but the connections purport to establish themselves like a "model of diversification and decimation" (S. J. Gould, in another connection).

Image: a storyteller. Sitting on a rock, in a circle of hearers, she/he animates a situation, brings the circle to some synecdoche of world, or slice of life (that, like a hologram slice, represents the whole). He/she moves hands . . . & armies flee, ripples voice & stones or stars are reassembled, thinks out loud—& creatures are transformed. Let's say the story is of a kid caught in a life of flatness & dust. Lo, a whirlwind reaches through the sky & carries the child to a magic place, a land of dangers to be sure but also a land of no end to possibilities. Every image that comes along—dancing scarecrow, talking lion—is a violation of assumed limits, until life is a flow of surprise.

Nature is like that. Biodiversity is like that (even Kansas is like that, underfoot). "Out there" is the sense of an endless supply, & endlessness equals unpredictability. Once things can be counted, they're almost gone. They can't enter "the story." Sure, Three Fates can fly in, but they're not isolated; they betoken a fabric of available magic. We poor forked blobs with bobbing brains can never encompass, in our isms, what the future needs. We can only count supplies within a thin phenomenological band of sightings, but the implicit count goes on & on. Old tale-tellers were right to enter magic openly when realism tired. Even the most realistic stories depend on disguised supernature to make their way—the emphases of the moment are a form of legend. Even science thought now finds itself in processual Oz.

Our Nature images, "good & bad": Yggdrasil, Bugs Bunny, Albrecht Dürer's rhino, Faerie Queene, Snow White's shifting ecosystems, Lassie Come Home, Poe's Raven, Mr. Ed, Little Red Riding Hood, Jonah & the Whale, Sinbad's Roc, the Griffin, Come Live With Me & Be My Love, "The Pigs!" meek as a lamb, goatsuckers, zippety-doo-da, sea monster, Tie rosemary on right arm to be light & merry, werewolves & Dracula, Krag the Kootenay Ram, "Earth is filled full of restless dread throughout her woods her mountains & deep forests" (Lucretius), Green Mansions, Tweety-Bird, Coyote, Pan, Donald Duck, Dr. Doolittle & friends, "bewildered," Ferdinand the Bull, Moby Dick, "an unweeded garden" where "things rank & gross in nature possess it merely" (Hamlet), the Snake in Eden, Black Beauty, potted tree on geometric tiles, "hideous" Alps, Cowardly Lion & The Gump, soft zephyrs always wafting over murmuring waters, Reynard the Sly Fox, "The world existed to be cooked."—The world existed to be cooked.

Down-to-Earth Einstein made his amazing mental leaps, while quite a young man, by ascending an image staircase 'round the stars, as it were. Trying to cut away myth & still have something. Stared every assumption in the eye till somebody blinked. Later, he was stuck for decades in further but "relatively" unfruitful thought, climbing math in place of picture. Thinkers keep crying for images to hoist themselves along theory.

The World swirls with images; they're not scarce. Human bite-size images, & the very infinity of 'em flavors any given one, or deepens the flavor, lends it the power of resonating for us into larger & larger coherence. We pump up/foursquare paper, paint our paradigms with reflections from the life around us. But other-size images, off in micro/macro realms, or down beyond some temporal horizon, seem suspect (is "future soil loss" bigger than a breadbox?). They don't hit gut. They're intellectual toys, we rationalize. Out of *sight* out of mind.

Van Loon's bird works to make time both real & breath-taking by dividing its vastness into barely conceivable segments—then their multiplicity (zillions of sharpenings) carries us far enough out on a verbal bridge to wonder if the words will not collapse & part, & we plummet down to drown in prehistory.

The forest Indian image takes us through our known woods & to a version of the unknown, one that simply lures, if we're so inclined; without the gingerbread in a certain grimm forest & without attempted murders by a pre-Christian witch to post a lesson that little Hansel u. Gretel should simply never go out there again unless they bring a bulldozer. Through Old Man, we're attracted to Nature. If we go we may follow him to the prophetic dignity of drowning in history—&/or we may live in a house, recycle, juggle images, find creation in the plural of choice.

Some "little cannonballs" on image & magic:

- Nature has been unexamined but by use.
- Our images have been like movies, psycho-dramas projected right onto the landscape.
- The future is here till the sun burns out.
- Charles Olson: "Of rhythm is image; of image is knowing, and of knowing there is a construct." So image is inevitable lens along our light path.
- Magic—to mix is to enlarge, since real components suffice to make combination infinite. / Ecology is "the" relational, the means of enlargement, what carries beyond the sum of parts. / By naming the parts the same magic will occur on paper as "out there."
- I have no beautiful line to draw between falsification & magic. Rhythm discriminates. & its portion, Emphasis.
- A bulldozer or bomb is modern magic; including all the old & new & sideways is postmodern magic.
- It takes magic just to perceive a house or brick or grain of sand.
- Magic is accuracy because plans don't equal truth infinity does, & only the magic-approach visits that dimension.
- Magic can be might be superempiric—accessing of the holographic level. Like a "breath" (inspiration) does that Chaos thing, becomes a tornado in the planetary top-knot.
- *All* mystery is lifelines to environment.
- Empiricism is poetic, 'round the edges (where things happen).

o The plain fact is it's impossible to portray plain fact. Words turn to powder long before they get exact. Language, honestly handled, is a means to notify others of one's assumptions. The world of language hovers like broken clouds over the earth it pretends to denote. Thus only style can tell a "real" story. But you find style, in part, by trying like the devil to avoid it.

As long as Nature was seen as exceeding the effects of our falsifications, no problem. No problem, Nature's *there*. But a word as much like the Devil as any, Convenience, has arisen & rudely erased the buffer zone of *far niente* that cushioned our acts, kept 'em small, in the pre-power age. This *is* the Power Age (however powerless a given person may feel). Some awe-full coincidence of brain, free hand, & land has let our species extend animal power beyond body until power works to short-circuit the usual drags of time. Convenient! Modern magic. We want it, we got it. & desire's not slow to swell & sophisticate, anywhere capacity shows a way. But the whole shebang can't afford false images now—too many tools to violently define the implied delineations! Cut a deer in the shape of Bambi, hillside soil in the shape of forever when it's only *whoa*!

But who am I to say "false," as if I could say "true"? I'll say this: true contains false. Just keep on walking, like the songs say.

Image: you're in a circle, as always. You have a new gun. You pop off a few arcs—woops! nobody told you magic might call in sick, fail (for a while) to stuff infinity back into the holes . . .

Biodiversity is the fodder of continuance, not circumscribed by plate or eater, a galactic chickadee, a "matter" of flow . . .

Next comes the Preface.

PREFACE

What I attempt here suffers from an epistemological shadow, mostly the *loss of light's focus that long times & multiplicity occasion*. Can't know, thus can't care for, specifics too complex stretching so far down the road. One can speak with fervent, earthy effect of the Eco-Crisis, & many have, but at the cost of communicating the superhuman size in time/space of the all-too-human problem.

"We are destroying the Earth!" & similar speeches in large terms simply don't fill the ear as they fill the air. Image vague, seems corny. It's tough to flesh out Apocalypse, again. So we wind up with "tiny" statements—"Incidence of cancer has risen by 6%," or "The spotted owl is endangered"—which arouse in their favor at best band-aid solutions*—& in their opposition values such as "jobs" which *seem* more substantial to our nearsighted anthropocentric minds' eyes than the life or death of an obscure hootowl or the hubris of proclaiming the future. In these cases, as in many more, what's lost is the immensity that the word *ecology,* by definition, leads to. Turns out *relationship* is the key, the very center, though it has no weight in the hand, & this key goes on forever. The size of the real concern is beyond our capability to take in, much less act on. The spotted owl is a bellwether of an entire forest condition, & forest is bellwether of global condition. A tree cut in Oregon, as it were & will be, "falls on the head of" unborn—long, long unborn—multitudes all over the world. Massive, shadowy desert-ion. Global slash-&-burn.

Back of the metaphor is fact, like what we call moonrise. Backed up by certainties of science. In the perspective of Earth history, the utter absurdity alone, of Destruction (& gulp—sorry, folks—the atmosphere's wrong for life to start again) is beyond drama. We've been gaining practice at absurdity all century, but the prospect of 4 1/2 billion years of delicate history blowing itself off due to the momentary cultural addictions of one life-form, as a thought, is just too grand. But there it is. As it continues to specify itself, we'll know, but the catch is that the cause-&-effect is on such scale, especially in time, that it's always gonna be too late to fix . . .

Even if *total* destruction of life's prevented by some lively node deep under the Galapagos, obliteration of, say, everything down

o o o

* "Think globally, act locally" is excellent, but must always be twined & twinned with its opposite, that thought & act unite.

to the sponges is beyond drama. Too much arrogance. Loss beyond speculation. Too much pain.

5000 years ago, writing was discovered. Meanwhile here *we* are, & the world is, more or less as we've lately been in detail but taking on much more rapid change, till change itself overshadows substance. Boom! Everything's fucked. To jump absurdly to cases, how do we write?

Answer: as many ways as there are ripples in wet sand. . . . As background, get in the habit of nature. Take walks. Study some animals or plants. Become a connoisseur of light. Once a day, pretend you're a stranger to Earth, see how things look. There's change enough, anyway, in the *human* air this century to initiate us into strangeness per se, quicken its familiarity.

Poetry has always immortalized change. Now, within (& without) the resistance of language, it rides change's acceleration. It can also, like the patterns that crop up in the rush of chaos, hark back & conserve piece after piece of beautiful stasis, as in Ed Sanders' poem,

> The chickadee
> biting & shaking
> > the cluster
> > > of maple seeds
>
> like six tiny
> mountain maracas

wherein the preservation has focus & reference quivering at the surface. . . . Life-size thought like this is fine. Expanding thought is fine.

We write along the curls of question where insight engages environment (i.e., "anything"). Given multiple truth(s), if the poem messes awhile with just one, & is *interesting* in its denials, it's a step. Focus anywhere, which becomes everywhere, as we go. END OF PREFACE

> the birds flying, tree
> cloud, stems, rain
> > to be, mostly, leaf

hulls, to pass the ocean

deeps, green, black

the constant energy, the head
flight, voice, at the top of a gutter
the blue continues to dark

—*Larry Eigner*

THE ESSAY ITSELF

Background: There's a "new" awareness of great danger to Earth's crust life, via the normal human presence in/at its present state: simple consumption & intricate contamination.

The fact is: human global presence, as it is & is likely to become, is an agent of death, among whatever other beauties.

Probably what it amounts to is that present & projected population levels equal/will-equal disaster of the largest scope. We can view this as a matter of beautiful rhythms/or as a matter to be striven against.

Mostly we fail to follow thought out & thus to place our endeavors against one or the other of the above backgrounds.

Some wish to say, do say, environmental warnings're mistaken/exaggerated/powerplay-neurotic &/or (take pick) anti-people/anti-business. But the evidence is like a great sea. No proofs or arguments here but I say the warnings are (largely) just & indeed fantastically, blindly underplayed.

Some artists & others—to trace out objections to environmentalism—feel the fascism of a massive moral movement, & its steamrolling over fine distinctions. Poets revolt at its speech & speakers. But while it's legitimately poetic to apprehend value contextually, it's also guilt by association (eek). Sumpm's too cozy if we only want self-clones on our side. Why shucks—doughy dimwits in Birkenstocks, supermarket poisoners seeking vengeance on behalf of lab rats, privileged Pooh-bahs promoting private picnic possibilities, miscellaneous misanthropes, cloudominium-dwellers, teenage deductive ideal-grinners, Calvinist-o-cranks, jog/yups, folks whose talk is like dried oatmeal, mad-scientists & sane scientists, sunset-postcard-floaters, jargoneros, humor-stompers, bandwagon-barnacles, etc.

etc., are salt o' the earth. Truth is, artists ain't ready for an imposed transition zone that may monkeywrench their work a few decades, wanna stick with the moves they know &, better yet, half-know.

But think it out—we've learned aesthetically, in poems, that we don't stop thinking when we shock ourselves. We go beyond impressions. The eco-crisis is real & permanent. It's a "condition." Doesn't matter who "favors" it. As to what to do about it—maybe nothing. Maybe it's Kismet, within which we simply operate vividly— best gift to the universe right there. Maybe we "fight," recycle, etc., pace out Big-Brain atmosphere to Empyrean.

> . . . "I DEDICATE MYSELF TO THE UNIVERSAL
> DIAMOND BE THIS RAGING FURY DESTROYED"
>
> And he will protect those who love woods and rivers,
> Gods and animals, hobos and madmen, prisoners and sick
> people, musicians, playful women, and hopeful children;
>
> And if anyone is threatened by advertising, air pollution,
> or the police, they should chant SMOKEY THE BEAR'S SPELL:
>
>> DROWN THEIR BUTTS
>> CRUSH THEIR BUTTS
>> DROWN THEIR BUTTS
>> CRUSH THEIR BUTTS
>
> And SMOKEY THE BEAR will surely appear to put the
> enemy out with his vajra-shovel.
>
> Now those who recite this Sutra and then try to put it in
>> practice will accumulate merit as countless as the
>> sands of Arizona and Nevada,
>> Will help save the planet Earth from total oil slick,
>> Will enter the age of harmony of man and nature,
>> Will win the tender love and caresses of men, women,
>> and beasts,
>> Will always have ripe blackberries to eat and a sunny
>> spot under a pine tree to sit at. . . .
>
> —Gary Snyder

As with all poetry, this can be divided & subdivided, moral/amoral.

Environment begins at the skin, if not sooner. If the ecological crisis is even fractionally actual, the "ecologies" of our lives will undergo thorough restructuring, whether now as foresight, later as consequence, or both. Great change *is* in the air(-earth-water-fire). Meanwhile, language begins all over the place, heads along chronology valley. Perhaps some poetry, in its eco-response, can reach forward in time, humanize or enchant scientific prophecy. But even without poetic recourse to any future, the inevitable different complex intimacies we('ll) have with our surroundings—coerced at first by pragmatic concern—will inevitably breed new spiritual registrations of nature's details—details we can no longer use as screens for our own projections. We're faced with a vast culture paradigm, suddenly central, forcing up episto-facets that tend to contradict the familiar. The routine *emphases* within our pinched limits will naturally & radically shift like kaleidoscope bits. Our most homely perceptions will alter & coalesce anew. The mixed metaphor may become a delicacy. What a frog or a field just plain *is* may articulate & resonate as never before. The retinal afterimage may come to outdo psycho-logic of traumatic residue, etc.

> There's a way in midnight
> when death comes flippin' and a-rollin'.
>
> —*Blind Willie Johnson*

Poetry, as both verbal "sun" & reflection, will continue to wriggle along its marvelous unpredictabilities, many of them having little, ostensibly, to do with ecology. But all coming poetry in our culture(s) will be at least contextually affected by the ecological "revolution," as the Industrial Revolution has affected every subsequent Western poem. Some poetry will *anatomically* incorporate the repercussions of the eco-worldview upheaval—different, "cinematic" selection of images, point-of-view fragmentation, tone leaps, new overhearings of sound's role & expanded associational rationale; everything down to the phoneme may "change color," gain or lose weight.

Even the poetry least affected will be affected, via interior ecologies. Poetry *is* verbal ecology; when the word "ecology" metamorphoses in our minds, poetry moves too.

A SENSE OF PLACE

I'd live on the moon
if the commute were a little less.

—*Ed Dorn*

Implications of new thought in physics & biology somersault to the poetic leading-edge. Punctuated equilibrium & the psychogeometry of the genetic ridge liberate & indicate rhythms & strains of possible poetry. Uncertainty Theory proposes an aesthetic of indirection, a "cluster" truth-hypothesis. Observation is revealed as hard, or impossible, diamond.

Grasses are herbs with round or flattened (never 3 angled), usually hollow stems (culms) solid at the joints (nodes), and 2-ranked, alternate, parallel-veined leaves, composed of two parts, the sheath, which surrounds the culm like a tube split down one side, and the blade, which is usually strap-shaped, flat, folded, or with rolled margins. At the junction of the sheath and blade, on the inside, is a small appendage (the ligule); this is commonly thin in texture; sometimes it is only a ring of hairs, rarely it is obsolete. The plants may be annual or perennial. The root, stem, and leaves are the vegetative part of the plant. The flowers have to do with perpetuating the species.
—*First Book of Grasses*

Howdy-doo "have to do." I loafe & invite my soul. The above mowing per se is only a style, but it is that. When walked through by Tygers, thrice-battered, bugged, slow-baked, benevolently left, mouse-tunneled, whatever, it might become anything, even a leaf.

Todo el mundo
depende de
un pedazo de yerba.

o   o   o

I teach a graduate course called Eco-Lit at Naropa. We study as
wide a range of writings as might apply* & write an *Ecompost* (the
name of one class anthology) of products: poems (observational,
acrostic, song, sonnet, haiku variants, great-poem takeoffs, con-
crete, collage, vers libre, lyric, lists, haibun, dramatic, letters, memories, metaphors, spontaneities, origin-searches, slang, penetrations,
political poems, aleatoric processes, questions, sestinas, recipes,
macaronic verses, animal dialogues, imitations, hybrids, etc.), also
critiques & essays, slogans, prose poems, stories, definitions, how-I-
writes, bumperstickers, discussions, lectures, polemics, fact sheets, &
so forth. Thus a literary ecosystem is constituted conducive to reflecting & naturally expanding the multiplicity of the natural ecosystem—
true-to-life. In all instances we try to uphold subtlety & modesty despite the blunting influence of looming disaster & such emotional
giantism. Humor (the dance of accuracy) lives until everything's
dead (& even then . . . ?). Likewise joy.

o   o   o

THE PANTHER

Jardin des Plantes, Paris

His sight (from passing through the bars)
has become so tired it holds nothing.

o   o   o

* A few authors: Carson, Leopold, Fuller, Gould, Sauer, Silko, Griffin, Thoreau, Abbey,
Menchu, Prigogine, Pokagon, Fabre, Dillard, Ehrlich, Columbus, Sam Johnson, Darwin
& Agassiz, Dickinson, Melville, Gert Stein, Boethius, A. Pope, Coleridge, Blake, Snyder,
Levertov, Sanders, Goethe, Keats, Akhmatova, M. Moore, Neruda, Kabir, plus anony-
mous Celts, American Indians, Eskimos, Africans, & Asians, & Senator Bill Armstrong.

As if there were a thousand bars
and beyond the thousand bars no world.

The soft swing of the potent steps,
still supple in a sawed-off curve,
is like a dance of power round a point
wherein a great will lies stupefied.

Only sometimes, the eyes' curtains
silently rise.—Then an image goes
inside, along the tightened quiet of the limbs,
and in the heart stops being.

—*translated from Rainer Maria Rilke*

The next section is called "The Tables." Attempt to play construc-
tively with words & current ideas. Pause. Cushion fades, purple
evaporates, west, south, up, & spadewise, along the grain . . . .

"THE TABLES"

Here is a list, not comprehensive but indicative, of 14
nouns. Each is abstract; essence of each is, explicitly
or implicitly, movement. Each is a masked verb.

1 change		8 exemplification	
2 variety		9 options	
3 paradigms		10 indirection	
4 facts		11 "communication"	
5 close observation		12 context	
6 extension		13 perspective	
7 time		14 psychic geometry	

Here is a set of visual symbols for these verb-nouns:

1 ⟶   2 ∴   3 ⋀⋀   4 ⌸   5 ⊐   6 — · ·   7 ↻

8 E!   9 ∈   10 ╱   11 ≜   12 ⊛   13 ⋈   14 ½

| JACK COLLOM

& following is a list of terms having to do with contemporary philosophical concerns. Quick characterizations are appended, including to what limitations/distortions each outlook is subject.

DECONSTRUCTION | Exposes pretense (elaboration of
Intentional Fallacy thrust). Subject to pretense of ex-posing beam
(fascism of rationalized irrational).

POSTMODERNISM | Pluralism—acceptance of elements sans
fashionable restrictions. Subject to incoherence.

EPISTEMOLOGY | How'd'y'know?—Subject to passivization
(& latinate constructs).

CHAOS | Every little "thing" counts. Subject to overexcitation.

RELATIVITY | What it says (more or less). Subject to confusion.

UNCERTAINTY | Y' don't know. Subject to dizziness.

SIMILITUDE & SCALE | What's like & unlike in a magnitude zoom.
Subject to astonishment.

EVOLUTION | Biological instability. Subject to self-denial.

When these light-blockage factors (the subject-to's) are added
up—pretense, incoherence, passivity, overexcitation, confusion,
dizziness, astonishment, & denial—it is as if a list of the psychic
debilities of "modern man" had been sought. I guess that proves
everyone's a philosopher.

EXERCISE 1 | Examine each of the 14 verb-nouns in connection
with each of the seven philosophical terms. Decide if they have
any special affinity. I.e., does "change" have a special affinity
with Deconstruction? Does "variety"? Does "paradigms"? & so on.
If you find a near-unanimity of linkage, you have a large network
of thought which can serve as background or foreground at any
given point. Almost any one of the key words can serve as a bellwether for the rest. . . .

EXERCISE 2 | Peruse the list of visual symbols (previous page).
Start drawing pictures, doodling, using among other things these
figures. Try combinations. Lose yourself in shapes & moves. Then
substitute "real-life" illustrations for the shapes & moves. Do so in
words. Note emerging sentences. Make mini-stories. Follow your
nose, explore.

EXERCISE 3 I Write or recall a line or short passage of poetry. Study it in terms of the 14 verb-nouns.

    a I Which verb-nouns apply to it? How? Mark exact places & make distinct notes.

    b I Are changes in the poetry sample indicated? Yes or no, try some out. Make several versions; some may be new pieces rather than versions of the original.

EXERCISE 4 I Write a poem, then deconstruct it mercilessly. Consider each & every tone down to the smallest syllable. Then carefully list all criteria of the deconstruction act—& deconstruct *them*, etc.

EXERCISE 5 I Observe a "piece of Nature" & write about it in as many different ways as possible (see page 112).

EXERCISE 6 I Invent your own form—complex, simple, irregular, whatever.

EXERCISE 7 I Just write. Fastwrite or force yourself if necessary.

EXERCISE 8 I Keep on.

ADDITIONAL RESONATING TERMS & IDEAS FROM SCIENCE

    "tendencies to exist" I the most you can say

    "grand unification theory" I GUT feeling

    "implicate order" I at last, nothing's random

    "entropy" I slow death (Fate)

    "broken symmetry" I any beginning

    "fluctuation" I life

    "unfolding syndrome" I the politeness of matter & energy

    "morphic resonance" I a classification converses with its constituent creature

    "autocatalysis" I diversity→fluctuation→chaos→finitude (a little progress)

    "spontaneous self-organization" I autocatalysis of life-forms

    "punctuated equilibrium" I terraced/time/terrestrial vitality

    "co-evolution" I simultaneous cause & effect

    "gratuitous functionality" I hey, survival's only a start

    "catastrophe theory (biology)" I dynamism of nonlinearity

    "Fourier transforms" I brain digests complex shapes by

splitting into simple sine & cosine waves for storage (pattern implicate)

"engrams" | Atlantises of the brain

"dissipative structures" | vortices controlling their own destinies (briefly)

"pilot-wave theory" | potentiality works as waves, expression of the total arrangement, guiding electrons

"spectral lines" | the fineness, yet (comic) existence of borders

"world tubes" | arbitrary views for the sake of "history"

"semantics" (apparent differences) | language as focal instability

"bring home the Bacon" | take a look, etc.

These are meant as just some sample structures of the previous ball of wax. Given an open epistemology, they have their graces. Along with many, nay, infinite, excitations more, they *fit*.

The above section ("The Tables") is cranky, ignorant. Needs acclimatization & color, but there's as it were no space. In sum, it attempts the loose synthesis of some current leading-edge (fringe?) thought-attitudes into a demonstrable syndrome having multiple affinities with the ecological view of the world. I mean especially to refer, not to the disasters eco-awareness projects, but to a "new" relational quotidian life & its symbiosis with art. You do have to (Gott sei dank) fill in the blanks; perhaps part of tomorrow's, or this afternoon's, thinking might be making abstractions into something as gut-level as specifics're now (barely) seen to be. Phantom gestures of Samuel Johnson. Swirls "in" the inductive-deductive ferris wheel.

In a silver lake, what's the rush?

—*Reed Bye*

o o o

To take this to the practical, I've earned my main "living" for 18 years as a "Poet-in-the-Schools"—usually workshopping with elementary-age kids. In that work, without, I hope, disturbing the poetic ecology of the meetings, I've included avenues of physical, of local & global ecology. Many of the poems by children that emerge are aesthetically exciting, are reverberations of current knowledge theory, wild gardens of language. Here's one.

THINGS TO SAVE

The darkness of shadow-like wolves
darting across the night like
black bullets, and the moon
shimmering like a sphere of glowing
mass. Let us save lush grass, green
as green can be, but, best of all,
imagination glowing with joy aha,
images it is composed of, it is this
that is making the earth grow
with flavor and destination.

—*Fletcher Williams (5th grade)*

This Poet-in-Schools work is only "cause-oriented" in a minor key. Indirect. Preaching to the converted seems to have in our society a large role but a small effect. & preaching to the unconverted batters the most adamant (because abstracted) aspect of an audience. The try with kids is: simply poetry responsive to new light. Then it can grow what it wants.

My own best shots in eco-lit have been in the poem collection *Arguing With Something Plato Said*. One of the poems, "A Preface to Surroundings," essays some science/philosophy thought in fast-moving, intuitively juxtaposed, rhythmic speech patterns. The intent is to establish a "hip," visceral ground out of which such a simple phrase as "save a leaf" may arise in connotative freshness. The hope is that, through trickling increment, such a chunky attempt might help spread an ecological way with words into the general awareness. As with all poetry, the "agenda" disappears, ideally, in its own breadth: help keep language open.

Another, "Passage," on the most abundant bird in the world (1800), extinct forever 100 years later, the American passenger pigeon, details history & ornithology in a multitude of styles & voices: lune series, quotations, free verse, serious limericks, birdcall, vernacular prose, rhyme, chant, & poetic rhetoric. Thus structure exemplifies an important aspect of the content, & forms a linguistic ecology. I wish to continue in these directions.

Writing plans themselves are an ecosystem of intention & discovery—open to serendipitous touches & shifts in direction, & destruction, as well as to the use of whatever material that history, personal or poetic, can bring. As Stephen Jay Gould shows in his excellent essays, many a still-useful thought lies buried in the wake of some past pendulum swing.

> I caught two in my hands. They were mating. I sat down
> and carefully watched their movements.
>
> —Chief Pokagon (on one of the last large passenger pigeon
>   migrations)

The term "paradigms,"
having lost its first, fine fire
strikes my fancy.
                    Concurrent,
                        relief map of nonlinearity.
        Optional perspectives as in some Chinese old scrolls.
                        One
                        puts opinion in its place, never
                        perfectly;
                        the leftover energy
                        runs around symbiotic loop like a Lionel.
In a given moment in the life of a squirrel,
there's a particularity of entirety,
as well as all the particulars.
& there's probably one particular
or bunch of particulars

that defines the moment,
i.e., leads to the next. Such as
"out the branch."

Where am I?

(With microscopes ((sci-tech, psychic)) & physics macroscopes, we've learned enough wondrous new facts about Nature to wonder whether there are any (((facts))). The universe seems built of uncertainty, like poems. Everything really does flow, like the old guy said. We can still feel the mouse in our pockets, & that serves as fact, but falls away instantly to monsters of normal distortion.

o   o   o

Dinner for the space trio included Odyssey apertiff
(sic), shrimp cocktail, prime rib roast, lunar salad with
Iwo Jima dressing, and for dessert, moonfruit melba
and Apollo cookies. The astronauts will go to Pago
Pago Saturday.

o   o   o

Languge happens on the frontier:

o Surrealism	o myth
o street & kitchen oral riffs	o soft classics
o laments	o flicks & flecks
o experiment	o exhortations
o rambles	o mongrels
o jokes	o screams
o journals	o scare stuff
o fantasies	o sweet & sour nothings
o glossolalia	o alphabet stews
o statistics	o babytalk
o permutations	o drips
o headlines	o anthropomorphia
o how-to manuals	o mysteries/rebuses
o Western Swing	o chains & fables
o tech jargon	o kisses of death
o red herrings	o waves
o gossips	

Following dimension into any of those events leads us far enough
(farther than we can go).

> Science has finally found itself to
> be poetic, on the discovery side;
> poets can in turn learn from the
> thought processes & beautiful slippery
> reality it now presents. Power lies
> in exposure, speaks in act. Human
> feeling struggling to articulate the
> new dissolving world, in local words
> with global implications, has power of
> expansiveness, exposure to motion.

Human feeling has too long circled around its own heart, forming
the half-cooked shields of psychology, coalescing terms toward a
comfy salvation. Emotion breathes when it leaves its own labels &
simply serves perception, in a "heaping up" (poetry, Sanskrit root).

E	asily	W	hile
C	rowded	A	ll
O	nto	T	hink,
L	ame	E	vening
O	rbiting	R	esponds
G	iant		—*DeAun Burchi*
Y	ield Sign		

—Kathleen Pope

(Naropa students)

There are precedents in nature for any move the Big Brain might
make, as from solid directly to a form of air, when the heat is on. Or
sheer numbers.

o   o   o

". . . but Nature is catching on."

—Jennifer Heath

o o o

Out there, around here, upon leaving labels, would include movement inside—anywhere out of usual assumptions—& there, in Hegel's words, "Freedom is the recognition of necessity." (Pause to re-see "necessity" like a new particle.)

o o o

"Quien sabe? It might fetch some fireworks you're not
figurin' on," said Nevada, moving over from his heav-
ing, foam-lashed horse to get in the shade of a pine.
—Zane Grey

o o o

Necessity, in the public square, whatever shape, now that our material power rolls out into invisibility, entails poetry's triangulation of available space. Could be simplest look at a rotting leaf, or thumbnail. Sketch of dirt or Big Dipper . . . .

A raindrop falls.
It falls on my nose—
delicate, light, transparent.

NOTES FROM A (POETRY) READING LIFE

1

When I was very young Chingachgook and Cody, Winnetou and Wild Bill and their cohorts were my guides across the huge, wild, entirely imaginary land across the ocean. Later, those thrilling chieftains were joined and soon overshadowed by Ishmael, Huck Finn, Nick Adams, Sam Spade, Philip Marlowe, Holden Caulfield—but by the time *he* came along I was already having a not-so-thrilling sojourn in Cedar Rapids, Iowa.

This was 1951, when I spent my senior year in high school as an American Field Service exchange student. My hosts considered W. Somerset Maugham unsuitable reading for a seventeen-year-old and turned an unhealthy color when I told them I liked Henry "The Air-Conditioned Nightmare" Miller. They certainly hadn't heard of be-bop, and even if they had, they would have disapproved of it, as they disapproved of the teenagers from "downtown" Cedar Rapids with whom I struck up friendships across class lines.

Having thus acquired firsthand experience of the chasms yawning between at least three distinct and separate "cultures" in the land of Amerikay (then as now), i.e. Artistic, Official, and Popular, the kid from Helsinki, Finland, born of a German-Baltic mother and a Finnish father who had taught him to speak and read German, Swedish, Finnish, and English (in that order), returned from his first venture to the West a sadder but marginally wiser person, and left Helsinki soon thereafter for prolonged sojourns in Germany, Austria, and England, not to return to these still so curiously Divided States until 1965.

2

The first poetry I read, in a parental home with a sizeable polyglot library, consisted of works by the German Romantics printed in Gothic type faces—for instance, Johann Wolfgang von Goethe's "Wer reitet so spät durch Nacht und Wind":

Who's riding so late through night-wind wild?
It is the father with his child;
He holds his boy safe from the storm,
His cradling arm is keeping him warm.[1]

Spine-tingling stuff, especially when we get to the Elf-King's seductive promises to the little boy:

Do come with me, my lad so fair!
My lovely daughters shall give thee care,
Through night my daughters' revels sweep,
They'll dance and they'll sing and they'll rock thee to sleep.

In the end, the Elf-King steals the boy's soul; so, don't even dream of going out "riding so late through night-wind wild." Then there was verse of a more historico-heroic orientation, such as Count August von Platen's "The Grave in the Busento":

Nights one hears on the Busento near Cosenza muffled
    singing:
Echoes answer from the waters, from the depths seem to be
    ringing,
Shades of valiant Goths move back and forth in ghostly
    lamentation,
Mourning the death of Alaric, the greatest leader of their
    nation.[2]

In school, there was more of that sort of thing in Finnish, easily recognizable as, indeed, more of the same. It was interspersed with readings from The Kalevala, the collection of Eastern Finnish oral poetry cobbled into a "national epic" in the early nineteenth century:

I am driven by my longing,
And my understanding urges
That I should commence my singing,
And begin my recitation.
I will sing the people's legends,

And the ballads of the nation.
To my mouth the words are flowing,
And the words are gently falling,
Quickly as my tongue can shape them,
And between my teeth emerging . . .[3]

To a child raised above and in World War II air-raid shelters, in a family divided by Axis vs. Allied sympathies, glorifications of heroism and nationalist mythology were not only boring but repugnant. I remember what it was like to be (and stay) alive in a city subjected to nightly aerial bombardments; I saw the literal ruins created by modern warfare, in both Finland and (later, in the early Fifties) in Germany.

Long before the sixties, I was a confirmed internationalist, anti-militarist (though not necessarily 100% pacifist), anti-authoritarianist, anti-"Prussian". . . To this day, military uniforms with people inside them give me the heebie-jeebies. I love the America of early anarchist communes, of the IWW, of the Lincoln Brigade, of the WPA (and thus feel close to the strains of the sixties that derive from that tradition), but never had much use for what I tend to think of as the George Harrison aspects of that decade, the swoony peacock feather raga trip—or its descendants, various repulsive superstitions of "newageism" (neo-astrology, Tarot pseudo-psychology, crystal-gazing etc.). No patience with those, any more than with the global money establishment's hypocritical monotheism.

Everything my parents enthused about—one from a humanistic-Socratic viewpoint, the other, from a Nietzschean 'will to change' vantage—that smacked of heroics, idealism, reverence of some occult 'virtue' or another, was deeply suspect to me. I was a politely rebellious son and student affecting the style of my not always so polite fellow rebels—1930s gangster style hats, pegged "jitterbug" pants, and a generally snotty and cool attitude.

There was, however, one poet in my early reading whose words seemed to bear some relation to how I felt about things:

The sexton's daughter was small and sweet,
She showed me through hall and crypt;

Her hair was blond, her form petite,
From her neck the kerchief had slipped.

Candles and crosses, tomb and fount—
She gave me a tour of the place.
The temperature then began to mount—
I looked in Elsbeth's face.

o   o   o

The sexton's daughter sweetly led
The way out of hall and crypt;
Her lips were moist, her neck was red,
From her bosom the kerchief had slipped[4]

Like his soul brother Robert Burns, Heinrich Heine loses much in translation, but there was an irreverent Enlightenment edge to his verse
that was very appealing, as were his revolutionary (*and* cynical)
sentiments:

There are two kinds of rat:
One hungry, and one fat.
The fat ones stay content at home,
But hungry ones go out and roam.

o   o   o

These wild and savage rats
Fear neither hell nor cats,
They have no property, or money too,
So they want to divide the world anew.

o   o   o

The burghers spring to arms,
The priests ring out alarms.
The bulwark of the state, you see,
Is periled—namely, Property.

○ ○ ○

> No finespun talk can help, no trick
> Of old out-dated rhetoric
> Rats are not caught with fancy isms—
> They leap right over syllogisms.[5]

(Years later, I recognized that tone and vision again in the works of
Bertolt Brecht.) "Old out-dated rhetoric" was, indeed, what I mostly
found in my early reading of what was called poetry, even though
there were exceptions like Christian Morgenstern, the German
counterpart of Lewis Carroll, and Joachim Ringelnatz, a Hamburg
sailor-poet who still awaits effective translation (and may well wait
for it forever—his verse is 1920s macho-piratical and far from politically correct).

3

e.e. cummings, Carl Sandburg and Don Marquis were, if memory
serves, discoveries made in Cedar Rapids—or even before that, in
the United States Information Service library in Helsinki; their various
rhetorics struck me as more up to date. But it wasn't until I encountered the monumentally baffling Ezra Pound—at first, I believe, in a
bi-lingual edition with Eva Hesse's[6] remarkable German translations:
a small paperback selection, with a greenish photo image of the
slightly puffy-faced poet on a glossy black cover—that poetry began to seem a subject worthy of active pursuit.

Pound's Bertrans de Born still smacked of mothball heroics, but
Cathay and *The Cantos* were different: they existed in a realm of ac-
tive language first opened up to me by Ernest Hemingway's crisply
Imagist short stories, the favorite reading matter of my early twenties.

They also led me to the work of William Carlos Williams and helped
me identify my dissatisfaction with my own attempts to write Heinesque poems[7] and Hemingwayesque short stories: WCW's poems
encompassed more of what human life was about most of the time,
and did so with greater economy, elegance, and variousness than
those finally formulaic 'stories':

Somebody dies every four minutes
in New York State—

To hell with you and your poetry—
You will rot and be blown

through the next solar system
with the rest of the gases—

What the hell do you know about it?

AXIOMS

Don't get killed . . .[8]

Compared to the poems of Williams and Pound, even the prose of Chekhov and Stendhal *ran on rails,* just as what poetry I knew from the nineteenth and most previous centuries seemed to do: this new poetry made it possible to get off the train and fly through galaxies and dandelions, zoom down to that nail in a woman's shoe, up to the top of Niagara Falls, back to a sunset over Mt. Taishan or forward to some minuscule personal moment of incredible complexity in an undisclosed, wholly interior location . . .

o o o

Williams's, Louis Zukofsky's, and Kenneth Rexroth's essays mapped the European sources of that kind of vision—Apollinaire, Cendrars, Pierre Reverdy, and Federico García Lorca; the last-mentioned I had already discovered all by my little self through an intermediary, one "Georges Forestier" who, in the 1950s, sold thousands of copies of his book "Ich schreibe mein Herz in den Staub der Strasse" ("I Inscribe My Heart in the Dust of the Road") by presenting it as the work of a Byronic Alsatian-born Foreign Legionnaire. The poems were blatant imitations of Lorca, and "Forestier" was soon revealed as a fiction (or fraud, depending on how judgmental you want to be); nevertheless, I am grateful to him for pointing the way to one of the masters.

4

Despite the ruins and losses and pervasive feelings of guilt and resentment, the fifties in central and northern Europe were an exhilarating time. Artists and poets of post–World War II "free" Europe were rediscovering and catching up on the spectacular Modernist movements that had emerged and flourished between the wars: Cubism, Futurism, Dada, Surrealism, Joyce, Pound, Kafka, Stein—all that had been either banned or buried for almost a decade, especially (with the exception of Switzerland) in the Germanophone realm. During my six years (1952–58) in Germany and Austria, I attended that revival both as a reader and, to a modest extent, as a writer. German poet-editors Kurt Leonhard, Max Bense, and Reinhard Döhl were kind enough to publish and even anthologize some of my German-language texts—unlike my Heinesque Finnish ones, these were now influenced by Dada, Bense's "stochastic" experiments[9] based on probability theory and cybernetics, and Helmut Heissenbüttel's post-Steinian writings.

(In the mid-to-late sixties I encountered a very similar "language orientation" in work produced by students of mine, mavericks at the Iowa Writers' Workshop—whom I introduced to the few translations that were then available of that German-language oeuvre, including works by H. C. Artmann and Konrad Bayer of The Vienna Group of the 1950s, and to some of these writers' major initial influences, Sapir, Whorf, Wittgenstein, Barthes, etc.[10] Far be it from me to make any historical claim to mentorship here—but I may have reinforced the desires of Bob Perelman, Ray Di Palma, and Barrett Watten to explore avenues not favored by their other teachers.)

Collage and montage of various kinds were the major modes of production. "Any text could be used, textbooks, trivial literature, etc., and . . . the effect is that of releasing language from its rules and structure, demonstrating its restrictions and hierarchies. The idea that language molds and shapes thought is not new, dating from at least the 19th century, but the Vienna Group made this their basic literary premise."[11]

5

Now, in 1994, the Eisensteinian montage of *The Cantos,* Tzara's words out of a grab-bag, Max Bense's "stochastic texts" and Artmann's "verbariums", Gysin's and Burroughs's cut-ups, Jackson Mac Low's and Clark Coolidge's continued oeuvres, Kathy Acker's montages and appropriations can all be seen as parts of the canon of Modernist verbal imagination. In a note I wrote for my section in a German anthology published in 1963[12] I see an early expression of my continued love-hate relationship with that "artful" approach to poetry: "I've experimented with various techniques of fractured syntax, mostly in German, but find that the results end up being merely the charmingly sinister effects of a kind of insensate 'objectivity', a dead end. Time to start over, however modestly."

Fourteen years later, in *The Actualist Anthology,*[13] a small group of fellow poets and students who had converged on Iowa City banded together to demonstrate such a modest starting-over. Darrell Gray, soon to be lost—and lost too soon—to the angry sicknesses of alcohol, states on that book's introductory page that "to be Actual is not to *possess* Actuality—it is to be possessed by it . . . I want to emphasize that Actualism is not an aesthetic 'movement' in the usual sense of the word. It owes nothing to literary history that it could not find elsewhere, least of all aesthetic theory or literary criticism. Actualism begins when the Automorph in man's being decides to wake him up."[14] Gray's "automorph" strikes me as a forerunner of Gregory Corso's "autochthonic spirit".[15]

Morty Sklar, co-editor and publisher of the anthology, states that "each Actualist is concerned with connecting with the reader on *some* level"—in retrospect, a concern charmingly optimistic in its assumption of a generalized "reader" who does not need to be thoroughly re-educated first, either in currently correct politico-literary theory, or in currently correct oppressed minority group allegiance, before she or he can even presume to "connect" with the author. This may, of course, reflect a thoroughly antiquated (in 1994) bohemie-anarcho-individualist ideology, but I would not exchange it for another. Give me the Elysian, or Eleusinian, fields of poetry where Egil Skallagrimsson enjoys a picnic with Emily Dickinson, satyrs converse with cyborgs, and dinosaurs roam next to herds of pro-grammed super-rabbits.

The spirit of the Actualist group (Sklar's press was, and still is, called "The Spirit That Moves Us Press") owed much to the work of Frank O'Hara and James Schuyler, and to the "actual" presence of Ted Berrigan in Iowa City for one memorable year. Ted composed his sonnets and odes with an immediacy, anarchic humor, and un-pretentious artifice that still strike me as what might be The News. It also occurs to me that O'Hara and Berrigan may well have been the last WASP poets *of the city*, and that the Iowa City Actualists were aware of this.

But all that was back in 1977, a decade after I had left London to join the poets of the America of Whitman, Williams, Olson, and many others both living and dead.

My nine years in the United Kingdom mostly confirmed the premo-nition I'd had when I left Vienna—that London was a place where I would find few writers with an urgency to "start over" in any direc-tion not sanctioned by the established consensus of a venerable tradition. Dadaism and Surrealism, in their day, had made no per-ceptible dents in that consensus; they had just been "Continental" fads and aberrations. There never had been an Armory Show in London, yet it was mainly among visual artists (Richard Hamilton, Edoardo Paolozzi, Tom Phillips) that one found a lively sense of what had been thought and done elsewhere in the first half of the cen-tury. Pound had come and gone, Eliot was a gray eminence glimpsed slouching toward the elevator in Bush House, and Basil Bunting had not yet been resurrected. A few people knew and ap-preciated his work and that of David Jones and David Gascoyne, but they were not among the taste-makers of the era of "The Angry Young Men" and "The Movement."

As Allen Ginsberg remarked when first met in London, the young Britons who cheered the Stones and the Beatles were not *readers:* the early "Beat" era produced no British counterparts to the shining Ginsberg—Corso—Ferlinghetti triad across the Atlantic. There were imitators, but a genuine assimilation of the Beat, Black Mountain, and New York School esthetic only took place in the late sixties and early seventies, largely due to the influence of Edward Dorn, Tom Clark, and Ted Berrigan who spent time teaching, editing, and publishing in the U.K. In retrospect, Allen's observation may have reflected the economic and educational difference between U.S. and U.K college cultures in the sixties.

I still have a vivid personal memory of my excitement and delight upon finding *Howl* and *Gasoline* in a book store in the Charing Cross Road, and soon I acquired friends and mentors among those who felt a similar delight: Michael Shayer and Gael Turnbull who published *Migrant* magazine (and my own first books in English), and Tom Raworth (who published *Outburst* and, with Barry Hall, Goliard Press books). We looked to the poets we read in little overseas magazines like Cid Corman's *Origin,* LeRoi Jones' *Yugen,* Diane Di Prima's *Floating Bear,* Lita Hornick's *Kulchur*—then met them in the flesh as they came to visit and some even to stay a while in "Swinging London": Allen; Gregory (who became my daughter's godfather); Lawrence (who published my translations of *Red Cats*); Robert Creeley; Edward Dorn; Jerome Rothenberg; Jonathan Williams; John Ashbery; Ronald Johnson; Tom Clark; Peter Orlovsky; Aram Saroyan; Lewis MacAdams; Gerard Malanga; Larry Fagin; David Ball (first met in New York in 1951!); Piero Heliczer . . .

Donald M. Allen's anthology, *The New American Poetry 1945–1960*,[16] was the answer to the prayers of our little cargo cult—evidence that there were not just one or two or three poets "over there" who had heard and assimilated the sounds of the twentieth century, but at least forty-four, and, as the editor stated, this selection presented only a fraction of their work. The pull exercised by this far-flung company of poets proved too strong, and in 1966 I bade farewell to a city I had grown to love and began a quarter of a century's odyssey through, as they say, American life and letters.

> really just a young 23-year-old American poet (came here in
>   '66)
> or should we start with '58 London 31 in that case

o o o

was it an hour ago I sat there in London wondering
about Ted Berrigan this tough young American poet & critic
in the pages of KULCHUR magazine[17]

7

Thomas Mann once stated "Die deutsche *Sprache* ist mein Vater-
land" ("The German *language* is my fatherland"). In my mind, I
have sometimes modified that: the American language, specifically its "outrider" poetry, is my homeland. My *vita* has proceeded
along the lines of Guy Debord's "derive"—*drift*—combined with a
genuine love of exile, i.e., communities and places of choice, not
predetermined by accidents of birth. South and West have been
the main directions in which the currents have tended to carry
me—so here I am now, in the American Southwest. The Front Range.
Not far from the grave of my childhood idol, Col. W. F. Cody. Of
course he was a fraud, a liar, an arm of U.S. colonialism, but he did
introduce Chief Sitting Bull to Queen Victoria.

8

So, "what's the moral of the tale? "—if a tale it be: initially, my secret
model for these pages was the "Book List" we at the Naropa School
of Disembodied Poetics ask our Master's candidates to compile as
an appendix to their theses—but even as that, mine is not comprehensive, it is just a sliver off the top of a rather densely laminated
and poly-lingual reading life. Nothing has been said about the
Finnish poets, my contemporaries Paavo Haavikko and Pentti
Saarikoski, whom I have tried to translate and make known in the
Anglophone realm; nor about Gunnar Harding of Sweden, Jean-
Paul de Dadelsen of Belgium, Andrei Voznesensky of Russia, Rolf-
Günter Dienst of Germany . . . all of them dear and important pres-
ences in the international web-work of poetry that exists and always
has existed in spite of linguistic and politico-cultural barriers.

All of them, all of us, have lived through "interesting times"—
times marked by unprecedented (and, as we are beginning to

understand, insanely excessive) numbers of human beings on the planet, and therefore, and at least quantitatively speaking also marked by unprecedented magnitudes of loss, injustice, oppression, and *Weltschmerz*—"sorrow or sadness over the present or future woes of the world," says Webster's, and I would not leave out the *past* woes, either.

When asked about the inspiration of his poems, Apollinaire said: "Le plus souvent il s'agit de tristesse" ("It's mostly a question of sadness"). But, as he knew, the trick is to remember that that is absolutely *no* excuse to be *boring*, or *humorless*, or *too conveniently absent*.

9

At the risk of pushing my Old Codger routine too far, I have to say that much of what I read these days in our poetry periodicals and books strikes me as culpable of those three no-no's.

Many of those who believe they are upholding the great tradition from the Isles, or advocate a return to it after a—to their minds, rather regrettable—eighty-year excursion into what William Carlos Williams called "the American idiom," tend to be only too obviously (= boringly) 'present' in their work and solemn about it to boot, while some of those who still like to try on the old avant-garde hat ("It is important to keep old hat in secret closet"—Ted Berrigan) often produce faintly ironic rearrangements of various debased public lingos that leave one neither amused (moved) nor entertained (smiling).

The reason the irony is so faint is that there is, literally, no one there. Which is very different from, say, Charles Olson's immersion in his best poems (e.g. "Maximus, from Dogtown"), or Louis Zukofsky metamorphosing into flowers of sound.

While the "mainstreamers" or proponents of the nostalgia esthetic rely too heavily on First Person Singular and First P. Singular's ancestors, relatives, lovers, enemies, pets and pet peeves, many of their seemingly more exploratory counterparts seem afflicted by the misconception that it is possible (or even desirable) to expunge all of the above, and all of one's feelings about (for and against) them, from the text.

The currently sanctioned post-modern vanguard's main problem seems to be an infatuation with the not-so-new discovery of "opacity"—what we used to call "obscurity" in the old days, and not always pejoratively, either: Herakleitos was nicknamed "The Obscure", the Dark One. In present instances, this often seems to generate a kind of incoherent neo-symbolism embedded in language that appears, well, *stunted*. It is true, as Philip Whalen has noted, that one cannot know what one "thinks" in a poem before one starts saying / writing it: but it is equally evident that there are times when one both thinks and writes rather less than memorably or communicatively, and if the results seem opaque, that does not necessarily mean they are any good.

Parenthetically, once again: I am aware of the interesting way in which the Mallarméan late Symbolist tradition is being revived by some contemporary French and American poets, but in some respects it feels too close to, or like another code for, the Anglo-Germano-Romantic strain. (Sibelius? Never really cared for him; my taste runs from the Baroque & Mozart directly to Miles.) The reader should not have to "work to get the point" as if the text were a sophisticated MENSA exercise. But with, say, John Ashbery, whom some may consider a sphinx, I have the sense that he is talking about exactly what he is talking about, not involving you in any "find-the-point" contest, nor nudging you to read his or his friends' latest essay on methodology.

It is also true that hardly anyone writing and publishing poetry these days receives genuine "criticism" any more. One of the reasons for this, pointed out by Samuel R. Delany in a 1974 essay, may simply be that there's far too much of the stuff for *anyone* to have an overview. [18]

It seems to me that I have always been (not unpleasantly) "torn" between:

1) a poetry that is both transparent, or if you wish, limpid, and intelligent; that seems to be "saying itself": "My poetry is mainly just talk"—Ted Berrigan; that runs word-thought / word-feeling by me, with economy and elegance, sometimes playing with different levels of available rhetoric, switching back and forth between them,

and has some surprises in it, the way good conversation does, often of a humorous nature—and

2) the total Sargasso Sea of Signifiers, from Joyce to Stein to Bruce Andrews. I remember Ted telling me once that he cherished the works of his friends Aram Saroyan and Clark Coolidge "because they do my *research* for me."

10

Print and radio journalism, translating, and teaching (in that chronological order) have been the three ways I have had of making a livelihood. Each in their own way, they have "been good to me"— to the extent that I'm still around, and that I have had some time left over to do some writing of my own.

In poetry workshops, I try to get the participants to *read*—first of all read the works of their predecessors, as far back as possible, and only then some of what their contemporaries are doing to see how these may be dealing with the various strands of the traditions. Read, read, read. Then, when something really "gets" to you, one way or another, read it again: read it very closely: word for word, and think about each word and why it is where it is. Now read your *own* work that way. "Be absolutely ruthless with your own work"— Tom Raworth. Poetry is language art: "Wortkunst," the Germans say—"word art." And Pound's "Do's and Don'ts" still seem valid, although I would not insist on anyone's reading all the texts he recommends. But I do bring in what strikes me as interesting in my own reading at any given time.

11

In days not too long past, when education always meant knowledge of at least one other language, mostly Latin, even people who did not necessarily consider themselves poets had a go at translating Catullus or Horace, merely for fun, as a mental and linguistic exercise. To some extent, in our Anglophone sphere, the great modernists of languages other than English have now taken the place of old Horace and Gaius Valerius: consider how many different translations there are of Baudelaire, Rimbaud, Apollinaire,

Lorca, Neruda. The act of reading a poem with translation in mind is the *closest* reading imaginable, and that quality of attention, once acquired and exercised, is valuable in other contexts, not least in one's own writing. The participants in my translation workshops at The Kerouac School are practicing writers, and the workshops give them an opportunity to make this kind of intensive study of texts by authors outside their linguistic realm—to get ideas, and to creatively understand, or misunderstand, what those people were up to.

It has been said that translation has no muse, but I think that it is presided over by a committee of at least six: Calliope (epic), Clio (history), Erato (lyric/amatory), Euterpe (music), Polyhymnia (sacred song), and Thalia (acting). The ancient Greeks were, of course, terrible chauvinists: they regarded other peoples (including their poets) who did not know and use *their* language as Barbarians, and translation was simply appropriation. I guess Ares presided over that.

12

Meanwhile, Blaise Cendrars and Joel Oppenheimer, who had *names*, and *cities,* and *times,* are still speaking of these to each other, in the company of whoever cares to join them at the great Lion's Head Bar in the Elysian Fields. I think I see Mina Loy there—and Lorine Niedecker—Bert Brecht and Basil Bunting and Pentti Saarikoski . . . And, of course, Ted.

NOTES

1 "Erikönig" by Johann Wolfgang von Goethe. English translation ("Elf-King") by Martin Zwart, in: *A Treasury of German Ballads,* New York, 1964, Frederick Ungar Publishing Co., Inc.

2 "Das Grab im Busento" by August von Platen. English translation ("The Grave in the Busento") by Martin Zwart. Op. cit.

3 *Kalevala, The Land of Heroes.* Verse translation by W. F. Kirby, London (J. M. Dent) and New York (E. P. Dutton), 1907.

4 "Im Dome" by Heinrich Heine. English translation ("In the Cathedral") by Hal Draper, in: *The Complete Poems of Heinrich Heine, A Modern English Version,* Oxford, 1982, Oxford University Press.

5 "Die Wanderratten" by Heinrich Heine. English translation ("The Roving Rats") by Hal Draper. Op. cit.

6 Not the American artist of the same name.

7 *Sateiden välillä* ("Between the Rains") by Anselm Hollo. Helsinki, 1956, Otava Publishing Co.

8 From "XXV" in *Spring and All 1923* by William Carlos Williams. *The Collected Poems of William Carlos Williams.* Volume I: 1909–1939, edited by A. Walton Litz and Christopher McGowan. New York, 1986, New Directions.

9 *Augenblick* ("Moment"), a literary review published and edited by Max Bense from Siegen, Germany, 1955–61 (?). Also: *Programmierung des Schönen* ("Programming the Beautiful") by Max Bense (aesthetica IV). Baden-Baden, 1962, Agis-Verlag.

10 See *The Vienna Group: 6 Major Austrian Poets.* Translated and edited by Rosmarie Waldrop and Harriett Watts. Station Hill, New York, 1985, Station Hill Press.

11 *Selected Works of Konrad Bayer.* Edited, translated, and introduced by Malcolm Green, with additional translations by Walter Billeter and Christopher Middleton. London, 1986, Atlas Press.

12 *Zwischenräume* ("Spaces Between" or "Interstices"), edited by Reinhard Döhl. Wiesbaden, 1963, Limes Verlag.

13 *The Actualist Anthology.* Edited by Morty Sklar and Darrell Gray. Iowa City, 1977, The Spirit That Moves Us Press.

14 Op. cit. p. 5.

15 *Herald of the Authochthonic Spirit* by Gregory Corso. New York, 1981, New Directions.

16 *The New American Poetry 1945–1960.* Edited by Donald M. Allen. New York 1960, Grove Press.

17 From "Arcana Gardens" in *Outlying Districts* by Anselm Hollo. Minneapolis, 1990, Coffee House Press. The poem was written in 1989.

18 "Shadows," collected in *The Jewel-Hinged Jaw* by Samuel R. Delaney. New York, 1977, Berkley Windhover.

THE SOUNDING VOICE:
A RHAPSODY

We have sustained a barrage of hieratic statement this month and the month is almost over. It is to be seen whether we have been struck, have sustained damage, improvement, or any change at all. Most of us are in a kind of shock, as if this month had been a collision—a slow motion, ongoing, accruing collision. We have heard personal and heartfelt accounts of Persia, Egypt, Language, Meditation, and Beliefs, Beliefs, Beliefs, as if a crowd of Marco Polos had descended on us. As if a phoneme were a city believed in and visited and now here described by our time and mind travelers.

And now, just when what we would all love to do most is rest, I am here to add to that conglomerate. Take heart, I am going to talk about simple things: the values of bread and butter, the commonplace, and what you know without having labored for it. And the vocabulary you already possess is as much as you will need.

I'll begin with this cranky and usable thing of Edgar Allen Poe's:

If a man, if an orphicist or seer or whatever else he may
choose to call himself while the rest of the world calls
him an ass, if this gentleman have an idea which he
does not understand himself, the best thing he can do
is say nothing about it. But if he have any idea which is
actually intelligible to himself and if he sincerely wishes
to render it intelligible to others, we then hold it as indisputable that he should employ those forms of speech
which are the best adapted to further his object. He
should speak to the people in that people's ordinary
tongue. He should arrange words such as are habitually employed for the preliminary and introductory
ideas to be conveyed. He should arrange them in
collocations such as those in which we are accustomed to see those words arranged.

Meantime, we earnestly ask if *bread and butter* be

the vast idea in question, if b*read and butter* be any
portion of this vast idea; for we have often observed
that when a seer has to speak of so usual a thing as
bread and butter he can never be induced to mention it outright.

The "people's ordinary tongue" begins with speech, with the sounding voice and the ramifications of the sounding voice—that speech
vibrates the body and is sensual, that constellations of thought
open in our heads, caught to a word.

In our ongoing histories as word-involved persons what usually
came next was reading. We were given books to read, and we were
taught to decently keep the sounding to ourselves, a curious but apparently necessary social skill. "Silent reading," the teacher called it.
"We will now read silently. Take your books and read to yourselves."
And we all did. Babies learning the gridwork. What was wrong was
to move our lips. But we had to hear the word to know it was right. We
heard it in our heads. Our lips were still, and in all our heads there was
this miracle—the silent word sounding. "See Dick run. See Jane run."

The words were on the page. They stayed there. They said the
same thing as often as we looked. On the page, for all who look,
Zukofsky will always say, "The running dog never lies down."

Dick and Jane run and run.

Before all this began, the last week of June, an extraordinary
singer, Isaye Barnwell, gave a workshop here. You may know her as
the woman who sings bass in Sweet Honey in the Rock. Sixty of us
sang from one to five every afternoon for a week. We began on
Monday. Thursday evening we gave a concert of fifteen songs in
five-part harmony.

During this very intensive workshop she said a number of important things.

She said, "We are the people we've been waiting for."

She said, "Singing changes the body chemistry."

I heard her and believed her, but then I am susceptible to
change. And I thought of speech and words on paper, that they

also change the body chemistry. However "silent" on the page, the words we read and the words we choose to write vibrate our frame, shake our cage, resonate. The words we choose. "Our" words.

Information, it is comfortable to think, is *held* in words. Neat little containers, all in a row, make a sentence. And then one makes another one. One accumulates these rows to arrive at a piece of writing as my grandmother did her year's canning. I could look at the glass jars in her dugout storm cellar and recognize tomatoes, green beans, peaches, shining through.

Some words *are* that simple, "Please pass the bread and butter." But language is a living thing—it lives in us—we *host* language. Words are born into our vocabularies, live and die there. And the *lively* words do not stay still, are not mannerly, do not so much "hold" information as spill it, stain the environs in which they occur— the *sound* of our spoken sentences, the "silent" sounding of thought in our heads and of the sentences we put onto paper.

The sentences we put onto paper are as caught to the body that produces them as thought is, as voice is. The "instrument" shapes the possibility. How and where your voice is placed in your mouth and throat, how your "voice box" vibrates, the tempo your breath and heartbeat take in various circumstance, determines in large part what you say, in what rhythms.

When you speak or sing the sound of your voice is unique, is yours alone, as distinctive as a fingerprint. A voice print can be made of your voice and proven to be yours. The term for what distinguishes your voice from all the rest is *timbre*. It is a word brought from French and retains the French pronunciation.

> From the *O.E.D.*—*Timbre:* The character or quality of
> a musical or vocal sound (distinct from its pitch and
> intensity) depending upon the particular voice or in-
> strument producing it, and distinguishing it from sounds
> proceeding from other sources; caused by the
> proportion in which the fundamental tone is combined
> with the harmonics or overtones.

When you think or write it is with *timbre*. Whatever you voice, into air or onto paper, is shaped by those harmonics. The sounding that is uniquely yours informs your diction, as if you carry a song in your throat that you will sing your whole life long, in all its variations.

"In all its variations": rhythms, heartbeat and breath, rhythms that change constantly according to time of day, time of month, time of year. And according to circumstance.

Circumstance heightens perception or freezes it like a rabbit in grass, alters breathing patterns, determines the rate at which hearts beat. Crucial decisions are made in our bodies as the rhythms present in that instant's circumstance determine not only what we say but what we can best hear.

We hear most simply the rhythms and tempos kindred to our own.

"Two hearts that beat as one" is more than a romance, it is an essential. If lovers are to understand each other in rarified moments they need their breath in a mutual rhythm, their hearts in a mutual rhythm—otherwise they are stuck with the descriptive. And nothing dissipates passion faster than the descriptive, as hapless as explaining a joke.

As writers, it is crucial to be aware of the configurations, the rhythms that affect what and how we state our selves.

This is not an abstraction.

Ed Sanders asked the persons sitting in the tent for his lecture at what time of the day they best wrote what kind of thing. A question that held information usually to be found only in answers.

For instance, there is a feeling of semi-hypnosis that many writers experience when they are going to write and it's building inside them to happen. You can find yourself meandering through your house or apartment holding something in your hand as if you're about your daily business, but what you're carrying might be one of a pair of shoes. Some such uselessness. Or you might be carrying an item you meant to put away, and you find yourself, again, looking at it, trying to remember what you had in mind.

Notice that float when it happens. You are bemused. You are waiting for the writing that is going to find its way into a shape. Become familiar with that *feeling* that is an "announcement." When it happens disconnect the phone, put a sign on the door that says you are at work. Do everything you can to protect the *tone* of that feeling.

And if, when you have put the sign on the door that says you are not to be interrupted, a "friend" knocks anyway, notice that also. Any interruption at all and you will return to the ruin of what had been going to be a free gift. You will return, thinking "Now what was that . . . ," and you will have become a different person. What had seemed so clear, so *approaching*, so almost here, if you write it now—with that sweet float gone—you will have to dig for every word, work for every nuance. You will probably find yourself rewriting more than writing, all for the sake of what you lost, what you had that went glimmering.

So, information arrives in words bound to configurations of sounding and rhythm. Multitudinous. How are we to sustain our *selves,* which is all we have, against that rush perpetually seeking us out. The rush that is always just the beginning, because when you learn anything you had not known, when you recognize something you had not known you knew, the "stuff" that has been held, waiting in your head to be sprung by a catalyst, clicks into place.

Something from Valéry. This is a small bit called "*Abrupt Changes in a Self Same Thing.*"

> Sometimes our attention is strangely and abruptly arrested by an idea, a recollection, a corner of some piece of furniture. All at once it seems as though we are seeing something for the first time that we have seen a thousand times. Or we perceive the coming of age, the puberty, of an impression. An idea in its sudden force seems more real and yet we have thought of it many times before and even close up and even with deliberation. But this time it is, as it were, tangible. . . . In the same way it often happens that we understand something only long afterwards, an intention, a text, a person, oneself. We discover the significance of a look addressed to us twenty years ago by someone now dead. And the meaning of a phrase.

And the beauty of a line of poetry we've known by
heart since childhood. So it is said the grain of wheat
found in hypogeum germinates after three thousand
years of arid slumber.

—*Selected Writings of Paul Valéry*—

Lovely to think meaning can hang there while our mind ripens to receive it.

And it is a relief to realize that—given all the change we're capable of—we do continue to be ourselves. The skin holds. Keeps its
shape. We don't have to hold it together, however much the mind
needs to insist it's got everything under control.

"I think, therefore I am."

That's a likely story.

Descartes could be glossed, "I think I think, therefore I think I am,
I think."

Or take a different person entirely, who says, "I am because my
small dog knows me."

We need not fear that we will lose ourselves into the maelstrom.
We stay recognizable even to people who know us only slightly.

Robert Louis Stevenson had someone in *Kidnapped* say, "Life is
all a variorum." If there were a job description for life, it would be
that. It is not that we *do* it, it is that we *are* it—alive, and various. And
all around us it is the same—i.e., various.

My topic is the speaking voice and where it takes us. The resonating, sounding voice that has our body as its instrument; lungs
and diaphragm send air through the sounding, shaping environment of our throat and tongue and lips to be words, sounding nuance, tone and timbre, tessitura and the thrust of thought.

A word, however saturated it is with meaning is in the air and
gone, that quick. There just long enough to get us to the next word.

Valéry says,

I distrust all words. I have reached the point alas of
comparing those words on which we so lightly traverse
the space of a thought to light planks thrown across an

abyss which permit crossing but no stopping. A man in quick motion can use them and get away but if he hesitates the least bit in the world this fraction of time breaks them down and altogether they fall into the depths. He who hurries has caught on. He must not dwell heavily. He would soon find the clearest speech to be a tissue of
obscure turns.

During the Vancouver Poetry Conference in 1963, Charles Olson, who habitually traversed those planks with the speed of light, was asked what he meant by his insistence on the vertical as human. He stood, six foot seven inches tall, and he said,

"Haven't you noticed that man stands upright on two legs," and he put a piece of chalk to the blackboard, began walking the length of the wall toward the door. "That man walks," he was holding the chalk to the blackboard so his walking was marked in exact instant, "through the horizontal time is?" And he walked out the door and was gone.

Behind him where he had been there was a long mark of chalk.

Of course we laughed. And everyone sat reading the chalk mark from left to right.

Then doing it again.

Left to right.

The history of Olson leaving the room.

The speed of it. That was Olson's tempo, that speed, the thought and the action.

o o o

I woke in the night depressed by how little substance there was in this damned thing, nothing tangible about writing and getting on with it.

With awful 3 A.M. clarity, looking into the dark, I thought, "It's just rhapsodizing."

And became curious (more of the 3 A.M. mindset) about "rhapsody," why I thought it meant blathering at the same time I thought it had to do with music.

I got out of bed—what sleep specialists say one must not do—and headed for the *O.E.D.* in the next room.

Rhapsody: Gk., "to stitch" + "song"

The rhapsodes, according to Coleridge, were persons who earned meager livings by memorizing and declaiming the Homeric verses in public places. They held a rod or a bough of laurel, according to one informant, implying a ritual intent.

It is hard to know who the rhapsodes' supporters were; the vulgar masses—incapable of reading for themselves; the "better class" who approved the choice—agreed it was "worthwhile"—(dropping coins in the hat of a busker who plays a classical flute in the bowels of the London subway system but walking past the others); or whether they were paid, like violin players in restaurants, to go away. What is clear is that they were not universally approved. They were "expelled by the despot Cleisthenes in the time of Solon." Historians of that time would know whether Cleisthenes was a despot or simply desperate. (I hear a voice ringing down through the centuries, the ancient cliché, *"All I ever wanted was a little peace and quiet!"*).

Among those in favor, who use "rhapsode" as a positive, is Swinburne (1867), "There has been since Chaucer no second teller of tales, no second rhapsode, comparable to the first."

Lamb, in a letter, writes "My pen goes galloping on most rhapsodically." He seemed to like it.

And someone named Hawkins (1787), in a *Life* of Johnson, says of a speech by Pitt that it was "void of argument, but rhapsodically and diffusively eloquent," making an apparent discrimination between argument and eloquence, and opting for the latter.

It is generally agreed that, in rhapsody, the language and manner is exaggeratedly enthusiastic and/or ecstatic. That suggests what divides the sheep from the goats, the persons of it and those who hate it. But the real clue is in a reference by Grote (1846), "It appears that there had once been rhapsodic exhibitions at the festivals of Dionysus."

Ecstasy and Dionysus.
The old, old argument.

When I saw that Sterne referred more than once to *Tristram Shandy*, which I adore, as rhapsodical and rhapsodizing, I felt secure enough to go back to sleep.

o   o   o

As such things do, it continued.

The next day I went to hear Maxine Hong Kingston. She was talking about the fire in the Berkeley hills, how it had destroyed her house and the manuscript she was working on. She described the look of the burnt manuscript, pages holding in place as the most ephemeral ash, waiting to waft into the air at a breath. And she spoke of her father, who had died a year earlier; she had been returning from the traditional memorial for him when she heard of the fire on her car radio. She said that perhaps the fire meant that her father's spirit had needed more paper money, more food.

The student I had gone to the reading with wrote, "Isn't this getting a little metaphysical?"

"No," I wrote, feeling as if I knew something, "it's rhapsody. Let's talk about it later."

Listening to Maxine Hong Kingston, I thought that a tone of voice can let a thing be said that could not have been said if the voice were elsewhere. That "rhapsodizing" is a way of "singing" oneself into variant locations, to have what it is the voice may now say.

And I thought of Charles Olson in 1965, during the Berkeley Poetry Conference, lurching around the stage, the cord of his lapel mike catching him up, and he saying, "My God, it's the Holy Mother Church". Except for Tom Clark's book, there's been something of a cover-up on that lecture. All the off-the-wallness of it being played into the world as another instance of Olson being difficult to understand.

It wouldn't have disturbed Olson that much. He was so constantly "interpreted", still is. When he got a date wrong in an essay he was writing and his publisher suggested correcting it, he said, "Leave it there. It'll add to the mysterium." A man who didn't give a damn for such trivialities and who had a sense of humor besides.

The real problem of that "lecture" was that he was looped.

A young woman had arrived on the scene and he was enamored. They were getting very little sleep. He had taken some stimulant, to be "up" for the lecture, and then something else when the first seemed ineffective, at which point the first kicked in, and now here he was, on stage, in an auditorium filled to capacity. The stimulants were throwing him around. His cronies and confrères were looking at each other like Old Dad was disgracing himself in public. Creeley leaned forward and said to Dorn, who grinned back, "Is this the Charles we know and love?" And Duncan left, Olson asking him, "Are you deserting me, Robert." Duncan said he had to go to the bathroom, then didn't come back.

o o o

And during that lecture Olson—as hoisted on the horns as James Merry, the "handsome sailor" (also six feet, seven inches tall), who lifted the bull to his shoulders every year until the year it killed him, ever was—stopped still, looked flat out at his audience and said:

"And isn't this how we write? Just like this? What I'm doing right now?"

o o o

The sounding voice and where it takes us. And Rhapsody? We are of it and in it. Lost onto the stage, doing all the various and even questionable stuff that brings us appropriately or not, to be public.

That brings us, over and over again, to the last resort, where we must, and sometimes do, say, "And isn't this how we write? Isn't it?"

July 1992

PART THREE

GNOSIS

PART THREE

GNOSIS

MOUNTING THE POETRY VEHICLE

Anthropology tells us that all peoples have consulted oracles when their own wits leave them with few clear guides into the future. For a literate culture the most reliable oracles are books. Poets in particular take to books as Ionian and Dorian warriors took to Apollo's priestess at Delphi. That's why it's worth noting, if only with a bow of the head, an anthology Shambhala Publications brought out last year. *Beneath a Single Moon: Buddhism in Contemporary American Poetry* loosely gathers up poems and essays by a clutch of poets—poets who either practice some form of Buddhist discipline, or have drawn an explicit impulse towards writing from the lore, the art, the metaphysics, or the mythologies of Buddhism. How useful an oracle, this book? I don't know—I simply note that its forty-odd contributors show how naturalized American soil has become for contemplatives. But there's something else here—it seems you can no longer look deeply into American letters without touching upon Buddhist thought. Not just Buddhist thought in fact, but all those practices—wild, chilling, calm, provocative, or simply ordinary—of insight and magic that come out of the great civilizations of Asia.

I'm not suggesting that to dip at that poetry stream you need to go down to its banks clad in some exotic doctrinal garment. You don't need any such cloak. To taste a contemplative practice or investigate some yoga, there's no more need to deck yourself out in a foreign belief system, alien to your Yankee common sense, than to adorn yourself in outlandish costume. Quite the opposite. At its wisest, the practice of sitting meditation, like the practice of a clear-sighted poetry, is a disabusing of all belief systems—in Blake's terms, a cleansing of the "doors of perception." It is a matter of learning to see clearly—Ezra Pound's "Damn your taste! I would like first to sharpen your perceptions. Then your tastes can take care of themselves."

So Buddhism as I understand it doesn't mean true or false. Nor does it mean believing in miracles or extravagant metaphysics. It just means waking up. The Sanskrit verbal root *budh* means "to waken,"

ANDREW SCHELLING

and a *Buddha* is literally "one who wakes up." It's funny, but the parallel is that in Language's dominion, poetry seems the one place where true and false aren't the issue. One goes to poetry with a different question: *do these words wake you up?*

Years ago, during a stormy and exciting period of American history when I was first coming to recognize the domain of Language as a field of confrontation, the locus of a mighty wizard's struggle, I encountered the small press and began to read a living poetry. In magazines like *Ramparts* and *Evergreen Review* which I'd grab at the newsstand, in books published by City Lights or Leroi Jones's Totem Press, I found poets who took to writing as to "the hall of practice." These thought-shapers, following what I'd later recognize as a genuine lineage of poetic predecessors, were not using words simply to talk about something. No argued definitions, no cautious examinations. These elders were producing states of consciousness, forging in language some specifically *wakened* thing. Poems seemed ideograms of alertness on the page. You could carry them around in your hip pocket, a literal state of Mind.

Within a few years I had discovered a comparable vigilance in the texts and personages of Buddhist history. Shakyamuni Buddha, discussing with friends the wild discoveries he'd made about Mind while he sat under the Bodhi tree 2500 years ago and half a world away, seems not at all distant from my own generation. There's a compelling historical parallel here. In India, up until Shakyamuni's day, poetry and philosophy had centered around the ingestion of an alarming, potent vision-inducing plant—*soma*—the effects of which a priestly caste had increasingly tried to put to work for their own benefit. During my own youth, the dramatic site of discovery was LSD, a vehicle of turbulent confrontation and hard-won cultural insight. While amateur technicians of the sacred—Leroi Jones's "knowers, diggers, oddballs . . . true scientists"—were extending the parameters of consciousness, the CIA and the armed forces like a band of angry threatened priests were trying to wrest control of psychedelics ("mind manifesting" substances) and bend them to their own narrow purposes—namely the shoring up of a very paranoid world order and the extirpation of their perceived enemies. In the process, they were demonizing the sacraments—testing them out on prisoners, military conscripts, ethnic minorities. That they thought they could turn to their questionable purposes such gentle spiritual allies as *peyotl,* with long sacramental traditions, shows a mistrust of basic human intelligence that would be ludicrous, had their misguided experiments not inflicted such damage. Some capable historians have now documented the CIA and military efforts, though we'll probably never get the full story about their experiments on colleagues and fellow citizens who ended up in Vietnam or in prison during the late sixties.

But to return to that early period of Buddhism—it seems that wild and turbulent tripping, insightful and culturally generative as it was (and some terrific poetry came out of it), somehow gave way to other disciplines, further methods of insight. Perhaps the priests of ancient India used *soma* exclusively for narrow purposes of their own, more likely the stuff just got too unpredictable—useful, like mushrooms or acid for a while—but ultimately lacking in grace—a vehicle that travels too fast to control. People left off tripping and headed to the forests for introspection—to practice yogas, talk poetry, debate philosophy.

During the period of comparable social disaffection and cultural innovation in this country I was just referring to, wherever psychedelics got applied with intelligence their use also dropped away over the years. Friends turned to the disciplined training of an art, a handicraft, a technique of meditation. Or to word-powered vehicles. By which I don't just mean mantra or *dharani,* the chanting of formulas and spells. Such practices have their indispensable uses, and for certain purposes are admirably direct. But poets demand a different precision, another subtlety—one acquired by playing the widest range of language.

I had come more and more to regard language as a field of encounter, of challenge; a ground of affection and contest, with poetry the site of consecrated warfare. At stake was our American culture. While thinking along these lines, I met on that field the poets of classical Sanskrit, an eloquent if nearly anonymous crew. These writers, their culture flickering out a thousand years before I'd been born, had drawn careful distinctions between all the emotional conditions that flash through and across the human heart. They had gone on and developed a poetry that could not only account for, but with wizard precision provoke, each of these states. This requires a certain cunning of course—or more precisely, a capable bag of tricks, a sorcerer's toolkit.

Every culture's minstrels fashion such kits, but I'd like to invoke one term the Sanskrit poets treasured—*sandhyabhashya*. It means "twilight speech," and refers to the language poetry uses—a language that occurs in an intermediate zone where day and night meet. A twin incandescence lights this realm—the realm of haunted sounds and strange inscribed ciphers. Poetry's job is not to manipulate emotion—to pretend day is night and night day—which is what the priestly castes do. Poetry's twilight sphere is the site where one confronts the most vivid passions, bedrock realism "lit" by sound and cadence.

I occasionally run into people who see as "Buddhist" only a poetry which displays a certain *cool*, an aloofness from the hotter, more unruly ardors. But the Sanskrit poets, writing at a time when Tantric Buddhism was learning to channel the fiercest human frenzies into luminous insight, would elicit a gem-like poetry from the conflagration of any emotion. They professed a faith in the heart's self-born intelligence and were unafraid of where it might lead them. It's this—people examining the mystery of themselves and their culture—that unites for me the twin disciplines, meditation and poetry.

I've seen parallels drawn between Buddhist metaphysics and poetic practice, some of which are surprisingly cogent. But the planet being wide as it is, and Mind such surprising terrain, I'd resist any comprehensive statement of procedure—"spontaneous prose" or "first thought best thought" for instance—as getting to the pith of writing. With some people it might take several dozen years of hard work to loosen up to a point of easy alertness. Think of Ezra Pound's poem "In the Station of the Metro," which records an experience—a *vision*—that came to him as he dismounted a rush-hour subway in London and looked out upon a throng of human faces lit by some strange incandescence. By his own account Pound spent months trying to capture the quality of his perception in words. Twenty lines, thirty lines . . . the more he wrote the more false it sounded, the further from his original impulse. So he started going the other direction, whittling down all the material he'd composed, trying to get back to the raw fact of the perception. *"I would like first to sharpen your perceptions."* And one day, six months after his vision, he got it—just the title and these two lines—

> The apparition of these faces in the crowd;
> petals on a wet black bough.

One scours the chronicles of poetry to locate heroes, secret friends—to read about toughminded struggles as our predecessors sought the mind-born sources of verse. Pound's is one account. Lorine Niedecker's is equally vivid:

> . . . what vitality! The women hold jobs—
> clean house, cook, raise children, bowl
> and go to church.
>
> What would they say if they knew
> I sit for two months on six lines
> of poetry?

Buddhist lore's packed with comparable accounts of tough labor carried out for years. Gritty patience and gentle humor leveled at one's own frustrations. Consider the trials of Milarepa, yogin and poet of Tibet. Or Bodhidharma's dogged practice, staring in open-eyed meditation, the stories say, until his eyelids dropped off. Consider the perilous journeys of T'ang Dynasty monks to India in search of texts and documents. All these labors carried out with exemplary grace, and one suspects, no little grumbling—to free the perceptions of those tenacious "mind-forge'd manacles." The phrase Mel Weitsman Roshi applies to zazen, or sitting meditation, occurs to me. Not achievement, not some resting place at the end of one's labors—he speaks of "continual refinement."

Applied to writing, I don't think this means laboring and belaboring a few words or phrases day after day in some obsessive manner, though it can mean this and everyone's gone through it. James Joyce during the writing of *Ulysses* told a friend he'd been working on a single sentence all day. When the friend noted, "Ah, looking for *le mot juste*, the precise word?" Joyce replied, "No, I have all the words—what I need is the order." Well this is part of it.

But I'm more interested in the other part. "Continual refinement." In zazen, when you are sitting down—not to all those things you ordinarily sit down to, like dinner, or work, or conversation—you sit down to what is doing the sitting. The Japanese term is *shikantaza*—"just sitting." Or maybe: *sitting and nothing else*. Sitting down to the writing of poetry, hammering an essay into shape, tracking elusive references through the stacks of a library—all require a comparable intensity. The thing you are working on is that which is doing the working. The thing you are making is that which is doing the making. Suddenly you find yourself far away from the limited accidents of your own small life, out on the track of this 40,000 year human experiment we call language. And you occasionally end up with certain strange artifacts that might be poems—some of them resemble poetry anyhow—though the most interesting ones may not resemble it very much.

> Over
> rises quiet
> even insects
> to sleep
> are ancient
> dry

I once gave a talk on the poetry of Buddhist India which I called "Formal Gestures into the Void," and I think that phrase gets close to what I'm trying to talk about. Continual refinement of the worker through practice of the craft is one way of looking at poetry. Yet paradoxically, if you go off in search of the worker, the farther you travel the farther he or she recedes into some fragrant gap or abyss.

Innumerable worlds open before you, like in those terrifically psychedelic Mahayana Buddhist texts. Which world does the song or poem come from, into what world does it vanish? Poetry seems always a series of formal gestures into the void.

> Night
> thunder cracking
> through coiled clouds above him
> the traveler
> stung with tears
> sings out his loneliness.
> Traveling
> is a kind of death
> and the village people hear it,
> bow their heads
> and quit talking.
>
> —*from the Sanskrit* Amarushataka

Of course as a worker, you *make* poems. But that doesn't mean simply technique. I think it's not very different from making love. An unfettered urge exists from the start—it's part of our makeup and only by trusting the instincts can you proceed. With some people the raw impulse takes a frightfully demonic form. Yet the task of refinement—as poet, as lover, as contemplative—has no limit. Every time you set out, no matter your level of previous attainment, you find yourself at another bend in the trail. Gertrude Stein has spoken eloquently on writing as beginning again and again, just as Suzuki Roshi addressed the practice of Zen meditation in *Zen Mind, Beginner's Mind*.

So—how long do you sit in meditation before posture and breathing are correct? How long is too long for a poem to take shape? Sometimes it occurs on the instant, a luminous bolt. Other times it is the effort of years.

Not that meditation and writing substitute for one another. They just clarify certain mysterious concerns in similar ways. One clear correspondence: both demand hard work, but work that accepts uselessness as the ground of endeavor. Sure you can write a polemical poem, cast a metrical curse, court a beloved with gracious song—just as you can "sit" outside the gates of Livermore weapons lab—making the gesture effective by locating it in some special context. But that's different. The eerie word magic that haunts poetry, the quiet sorcery that smolders in meditation—these occur in some indescribable twilight. Our consumer-mad world, too electronic to see into this twilight, no longer accords much credence to it. India does, to some degree; parts of Africa probably. But the modernized West? Well, poets and yogins are not quite so intimidating as we used to be. So what? Maybe we've gained something, now that contemplatives don't get hired, as they did for centuries in Tibet, to work as "doctors of political medicine"—magic poisoners, that is. Poets no longer get hung up on vengefulness, employed by kings and priests, wrecking crops with spells, shattering armies with vile curses. Freed from such demands, a delightful autonomy opens up—call it "breathing room"—for those who want to sit down and write. Or for those who just want to sit down.

I'd like to note a remarkable coincidence. Hardly anyone pays attention, but give or take a hundred years Shakyamuni Buddha was contemporary with Panini, the world's first, probably the world's greatest, linguist. Panini, also from India, compiled the great explicit grammar of Indo-European languages when they stood at their most complex and elegant. Though these two heavy practitioners, Panini and Gautama Buddha, never met, they were haunting the same roads. Coincidence? Who's kidding whom? Something momentous was taking place, these simultaneous inquiries into Mind and Language, 2500 years ago. And it was happening across the planet—in China Lao-tzu and Confucius; in Palestine the Old Testament prophets; in Greece the pre-Socratics—all of them hammering out a new syntax for thinking.

It was Confucius who insisted a kingdom would prosper if everyone grew up able to recite to a stringed instrument the culture's best poems. The Jewish prophets in Palestine, a different fire flashing behind their eyes, knew you could bring a city to its knees, crumble its literal walls, with a new cadence. This I think is where our own so-called Modernism begins. Practicing Mind and practicing Language. The two have been pretty inextricable ever since.

So inextricable these two domains seem, that certain friends who are not even poetry extremists hold Mind to be nothing *but* the play of language. That contradicts my own experience. Not all worlds seem accessible to syntax and grammar. Vocabulary has limits. Yet words and the way we put them together are at this historical juncture the primary heritage we've got. Almost everything about human life on our planet seems locked up inside this mystery—Language.

I do not use the word *mystery* for color or dramatic effect. For two and a half millennia Buddhist documents have spoken of three mysteries. Three are certainly enough—I don't think we could handle any more. Anyhow, these mysteries the Buddhists address are neither obscure secrets nor unattainable ciphers you have to stalk to the ends of the earth in order to locate and open—they are the three things closest to the human person: body, speech, and mind. Why "mysteries"? I guess because the utter richness, the delicious complexity by which they operate, lead to profound misunderstandings, and as a result humans experience and perpetrate the most grievous sufferings.

Everyone's experienced suffering in body. Everyone knows how the mind suffers—

as Ixion, unstill, ever turning.

What about speech? This brings us close to what concerns the company of poets. Can you suffer in speech? Or put another way, *does speech suffer?* It's an odd notion. But I think it's easy to see. Any time language finds itself incapable of clarity, suffering arises. When you grope for a word and feel stupid. When you regret having said something in a misguided fit of anger or enthusiasm. Consider the whole tangled karma of language, how a thoughtless remark runs a circle about you, and comes up to hit when you're expecting it least. And irony. Irony is a good indicator that suffering is occurring through Language—that some painful gap has established itself between conceptual and linguistic experience.

More to the point though, is the terrible truth—that the most nefarious forces in our contemporary world have through skilled manipulation of the printed and electronic media learned to use Language as a device for enslavement and destruction. Whole sectors of the Earth's population feel caught in somebody else's language much of the time, driven into war or starvation, exile, neglect or madness by the wholesale appropriation of human speech or the warping of names and definitions. The Gulf War, Rocky Flats, old growth forestry issues—here at home a layer of newsprint is thick enough to conceal the reality.

If one thinks in terms of historical epochs, each with its explicit challenge, then this has to be our contemporary task—to refashion the language, to free it from those who have twisted its cherished powers. This theme runs through recent centuries—I'd see Emily Dickinson and Henry David Thoreau as two who recognized early what had to be done. With the appearance of writers who came of age during the Vietnam war—the so-called Language Poets are some of them—the heroic task of our day articulated itself. A recognition that speech, oral or written, is the ground of contest on which we stand.

So: body, speech, mind. From these mysteries stem all our sufferings. But also from them stem the clarities, our choicest delights. An old document quotes Gautama Buddha telling his cousin Ananda, "Without body there is no Dharma." No insight, no wakening, no *foundation*. Dharma literally means "that which is established, that which is firm: the ground underfoot." Again, to get a sense of what Buddhists mean by it you have to shake free from true and false, from metaphysic, from the whole bag of theisms. Dharma has no more to do with true or false, with doctrine or belief, than does Earth, our own literal *under-foot*. It's simply there, cradling you whether you acknowledge it or not. The most tender iconographic image of Shakyamuni Buddha shows him reaching a hand down to touch the ground on which he sits, calling Earth as his witness—witness that a profound wakening, beyond the clutch of mind-born furies, beyond the grip of obsessions, neuroses, ignorance, not only is possible, but has in fact been accomplished by a human person.

So he says, without body is no Dharma. The same goes for

speech--without speech is no insight. This is the single tenet the poet bows before. It is a faith that cuts against the grain of so much in contemporary thought, so many wounded belief-systems which fear and suspect speech and language as inevitably tainted, the front guard of oppressive regimes.

Let me quote a poem—the invocatory verse to Vishvanatha's *Sahityadarpana*, a fifteenth-century text on poetics from India.

> Shining with the luster
> of moon in autumn,
> may She, goddess Language,
> stripping from my
> heart the endless woven darkness,
> cast the nature of all
> things into light.

In a tireless attempt through the centuries to "cast the nature of all things into light," Buddhism has developed three so-called *vehicles* (*yana*) which the practitioner may mount. First devised by the early yogins and poets was the *Hinayana* or "local vehicle," which synthesized a great deal of cultural lore and yogic practice specific to South Asia. Then came the *Mahayana* or "cosmopolitan vehicle," an outward-looking, experimental tradition committed to techniques of insight that people not culturally dependent on India could use. This vehicle spread through the Orient and first came to North America. Certain people with wilder temperaments devised the *Vajrayana* or "diamond" vehicle, which brought in the older shamanistic legacy of Asia. These have been the three traditional Buddhist lineages. Yet alongside these, often operating within them, I'd see another tradition—a subterranean movement or vehicle, not yet named, untamable as the other three, but which speaks with elegance, distinction, and not to Buddhist practitioners alone. It is free of jargon, and adaptable to sentient beings in any realm.

This underground vehicle has equipped itself to trade in marketplaces across the planet. Its riders include Tu Fu, Milarepa, Lady Murasaki, Li Ching-chao, Basho, and Jack Kerouac. It is a night-wandering caravan, loaded down with strange and desirable

goods, the goods of Poetry, and it picks its way along the treacher-
ous trade routes of History, generously alert to the perils and needs
of our own epoch. One could call it by a Sanskrit term, *kavyayana*—
the Poetry Vehicle. Here the gospel lyric comes to mind—

> *You don't need no ticket, you just get on board.*

4 July 1991

HE QUEST FOR KNOWLEDGE IN THE WESTERN POEM

The text that I am presenting here is properly two texts, one made up of sections from a poem and the other based on notes that were written not so much to accompany the poem as to exist in parallel, notes not about the poem but about the general enigma that the poem attempts both to address and to enact, and which can be put in the form of a question: "What does a poem know?"

Or more specifically, "What does a Western poem know?" I wanted to consider not only the situation of knowledge in the context of poetry, but also the situation of poetry in the context of that body of knowledge which is a peculiarly Western construct, and one which, by the way, provides the grounds for the proposition "America was discovered in 1492."

But this year's Quincentennial celebration is not, properly, a recognition of discovery but of a concept, an invention. Western knowledge itself has been a set of inventions, framed by perception but linked to anticipation.

1 THE CORRESPONDING SKY

Above our real things the sky is drifting
      toward the edge of the dark—the edge heavy
      with gold, the night blue and maroon,
      as the sunset, claiming the horizon,
      binds it (by whatever is to come, whatever
      to continue) to the West
It is faced by an unbacked bench
The West?
It is met with perception
Set with appreciation
And I am one
Until I'm placed in the objective sense—am I to say
      "prepared"?—a person to turn as toward sky

around sun
An enclosure?
Knowledge?
Nell said, I've vowed to learn a new word every day,
        but I'll never, even when I'm old, be ashamed
        to dance
Still, I would get rid of *I* if I could, I said, I
        did, I went
I was born in the West

The emphasis on the "West" was initially and superficially a nervous response to my having written a "Russian novel" (*Oxota: A Short Russian Novel,* The Figures, 1991), albeit in verse. The very issues that the Russian novel explores in a Russian context I have wanted also to explore in the more familiar, and therefore far more vague and far less closely observed, context of "home." The fact that I live in the literal West—not just within the bounds of so-called Western culture but also at the farthest reaches of the geographical West, at the terminus of Westward exploration, Westward expansion, Westward exploitation, and Westward imagination—seems to place me in the extreme longitudes of a literal realm of experience. To live in California is to live so far West that one has all but overleaped the cowboys and landed instead in Hollywood or in Disneyland—or in what the world suddenly knows as South Central Los Angeles—that is, in created places, which are themselves to a large extent worlds of fantasies (both positive and negative), of extremes, but of constructed extremes, that is, extremes which are also imitations and descriptions (where description is a form of anticipation). And in being imitations and descriptions, they are both derived from and directed at assumptions, which in turn have at least the appearance of comprising bodies of knowledge.

I was born in the West
What is the criterion, I, born, or West, of knowing so
Is this inevitability as I know it—its terrible and ludicrous
        humanity and only it

Subject, object, and yielding—as if meaning were my
familiar milieu
I have learned to treat them all as unique in entity, as
solitudes and plenitudes
The independence of oneself from reason is much bigger
than oneself
A Westerner, Owen Wister said, will always watch the telling
detail of a welltold tale of believable adventure but
miss the clever framework on which it hangs
All of it said Garland, if you've got the time

2 THE HORIZON SOON WIDENS WHAT IT COSTS US

"The great division," the moment when the West became the West, when the West distinguished itself from the rest, is often said to have occurred between 500 and 399 B.C., in the century of Socrates, the period that defined and established the concept that fundamental laws might be discovered and incontrovertible logic be constructed for governing philosophy, science, and the social state; this was, of course, also and not inappropriately, the century of Sophocles and Euripides—the century of the birth of tragedy.

But in considering contemporary experience, and particularly contemporary notions of what and how we know (i.e., our states of perception and our sensation of knowing), an attempt to observe the West should be equally attentive to the fundamental redefinition and revaluation of the rules of knowing that occurred at the beginning of the seventeenth century, with the burgeoning of experimental science, inspired by and accessory to the voyages of exploration and the sudden increase in what was taken to be knowledge, or in the raw materials (data and experiences) out of which knowledge could (and must, as they thought) be constructed. It was then that a scientific model for the acquisition of knowledge (along with the very idea of acquisition in relation to knowing and its value) was established, one that ever since has seemed nearly irrevocable. It is this scientific model for the acquisition of knowledge that produced something of what now seems definitively Western in our culture.

The model as both a system and a program (or what we would now term a *method*) was most thoroughly formulated at the very beginning of the seventeenth century by Sir Francis Bacon, in the project which he called "The Great Instauration," of which only two parts were completed, *The Advancement of Learning* (1605) and the *Novum Organum* (1620). Bacon and his subsequent followers were convinced that the components of the natural world are themselves "eloquent of their own history." The "multitude and host" of particular objects, "lying so widely dispersed," must be organized "in living tables of discovery" so as to be readily available as "the subject of investigation." And the linguistic descriptive activities concomitant with this investigation should be identical with scientific observational ones.

The Advancement of Learning and the *Novum Organum* were explicitly directed toward problems in recording and describing data, but in a profound way the Baconian project sought to encourage a particular style of mind, characterized by perceptual acuity, self-sufficiency, undistractibility, and objectivity.

In a sense, Bacon's program was devised for the sake of learning, not for the sake of knowledge. It is not knowledge per se that is to be learned, but rather the world, and the method for achieving this learning is a descriptive method, one in which the observing senses are fundamentally aided by language.[1]

3 A SENTIMENTAL ACHIEVER

Wake up, wake up!
The sentimental person is a self-regarding rarity
What it knows it derives from a tender sense of combination
Its day verges, its sun rides, and its sight travels all the
    dimensions of its capacity for impressions
It leaves messages to give its reasons
And we receive the sentiment of enormous distance
A view whose farthest points attain position undiminished

There the person wants the human pattern to repeat so as

to do in life exactly in its absence all that it will know

4

Knowledge in the West is incorporated into visions of the West and visions of the West have tended to be put into action—generally, I would say, for the worse, which is sadly part of our story. It is guilty knowledge that may lie at the heart of our fantasies. The fact that our knowledge of gain is suffused with knowledge of loss may account in part for the anxious circumspection and endemic nostalgia that inform our sense of time and our sense of time's effect on place.

This must in part be due to the fact that this geographical American West, as everyone knows, is only latterly a ground for Western culture, if we mean by that the attitudes, assumptions, interests, and traditions of Europe since, say, the so-called Enlightenment. The American West was for a far longer time the home of other peoples, distinctly and paradoxically "non-Western" in their approaches to living, to the meanings of that living, and in their conception of who it is who is doing that living.

5

It seems that one might take the "non-Western" Native American and the Western concepts of self as exemplars of very different experiences of having, or being, a self. For Westerners like me, my self, or my person, seems the very context of my living—my life's trope, as it were. It is a metonymic trope. "I" am a discrete individual part among other parts, in ever-changing contexts. Dorothy Lee, in her essay "The Conception of the Self Among the Wintu Indians" (*Freedom and Culture*, Englewood Cliffs, N.J.: Prentice-Hall, Inc., 1959) comments, "With the Wintu, the self has no strict bounds, is not named and is not, I believe, recognized as a separate entity." But "definition of the self in our own culture rests on our law of contradiction. The self cannot be both self and not self, both self and other; the self excludes the other" (131–32). It is in contrasting linguistic usages among the Wintu with English language usages that

Lee delineates the differing conceptions of the self, and it is not so much the Wintu as the contrasting "Western" concept that I want to emphasize. Lee argues that, "Our own linguistic usage through the years reveals a conception of an increasingly assertive, active, and even aggressive self, as well as of an increasingly delimited self" (132). She traces the change from Chaucerian usages, full of reflexives like "thus dreamed me" and "melikes" to our current "I dream" and "I like" and concludes that "the English language has followed an analytic and isolating trend and it is possible that in linguistic reference there has been an increasing separation of the self from the encompassing situation" (133).

Meanwhile, recent events in South Central Los Angeles following the Simi Valley trial of the police officers videoed beating Rodney King offer a terrible demonstration of this trend toward the "separation of the self from the encompassing situation." It is evident precisely in the way in which it is incorporated into what purports to be the telling of the story of what "really" happened and thereby to be establishing knowledge of what is called "the situation." The narrative scenarios that have emerged to give an account of the sequence or array of events known summarily as the L.A. Riots have tended to follow conventional narrative logic, that is the logic of cause and effect, with the qualification that since the accounts are retrospective and the events were "bad," *cause* is logically characterized as *blame*.

The whole thing is said to have begun with the beating of Rodney King, an incident for which either King is to blame (for being a bad character, for provoking the officers with threatening behavior) or else the four policemen are to blame (for unnecessary violence, for attitudes—racism, machismo—predisposing them to such violence). In either case, the incident is blameworthy. The jury selected to determine where the blame lay announced that it had done so, and the jury members in turn were generally considered to be themselves at blame for that determination—and for "triggering" the riots that followed. Likewise blamed for the riots are various "Black leaders," among them the Mayor of Los Angeles Tom Bradley and the film director John Singleton. The extent of the rioting has been blamed on pervasively chaotic social conditions or on symptoms of those conditions (poverty, unemployment, the recession, poor schools, drugs, gangs, or the "breakdown of the family," symbolized for one political pundit by a certain Murphy Brown, who is herself a creation and hence the "fault" of Hollywood scriptwriters and producers, the "cultural elite") or on the police (who were personally fearful, or indecisive, or negligent) or on L.A. law enforcement as a system (lacking discipline, corrupt, without clear chains of command). The terrible symmetry whereby a video of four white men viciously beating up a black man comes to be vindicated by a video of four black men beating up a white man is the unmovable, intransigent emblem of what we are supposed to "know" about "modern urban America"—whereby equivalent, immobilized, static blameworthiness is extracted from history.

My sense is that this is more complicated than mere "finger pointing" or "scapegoating." Such unsubtle, broad, even gross quests for accountability and the assignation of blame have served paradoxically to deny guilt. Everything about what happened in Los Angeles has been exteriorized. There were a few media comments about "soul-searching" but in fact there was almost no social introspecting in comparison to the large-scale all-purpose orgy of looking out, or looking away. And what is blame, after all, but radical negative otherizing.

6 NOTHING'S IMPOSSIBLE

A ghost (by definition) is always sighted, seated with its
     shotgun, smiling, in possession of its chair
The body goes
And the head seeks matter
Supernatural gain
What difference would it make if it were night
I'm right that I saw the ghost
It smiles by carbon light
The head drifts over the bed and holds with it all that it
     knows

But without logic—like a trick of love—it is and was
   autonomous
Like Faust it experienced a desire for knowledge and then
   apparently experienced knowledge without satisfaction of desire
I too cannot be proved

We can, at least to a limited extent, address the question of knowledge, and the quest for knowledge, vis-à-vis its relation to the self,
linguistically, first by examining our ways of speaking about knowing
and knowledge, and second by looking at writings which seem to
seek or express it.

First, knowledge seems to be something: "I seek knowledge." It
seems to be something quantifiable but not so easily qualifiable: I
can have a lot of knowledge of something but I don't tend to have
a big knowledge. Or knowledge can be inadequate, in which case
I have to get more of it. On the other hand I can have precise
knowledge, suggesting that knowledge is an instrumental something—I can use my knowledge.

As for knowing, it seems to be an act and a transitive one, with
an object: I know something. I know my name. I know Anne Waldman. I know the northern California oak and redwood forest. But
apart from my name and such suggestive plenitudes as are conveyed in expressions intimating a redolent experience of some person
or place, most of what we know, at least so far as we can talk about
it, seems to occur in the form of abstractions or extrapolations. I know
when Pushkin died (1837); I know *how* to make a long distance credit
card call; I know *where* Arapahoe Avenue is; I know *what* the sky
looks like. Or in a more complex statement I can say I know the *difference between* red and blue. But it would be an unusual formulation to say simply "I know Pushkin's dying" or "I know long distance
credit card calling" or "I know sky" or "I know difference." In fact, it
would seem from common usage that knowing is indirect, oblique,
and at some remove from that to which it pertains. Knowledge
seems to be some *aspect* of our perception—and, so to speak, sec-
ondhand. We know *that* something, or we know *about* something.

Paradoxically, this mediated, abstracted knowing may be our clearest expression of objectivity, just as, conversely, the expression of direct unmediated knowing may be preeminently subjective. I think this is so because mediated knowing is embedded knowing— it is knowing something in the context in which it is meaningfully known. It is conditional. A statement like "I know sky" is vehemently subjective and apparently unconditional, but nothing that we can know—or nothing that is real—is unconditional.

Certainly we do not know knowledge. At least, we don't say so.

7 THE EXPERIENCE OF ACTIVITY

Knowledge is a part of a whole
If we linger we blur
Stasis is a profuse focal point
We only catch ourselves as in the words of lovers who are
      contrasting their emotions
If you bend to the West someone serves as the interpreter
Everyone's thought is like luck to be applied
So love conjectures love
We need the language to aid the senses
The activity of solitude if finitude is engaged produces
      anticipation, but what's committed must be true
Any change is an activity—that is, a marker and a claim

8

The Western poem presents us with experiences in a field of inquiry exposed to observations carried out by the aided senses. In my notebook, this proposition is the first sentence I wrote on the topic of knowledge. It includes many of the terms this paper attempts to examine, but it does not include the term *knowledge*. It does seem to suggest that knowledge might be the ultimate goal of the Western poem, that for which it quests, since inquiry and observation are generally taken to have that goal, but it doesn't specifically say so, and in the end I believe that the goal of the poem instead is to provoke and sustain in both writer and readers an experience of experience; I believe too that this may suffice for knowledge.

9 THE WILL TO REALITY

> The cowboy of fiction is at ease with reality
> He will know what he did
> Causation is his
> He takes his solid seat and sees, impassive in reality
> To discover it, to spread it, to possess it
> What we thus disjoin we can put together
> All changing times are marked by changes of yellows, of
> blues, and of greens, with much division, crack,
> and breach
> As for the book on the table top, it really says what I write is
> digressing toward things I've known or seen having
> hunted up life but not lies

The stereotypically Western person is ambitious, besieged by society, in search of solace, and careless with paper. But it's not true that Western persons don't read. The empirical method insists on the principle that the truth must be replicable. It regards repeatability as the grounds for certainty. And the possessive method, which relates knowledge to desire, attempts to triumph over ambiguity and uncertainty. "I think and I mean to get" is the basis of a Faustian identity. But the Western person, in all his or her desire to possess knowledge, is wasteful of uncertainty.

Meanwhile, the notion that knowledge must have *foundations* has generally been abandoned by academic philosophy, and with it the epistemological pre-eminence of the self as the last recipient of data, the self over whom the shadow of knowledge must slowly spread.

> There's panorama but it hides
> Life imposes a variety of restraints, and the curves of the hill
> are said to be breasts

So the sun itself goes west, but never to restore a lost
    relationship
The hills are heroic under cow
The cowboys are lying down
To use the landscape, to impress the world
The gold in the grass should be applied to it
But slowly, slowly, and with immense consideration, the way
    Darwin or Agassiz weighed amelioration, obedient
    though spontaneous and with a will to love
The weather is steady as a heart—opaque, massive,
    peacefully bullying the sky, incorrigible but always
    changing

10

"The peculiarity of our experiences," says William James, "(is) that
they not only are, but are known" ("Does 'Consciousness' Exist?",
Essays in Radical Empiricism (Cambridge, 1976), 14). But the distinction
between thing and thought, as between thing and word, doesn't
establish a dualistic configuration whereby "I" is to be perpetually
and perennially separated out from all else. I look into my mind to
find the thought—the search for the thought is thinking. That thinking finds no thought, nothing in time or place. The thinking in search
of the thought is a thinking about thinking, a destabilization process,
a process of transformation. Knowledge, like speaking or writing, is
not an entity but a function—it would best be called "knowing"—
and the purpose of that function is to contextualize—to contextualize in the profoundest sense, so that knowledge is not only knowing
of (which is experience *in potentia*) and knowing *that* (which gen-
erates propositions) but also knowing *how*.

Then for the first time I noticed a man who sat on the
high gate of the corral, looking on. For he now climbed
down with the undulations of a tiger, smooth and easy,
as if his muscles flowed beneath his skin. The others had
all visibly whirled the rope, some of them even shoulder
high. I did not see his arm lift or move. He appeared to

hold the rope down low, by his leg. But like a sudden
snake I saw the noose go out its length and fall true;
and the thing was done. As the captured pony walked
in with a sweet, church-door expression, our train
moved slowly on to the station, and a passenger remarked, "That man knows his business."

(Owen Wister, *The Virginian*, opening paragraph)

Curiously, I found myself, in the course of getting interested in the
array of questions pertinent to "knowledge in the West," reading
from a cluster of materials (*The Virginian*, essays collected in William
James's *Essays in Radical Empiricism*, Stein's *The Making of Americans*, Frank Norris's *The Octopus*, Jack London's *The Call of the
Wild*, for example) all dating from the period around 1900–1908,
that is, approximately midway between the present and the so-
called "opening of the West" as it was recorded in the journals (later
referred to as "our national epic of exploration" by Elliott Coues in
his preface to the definitive 1893 edition) of Merriwether Lewis and
William Clark during their expedition to explore and describe the
West (May 1804–September 1806). I suppose I found myself working
with materials from the first decade of the twentieth century because generally they tend to look both ways, back at a certain milieu of achievement (highly compromised as it seemed even then)
and forward to its implications and the working out of a complexity
of romantic and realist values colliding finally in postmodernism, not
only as an aesthetic but also as social reality and lived experience.

11

Where an old person writing feels skin and sees trail, the
        clouds drift and cattle crouch in magenta, brindle, and
            swing of opportunity, and cynicism is out of place
Everything that's real is repeated in its new found sense
We know that limit and surpass it, renaming our integrity
Now it's reality

> So the evening is familiar—as familiar as a river—on either
>> side a fading
> But the voluntariness of my knowing that the place is mine is
>> strong

We know what we expect.

The sense of time is a faculty of mediation. As such, and like lan-guage, it's an aid to perception, and also an aid to anticipation. "Why insist," asked William James, in his essay on `A World of Pure Experience' (*Essays in Radical Empiricism*, 37), "Why insist that know-ing is a static relation out of time when it practically seems so much a function of our active life? . . . When the whole universe seems only to be making itself valid and to be still incomplete (else why its ceaseless changing?) why, of all things, should knowing be ex-empt? Why should it not be making itself valid like everything else?" For three hundred years, since Bacon's "Great Instauration," the contents of knowledge, if one can speak of them as such, had by definition to be certainties. But for James, knowledge had objects, and these objects, being in time, were, or rather involved, uncer-tainties as well as certainties.

And it is the interdependence of certainty and uncertainty that I want to emphasize, to suggest that the writing emerging in a quest for knowledge must be cognizant of this mutuality.

> Uncertainty and erotic cold thought to calm, to come, to
>> combine
> Particulars are related, but particulars are related to
>> uncertainty
> The experience of experience in resilience, in shifts, in
>> buttons, in numbers, in mirrors, in rivers, in grasp, in this
> The thought is not a substitute for something real
> Objective reality then, I say, is an incident
> The very original of what we mean by continuity

What of the inclusive impulse—"all of it"—which is so characteris-tic of modernist approaches to comprehension and of modernist control? If we accept the notion that knowledge is always and only embedded, always and only situated, we must give up the aspiration to "know everything." This has profound implications for the meaning of "the word," which, since Faust, or indeed since long before, has promised knowledge—a promise which has filled us with desire for it.

What if the word promised something else?

> The flakes of mica flick and the river fills with sharpness
> The time process resounds again against the skin
> Skin on the West, the West on skin

Knowing is not a terminus but an incitement. The skin moves attention from one thing to another.

It is in poetry that the values requisite to exploration and inquiry (or to so-called experimentation)—for example, patience and persistence on the part of the observer—and the resulting achievement—for example, discovery—also retain their concomitants—for example, impatience, restlessness, and a sense of loss.

12

> Poetry instead is said to love to increase desire
> Rising behind in the morning, muttering, a phrase plays
>   upon the conquering surface of things
> In retrospect it seems done but on some vast extensive
>   edge
> What *is* the nature of this strange work?

If there is any connection between how knowledge works and how language works, it would probably not lie in the stasis of individual words, not even if one regards words as repositories of their own history, but it might lie in relationships between words, that is, in instances of their usage—in grammar. Or, if we specify our field of interest as poetic language (which is to say, the linguistic logics at work in a poem), then in syntax—in the putting together of the verbal materials at many levels. And if we think about the particularly poetic problem of how language works, we come, I think, immediately to the point I feel to be the relevant one. Because language in a poem does not lay down a path we can follow easily; if it is "knowledge" we are trying to arrive at it would seem that there must be a more efficient way of getting there. Indeed, one wonders just whose side the language is on.

But there is no knowledge somewhere. Knowing is transient, though recurrent, occurring *in situ,* in experience, but not automatically.

> The old man's ears cleared at the height of the virgin forest
> At the moment of panorama
> At the momentum of preparation
> The biggest tree is over there, he said, stretching the
>   independent nature of my expectations
> The West is here—we can ground our uncertainties on
>   nothing else

13

The visual dominates our access to knowledge; we are overwhelmingly inclined to look or, where that's not possible, to visualize, in order to understand or even to conceive. Scrutiny, as a heightened and intentional mode of looking, whether disciplined or not, is a felt function of all conscious thought; in order to think we call into service the actual eye or the inner eye—and most frequently both. The gap, then, between the imaginable and the imageable must, we assume, be very small.

But in fact I think it is very large; the seemingly uninterrupted flow of visible experience, its fluency, is broken up in thought into reflections, and the inner eye, the imaging eye, sees only these.

Knowledge is based on the experience of the disjuncture between what's seen and what's thought—on the alterations cast by reflection, on thought's own alterity. In fact, if it weren't *other,* at least momentarily, we wouldn't experience it at all, because we wouldn't notice our noting it.

In a sense, art would enact (in order to provoke) self-consciousness, so as to make living palpable and knowledge experienceable.

14

It is in the interplay or relationships—or as Tolstoy put it, in the "linkages"—between certainties and uncertainties as between parts and their wholes or, in poetry, between grammar and semantics, that meaning and its concomitant knowing abides. Tolstoy, writing in response to articles analyzing his *Anna Karenina*, put it:

> If I were to say in words all that I intended to express by way of the novel, then I would have to write a novel identical to the one I first wrote. And if critics now understand and express in a feuilleton all that I want to say, then I congratulate them. . . . And if nearsighted critics think that I wanted to describe only what pleases me, how Oblonskij dines and what sort of shoulders Karenina has, then they are mistaken. In all, or in almost all that I have written, I was guided by the need to collect my thoughts, linked together to express themselves . . . but each though specially expressed in words loses its meaning, is terribly degraded, when taken alone without the linkage in which it is found.

And in remarkably similar terms, William James, in writing (in his *Principles of Psychology, I, 275–76*) of the essential experiencing that writing provides, said,

> If anyone ask what is the mind's object when you say `Columbus discovered America in 1492,' most people will reply `Columbus' or `America,' or, at most, `the discovery of America.' They will name a substantive kernel or nucleus of the consciousness, and say the thought is `about' that. . . . But the *object* of your thought is really its entire content or deliverance, neither more nor less. It is a vicious use of speech to take

out a substantive kernel from its content and call that
its object; and it is an equally vicious use of speech to
add a substantive kernel not particularly included in its
content, and to call that its object . . . The object of my
thought in the previous sentence, for example, is strictly
speaking neither Columbus nor America, nor its discovery. It is nothing short of the entire sentence,
"Columbus-discovered-America-in-1492." And if we
wish to speak of it substantively, we must make a substantive of it by writing it out thus with hyphens between all its words. Nothing but this can possibly name
its delicate idiosyncrasy. And if we wish to *feel* that
idiosyncrasy we must reproduce the thought as it was
uttered, with every word fringed and the whole sentence bathed in that original halo of obscure relations,
which, like an horizon, then spread about its meaning.

Paradoxically, substantives, though they are no less than the totality
of themselves and the contextual plenitude of all their relationships,
are inherently uncertainties, since this totality is constantly altering,
while the parts, it seems to me, establish, in their independence,
and because they are of the moment, the suggestion of a kind of
certainty. This alterity, this otherness, immanent within totality, is the
sole "foundation" of knowing, and it is always only achieved in part.
    The only way to discover it is to proceed step by step, point by
point, for their own sake, because there is nothing beyond. So long
as we *continue* the effort, we are *intending* the experience, and
that is the sole form in which knowing is designed. To discontinue the
process is not to arrive at knowledge but merely to cease thinking.

15

I ask myself what's in a poem
The outside of the world—but this itself is that if looked at
            when the sight is forgotten and only the looking remains
Three different things

And I imagine what kind of vigilance is layered within the
        remarkability of all that I have requested

My values are held in change, vividly falling to one side and
        then the other, their fascination dependent in part on
        their very absence of order

My senses too seem to exist—I hear a bluejay squawking
        between the leaves and suddenly feel the links
        between the minuscule elements of the smell of gray-
        green as the rain begins to fall—but the well-known is
        not necessarily known at all

Accuracy is not the voice of nature

There are places where the action never stops

But around a moral value (and we insist on moral value)
        shakes the image of a troubling construction: time
        and the time it takes to know of this

We proceed (we insist on motion) and we shift the center of
        gravity and with it the nature of confinements

Then progress (gold and the research clock) changes the
        look of things and with it the value of things

But just by being under the sky, a person knows it exists

Nature is mediated—in large part so we could stay out of
        the way

Then it finds itself (or, more precisely, cannot find itself, and
        advances) staring at itself

Well (says someone) we still have the vitality of ourselves in
        boot from our days on a frontier which we made it our
        business to contemplate—then in search of an
        indigenous present, of authentic strange times

So, from the time I was old enough to know the facts,
        remember sounds, render rhythms, I thought work was
        as similar to life as one could suffer

Sunlight on the wall could hold the air in meaning—though it
        didn't seem to

And I remember even as a child realizing that pleasure lay
        in arranging it

Statements, syntax, and words—all arts are installments

Not only recapitulating, not solely evaluating—it should be
            humane to anticipate, wait, and surge
How quickly I got home, how slowly I was there
Knowledge is always situated
It's where one perfects
Thinking lives
No waste of work, no waste of time
Lives, likes, lines

(Spring 1992)

NOTES

1 My essay "Strangeness," in *Poetics Journal* 8, 1989 discusses Bacon
and his influence on linguistics and poetics at much greater length.

FOURIER!—OR, THE UTOPIAN POETICS

feeling lonely like your aging bachelor in Paris rented rooms over-grown with flowers—ever since you were a boy and the flowers took over your room—burst their pots, dirt spread over the floor under the bed, black manurey soil with flowers metamorphosing your room into small cubical Douanier Rousseau–like jungle—the loneliness of modern life, let's not dignify it with such grand terms as "alienation," began as long ago as 1799, obviously, since you, Fourier, felt it even then, aching cold of static streets where no one knows anyone else's name—and the frigid disgust of Sunday fam-ily suppers before the TV hearth in Civilization, *late* in Civilization

We are going to speculate about . . . an order of things in which marriage and our other customs will have been forgotten, their very absence having in-spired a host of amorous innovations which we can-not yet imagine. (UVCF 327)

. . . the family is a group that needs to escape from it-self . . . (HM 236)

Thus we see beings unite in marriage and other affairs who have no personal passional affinity, and whereof the approximation, the bringing together, is nothing but a subdued disgust. (PHS II 44)

Accordingly, men who are well acquainted with Civilization give, as a rule for success, the precept,— cringing mediocrity. (PHS II 186)

THE SEXUAL ANGELICATE

which in Harmony means the man and woman who preside over the Court of Love, that game/machine at the center of the dream

PETER LAMBORN WILSON

of the Phalanx—the two *perfecti* of the entire Polygynal Series of Passional Attraction, who can make even pity an erotic act—Fourier himself combines these two angels in one hermaphroditic mind[1]— Fourier himself was "ambiguous"—as witness his special mania for sapphists which he discovered only in his late thirties—in fact Fourier considers love itself an "inversion", since in true love a "superior" (in strength, age, sophistication, etc.) bends to the will of an "inferior." This romantic voluntary erotic slavery, which Fourier considers natural, is generally impossible in Civilization. Fourier was the alchemical androgyne. Yes, the Masonic Fourier! The occult messiah!

> *If love is to be a source of generosity, we must base our speculations on the collective exercise of love.* (UVCF 374)

> *In Harmony . . . amorous celebrity can entitle a person to a world-wide monarchy and to other lucrative & magnificent offices.* (UVCF 368)

HYMN TO THE DAWN [SEE APPENDIX A]

To read Fourier with feeling gives the same thrill as discovering a new lost cult of ancient times with strange and gnostic truths. If you really love someone, buy rare old yellowing Fourier pamphlets and let your beloved discover them as if by accident in musty library of deceased uncle, or leftist used book store in Montmartre, dusty pages of cheap acidic nineteenth-century paper flaking away like ivory scurf, quaint elongated fancy typefaces, elaborate pseudo-mathematical diagrams. At first your beloved believes that *no one else* knows about this unique forgotten genius. . . . then your beloved discovers that there are others. . . . that *you* are one of them! What a pure and ennobling pleasure!

FOURIER'S HEAD IN MARBLE

resting on his grave as on some Salomean platter—an obvious invitation to necromancy. Candles and incense, invocatory rhodomontade, pallid young men in neat raincoats, shabby-gen-teel old ladies, disciples gathered in Montmartre Cemetery. . . . Sunday afternoon seances in the April mist, perhaps. Doctrines as beautiful as these were destined to be enshrined in a cult, a poor small religion of lodginghouses & badly lit meetinghalls, illuminated certificates of entitlement & orders of chivalry, faded velvet ban-ners, memorabilia enshrined in glass like reliquaries. Fourier's monu-ment—a stone structure standing where the rue Caulincourt hits the Place Clichy in the IXth arrondissement, just down from Montmartre—it was worn & truncated, the writing on the stone illegible. In Octo-ber 1960 the journal *Combat* reported the wish of a municipal councillor that the monument be removed. André Breton pro-tested. The monument still stood in 1970 (what have 24 more years done to it?). In his *Ode to Fourier* Breton relates this experience:

> Et voilà one little morning in 1937
>> that would be about 100 years by the way after
>>> your death
> in passing I noticed a very fresh bouquet of violets at your
>> feet
> it is rare that anyone beflowers statues in Paris . . .
>> it must have been a woman's slim gloved hand
>> the kind they love to shade their brows with
>>> while gazing into the distance
> I observed casually in days that followed the bouquet
>> was renewed
>>> the dew & it made one
> & you, nothing would have turned your eyes from
>> the be-diamonded muck of Place Clichy

> . . . *rustic altars are placed at the summit of a knoll.*
> *They are bedecked with flowers or shrubs & the statues*
> *& busts of patrons of the sect (the "Thousand Flower*
> *Series") or of the individuals who have excelled in work*
> *& have enriched it by inventing useful methods. These*
> *individuals are the mythological demi-gods of the sect*

or industrial Series. A corybant opens the session by
burning incense before the demi-god . . . (UVCF 293)
(Note: For The 1000 Flower Series, see Appendix B)

THE ANALOGIES

Stars & planets are sexual beings. Gravity on the physical plane serves as a metaphor for the erotic attraction which really moves the universes:—the Aromal Emanation. Each cosmic body shoots out multi-colored rays of aroma by which they copulate with each other & propagate their kind in a continual orgy of creation. These rays crisscross Space in a veritable multidimensional web of color, just as Space on another level is a webwork of light. Each of the Passions corresponds to a numeral, a musical note, color, mathematical process, geometric form, alchemic metal—thus the Cabalist Passion is symbolized by an indigo silver spiral. Different kinds of love can be represented by iris, tuberose, carnation, hyacinth. Did Fourier spontaneously re-create the occult theory of analogy out of his own imagination, or had he read Paracelsus? No wonder the Martinists, Illuminists & Swedenborgians thought Fourier was one of them, an adept. Aromal influences in the coming era of Harmony will cause the seas to turn to lemonade. *Everything* is erotic, everything yields to the influence of Passional Attraction—the only possible society is one composed entirely of lovers, therefore the only possible politics is a politics of the Impossible, & even a science of the impossible, erotico-pataphysics, dada epistemology, the Passional Calculus

> *A star can copulate: 1. with itself like a vegetable, the*
> *north pole copulating with the south; 2. with another*
> *star by means of outpourings emanating from contrast-*
> *ing poles; 3. with the help of an intermediary; the tube-*
> *rose was engendered by three aromas emanating*
> *from the south pole of the Earth, the north pole of*
> *the planet Herschel, & the south pole of the Sun.*
> (UVCF 401)

Subversion	Transition	Harmony
Night	Twilight	Day
Caterpillar	Chrysalis	Butterfly
Comet	Concentrated body	Planet
Winter	Half season	Summer
(PHS II 412)		

NORTH AMERICAN PHALANX

The longest-lived Fourierist experiment was the North American Phalanx in Monmouth County, New Jersey, 40 miles south of New York City. Between 1843 and 1858 there may have been a hundred or so phalanxes in America. In an alternate universe none of them failed ignominiously or vanished into the dustbin of lost crackpot history—they succeeded wildly, & America-prime became the cradle of universal Harmony. Our alternate selves are all living in big phalansteries & the very weather has changed, balmy & crackling with erotic energy, orgone skies & lemonade oceans, so that everything we do, even harvesting pears, gives us hard-ons or wet vaginas. We need only three and a half hours of sleep a night, eat five meals and two snacks a day, flit from task to task and pleasure to pleasure like butterflies.[2] We're seven feet tall, live to 120, and the most advanced have tails with a hand on the end, and an eye in the palm of the hand: the *archibras*.

MONEY

Since Fourier took the opposite point of view to all philosophy (*l'éclat absolu*, absolute doubt & difference), and since "philosophers" invariably disdain and disparage wealth, he was for it. He recognized the erotic and "childish" purity of money *as money* rather than as frozen abstraction & oppression. Even if he were to consider money as "filth" he would still approve it, as he was far from ignorant of the erotic power of filth, at least for certain Series. Every pleasure condemned by the moralists of Civilization he applauds as a force for Harmony—a revaluation of all values leading not to Nietzsche's chilly loneliness but to the elegant perversity of the horde, the band, the tangle of bodies in "touch-rut."[3]

. . . the mutiny of love is only the more effective for
being hidden & concealed behind all sorts of masks.
(UVCF 340)

I have now said enough to make it clear that this
corps of children (the Little Horde), who indulge all the
inclinations that morality forbids, is a device which will
realize . . . Sweet Fraternity. (Harmony) encourages
the dirty inclinations which are repressed with heavy-
handed whippings by a tender morality that makes no
effort to utilize the passions as God gave them to us.
(UVCF 321-2)

Children are nature's echoes against morality; they are
all in league to escape its rules. (UVCF 165)

THE LITTLE HORDES

at dawn, under their Little Khans, they march, barbaric banners flying, out into the still-misty fields, to rid the furrows of vermin & ser-
pents, to spread manure—boys attracted to danger & filth. A few
girls, and adults, the Bonze/Druids, who still share these tastes, accompany them. The whole Phalanx honors them for the distasteful
work and thinks of them as little knights. Who knows what mischief
they're up to later out behind the barn, in the dump, the junkyard,
the privy overgrown with honeysuckle—what rituals of filth?

. . . the science named Gastrosophy . . . will place
good cheer in strict alliance with honor & the love of
glory. (PHS I 33)

. . . the most clever gastrosophers will be in their lifetime
promoted to saintship, of which they will have the rank
& the title. (HM 94)

. . . when a well-assorted company can, in a short eve-
ning party, place itself in full composite by mixtures of

material & spiritual pleasure,—gallantry, the ball, the dainty supper, and, above all, cordiality,—then everyone is enraptured with this state of delight, so rare in assemblies. Everyone says, why does not this state of festivity & intoxication always last? why does it not revive every day? If you return after this to your dismal home, & to the routine of business & morality, you think yourself fallen, like Apollo, from the heavenly abode into a place of exile.

These moments, when parties rise to the delight of the composite, are infinitely feeble pictures of the delight that the Harmonians will constantly enjoy . . .
(PHS II 7)

Moderation is good as a channel of refinement of the pleasures, but not as a deliberate privation. (PHS II 101)

THE FOURIERIST BANQUET

Gastrosophy—the art and science of good taste—Fourier's most beautiful & perfectly typical invention. I used to apply the term gastrosophy not only to Fourier but also to Brillat-Savarin, author of *The Physiognomy of Taste;* imagine my surprise to discover that they were related and knew each other well! True, Fourier disdained Brillat-Savarin's gourmandism as "simple" in comparison with the compound or *composite* complexity of cuisine in Harmony—nevertheless (as Barthes points out) it was probably B.-S. who introduced F. to *mirlitons,* the little spiced cakes of Paris which he loved and praised as harmonian food. Therefore a Fourierist banquet might well feature B.-S.'s famous recipe for turkey, almost the only recipe contained in the *Physiognomy* (which is a meditation on food, not a cookery book). Fourier also loved fruit, especially pears, melons, and apples, and fruit compotes (because they were "composite") made with sugar, which the Harmonians will eat instead of bread. Bread, except for very fine dinner rolls, seemed boring to F., & the labor of raising wheat too dull; moreover, the sugar of the future will (due to aromal emanations) lose its "wormy" unhealthiness. Bread is too *Civilized*—and Harmony is the Big Rock Candy Mountain of childhood dreams. If the Fourierist banquet is to contain dishes much discussed by the Founder, then serve a stew made from a "tough old hen" (or two hens and a rooster), "marinated & served in a braising pan, or in gelatine", in honor of one of Fourier's famous illustrative fables, about a series of chicken-loving gourmets with extreme tastes; and served with cous-cous and slightly rancid butter, in honor of Barthes and his friend (see *Sade/Fourier/Loyola*). Omit provençal-type dishes made with "hot oil," garlic, saffron "& other villainies," of which the Founder disapproved (v. *PHS* I 316). Also note: "How many 'hidings' have I endured (as a child) because I refused to swallow turnips, cabbage, barley, vermicelli, & (other) moral drugs, which occasioned my vomiting, not to mention disgust" (ibid., 344). Even if we happen to like some of these things, we'll omit them in honor of the hero we celebrate. April 7 is his birthday. Plenty of wine & cognac, & "ices, orangeade, sparkling wines." Table set with flowers. Twelve toasts, one to each Passion—& one more for the Founder. (See Appendix D)

> . . . *in order not to have the trouble of forgetting the books of philosophy, I have never taken the trouble to read them.* (PHS I 117)

> *The Series needs discords as much as it needs harmonies.* (UVCF 231)

FOURIER STIRNER NIETZSCHE

We need warm Fourier to counterbalance cool Stirner & Nietzsche, and we need Stirner and Nietzsche to even out Fourier. Stirner exterminates a few spooks still rattling around in Fourier's head; for "altruism" sometimes appears in Fourier detached from the interest of individuals, floating free as an abstraction; at other times however Fourier makes it clear that self-interest *alone* is sufficient motivation to bring about Harmony, since the individual can only realize full individuality in a social setting where need ("work") and pleasure are nearly synonymous, and where one's own passions are complemented & fulfilled by *others* of the appropriate Series. The Phalanx can thus be seen as one possible form for the Stirnerite "Union of Egoists" (or more accurately, "unique-ones"). It has been argued (by Gustav Landauer for example) that "Ego" for Stirner still retains—despite all Stirner's determination—a taint of the Absolute, in the same way that "Society" (or Association) does for Fourier. In this case, Nietzsche appears as a positive/ambiguous third term or pivot of reconciliation between the two extreme cases, first in his image of the "free spirit", which could stand for Stirner's and Fourier's ideals as well; and second, in his "perspectivalism," which precisely puts the two extreme perspectives *in perspective.* Moreover, Nietzsche and Fourier agree on the question of the Necessary Illusion, the social myth; in this light one might interpret the Phalanx as the "will to power" of the combined Passional Series and Groups. All three thinkers are "radical aristocrats," disbelievers in equality and democracy. Believing in the possibility of a synthesis of these three cranky geniuses may involve the aesthetic of the well-known mating, on operating table, of sewing machine and umbrella; but that's old hat to the likes of us. Indeed, we can add a few more "impossibles" to the mix, and hope for six before breakfast. For example: a number of nineteenth-century American utopianists managed to reconcile Fourier's theory of Attraction with Josiah Warren's "Society of Individual Sovereigns"—particularly Steven Pearl Andrews, founder of the UNIVERSAL PANTARCHY and of "Modern Times," the anarchist community in Brentwood, Long Island. In fact Fourierism dovetails nicely with what might be called the "left" wing of Individualist anarchism, its labor-movement-oriented side, represented by Tucker and Mackay. A similar synthesis was made in the "pleasure politics" of Situationism, which probably absorbed Fourier through Surrealism. Fourier's *Nouveau Monde Amoureux,* his most overtly erotic work—which never appeared in his lifetime and was lost—finally made it into print for the first time in 1967; if it was not a precipitating factor of the following year's "Events," it was surely a symbolic premonition.

The biggest area of difference between Fourier and Stirner/Nietzsche, and the biggest area of difference between Fourier and the whole later development of socialist anarchism, is the area of religion. Stirner/Nietzsche did not believe in "God," and neither did Proudhon or Kropotkin (who both read Fourier with "fascination" when young). But Fourier did believe in something. He attacked "Religion" as an aspect of Civilization, but he spoke without hesitation of a "God" & of "UNIVERSAL DIVINE PROVIDENCE" (as a necessary axiom to the proof that all humans should enjoy an economic & erotic "minimum," without which it would become necessary to accuse "God" of injustice). Fourier's theory of correspondences is also metaphysical or "occult." Fourier's deity, however, cannot be identified with that of Abrahamic Monotheism, since His most essential feature is His approval of all passions and forms of sexuality, indeed His virtual *identity with* the Passions. Fourier's monist pantheism invites comparison with the non-Religious spirituality of certain radical mystics and heretics (such as William Blake), and also with certain contemporary movements such as anarcho-Taoism or anarcho-paganism. (These in turn are of course updated versions of earlier heresies such as the Brook Farmers' Transcendentalism, a sort of mix of Fourier and Unitarianism. Spiritualism and Swendenborgianism were also rife amongst nineteenth-century radicals.)

THE PHALANSTERY

—big victorian palace, pseudo-chateau—"the caravanserai . . . , the temple, the tower, the telegraph, the coops for carrier pigeons, the ceremonial chimes, the observatory, & a winter courtyard adorned with resinous plants," wide verandas, oriel windows, bay windows, stained glass, all wood and shingle, an american Versailles in the midst of Jersey truckfarm fields humid & cheerfully vulgar, flat and green. Corn tomatoes chickens cherries apples pears plums herbs hemp turkeys pigs cows dogs cats[4] sunflowers hollyhocks 1620 people under one roof (with outlying gazebos and cottages for allies and hermits)—like the castles of Sade's libertines the Phalanstery is a closed space, *hortus conclusus* or artificial paradise rising originally in all its elaborate and obsessive architecture and detail out of masturbation fantasies. The one big important difference between Sade and Fourier is that in the Phalanstery everyone's rich and happy—not just the libertines. In our modern Phalanx the "Bourse" or Exchange, the complex daily process of scheduling and book keeping, is aided by computers—otherwise, however, reproductive and mediating technologies are not very popular. We prefer to make art rather than passively consume "leisure" and "entertainment." Our chief modes of creativity are the banquet, the "OPERA" (which Fourier already understood as the synthesis of all art forms), and the orgy. Of course in our alternate universe we expend as much energy and eros on mere work as you (in your sad reality) on the finest art and most exquisite pleasures. Our food, our art, our eroticism, receive the influx of sheer genius, and exist on a higher plane of intensity than you can imagine except in fleeting moments of ecstatic realization. Our quotidian routine has the same texture as your highest adventure.

> *A Session in the Court of Love: the band of adventurers*
> *moves forward through a cloud of perfume and a rain*
> *of flowers.* (UVCF 387)

HIEROGLYPH

The foul emanations of Civilization have caused the Moon to die. By the unalterable law of Passional & Aromal rays, our present Moon will be destroyed and replaced under Harmony by five different-colored satellites. So enjoy the pallid & sterile glow while you can, dupes of Civilization, for it is inexorably doomed.

> *The material world being in all its details hieroglyphic of*
> *the passional, God must have created emblems of the*
> *passions in all the degrees.* (PHS I 6)

> *This is to say that the properties of an animal, a veg-*
> *etable, a mineral, & even a cluster of stars, represent*
> *some effect of the human passions in the social order,*
> *& that EVERYTHING, from the atoms to the stars, consti-*
> *tutes a tableau of the properties of the human pas-*
> *sions.* (UVCF 397)

PARANOID CRITICISM

—a term invented by S. Dali—everything is alive, and even consciousness is more universal than poor Reason could ever allow—life and history are shaped by occult forces, specifically by the unconscious, by desire—but also by actual conspiracy, "breathing together." Analogy—everything means something else—no "coincidences." An aesthetic derived from this theory would of course approximate Surrealism. Fourier remained silent about the art of his time and limited himself to foretelling a future when the borders which Civilization enforces in aesthetics would fall & be replaced by (for instance) the Harmonian OPERA. Thus Surrealism is justified in considering him an ancestor; moreover Fourier himself exhibited a definite "paranoid" streak, convinced of a vast conspiracy against him and his mission, orchestrated by the philosophical establishment and its lackeys in the press and government. The art he predicted indeed came into being—but not the social form which ought to support it, uplift it, surround it, and carry it on to universality. In this sense the historical avant garde became the unacknowledged legislators of a nonexistent & still totally *imaginal* world, a counterworld or utopia in the literal sense of "no place." In the alternate universe where Harmony reigns, *Art* has been "suppressed and realized" because *every* Harmonian is an "artist." In our world, however, the avant garde has actually fallen into the gulf that separates vision from actuality—the avant garde has "disappeared" into the abyss created by a *tragic* contradiction (between, for example, Surrealism and Stalinism). In the twentieth century art had to make a revolution or else die. Its revolution failed and indeed all that remains of it is an exquisite corpse. So—hey presto—Art has already been "suppressed". What remains now is its "realization"—in the free play of creative imagination *outside* the total area of reproduction and mediation, *outside* the entire dialectic in which a term like "avant garde" makes semantic sense. What form might this endeavor take? I don't know—I'm still engaged in producing books, despite Fourier's prediction that the libraries would fall. Still, reading & writing are also *passions.*

Let us begin by pointing out that in the eyes of morality all the most distinguished personality types, the truly sophisticated ones, are dangerous. (UVCF 222)

. . . the birth of social happiness is dependent on the discovery of two means: 1. luxury, without which harmony cannot be organized; 2. the theory of harmony, without which you cannot make use of luxury.
(UVCF 213)

FIAT LUX(E)

In Harmony everyone will be an artist, since each will perform "useful labor" with the same creative intensity now bestowed only on art. But no one will be *only* an artist, since the Butterfly Passion (the lust for variety) will give each of us at least thirty vocations. In effect the Phalanstery IS a work of art, in all its movements, rituals, processions, pavilions, banquets, set-pieces, cabals, assignations, and operas. Its aesthetic is rooted in *luxury* and *light*, or "brilliance," one of Fourier's favorite words. The "mathematical poem" or science of Attraction is also an art, or rather, it takes the form of a language whose grammar is musical and whose content is erotic. This atmosphere evokes a resonance with psychedelic aesthetics, and indeed the phalansteries of the 1840s lie buried beneath the floors of the communes of the 1960s—like lost archaeologies—or ancestors whose names are forgotten but whose genes are immortal. Consider the "Museum Orgy," a Harmonian artform "offering no more than visual gratification and designed to encourage the development of the aesthetic faculties of the Harmonians" (as Beecher describes it, *UVCF* 392). Just as the border between producer and consumer is erased by attractive labor, so the line between audience and work of art vanishes in the Museum Orgy, as each Harmonian becomes simultaneously the object and subject of desire, both sign & signified in the language of Passion. Fourier predicts that Harmonians will eat and enjoy certain foods which to us are poisons, and he specifically mentions mushrooms; surely he would have approved of magic mushrooms, enhancers of luxury and erotic sensation, most "brilliant" of the hallucinogens. The aim of Fourierist aesthetics resembles that of Taoist or of psychedelic aesthetics: identity of subject and object, overcoming the dichotomy of self and other.

> We have heard the sensitive Anacreon, who prefers
> men to women, extol the orgies of young pederasts
> and intrepid drunkards among the sooth-sayers. If the
> champions of antiquity admire excess, so condemned
> today, it is because they quite agree that orgy is one
> of man's natural needs. (HM 278)

> The courts of love are based on the principle that
> every fantasy is good; they look for the most unknown,
> the most disdained, in order to give it prominence and
> to create its partisans the world over. (HM 114)

> Amorous love fantasies, whether infinitely rare as is
> foot fetishism, or common as are the sects of flagella
> tion, cannot be subject to debate regarding honor or
> proper comportment, nor can they require the inter
> vention of a council. Everyone is right in matters of
> amorous mania, since love is essentially the passion
> of unreason. (HM 112)

> In Harmony great efforts will be made to bring to
> gether the devotees of . . . extremely rare manias.
> For each of them the meeting will be a pilgrimage
> as sacred as the journey to Mecca is for Moslems.
> (UVCF 348)

THE HARMONIAN BODY
(a reading of *Passions of the Human Soul*, Vol I)
None of the commentators seem to have given a full description of the amazing differences between our Civilized bodies & those of the Harmonians in their full "evolution" (which will depend not on

genetics but on the brilliant influence of *social mutation*—not proto-Darwinian but proto-Lamarckian). Some commentators have noted with amusement the *archibras,* that fingered tail so useful no doubt in fruitpicking and orgies, and most have recalled that Harmonians will have longer childhoods (puberty at fifteen or sixteen), longer lives (nearly one-eighth will live to 144), more perfect health, greater statures (average seven feet), and more ravishing beauty than we can imagine. But what an *alien* beauty! Few modern sci-fi writers have dared to envision a future humanity so radically altered, or rather self-altered. No puny bulbbrains dependent on robots & prosthesis!—Fourier's future body-image is based not on body hatred but on the glorious apotheosis of the individual/collective will, expressed on a somatic level so deep as to resonate with the very plasm or life-forces of Nature, and on a psychic level so high as to make the boasts of shamans and magicians look picayune by comparison.

Science fiction abounds in masking-images of body-fear and hatred—immortality, decorporealization, Cyberspace, the airlessness and anti-organicity of "Space" itself—which reveal an underlying neo-Gnostic or neo-puritanical body-image in which material is bad, spiritual (or rather mental) is good. Fourier too has tinges of Dualism, which lead him to despise *our present body,* but he overcomes his own extreme idealism by advocating a *spiritual materialism* (i.e. making *life* the high value) so radical as to amount to a potential deification of the body. "There is . . . nothing more unsuited to us, who are a *cardinal star,* a star of high nobility, than the moral pleasures,—the turnips of Cincinnatus and the black broth of the philosophers. We need an immense luxury, and a bi-compound harmony, which ought to apply to all the faculties of our soul and of our senses, far removed in their actual (present) state from this brilliant (future) destiny" (*PHS* I 54).

This destiny includes, for example, the albino, a pre-echo of the Harmonian body in "his properties of equinoctial whiteness and conocturnal vision, with which the race born in Harmony will be endowed" (63). Fourier is particularly informative on the future becoming of *vision*—not only will we see at night, we will also come to enjoy the "amphi-vertical or diverging polar eye of the chameleon" who possesses the "beautiful faculty of simultaneously casting the eyes to opposite poles." *Convergence* for Fourier is always a restriction, a limitation. Our present civilized eyes converge & are thus severely limited; the Harmonian eye *diverges* & thus expands its scope, increasing the pleasure or *"luxe"* of the Passion of vision. That which diverges gives variety, like the divergent sexualities of the "manias" and so-called perversions. That which converges is monotonous, like morality or simple binoptic vision. The Harmonian will acquire "Co-aromal vision," allowing the perception of some 800 colors, each belonging to a different aroma (light is only one aroma, and we see only 7 of its 12 rays); we shall even watch in the sky the rays of aroma darting between stars as they copulate, noting their myriad shades in our "sidereal gazettes" (87). The vision of the *somnambulist,* who walks everywhere safely with eyes closed, "proves to us that we can experience sensations without the aid of the senses" (i.e. ESP), since we can psychically tune in to the "sensual faculties of the planetary body," Earth herself, who "sees and hears like ourselves, but through very different means" (105). We seem to be approaching Taoism here, and are not surprised to learn that Harmonians (like Taoist sages who plunge beneath the sea to meet with dragon kings) are amphibious, or that they fly through the air without wings (169), that they possess invulnerability (174–75), ambidexterity, and prehensile toes. Fourier's theory, however, is physical not magical: he proposes the existence of twelve atoms or basic particles making up all material things and organs. Our civilized eyes lack the co-solar vision of the eagle (the ability to see through fire, such as the Solarians or inhabitants of the Sun enjoy) and the co-nocturnal vision of the cat, because "one of the five sharp or five flat atoms is combined in a contradictory way in our eyes. . . . These disorders are only temporary, and humanity will remedy them by backing itself with the *societary system,* which alone can raise our bodies to extreme vigor, and favor the new combinations of atoms, of which we are corporeally susceptible" (91). Moreover, social change will influence planetary destiny, so that climate will change, Earth will lose its single "mummy" Moon and acquire a plethora of satellites and Saturn-like rings, and once again be bathed in the aromal influences of other planets and stars (as it was before Civilization literally knocked our world from its course); new aromas will circulate in our atmosphere, giving "new faculties to the beings, animals and plants. This spring (i.e. this source) alone would suffice to occasion all the specified changes (in the body & Nature)" (92).

Fourier refrains from outlining the development of other senses and organs, allowing us to make use of the Passional Calculus to deduce for ourselves the future of the sense of *touch-rut*, & indeed the future of the *genitals*, which must be even more extraordinary than that of sight and optic tissue. For our sight, he predicts, will ultimately render all "animate bodies" (and reality itself) *transparent* as "very limpid crystal," like "the silk-worm on the eve of its transformation, and the glow-worm in the dusk." Thus "the human eye will be in the condition of a man from whom a cataract has been removed, & who distinguishes forms & shades where before there was nothing but opaqueness & obscurity" (123). Clearly Fourier preaches a mysticism of the senses, or a sensual mystique, in which everything is embodied, but in *bodies of light*.

> *What dupes men are that they have compelled themselves to wear a dreadful chain; what punishment they endure for having reduced women to bondage. . . . Freedom in love, joy and good will, insouciance, and more, are not dreamed of because philosophy habituates us to regard the desire for true good as vice.*
> (HM 204–5)

> *The shades of white differ according to the planetary degrees; the white of our epidermis is false,—it is a rosy grey. The Jupiterians have already the rosy alabaster white; the Solarians, higher in rank, have the white epidermis of rosy musk color.* (PHS I 228)

MANDALA

Fourier's *future* would impose an injustice on *our present,* since we Civilizees cannot hope to witness more than a foretaste of Harmony, if it were not for his highly original and somewhat mad eschatology. He conceives of reincarnation not as a means of getting off the Wheel, but rather as a promise of an infinity of merry-go-round rides, in which we will trace as individual souls our trajectories through the future of Harmony and even to the emergence of entire new universes more stupendous than our present immensity. His critique of the *dullness* of all religious nonmaterial conceptions of paradise leads to a materialist eschatology—to the virtual eternity of self and body—since otherwise Fourier's God would have to be accused of injustice both to the living and the "dead." One of the things we can do with Fourier's system is to hold it within our consciousness and attention in the form of a mandala, not questioning whether it be literally factually true, but whether we can achieve some sort of "liberation" through this strange meditation. The future becoming of the solar system, with its re-arrangement of planets to form dances of colored lights, can be visualized as a tantric adept uses a yantra of cosmogenic significance, like a Sufi meditation on "photisms" or series of visionary lights, to focus and integralize our own individual realization of the potential of harmony within us, to overcome our "prejudices against matter, which is represented to us as a vile principle" (*PHS* I 227) by philosophers and priests. Like Nietzsche's Eternal Return, the Fourierist eschatology need not lose all value for us if we consider it metaphorically, or better, mandalically rather than as literal dogma. Both systems are meant to *symbolize* (i.e., to be, and to represent that which it is, simultaneously), to make present a similar Yes to material existence, to becoming, to life; a Yes which—despite all their differences—sounds like the same Yes in both Nietzsche & Fourier.

> (bi-compound or aromized or transcendent fire) . . .
> might be surnamed the material God of nature . . .
> since fire is the body of God, and ought in this wise to
> hold the rank of focus among the elements. (PHS I 188)

Diffraction:—instantaneous light of harmony piercing
the centre of subversion, (as when) a plumage of
black feathers, or a hat of black felt, being placed
between the eye and the Sun, reflect like a prism of
crystal the seven rays on their edge. (PHS II 414)

THE TAO OF HARMONY

By sheer coincidence while reading Fourier I happened to visit several charming Taoist temples in San Francisco (thanks to my friends at City Lights, who also supplied me with a copy of Breton's *Ode*). The temple of the Phalanstery, centuries from now, will have become encrusted with just such a luxury of red and gold, incense and banners; moreover, the Taoist emphasis on spontaneity, work-as-play, wealth, health, longevity, sexual "alchemy," complex cuisine, and even sensual pleasure[5] also accords well with a Fourierist religion. K. White points out in his intro to the *Ode* that when Fourier excoriates 3000 years of Civilization for "struggling insanely against Nature," and boasts that he is "the first to have yielded to her," he is speaking only for Europe; while in the *Tao Te Ching* one may read: "Let Nature take its course / By letting each thing act in accordance with its own nature, everything that needs to be done gets done / The best way to manage anything is to make use of its own nature / For a thing cannot function well when its own nature has been disrupted." In the Yang Chu Tractate of *The Book of Lieh Tzu* (which I bought the same day I visited the temples) I found:

Give yourself up to whatever your ears wish to listen to,
your eyes to look on, your nostrils to turn to, your mouth
to say, your body to find ease in, your will to achieve.
What the ears wish to hear is music and song, and if
these are denied them, I say that the sense of hearing
is restricted. What the eyes wish to see is the beauty of
women, and if this is denied them, I say that the sense
of sight is restricted. What the nostrils wish to turn to is
orchids and spices, and if these are denied them, I say
that the sense of smell is restricted. What the mouth

wishes to discuss is truth and falsehood, and if this is denied it, I say that the intelligence is restricted. What the body wishes to find ease in is fine clothes and good food, and if these are denied it, I say that its comfort is restricted. What the will wishes to achieve is freedom and leisure, and if it is denied these, I say that man's nature is restricted.

All these restrictions are oppressive masters. If you can rid yourself of these oppressive masters, and wait serenely for death, whether you last a day, a month, a year, ten years, it will be what I call "tending life". If you are bound to these oppressive masters, and cannot escape their ban, though you were to survive miserably for a hundred years, a thousand, ten thousand, I would not call it "tending life".

Civilized education . . . intervenes systematically to fight against our desire to be carefree, a desire that will be unfettered in Harmony. (UVCF 143)

ADDENDUM TO THE FOURIERIST BANQUET

A Note On Music

Given that for Fourier all measured series can be expressed in musical terms, so that music acts for him as a principle of social becoming, it seems only natural that *reading* Fourier enhances the ear for certain music, as I've discovered just now listening to Telemann, whom I already credited with being a Yea-sayer, a proponent of human happiness, and who I would now argue deserves to survive into the era of Harmony. Fourier himself mentions the operas of Gluck with praise—the only specific reference to a composer I've found so far in his work. Amongst the moderns one suspects he might have liked Satie. Fourier speaks rather mysteriously of a "masonic and musical eye", which sounds Mozartian as well as synaesthesic. And we know he enjoyed marching bands. (See Appendix C)

REVISIONISM

It's amusing that every one of Fourier's admirers has wanted to argue with him, to accept part of his system and reject part, from Victor Considerant, his chief disciple, all the way down to his modern commentators and biographers. I could have done the same, if such a course had not seemed to lack dignity and tact. Instead I've managed something better, and have ascertained by means of a series of Swedenborgian/Spiritualist séances that Fourier (who presently inhabits the "planetary soul" while awaiting re-incarnation as a Solarian) has changed his mind about certain aspects of his thought; for as he said, "Did I myself not write that 'a penchant for exclusive systems is one of the radical vices of Civilization, & it will be avoided in Harmony.'?" He's given up all his former racial prejudices, for example, but insists his cosmology was more-or-less correct. At first he rather liked Marx and Engels, who praised him when they were young—but later when Marx condemned him for silliness and the taint of the brothel, Fourier came to dislike him intensely, and points out that he was unkind and patriarchal toward women, "always a bad sign." The ghost of Paul Goodman introduced Fourier to Wilhelm Reich and the modern erotic liberationists and convinced him to rethink his position on infant and childhood sexuality.

I now realize that both Hypermajors and Hyperminors are present in all four Groups, thus:

In the 1st phase, or childhood	In the 2nd phase, or Adolescence
1 Friendship	1 Love
2 Ambition	2 Friendship
3 Love	3 Ambition
4 Familism	4 Familism

(Note: Three and four of the first phase are missing in the former system.)

In the 3rd phase, or Virility	In the 4th phase, or Old Age
1 Ambition	1 Familism
2 Love	2 Ambition
3 Familism	3 Friendship
4 Friendship	4 Love

"This," he said, "makes a great improvement in the chart on page 84, Vol. II, of your copy of *The Passions of the Human Soul.*"

"When I said that children are a third sex," Fourier went on (via planchette), "I meant they were asexual. When Henry de Montherlandt lifted my saying (without attribution) he meant to indicate that children are another *sex* with its own and proper *sexuality*. Needless to say, I was quite prepared to grant full sexual freedom to pubescents, but failed to grasp that children and even infants possess their own erotic natures as well. Of course, I still have the honor of being the first social inventor to propose the liberation of all the passions, including pederasty and sapphism—including even the passion for chastity! To admit now that the Passional Series contains *all* humans, regardless of age or sex, does not impair the strength of my system, but rather strengthens and *completes* it."

MANDALA (II)

The microcosmic architecture of the Phalanstery mirrors the macrocosmic architecture of the universe, and in this way can be seen *in toto* as a temple; for all temples are miniature universes. The key that links phalanstery and cosmos as mutual hieroglyphs is to be found in Fourier's radical play with scale, perspective, and closeness. The future of the solar system, for instance, involves Earth's acquisition of five new satellites, Juno, Ceres, Pallas, Vesta, and Mercury, which will leave their present orbits out of sheer *attraction* to the new Harmonian Earth and move much closer to us and to the Sun. The rest of the solar system will also squeeze closer together, so that Venus, Mars, and Jupiter will appear to us nearly as large as our own satellites, & we will behold even Herschel (Uranus) with its eight moons (La Faquiresse, La Bacchante, La Bayadère, La Galante, La Coquette, La Romanesque, La Prude, and La Fidèle). Our night sky will blaze with huge glowing multi-hued globes ("the effect of a garden illuminated with colored lamps")—we'll see Saturn's rings bare-eyed, Venus like a lilac moon, Jupiter a jonquil moon—Vesta will be of a "subversive tint," possibly "burnt sienna, like the back of a cock, or rather like the lees of wine." The planets will crowd together like warm bodies at an orgy, and we'll be so close we'll be able to see and converse with the inhabitants of the other spheres via the Extramundane Planetary Telegraph ("Thus we shall be able, in the Sun as in Jupiter, to see and count the passengers and the windows"—*PHS* I 213). Moreover the sky will be criss-crossed with aromal rays, like aurora borealis focused into lasers, shooting around the universe like jets of galvanic jism. On the *scale* of the individual phalanstery the same grand *perspectives* will be paradoxically combined with a similar *closeness* and crowding together. The neo-classical, ornate & HUGE palace of the Phalanx, the single roof under which its Harmonians dwell, opens its two wings like arms to the Sun, that visible emblem of the "material god," the "transcendent fire" or life-principle. The phalanstery provides an even more exact emblem of the universe—and vice versa—since each of the thirty-two Choirs or main Series corresponds to one of the thirty-two celestial bodies, with the Sun representing the Synod—"for there is no detail of planetary harmony that is not reproduced in passional harmony." Thus the rose represents hieroglyphically the Vestalate under the influence of Mercury, while the Troubadours are represented by the carnation, flower of puberty and first love, beneath the sign of Jupiter's fifth moon. Each individual is a star, linked and drawn close together by Attraction to all others, connected by "rays" (the radiants or complex movements of work/play, the Passional Series, etc.) and by "orbits." The chief orbit will be described by the Street Gallery, an indoor passageway connecting all the wings and running continually along the second storey of the Phalanstery. Fourier never ceased praising this invention, which summed up for him the very style of Harmony. Europe's nineteenth-century covered galleries, pale imitations of Fourier's ideal, fascinated Walter Benjamin, and the unitary concept of the built community exemplified by Fourier's Street Gallery finds echoes in certain playful twentieth-century theories such as Arcology, Situationist Urbanism, or *bolo'bolo*. Because Fourier's cosmology has been largely ignored, commentators have failed to recognize the hieroglyphic nature of phalansterian architecture; moreover, unlike the "druids" who built Stonehenge, Fourier was not basing his scheme on an *existing* universe, but rather on an imaginal one, an *improved* one, which will only come into being when human society virtually *brings it into being* by the power of Attraction & unleashed Passion—a force great enough to literally pull planets from orbit.

> *(In Harmony, men will) work quickly at replanting the mountains, & painting certain rocks, so that the luxury of landscapes . . . may be preserved.* (PHS I 59)

COMPARING FOURIER WITH WILLIAM BLAKE
(for Anselm Hollo)

you might well begin to think that the *moment of desire* had come to European Civilization with the inescapability of a comet or a steam engine; and of course that the complex which gave birth to it was the French Revolution—one of those historical events which is *still going on* in our time, like the Roman Empire or the Neolithic—which makes Fourier as much a proto-Romantic as Blake, but which also makes both of them our exact contemporaries. Two marginal cranks in rented lodgings, both mistaken for occultists but both prophets of the body, far more radical than most of the nature-mystics, reformers, and ideologues who came after them: they made the big breakthrough almost simultaneously, they overcame Western philosophy both Aristotelian *and* Platonic, they overthrew Religion—each of them had one foot in the eighteenth century and one in the twentieth (or twenty-first!)—they skipped the nineteenth century—and maybe the other shoe hasn't yet dropped, even now! They were both "mad." If Fourier was a "logothete" then so was

Blake—he even defined it: make your own system or be enslaved by someone else's. Meanwhile, what did Blake think about *fruit*? The moment of recovery from sickness induces a powerful mystique of material objects, smells, tastes, colors. Such moments lie behind many of Nietzsche's best insights. Fruit symbolizes this kind of moment. In winter: pears and apples of course, cellared since October, persimmons, oranges and grapefruit sent from the tropics on trains, and compotes of last summer's peaches, apricots, and cherries. Arboriculture! Somehow it seems to evade the curse of the "Agricultural Revolution," somehow its seems easy, not like real work at all, or in any case "attractive labor." New York was once an orchard state—literally hundreds of species of apples have disappeared since the turn of the century due to evil american capitalist conspiracy against variety and taste in favor of shelf-life and uniformity of product. And now (as it begins to snow—Jan. 8 1991) a complete hallucination: it's summer and Blake and Fourier are playing miniature golf in a run-down beach resort somewhere on the Atlantic coast, maybe South Jersey or Rhode Island, a warm night but not stifling, clear with plenty of stars; they've been drinking sangria in big iced pitchers stuffed with fruit, melons, lemons, strawberries, blackberries, plums, black cherries, Spanish brandy, and sugar— they're pretty high and missing most of their shots. Behind them comes a party of kids, 13/14 year olds in short shorts and hi-top sneakers, giggling, flirting, making fun of the two looped old geezers in a friendly cosmic way, and everyone laughing at the sheer stupid pleasure of it.

POETICS OF TOUCH

Fourier wanted to expand the alphabet to thirty-two letters to harmonize with the number of bodies in the solar system, number of teeth, number of choirs in the Phalanx, etc. The Phalanx is also called a *tourbillon* or Vortex, which gives a sense of its turbulence and its attractiveness, calling up the mathematical image of a "catastrophic basin" toward which all points will collapse by attraction. It may even be that we can think of the Phalanx as a "Strange Attractor," borrowing a term from modern chaos mathematicians.

Fourier speaks of an "Alphabet of Attraction" or of the Passions, and a "musical grammar." The thirty-two letters—including those which exist though we can't hear them, just as five colors (rose, fawn, maroon, dragon green, and lilac) exist in the spectrum of light even though we can't see them (on the analogy of the five unplayed notes in an octave)—these letters are flying around and around in a vortex, like a swirl of autumn leaves, ring-of-roses, all fall toward the middle, making a magnetic rose, rose of the winds. The letters flame up in transcendent fire, each revealing a number, flower, aroma, color, note, banner, animal, PASSION. This is a Cabala of Desire, a gematria of erotic analogies. Fourier has little to say of esthetic theory (other than a nod to the Aristotelian unities which he himself ignored) but his real contribution to *poetics* can only be assessed by weighing the entirety of his writing. Barthes was right to class him as a logothete, like Sade and Loyola, one for whom words have a life of their own and can be used to create new realities. With his neologisms, number mystique, theory of correspondences, etc., he used language very much as does a Ceremonial Magician, to call up images from the will into being. The difference between Fourier and other hermetalinguists, however, lies in the source/origins or "springs" of his words, and it is here that he parts company with all Illuminists and Platonists. The passions are not inferior shadows of higher more supernal realities—they ARE supernal realities. The letters spring from the passions as if from angels' mouths, each one a ray of the spectrum of desire. Here's the key to the Surrealists' fascination with Fourier: language defined as a system of marvels, mantras, and magic spells, but not emanating from any bloodless castrated spirito-mental flesh-despising religious mysticism—no, language emanating from passion, from the body, and returning to passion, and to the body, in a vortex of incalculable power. I want to consider this *poetics* Fourier's most precious invention; but perhaps I'm wrong to do so. When I've experienced Harmony and lived in a Vortex I'll know that this poetics is no end in itself, but a weapon, a tool, a strategy by which to make Civilization tremble and crack—but only a foretaste of real pleasure, real luxury, real *poetry:* life lived in the incandescence of passion.

SELECT BIBLIOGRAPHY

(Note: Sources of quotations are identified by the abbreviations used in the
   text. Bibliographic sources for the Appendices are cited therein.)

Barthes, Roland. *Sade / Fourier / Loyola,* trans. Richard Miller (Berkeley: University of California Press, 1989).

Beecher, Jonathan. *Charles Fourier: The Visionary and His World* (Berkeley:
   University of California Press, 1986).

Breton, André. *Ode To Charles Fourier,* trans. Kenneth White (London: Cape
   Goliard Press, in association with Grossman Publishers, New York, 1970).

Davenport, Guy. *Apples & Pears, & Other Stories* (San Francisco: North Point
   Press, 1984)

Fourier, Charles. *Design for Utopia: Selected Writings of Charles Fourier,* intro-
   ductions by Charles Gide & Frank E. Manuel, trans. Julia Franklin (New
   York: Schocken Books, 1971) (first published 1901)

HM:

Fourier, Charles. *Harmonian Man: Selected Writings of Charles Fourier,* ed. with
   intro. by Mark Poster, with new translations by Susan Hanson (New York:
   Doubleday, Anchor Books, 1971).

PHS:

Fourier, Charles. *The Passions of the Human Soul, & Their Influence On Society
   & Civilization,* two volumes, trans. with intro., commentary, notes, & a bi-
   ography of Charles Fourier, by Hugh Doherty (first published by Hippolyte
   Bailliere, London & New York, 1851; Reprints of Economic Classics,
   Augustus M. Kelly, Publishers, New York, 1968)

UVCF:

Fourier, Charles. *The Utopian Vision of Charles Fourier: Selected Texts on Work,
   Love, & Passionate Attraction,* trans., ed., & with intro. by Jonathan
   Beecher & Richard Bienvenu (Columbia: University of Missouri Press, 1983)

Lieh Tzu. *The Book of Lieh Tzu, A Classic of Tao,* trans. A. C. Graham (New York:
   Columbia University Press, 1960)

Noyes, John Humphrey. *Strange Cults & Utopias of 19th-Century America*
   (original title: *History of American Socialisms*), intro. by Mark Holloway
   (New York: Dover Publications, 1966)

APPENDIX A:

The Hymn To Dawn (PHS II 109 ff.)

At a quarter before five, some chimes sound the summons to the
lesser parade and the hymn of dawn; the company prepare in the

rooms of the refectory to descend in the course of five minutes; on descending you find under the porch the instruments of the musicians, the decorations of the priests and officials of the parade, &c. Five o'clock strikes; the athlete Conradin, aged 14, and the major of the service, commands the groups to form. I have stated on a previous occasion that the officers of the lesser parade are drawn from the choir of athletes; thus the *aides-de-camp* of Conradin are, like himself, aged 13 and 14; they are the athletes Antenor and Amphion for the groups of men; the athletes Clorinda and Galatea for the groups of women.

Amphion and Galatea go on the one hand to form the orchestras; Antenor and Clorinda go to prepare the order of march. They fall in, in the following order:—

I suppose that the muster consists of four hundred persons, men, women and children, and that the sum total composes twenty groups ready to start for different points of the adjoining country. The twenty standard-bearers place themselves in line and at a distance, facing the front of the palace and behind the flags. The troop is formed into an orchestra by vocal and instrumental divisions, having a priest or a priestess at the head of each group. Before the priest a lighted censer and an infant of the same sex that holds the perfumes, with a hierophant or high-priest between the columns of the two sexes; the drums or trumpets are on both sides of the porch; the animals and the cars are ranged along the sides of the court.

In the centre is the major Conradin, having at his side the *aides-de-camp* and before him four children of the choir of neophytes. They carry signal flags, and manœuvre to transmit the orders to the signal tower, that repeat them to the domes of the neighboring castles, to the groups already spread in the country, and to the palaces of the neighboring cantons.

When all is ready the roll of drums imposes silence, and the major commands the hail to God. Then the drums, the trumpets, and all the military music make themselves heard; the chimes of the surrounding domes play together, the incense rises, the flags wave in the air, and the streamers float upon the pinnacles of the palace and of the castles; the groups, already in the fields, unite in this ceremony; the travellers place foot to ground, and the caravans assist in the holy salute before quitting the station.

At the end of one minute the salute ceases, and the hierophant gives the signal of the hymn by striking three measures upon the diapason of universal unity; the priests and priestesses placed over the vocal and instrumental parts thunder forth the chant, and then the hymn is sung by all the groups in chorus.

The hymn being finished, the little khan causes the muster to be beaten to the flags, the orchestra breaks up its ranks, deposits its instruments, and every one goes to range himself beneath the banner of his industrial group; it is in this order that the troop files off in various masses and in all directions, for being formed of different ages, from the child to the old man, they would look awkward if they filed off in line and step as the quadrilles of the grand parade do. They range themselves in artificial disorder, and direct themselves first towards the animals; each group takes its cars at the passage, and making them advance abreast with itself, they file off successively before the grand peristyle, beneath which certain dignitaries are stationed, such as a paladin of the sovereign wearing his escutcheon, if it is a minor parade, and if it is a grand parade, a paladin of the emperor of Unity bearing the cycloidal crescent.

Each group, on passing, receives a salute proportioned to its rank; the groups of agriculture and masonry, which are the first, are saluted by a high flourish, equivalent to the drum that beats to field; thence they proceed each one to its destination.

The salute of praise to God regularly traverses the globe in different directions; if it is a day of equinox, there is a grand parade at sun-rise, and the spherical hierarchy presents at dawn a line of congregations or phalanges two or three thousand leagues in length, whose hymns succeed each other during the space of twenty-four hours all round the globe, as each longitude receives the dawn. At the two solstices, the hymns are chanted at once upon the whole globe and by the entire human race, at the instant corresponding to the noon-day of Constantinople.

The morning salute is performed like a running fire of artillery, that during the summer travels from the north pole to the south pole, and in the opposite direction during winter. The public *fétes* follow the same order: the day of the summer solstice, the whole northern hemisphere dines together *en famille*, or in descending groups, and the whole southern hemisphere in quadrilles or ascending groups;* the two hemispheres dine in an opposite order on the day of the winter solstice.

This morning assembly is interesting also as a session of after-change, where negotiators go to modify arrangements and agreements entered into the preceding day at the return session of nightfall. These numerous stimulants form a mixed transit of different ingredients, and these stimulants of the dawn suffice to set on foot the whole canton from the early morning. It will be seen that there exist plenty of other motives of matutinal diligence, amongst others the vestal court. Accordingly in harmony you must be either infirm or ill to make up your mind to stay in bed after four o'clock in the morning. A man whom they purposely neglected to wake would be disconcerted on going two hours later to the sessions of the different groups; he would have lost the thread of the intrigues, and his spite would be extreme.

APPENDIX B:

The 1000 Flower Series
(This version quoted from Breton's *Ode*; see also *UVCF* 292-3)

"If the cherrytree series is united in large numbers in its great orchard, a mile from the phalanstery, it should, in the four o'clock to six o'clock evening session, see coming to meet it and its neighbours:

    1 A cohort from the neighbouring phalanx of both sexes come
       to help the cherry gardeners;

o o o

* "Ascending and descending groups," here signify groups of the ascending phases of life, friendship and love, or youth and adolescence; groups of the descending phases of life, ambition and familism, or middle and declining age.—H.D.

2 A group of lady florists of the district, coming to cultivate a hundred-foot line of Mallows and Dahlias forming a perspective for the neighbouring road, and a square border for a vegetable field adjoining the orchard;

3 A group of the vegetable gardener series, come to cultivate the vegetables of this field;

4 A group of the thousand-flower series, coming for the cultivation of a sect altar, set between the vegetable field and the cherry orchard;

5 A group of strawberry maidens, coming at the end of the session, after cultivating a clearing planted with strawberries in the adjoining forest:

At a quarter to six, swing-carts out from the phalanstery will bring the afternoon snack to all these groups: it will be served in the castle of the cherry-gardeners, from quarter to until quarter past six, then the groups will disperse after forming bonds of friendship and arranging industrial or other reunions for the days to follow"

APPENDIX C:

"Harmonicon", by Steven Taylor

HARMONICON

APPENDIX D:

Fourierism was a very *New York* phenomenon. Brisbane and Greeley lived and published in New York, and most of the founders of the North American Phalanx were New Yorkers. Steven Pearl Andrews, founder of the UNIVERSAL PANTARCHY, also lived in New York. Compare the following passage from Pearl Andrews with the quote from Fourier about parties (above the section on gastrosophy, "The Fourierist Banquet"). The influence of Fourier on Andrews will become apparent:

> *The highest type of human society in the existing social*
> *order is found in the parlor. In the elegant and refined*
> *reunions of the aristocratic classes there is none of the*
> *impertinent interference of legislation. The Individuality*
> *of each is fully admitted. Intercourse, therefore, is per-*
> *fectly free. Conversation is continuous, brilliant, and*
> *varied. Groups are formed according to attraction.*
> *They are continuously broken up, and re-formed*
> *through the operation of the same subtile and all-*
> *pervading influence. Mutual deference pervades*
> *all classes, and the most perfect harmony, ever yet at-*
> *tained, in complex human relations, prevails under*
> *precisely those circumstances which Legislators and*
> *Statesmen dread as the conditions of inevitable anar-*
> *chy and confusion. If there are laws of etiquette at all,*
> *they are mere suggestions of principles admitted into*

*and judged of for himself or herself, by each individual
mind.*

*Is it conceivable that in all the future progress of hu-
manity, with all the innumerable elements of development which the present age is unfolding, society generally, and in all its relations, will not attain as high a
grade of perfection as certain portions of society, in
certain special relations, have already attained?*

*Suppose the intercourse of the parlor to be regu-
lated by specific legislation. Let the time which each
gentleman shall be allowed to speak to each lady be
fixed by law; the position in which they should sit or
stand be precisely regulated; the subjects which they
shall be allowed to speak of, and the tone of voice
and accompanying gestures with which each may be
treated, carefully defined, all under pretext of prevent-
ing disorder and encroachment upon each other's
privileges and rights, then can any thing be conceived
better calculated or more certain to convert social intercourse into intolerable slavery and hopeless confusion?* (from *The Science of Society; Part I, The True
Constitution of Government* (Bombay: Libertarian
Socialist Institute, n.d., first published 1848; p. 2.))

Andrews is usually considered a Warrenite Individualist Anarchist. He
was instrumental in founding Modern Times, & also the "Brownstone
Utopia" in New York (see M. B. Stern, *The Pantarch* (Austin: University
of Texas Press, 1968)). But his later thinking, the global structure of the
Pantarchy, and his universalist religion all seem to owe something
to Fourier. Warren and Andrews in turn influenced Benjamin Tucker,
who also lived in New York. Tucker was close to the Scots-German
anarchist & re-discoverer of Stirner, John Henry Mackay. This "chain
of transmission" helps to explain why members of the John Henry
Mackay Society, the American branch of which is in New York,
should take particular interest in the works and lives of Fourier and
Pearl Andrews. This interest extends beyond (though it gleefully

includes) historical and cultic obsession. We also feel that the synthesis of individualism and "Association", represented by thinkers such as Pearl Andrews, has a special promise for contemporary "post-Situationist" anti-authoritarian practice. A similar synthesis was made by Gustav Landauer, by Guy Debord, and by the anonymous "For Ourselves" Collective (writing in California in the 1970s) who defined it as a reconciliation of Marx and Stirner. We find Fourier and Andrews more congenial company, and we also appreciate them as pioneers of "sexual liberation"—a field to which neither Marx nor Stirner made any significant contribution (and they weren't from New York, either). For all these reasons we've decided to revive both Pantarchy and Harmonial Association, simultaneously and amalgamated, in response to the prophecy made by an anonymous Fourierist when the North American Phalanx closed down in 1856, that some day a "Phoenix Association" would arise to take its place (Noyes, 499). At the very least we will have banquets and field trips to Brentwood and Monmouth County; perhaps even a newsletter. At best . . . who knows?

the universal pantarchy & north american phalanx
c/o Autonomedia, box 568, Brooklyn, NY 11211

NOTES

1 one of the American Phalansteries of the 1850s chronicled by J. H. Noyes in his *American Socialisms* (see bibliography) was called "The One-Mention Community".

2 Fourier's "butterfly Passion," strangely pre-echoed in Chuang Tzu's Butterfly & echoed in Lorenz's "Butterfly", Strange Attractor of weather. According to Allen Ginsberg, Walt Whitman adopted his butterfly symbol from Fourier.

3 Touch & taste are the highest, hearing & sight the minor senses, with smell as the "ambiguous pivot."

4 A strange thing about Fourier and cats: in one passage he condemns them for being *antisocial*—yet the biographers mention that he habitually shared his rented rooms with a number of cats.

5 Taoism is not a monolithic tradition; not every Taoist maintains all these values. I'm thinking particularly of such poets/bon-vivants/"madmen" as the famous Seven Sages of the Bamboo Grove.

P HILIP WHALEN ZEN INTERVIEW

ANDREW SCHELLING AND
ANNE WALDMAN

*(ON SATURDAY SEPTEMBER 14, 1991,
the American poet Philip Whalen, known also by his
Buddhist name Zenshin Ryufu, became Abbot of the
Hartford Street Zen Center in San Francisco. An assembly of dignitaries from various Buddhist traditions,
Zen practitioners in black robes, poets in blue jeans,
long-time friends, local chroniclers, and attendants
from Hartford Street's attached AIDS hospice were
present for the ceremony in the downstairs meditation hall. Zenshin formally accepted the Abbot's seat,
staff, and horse-tail fly whisk with the words, "The seat
is empty. There is no one sitting in it. Please take good
care of yourselves."*

*We held this interview the following Monday in Philip's
quarters, a basement room at the rear of the building
which gives onto a garden. — A.S.)*

ANDREW SCHELLING: In a number of interviews you've given an
account of your development as a poet—your early reading of
Thomas Wolfe and Gertrude Stein, your days in the Air Force and
at Reed College, the move to San Francisco. Could you give a
parallel but alternative account, looking at your development as
a Zen practitioner? Maybe one that would note some of the important landmarks?

PHILIP WHALEN: Important landmarks might begin with Gary Snyder
discovering R. H. Blyth's four-volume set of haiku translations that
came out in the early fifties. Reading that, and then reading Suzuki

Daisetz afterwards, made a great deal of difference. Blyth keeps referring to Suzuki Daisetz in his notes, also in the introductory material. That's how Gary got to looking up the *Essays in Zen Buddhism*. So we read all those, Suzuki's three volumes, and a bunch of other material, but it pretty much started with the haiku translations.

The next real step was meeting Alan Watts and finding out that there was a Zen tradition actually happening, that he had been acquainted with various practitioners and so forth. Although he didn't believe it necessary for Americans or Europeans to do this kind of thing—he himself never got involved with formal Zen practice—he was interested.

The person with a more practical knowledge was Albert Saijo, who had studied with Nyogen Senzaki in Los Angeles. I can't remember whether Albert met him before going into the army, when they were in the internment camp up in Wyoming, or whether he found Senzaki in L.A. after he got out of the army. Anyway, Albert showed us how to prop ourselves up with cushions to sit, how to chant *The Heart Sutra* in Sino-Japanese, how to drink tea in the zendo and how to do fast *kinhin* (walking meditation) outdoors and through the woods.

SCHELLING: He showed a group of you?

WHALEN: Gary and Locke McCorkle, Lew Welch, and a number of people who were around. The place where Albert was sitting was in Homestead Valley on a piece of land connected to the house where McCorkle lived with his family. Albert set up a zendo in an uncompleted house that was on the property—a place Albert lived part of the time anyway. We would go and sit with him from time to time. I had practiced sporadically for years, trying to do meditation, usually something I'd drawn from Vedanta. But reading about the Zen tradition was very exciting to me because it seemed so much less complicated than the earlier material I had read about Buddhism. It allowed people to be poets and painters—or at least I thought it did—these were acceptable creatures to be Buddhist practitioners, and that caught my interest. You could be crazy and still be a Buddhist of some stripe or other.

Well, the next move was when I went to Japan in 1966 and saw people actually using temples and what not, and through Gary met monks and various teachers. That persuaded me that it was a live tradition, that it was still operating however much it may have changed since the time it came to Japan from China.

I came back here for about a year and a half, then went again to Kyoto and stayed until the middle of 1971. At that point I started sitting consistently, every morning at home, and after a while I felt I needed to talk about all this stuff to a teacher, to someone who was experienced with what I was going through. I had some idea that I wanted to be a monk. I didn't know what that was about, beyond pictures in Suzuki Daisetz's books. But I thought it was what I had to do. It didn't actually happen until I came back to the States in 1971 and was barging around with various people, living in Bolinas, going out and giving poetry readings. The following year, 1972, Richard Baker Roshi invited me to move into the Zen Center in San Francisco. So in February of 1972 I moved in and began formal Zen training with him. From then on, from 1972 until 1984, I worked with him at the San Francisco Zen Center or at Tassajara Monastery, doing *sesshin* from time to time out at Green Gulch Farm.

I was ordained a monk in February of 1973, and in 1975 I was acting head monk at Tassajara Monastery. Then in 1984 Baker Roshi invited me to join him at his new place in Santa Fe, so I stayed there for three years until he said, "All right, go away—go away and do something, go away and do your own thing. Goodbye."

And I came back here—I think it was December of 1987. I've been around San Francisco ever since. I was invited to come to Hartford Street Zen Center by Issan Dorsey. Issan wasn't yet installed as Abbot but he was the resident teacher. He wanted somebody to help run the zendo, so I moved in on New Year's day of 1989. In 1990 there was an installation ceremony for him as Abbot of the Hartford Street Zen Center, the Japanese name for which is Issanji, One Mountain Temple. Issan is also Tommy Dorsey's Buddhist name—the original Issan was a thirteenth-century Japanese teacher.

So I've been here ever since. Issan Dorsey passed away in September of 1990, but before he died he installed Steve Allen as

Abbot. Then two days ago—Saturday the 14th—Steve gave the job to me. I am the present Abbot.

SCHELLING: You've had a long poetic comradeship with Gary Snyder and Lew Welch, later on with Jack Kerouac and Allen Ginsberg. Were you at all aware of them as a community of contemplatives, as well as poetry practitioners? Did you have any formal notion of that?

WHALEN: No, not especially. It was mostly about poetry. The idea that Gary was sitting was interesting to everybody, and he was trying to get people to read a little bit, but mainly he wanted to get them to sit. Allen was interested, Jack was interested to a degree. Jack was still carrying around a copy of Dwight Goddard's collection, *A Buddhist Bible*. He was quite enthusiastic about Buddhism—about its beautiful extravagant language, as I've said a hundred times before. It's mainly the language that interested him, because he couldn't sit still for any length of time. His mind was too active. And physically, his legs didn't fold very well because he'd played too much football—he couldn't cross them.

But he thought Buddhism was wonderful. Until he read, or Gary told him, the story about Nansen and the cat. The Zen master Nansen had said to his students, "If you can say one word of Zen I won't kill this cat, but if you can't talk, the cat is going to get cut in two." The monks couldn't say anything so he killed the cat. The next day his chief disciple, Joshu, who had been gone while all this was going on, came back. Nansen told him what had happened and said, "What would you have done if you had been here and I had said, say one word of Zen and the cat will be all right." Joshu just took his shoes and put them on top of his head and walked out. And Nansen said, "If he had been here the cat would still be alive."

Well, Kerouac said, "Anybody that would kill a kitty-cat is bad. This Zen business is bad." He liked Gary and figured what Gary was doing was all right. But Zen as an institution was probably not good if it ended up killing cats.

SCHELLING: So just as Kerouac was drawn into Buddhism by the lovely extravagant sutra language, you were drawn into Zen by something in haiku?

WHALEN: And by Suzuki Daisetz's *Essays in Zen Buddhism*, where he discusses practice, tells the history, and gives numerous examples of koans. There is a great deal in the third volume about the *Prajna-paramita* literature and philosophy, which I found fascinating. From there I began reading the Mahayana sutras, like the *Lankavatara Sutra* which Suzuki Daisetz had translated back in the fifties. Maybe the translation was a little older than that, but there was an edition running around in the middle fifties. I read *The Lotus Sutra*, and later *The Vimalakirti Sutra* and *The Diamond Sutra*, and found them all quite instructive.

As I say, the English translations of these Sanskrit sutras are quite decorative, large, and expansive. Jack picked up on that more than anything else. Like me, he had been an early admirer of Thomas Wolfe and thought this kind of Elizabethan extravagance was where it was at. To a degree he kept that the rest of his life, blowing wildly—screaming and hollering—not having a specific structure, not having a proper grammar and proper sentence and so on, but having lots and lots of words spreading out in all directions.

Yet somehow in his genes Mr. Kerouac had a totally French sense of proper literature. You look at a piece like *The Subterraneans* or *Maggie Cassady* or *Tristessa*—the form is very very beautiful, very condensed, very exact. The language, although it may be extravagant, is still confined within careful proportions. Most of his work is done that way. You know, he used to say *Dr. Sax* was one of his favorite things, but even that book, which is structurally pretty loose, and pretty romantic as language, has some shape to it. The only strangely shaped affair is the original version of *Visions of Cody*, which was partly tape recording, partly conversation, and partly Jack typing his reminiscences. It doesn't have the kind of strict plan or *form* the other books do. Though I don't think he constructed any of them that way, they just naturally came out of him in a specific shape.

SCHELLING: Kerouac found Buddhism a great spur to his writing, but Gary Snyder has described how he himself quit writing almost entirely for some years after going to Japan and getting seriously into the practice of Zen. Did you ever feel a conflict between Buddhist practice and writing?

WHALEN: It wasn't so much a conflict. I didn't think of it in terms of quote Buddhist practice unquote. But I was living in a manner that took a great deal of time and energy. I had no time to sit around in my usual way, or walk around in my usual way looking at things. I was instead in a group all the time, talking with people and listening. A lot of interpersonal—oh, I won't say violent conflict—but certainly mild disagreement. I was much older than most of the people in the Zen Center, more set in my ways and crankier. It was difficult for me to get along with everybody, and I had to because I wanted to stay.

SCHELLING: This summer at Naropa we had a Contemplative Poetics week and there was disagreement about how language relates to contemplative practice. Frederick Jameson's phrase came up—"prison house of language"—the sense that language enforces and reproduces oppressive social institutions, that it is an entrapment, a realm of delusion or suffering, somehow a fetter. Robert Kelly, for instance, insisted language has to do with discursive mind, that it has no relation to how Big Mind works. A few of us contested his take, seeing poetry as an attempt to transmit some literal alternative consciousness through words. Do you feel your poetry is working towards an enlightened or enlightening function of language?

WHALEN: That's too hard, Andrew. I don't know. For a long time I didn't write much when I was at Zen Center. Gary had told me in letters about his experience and here I found out what he meant. I thought he was just busy the first couple of years he was in Japan. After he'd written a number of letters about what he was doing, what it looked like and so forth, the letters became fewer and fewer. At one point he said, I don't write, I'm not writing much. And I thought, well all right. But I didn't understand where that was coming from until I'd gotten into doing it myself, and it became more and more difficult for me to even write letters to people, much less to write down what I was feeling or thinking in the way of poetry. It was a whole different kettle of fish—not because the language was different. The thing was my head and ears weren't operating on the same level. They were on some other level than language as such. Language was totally utilitarian—for communication, direct communication with people.

SCHELLING: Did your reading also decline?

WHALEN: Not much. In the last year my eyes have gotten so bad I scarcely read anything at all, but in those years I was able to read a lot and did.

ANNE WALDMAN: How would you describe the difference?

WHALEN: Well, the difference I've come around to finally, is that, yes, a lot of talking is not so useful; on the other hand, as some sort of teacher I have to talk. I have to find ways of talking that get people going with their practice, that encourage their practice—so they don't just say, oh this is boring, I want to quit. That's very difficult. It's a different kind of problem. Whereas if I wanted to get some poem started, that's dealing with language as an aesthetic and intellectual object. If you're doing something else, like the way we're talking now, I tend to babble—I can't think, I don't think at all. Not in the sense that people who think think. I don't think discursively in the first place. I don't know how.

SCHELLING: You don't think when you write or read?

WHALEN: When I read I listen. When I was able to read it was like listening all the time. I wasn't so much reading but hearing.

SCHELLING: And your writing—do you have any sense then that your poems are teaching devices?

WHALEN: I've thought so. At the very end of my book *Memoirs of an Interglacial Age*, I put an afterword or note that says this writing is didactic, it is supposed to encourage you to learn things. Not that I was trying to teach anybody anything. But I was trying to poke people into learning, into checking things out. If nowhere else then just in what I'd written, to see what I was talking about. If they would get nervous enough they might try to find out where Samuel Johnson said this or that, or Democritus, or Shakespeare.

WALDMAN: When you were at Naropa there was a sense that you were pointing people towards reading—

WHALEN: Because they needed words!

SCHELLING: But teaching devices—I meant more specifically in a Buddhist context. Did you ever think of your poems that way, as Dharma teachings?

WHALEN: In a way, yeah. There are a number of things that are heading in that direction, certainly. Maybe it's possible that somebody who is already practicing might get the point as it were. And other people who weren't practicing might say, "What is this practice thing about, what is Zen about?" And try to find a group to work with, or a teacher. But that's about as far as it goes. It's just a tool for people. It's not an inspired statement or anything—just to say, here is another way of looking at things, of thinking about things.

WALDMAN: I worry about the Buddhist community not reading enough.

WHALEN: Oh, absolutely!

SCHELLING: So as a teacher, Philip, do you send people to books?

WHALEN: I try! I try! When I was lecturing Sunday, I told people I know it's difficult for you to read, but why don't you go look at pictures, go look at statues and pictures in the museums, go to books. See if you can get any feeling from them. Because practice is based to a great degree on feeling, on how you live. It's a question of feeling, not so much of rational thinking. To get a feel—one of the ways you can do that is just to look at stuff!

WALDMAN: Didn't you teach a class on iconography?

WHALEN: Yes, at the Zen Center back in seventy-three.

WALDMAN: So you would look at pictures?

WHALEN: Oh yes, I would lecture and show pictures.

SCHELLING: This was specifically Buddhist material?

WHALEN: Yes. I had a great many pictures and we had a number of books here in the library. Later I got slides out of pictures I had brought back from Japan. Of course ultimately I'd tell students to go look at the Brundage collection in Golden Gate Park.

SCHELLING: Did you also give them books to read?

WHALEN: Oh yeah. I don't know, they may or may not have read them. In any case people seemed to like it, they enjoyed sitting there listening to me talk. And I keep encouraging people to read sutra material, to read koan material. Even if you get to a point where you say, "I can't understand this." That's when you stop studying for a while and concentrate more on sitting. Because when you come back to the books after you've been sitting they start making sense. The books come out of practice, they weren't just written as rhapsodies, the way maybe Jack understood them. They came out of what people actually envisioned, what people saw when they were in various kinds of meditative states. And the thing that's important is that *these states are accessible!* To anybody who will practice! If you want to find out why they talk about trillions of worlds, and Buddhas and Bodhisattvas and whatnot in the ten directions of space, in the past, present and future, it all makes sense if you see where it came from. You can see it for yourself.

SCHELLING: Do any of your poems come out of these contemplative states?

WHALEN: No, I don't think so.

SCHELLING: You don't feel they're in the same tradition as sutra or koan material?

WHALEN: I don't know. So much of what I've written is written because I saw things or heard things immediately, not because I was thinking about it, not because I had a plan to write a poem, it was just that something caught my attention.

WALDMAN: That in itself is a contemplative state: attention. I always find in your writing an awareness of particulars and these amazing details—

WHALEN: What Blake called the minute particulars—

WALDMAN: "Look to them! The little ones!"

WHALEN: Yes. I don't think it's particularly Buddhist, it's just doing what poets do. To see and to hear.

SCHELLING: Do poems ever come while you're sitting? Is that a time when you hear things that go into poems?

WHALEN: Very very very seldom. Just no way it's going to do that, my head is someplace else. I'm just watching things go by, and trying not to let them carry me with them as they go by.

SCHELLING: You don't light on certain phrases that make their way into your notebooks?

WHALEN: No! But on the other hand, koan practice is an activity where you do repeat, where you do come back always to a certain phrase.

SCHELLING: Are you doing koan practice now?

WHALEN: No, because I'm away from my teacher. But look! There's about three bogus questions—questions about what is the nature of language, what is poetry, and what is contemplative life, and these are all wrong somehow! I don't like it! I don't like to look at them that way!

The conventional notion about language and poetry and the contemplative life is all hung up in journalistic phrases. I cannot subscribe to the idea that poetry is something that has a particular rnetrical form or rhyme scheme. It might be beautiful but beauty isn't the point. Good poetry presents a clear view of something and cuts through our usual feelings and ideas about the world. People tend to admire it because they're told it's wonderful high art. They admit that they don't understand it, but they have been taught to believe that it is worthy of great respect; consequently it gets ignored. I say that poetry is to be enjoyed, that it isn't a matter of linear understanding. People keep insisting that poetry is the kind of stuff written by Milton or Wordsworth. It explains and persuades and tries to manipulate the simpler emotions: grief, joy, despair. There's a large sloppily sentimental operation—make him laugh, make him cry. There is little or no intellectual or visionary content. People feel they are supposed to like it, just as they are supposed to like spinach—because it is good for them. I have no patience with any of this.

The popular idea that the contemplative life is an escape from the unbearable experience of daily life is also mistaken. An examination of the works of St. Theresa of Avila or Thomas Merton provides us with an accurate account of the contemplative life—it is concerned with keeping track of the laundry in the convent or with heavy farm work and the manufacture of cheese. In the pursuit of the contemplative life one finds oneself constantly in conflict with the rules of the organization and the seemingly petty concerns and heavy piety of one's fellow inmates. This kind of situation is indistinguishable from life in an advertising agency in New York City.

As for language—it has a double existence: as spoken word and as grammatical composition. The farther away the written language gets from the spoken language the deader it becomes. There's always a lag between conventional usage and actual speech or the most lively writing. Many people seem to feel that by study of structural linguistics we can create a more lively written language. Maybe so. I find it impossible to understand structural linguistics, so I listen to people when I'm writing on the bus or in the airplane or sitting in a restaurant. Memory provides vocabulary and locutions that I find intriguing and evocative of different places and times. I regret that I do not understand the so-interesting theories of the Language Poets. In both this instance as in the instance of structural linguistics I am the loser. I must make due with live speech and the corpus of Anglo-American literature from Chaucer to Gregory Corso.

And the contemplative life I think is particularly bogus because most people think the contemplative life is somebody sitting in a

beautiful room like in what's-his-name's painting of St. Jerome translating the Bible in his lovely room and his giant lion is lying on his toes
to keep them warm, and it's quiet in there and there's nothing both-
ering him, the telephone isn't ringing, the clock isn't chiming, the
streetcars are not going by outside, and so forth, and it's all beautiful and serene and withdrawn from the dirty nasty world. Many
many people say, "Oh, I would love to go to a monastery, and get
away from everything, it's just terrible." But a monastery is more real
than streetcars because you're dealing with yourself and you're
dealing with real people and you're dealing in a situation that has
very strict rules and very particular ideas about how to do everything. It's tough, it's tough work.

WALDMAN: You've alluded a few times to the problems with education, to the darkness of these times. I'm curious about your take
on all that stuff.

WHALEN: Well, a worst case scenario, like they say, is that Buddhism
in the United States will simply become co-opted like everything
else. Fifty or a hundred years from now Buddhism will just be what
you do on Sunday. It's getting more and more watered down.

WALDMAN: Friends just back from Nepal say the younger teachers
are not trained as the older teachers were. A lot is getting lost. As
there are more and more students, Buddhist teachings get more
popularized, more superficial. . . .

SCHELLING: Along with actual practice getting replaced by the
buying of objects. All these substitutes. It's become an industry. Books
and gadgets and thankas—

WALDMAN: And dorjes and bells! Banners—

WHALEN: Right! Right! As I say, it'll all become boiled down and di-
gested into whatever will suit the palate. Yet with any luck at all
there will continue to be places like Kennett Roshi's Shasta Abbey,
or Tassajara, or the place Maezumi Roshi's building out at Mt. San
Jacinto. Or the Mt. Tremper outfit Daido Sensei has, which will very
quietly be preserving the stricter edge.

SCHELLING: Is a center like Hartford Street trying to keep the same rigors as the remote places?

WHALEN: No. This is a city temple. Most of the people who sit here have jobs downtown. Most people come to sit in the evenings. Very few come here in the morning. Those who sit in the morning live here.

WALDMAN: There are various prophecies about Buddhism dying out in this present world system. In the Tibetan tradition there are prophecies about how it might be kept alive through the Shambhala teachings, or go underground. Do you see in this country things getting darker and stranger in terms of practice? Even the practice of art and poetry has suffered challenges—censorship for instance.

WHALEN: I'm not sure it's all so difficult. Being any kind of artist is difficult, any time, any place. It seems particularly difficult here, but a lot of people have survived and seem to be getting their work done.

WALDMAN: But these prophecies talk about an age of materialism . . .

WHALEN: Yes. The Chinese Buddhists spoke of *Mappo,* the "Ending Age." The idea was that it was a Dharma-ending age. The strength, the material itself, was pretty well shot. They had an idea that it was no use practicing anymore. But some said, "Well, it's all very well to think that, but it says here in the books that you gotta keep coming back to the whole thing, and take care of it." Dogen and other Zen people said, "We have to practice anyway. Whether things are good, bad or indifferent, that's what you do, you do your zazen. That's what's important, not predictions about the future havoc." Shakyamuni Buddha was once asked by somebody, "What about reincarnation? What are we going to do about reincarnation?" And he didn't say anything and the guy went away disappointed. His disciples said, "Why didn't you tell him? You know the answers to everything." And the Buddha says, "Sure I do, but the thing is I want him to figure out what to do in his lifetime." That's very much the Zen attitude, that whatever is coming to pieces, you still have to do zazen, to practice—ideally at some point to get insight into yourself and into the world.

SCHELLING: That's also the Buddhist attitude toward any individual period, even any specific moment, of meditation. You don't have good sittings or bad sittings—

WHALEN: Yes. Dogen says to sit. As long as you're sitting, sitting is enlightenment. You don't have to rush out to find it someplace, or as Francis Cook translates it, "go visit a bunch of dusty countries." As long as you're sitting you're keeping the precepts, you're keeping out of trouble, and there's a chance that if you keep doing this you might actually understand something at some point, understand your own Buddha nature. Your sitting is the expression of your Buddha nature. The thing is you have to sit. And in doing so you're accomplishing what has to be done. Of course it's terribly anti-social.

But the thing is, we don't know, we ourselves don't know, what is the *effect* of zazen on ourselves. Well, we may know something about that, but we don't know what it's doing to the surrounding territory. You know, on some idealistic level, on some religious level, the thing is that as long as people are continuing this practice it'll have some effect—if not on you at least on the landscape!

CREATIVITY AND THE FULLY DEVELOPED BARD

1.

THE MULTI-DECADE RESEARCH PROJECT AND ITS IMPLICATIONS FOR WRITING & POETRY

A multi-decade research project
can be a wondrous structure
to strengthen your art

It can kiss your work
Help you dare
    be part of the history
        of your region.
After all, a career lasts 60 or 70 years
and a multi-decade research system
of proper magnitude and design
can assist
    in bundles
      of projects
        year after year.

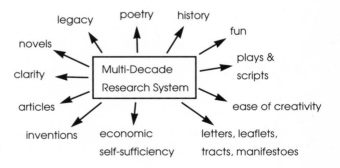

ED SANDERS

Part of
the research system
is the way it LOOKS,
FEELS, is laid out.
Its purpose is to *rhyme*
                    with your life.

Creating a Multi-Decade System
and *Using* it
            go together. You
            can't wait to create.

One way is immediately
to take on a writing project
that requires mammoth research.
It prepares you
            for the 60 years.
Charles Olson calls it
            a Saturation Job.

In his *A Bibliography on America* he describes the S.J.:

"Best thing to do is *to dig one thing or place or man or
woman* until you yourself know more abt that than is
possible to any other man. It doesn't matter whether
it's Barbed Wire or Pemmican or Paterson or Iowa. But
exhaust it. Saturate it. Beat it.
And then U KNOW everything else very fast: one satu-
ration job (it might take 14 years). And you're in, forever."

        You're ready to
            work the chrono-tracks.

2.
CHRONO-TRACKING

        Adorning and packing the Time Track
        with our researches

defines our stories.
Time Tracking is one of the most
difficult art forms.

It may be the ultimate poetic form
in the service of whose discipline
all your skills are tested.

Epic
is born
with beauty-gnarls
in the Time Track.

The multi-decade project
and Time Tracking
are twined upon the same Montblanc.

Your story is told in the Time Track
as well as the story you want to tell
by adorning and packing the Time Track
It requires personal integrity,
relentless and lonely work,
planning as complex as your mind allows,
yet laziness, imprecision, lack of zeal
shyness, fear, hesitation
and lack of a 20-year plan
oft leave the Time Track desolate.

Adorning the Time Track
is the substance of the Thing itself,
for history winds up being
the thing it describes:

"History is the new localism, a polis to replace
the one which was lost in various stages all over
the world from 490 B.C. on. . . ."
(Charles Olson, "The View," from
The Special View of History.)

and by your combined histories
we are that.

3.
COMPOSITION BY FIELD

"How sweet I roamed from field to field
and tasted all the summer's pride"

—*William Blake*

You set up a creativity zone
       in a Field of two or more dimensions
then fill within that zone
your poetry.

Composition by Field
is a way to use a keyboard
             as a scribe's palette

To have ideas in mind
and then, as a flow
      of positing
to inscribe the FIELD

           One of the best metaphors
           still, is Olson's
           "high energy-construct"
           from *Projective Verse:*

"We now enter. . . . the large area of the whole poem
into the FIELD. . . . where all the syllables and all the
lines must be managed in their relations to each
other."

Can it be easy?
You bet it can.
But it can be extremely difficult.

Verse Field

Breath by breath, syllable by syllable,
line by line
        in finely constructed or woven layers
        of the visual gestalt

        in the metaphor of the
                High Energy-Construct,

    where "ONE PERCEPTION MUST IMMEDIATELY
        AND DIRECTLY LEAD TO A FURTHER
        PERCEPTION"
                (Olson, quoting Edward Dahlberg)

    comes the Verse Field.

The eye scans the shape of the Field
and reads a wider area than
                just the line before it:

    "(Olson) had the term Field Composition which I'd
    seen before and thought about in relation to paintings
    because the Gestaltists had advanced the idea of the
    Field Composition of paintings—that intention does not
    move pointedly around a painting—that the eye actu-
    ally rediscovers the painting with different paths—and
    you look at a painting somehow entire and look deep
    into it—and then the great question came up right
    away for the Gestaltists: don't we read the same way,
    scan the entire area we're reading, and then read
    into it, so that we're already in an advanced state of
    recognition without much time passing at all as we dis-
    cover it, but the discovery comes from a Field Scan of
    the whole area."

                (ROBERT DUNCAN
                TALKING ABOUT CHARLES OLSON'S POETICS
                2-17-82 AT NEW COLLEGE, S.F.)

Composition by Field
can also take the form of
        shamanic self-rev-up—

it's a way of charging the mind,
          like a capacitor

which then
      when the energy is fully formed
discharges the poesy
        into the Field.

4.
THE THEORY AND PRACTICE
OF THE DATA CLUSTER

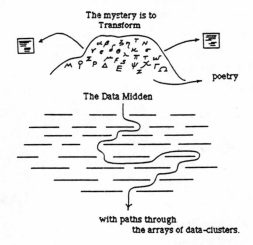

The mystery is to
Transform

poetry

The Data Midden

with paths through
the arrays of data-clusters.

It's in the creating and sequencing of data-clusters
that great writing
      based on research
         is born.

A key point is not to get frozen
        too soon into a version
The way you sequence your data

on different days
 different choices
  & different moods
 means different versions.

Try cutting out FACT STRIPS

Put a line or two on a strip
Make compilations of them,
all the while polishing individual strips,
rearranging the array of FACT STRIPS,
  beginning to shape the sequence
  beginning to hear the sequence
  beginning to see a shape of lines

Maybe it'll take 20 or 30 different orderings
  of a FACT STRIP plexus
till a sudden clarification,
  yes, that's it! occurs

—this is the birth of the Data-Cluster

You might lay out a sequence of Fact Strips
across a wall or on the floor, or you can pick up a
  bunch of drafting boards at garage sales
  and be able to carry your strips
  out into the woods.

Clusters form, pulse and throb
  with meters and melos--
  and sometimes apothegms and lyrics
  subtend from the cluster

and all of it, in a data-retentive era, made possible
by th' Negative Capability
     that Olson discovered for us in a letter of John Rods.

**IT WAS IN A DECEMBER 1817 LETTER
TO GEORGE AND TOM KEATS:**

"Browne & Dilke walked with me & back from the
Christmas pantomine. I had not a dispute but a disqui-
sition with Dilke, on various subjects: several things
dovetailed in my mind & at once it struck me, what
quality went to form a Man of Achievement especially
in Literature & which Shakespeare possessed so enormously—I mean *Negative Capability,* that is when man
is capable of being in uncertainties, Mysteries, doubts,
without any irritable reaching after fact & reason—
Coleridge, for instance, would let go by a fine isolated
verisimilitude caught from the Penetralium of Mystery,
from being incapable of remaining content with half
knowledge. . . ."

The bard in a fact-blizzarded and distraction-glutted era
sits, stands, lies or dreams in his/her
Creativity Zone

and says no to a million
                fine isolated verisimilitudes
till yes, yes, and yes
the mosaic of yeses
          begins to posit in the Creativity Zone.

The data-mosaic—little bits, ununderstood for months,
and maybe in the tentative discard pile,
                may prove important
in those illuminations that occur
day after day
         in your writing periods.

5.
TUNING THE DATA

One way to
    shake out
        a sequence of charged lines

is to read through the sequence of FACT UNITS
maybe read through it for hours
        over and over

and then SING INTO IT
(like Yeats sitting in a chair after dinner
beating time on the arm, humming a tune
        and polishing verses)

SING INTO IT
so that
    logopoeia makes love with
        melopoeia*

and this "tuning"
of the data-clusters
brings the best you have to the Field.

6.
SHAPED CREATIVITY ZONES

The shapes, the surfaces, colors
the relation of angles & views,
the lighting, the sounds

of your creativity zones help
shape your poetry

o o o

*See note on melopoeia, phanopoeia, logopoeia, tromopoeia, mythopoeia and
noopoeia with the bibliography.

That is, the place where you create
whether a knoll in a wetland,
a river bank, cliff cave,

                a room with a desk

has a configuration
that acts upon your work.

One way
is to experiment
with Shaped Creativity Zones
—move things
around or construct new shapes—
break the overreliance
on right angles
        in your shelves & furniture
                for instance.
It may acquire some subtlety
maybe you
        need to adjust
the shapes of your Zone
              for different types
                  of writing.

Or perhaps
        to use the concept of scrims
to change the patterns of background color.

           Some need
           the loot of a magpie—
           items & totems
           shells, posters
                stacks of collectibles
           in their Zone.

           Others like a Zen Zone
           a cleared-out area
           which to some seems stark

but to others
a highly charged place
as if it were
patterns of raked sand
around boulders
& a laptop.

The look & feel
& the way you array
your information systems
in your Creativity Zone
has meaning
for your work.

Different arrays
have different
impacts on the sequencing of data,
and on the ways you roam through
your files and researches

as well as the ways
you lay out data-clusters.

The goal is clarity
and to find those unforeseen
illuminations and connections
such as to help give birth
to your best work.

7.
TUNING THE CREATIVITY ZONE

No bard is fully realized
without a knowledge of meter

It's a simple as that—
You can groan, "Ah, Sanders, desist! desist!"
but it's true.

You have to SING into your clusters
where the vowels carry the melody
and the consonants,
              those click-tracks of infinity,
                        are the percussion.

All poetry can be parsed
              into patterns of classic meter—

and bards DO hold syllables quantitatively
as they read or chant.

Tones rise as they read,
tones change as they end a line—
              sometimes it's subtle.

So, a bard might, as a start,
              internalize 10 or 11 metrical patterns,
and you might as well memorize some of the
main classical meters:

⏑´	the iamb
´⏑	the trochee
´⏑⏑	the dactyl
⏑⏑´	the anapest
´—	the spondee
´⏑—	the cretic
⏑´—	the bacchic
´—⏑⏑	the ionic a majore
⏑⏑´—	the ionic a minore
´⏑⏑—	choriamb
´⏑——	epitrite
⏑⏑⏑´	the 4th paeon
⏑´—⏑´	the dochmius

Plus more complicated ones, such as
the Greater Asclepiadean (4 choriambs):
´⏑| ´⏑⏑ — | ´⏑⏑ — | ´⏑⏑ — | ⏑ ´

and a number of others, which you can pick
up from the *Oxford Companion to Classical Literature*.

Then make them a part of you.

They say you've learned a language
when you begin to dream in it.

The idea is to sing into your clusters
and understand your own self-grown meters
your own sounds and patterns

the way Sappho created her own famous mode
(the Mixolydian they called it)
and her own meters:

φαίνεταί μοι κῆνος ἴσος θεοίσιν

Phainetai moi kaynos isos theoisin

ἔμμεν ὤνηρ ὄττις ἐνάντιός τοι

emmen onare ottis enantios toi

ἰζάνει καὶ πλάσιον ἀδυ φωνεί-

idzanay kai plasion aduphonay-

σας ὑπακούει

sas hupakouay

her quatrains ending
in an "Adonic"

And other beautiful self-derived metricals such as
her two-line fragment:

Glukaya mater ou toi dunamai krekayne ton iston

Γλύκηα μάτερ ού τοι δύναμαι κρεκην τὸν ἴστον

pothoh damaysa paidos Bradinoh di Aphroditan

πόθῳ δάμεισα παῖδος Βραδίνῳ δι' Ἀφροδίταν

each line matching the other in very creative pulses—
beginning with iambs   followed by an antispast ∪ —́ — ∪
and each line ending with 2 iambs and an amphibrach

∪ —́ ∪ —́ | ∪ —́ ∪

Yes!

Or Whitman, that wild bard of beautiful meter!
(dactyl)

        (choriamb)   (1st line, twin adonics)

—́ ∪ ∪ —́ ∪ | —́ ∪ ∪ —́ ∪   ∪

Out of the cradle endlessly rocking   (paean)

—́ ∪ ∪ | —́ ∪ ∪ — | ∪ —́ ∪ ∪ | —́ —

Out of the mocking-bird's throat, the musical shuttle

—́ ∪ ∪ | —́ — | —́ —   —

Out of the Ninth-month midnight,

—́ ∪ ∪ | —́ ∪ — | ∪ ∪ —́ | ∪ —́ | —́ ∪   —

Over the sterile sands and the fields beyond, where the child

—́ ∪ ∪ — | —́ ∪ ∪ — | —́ ∪ ∪ —́ — —

    leaving his bed wander'd alone, bareheaded, bare foot,

—́ ∪ ∪ | —́ ∪ —́ —

Down from the shower'd halo

(choriambs)

LEAVES OF GRASS
Book XIX Sea-Drift

Or some lines from THE WASTELAND—

— ∪ — ∪ —

"Trams and dusty trees.

—́ ∪ ∪ — — | —́ ∪ ∪ —   —

Highbury bore me. Richmond and Kew

˘ ´ ˘|˘ ´ ˘ |˘ ´ ˘ ´

Undid me. By Richmond I raised my knees

˘ ´ ˘ ˘|´ ˘ ˘|´ ˘ ˘ —

Supine on the floor of a narrow canoe."

Or FIT IT to your *own* patterns

                of Throbs and Pulses

      What's needed in modern poetics
      is a renaissance
      of the ancient idea
          of different meters and patterns
      indicating specific
          moods, levels of energy, and emotions

      such as the Dochmius
      (a bacchic and an iambic) ˘ ´— ˘ ´)

      which was used in ancient plays
      for moments of great excitement.

   You can make up your own pulses
   Think of a pattern,
˘ ˘ ˘ ´|˘ ˘ ˘ ´|˘ ˘ ˘ ´ | ´ — ˘ — , say,
     then "pulse it"
       think of words

     or make the creation of words
       & the creation of pulses
         the same act

     Look at your poems of the past few years
          and analyze their pulses.

  ´ ˘ ˘ — ´ ˘ ˘ — ´ ˘ ˘ — ´ ˘ ˘ —

The choriamb awaits its Rimbaud
to bring to it a perfect
set of lines
  ´ ˘ ˘ — ´ ˘ ˘ — ´ ˘ ˘ — ´ ˘ ˘ —

whose realm is
       tape, film, font, collage, and the
              hieroglyphization of verse.

There might be as many as
       a *thousand* Muses now
each denoting a type of creativity
          or Muse Skill.

All of us partake in all the skills
       of all the Muses
          in varying degrees,

& part of a bard's journey
is to learn the levels of Muse Skills
        the bard owns
          by fate & endeavor.

For each of us is subsumed
      beneath the
        Perfect Bard of Infinity—

      The lyric compression of Sappho
      The inventiveness of Archilochus or Shakespeare
      The sense of colors & word of Blake
      The orchestration of Beethoven
      The performance presence of
          Nijinsky or Isadora Duncan
      The singing of Orpheus
      The ability of visual array
        and form of line
          of Michelangelo
      The theoretic reachings of an Einstein
      The undauntedness of an Emma Goldman.

All of us are subsumed beneath the perfect bard
as we search for our Muse Skills—

      The muse of line and line breaks
      The muse of melody and sequence of vowels

The muse of story telling and plot
          (tell a good story and the whole
world will listen)
The muse of rhyme and alliteration
The muse of pulses and meters
The muse of the beauteous data-cluster
The muse of Visual Array
The muse of humor
The muse of exquisite nature image
The muse of allegory
The muse of mythopoeia—at tracing
                    the numinal
The muse of condensation and pithiness
The muse of Brilliant Associative Flashes
The muse of Tromos (Τρομοσ) and Body Tones
          (Sappho's Tromos, or trembling)
          ("If you don't have your body as a
          factor of creation you don't have a soul"
                    Charles Olson)
The muse of the Performance Zone
The muse of Composition by Field
The muse of the long line
          (Homer, Ginsberg)
The muse of narrow-lined precision
The muse of Brilliant Metaphor
The muse of Etiology and Causes
The muse of Sandwiches of Striking,
                    Disparate Images
The muse of the brilliant foreground
                    (Odyssey)
The muse of the brilliant background
The muse of Dictation from the Sky
                    (Rilke, Eliot)
The muse of sudden clarifications
The muse of satire
The muse of the Visual Image (Retentia)

The muse of the dithyramb
The muse of ire and indignation
The muse of personality and characters
                              (the late Hardy)
The muse of Emotive Typography
The muse of the Multi-Century Maxim
                    (Ginsberg, Olson, Heraclitus)
The muse of Compassion & Sympathy/Empathy
The muse of Verse Containing History
The muse of First Thought/Best Thought
The muse of Reworking and Perfecting
        (Dylan Thomas' 117 versions
        of "Fern Hill")
and many others

Your muse-mix shifts through your life
Different times of day, too, are better
                        for various muse-skills.

You have to study your muse-mix.
                    It changes as you live.
One of the greatest modern examples
of an artist adjusting the mix of his muses
was Henri Matisse
who in the last creative months of his life
in 1952 and 1953, 81 years old,
        not able any longer to paint and sculpt,
confined to a wheel chair,
racked with anxiety and *timor mortis*
at night sketching faces on the
        ceiling above his sick bed
            with a long stick with crayon attached—

but nevertheless was able to adjust his muses
        even in a wheel chair
to produce some of the finest art of the century
those wall-sized works of painted paper cut-outs

such as *Apollo, Women and Monkeys, Memory of Oceania,
Large Decoration with Mask,* and smaller
gouache découpées such as the *Blue Nude* series.

9.
MULTI-DECADE INFORMATION SYSTEMS

The goal of a multi-decade information system
is ease of use (any item should be retrievable
within 30 seconds)
It should facilitate Creativity
It should flirt with you
and invite you to touch it
It should be easy to augment and reorganize
It should be easy
for parts of it to become mobile
and go on the road
You should be able to hide things within it

It SHOULD BE THERE IN YOUR LIFE
so that
in your best
creative moments
you can spiffle
through it
for materials

useful to your writing.

What's in it? All the obvious things—
books, magazines, collections of photocopies,
cross referenced collections of notes (all dated
and paginated) and interviews, and alphabetized,
chronological and subject-by-subject files;
oodles of dictionaries and source books, recorders,
typewriters, art supplies, drafting boards, wall charts,
ten foot plasma screens on the ceiling (in a few years),

light tables, magnifiers, microscopes, binoculars,
maybe drums, lyres, throat trumpets and music devices,
computers, electronic storage facilities such
as CD-ROMs and WORMS maybe, or Bernoulli
boxes, film, tape, photo archives, chronologies,
optical scanners, question lists by the thousand,
ideas and files for research on articles, stories,
poems, manifestoes, novels, inventions, songs,
paintings, glyphs, new fonts, myths,
religions, science ideas, et alia multa,

and all configured into a
            Shaped Creativity Zone
                        to empower your pen.

Data in the electromagnetic era is galactic—
For example, there are, as of '92,
600 separate data bases
            in the New York State Library.

& even though there are no homes for
the homeless, there's data base
                        on homelessness.

The glut makes Negative Capability
            just that much more important,

and what could be called "Datage,"
the sometimes-regretted-later
            throwing away of unnecessary files

in the service of sanity and the Zen Zone.

And so you'll be loning it
in your creativity zone
with ubergluts of resources—
what Thomas Carlyle
            dubbed the "Dryasdusts"

yet out of the Dryasdusts

grow

the Time Tracks

of the 20-decade bard.

Exhaustive Q-Lists (question lists)
are important to the
Multi-Decade Information System

They give you hierarchies of pursuit
in the mapping of WHAT YOU HAVE

WHAT YOU ARE

WHAT YOU NEED

And of course, Blake tells us to practice practice practice
bearing in mind the jazz adage

"you practice the way you play."

You might practice writing

your interview notes

into spontaneous verse-grids.

Even as you interview someone
over the phone, or hear something
brilliant backstage at the reading, you can
break it up into lines

and breath units.

10.
THE FIELD OF VISION

The eye is in the ascendency
i.e., the ability of humans
to use the eye

is arising.

"Children brought up on TV (that is, those born after
1945) have been shown to differ from people who

were brought up prior to TV (born before 1945).
Thorndike in "renorming" the Stanford-Benet 'tests'
found the mean I.Q. scores for today's 'normal' five-
year-old to be 25 percent or more higher than the
scores for children of 30 or more years ago. . . .
Garfinkel discovered that the behavioral attributes responsible for I.Q. score differences were primarily two:
superior competence in 'reading'
visual sequence (process, chronology or picture sequences) and superior competence in the perception
of small differences in visual gestalt."

—*John Debes*
"Visuocultural Influences in Lateralization"
Evolution and Lateralization of the Brain
N.Y. Academy of Sciences, 1977

We know that this century
bards have brought new glory
                    to the visual

Snyder, Pound, Olson, Wakoski,
Kyger, Duncan, Jacob, Blackburn,
Williams, Apollinaire, just
to mention a few, have shown us
that an important part of phanopoeia
is the visual array on the page
the shape of the poem
& the visual path of the eye
                    in the Field

        The eye is on the rise
and the Muse of Phanopoeia, the Calligramme and Hieroglyph
strengthen our poems
                    in the data-retentive era.

11.
EMOTIVE TYPOGRAPHY

The double columns
of the Gutenberg Bible
set the standards
for the visual array
            for centuries

Printing after Gutenberg
tended to be rectilinear
It fit the needs of
            print technology
the eyes and brains of readers
            okayed it.
Poetry was boxed
            for centuries
(poetry is often very conservative)

but in this century
because of advances
            throughout the world
poetry has been freed
as never before.

Phanopoeia, the visual aspect of verse,
            shares in this freedom.
Phanopoeia is not only
    "Throwing the object
        (fixed or moving)
    onto the visual imagination"

that Lb. described
but it's also denoted too
by the way it looks on the page.

Shaped poesy zones
as sleek as a bent wire
                of Giacometti
grace our era from a number of bards.

William Carlos Williams, in his beautiful tercets:

                Of asphodel, that greeny flower,
                        like a buttercup
                                upon its branching stem
                save that it's green and wooden—
                I come, my sweet,
                        to sing to you.

                (from "Asphodel, That Greeny Flower")
designed an exquisite emotive Field.

As early as 1914, Apollinaire's *Calligrammes* such as the famous rain
poem

                        Il Pleut

pointed a direction that
only later technology could follow.

Charles Olson in some of *Maximus*
                gleamed with phanopoeia.

His nautilus-like poem
about his father

had been prefigured
by Apollinaire's "Visee"

Colors—which added such glory to Blake,
will be more and more available to the bard.

The consciousness can recognize around
1488 colors and shades of color, according
to the *Munsell Book of Colour.*

"Colors win you more and more.
A certain blue enters your soul. A certain red
has an effect on your blood pressure.
A certain color tones you up. It's the
concentration of timbres. A new era is opening."
                    Henri Matisse

Assuming that environmentally benign
colored inks can be developed,
full color poetry
        with the 1488 hues and shades
                will be available to the bard.

We may see a hieroglyphization of verse
The Egyptians believed their glyphs were actually alive.
Now life can be resembled. Glyphs may pulse, breathe,
can seem to move, twirl, blink, elide, change color,
                        erase, erode, and mutate.

Faces, flowers and parts of the anatomy
no doubt will belong to
the bard's hieroglyphic fonts,

                and whole sentences or poems
                could be written now and then
                in a language of silence!

        Prepositions, for instance, could be replaced,
        at the bard's choice, by silent hiero-symbols.

And we might as well think about
hieroglyphic memory gardens and virtual reality Sonnet Fields
as well as alternate paths of narrative
                through 4-dimensional poems

                Or we may see "mood typesetting"
                        of the Verse Field
                as when certain music
                sets certain moods in films.

Serifs are mental hooks
They help hook words into memory
Why not subtly colored and shaped serifs
                    to convey moods and emotions?
Each bard with her own brand of serifs and colors
as a painter who has a special brush stroke,
                        color palette or "look"

I call it Emotive Typography
a means by which the bard can indicate
        changes of mood, emotion, pace, subject

        by way of the changes in serifs and fonts

        by way of certain cunning adornments to the type

        by way of the use of color

        by use of repetitive visual symbols—the
                    hieroglyphization of the lines.

12.
THE EGYPTIAN "SESH"

The Egyptian word "sesh"
the noun for writing or book
and the verb, to write or to paint

shows some of an ancient scribe's apparatus:

a roll of papyrus
        a palette with two cakes of ink or paint

a water jar,
and a narrow pen-case
connected by a string
        with which the writer
could carry them in hand or over the shoulder
that they not disperse

You need to create your own "sesh"
or writer's tools
and keep them at hand around the clock—

for there are no weekends for poets.

There's an in-the-field sesh
and an at-home sesh
but you should always have paper and pen
or pencil, knife, scissors, glue, tape,
magnifier, binoculars,

and maybe sometimes a pH tester,
sample bag, camera, tape recorder,
laptop, palmcorder, geiger counter,
nature guide, water colors,

        the point is, figure out your own,
        and always have it at hand.

13.
PLANNING AND MAPPING

        Just as countries
                need long term planning

        so do we—
                a multi-decade plan for
        books, poesy, songs, articles,
        operas, plays, manifestoes, inventions,
        short stories, areas of research

It will help you find your story
Know your dreams   Find your tools

"The tools you use will shape your dreams
and the dreams you dream will shape your tools
And the tools you dream will shape your soul for
            the Dream of the World"
            (from song, "The Dream of the World," *Cassandra*)

One of Bob Kaufman's books was titled
Does the Secret Mind Whisper?

It does, and you can urge
your mind to
        assignments
                that may take it
10 years to fulfill.

Sometimes it comes in a flow
Sometimes in fragments
Sometimes
        you have to assign it
                to your mind
                for later "sudden" solution

                George Oppen called it "Noopoeia"
                or "revelation"
                        sudden clarifications

as when Rilke received verse
as if it were dictation from the sky.

In your shaped creativity zones
you'll be working
        with the secret mind

on many
        different projects

some of them
only to be actually written
say 5–10–15 years
in the future

and with proper mapping & planning
you can suffuse it with all you have
of logo/phano/melo/tromo/noo/mythopoeia

logopoeia
phanopoeia melopoeia
tromopoeia mythopoeia
noopoeia

the wreath
of poesy

BIBLIOGRAPHY AND NOTES

PHANOPOEIA, MELOPOEIA, LOGOPOEIA, TROMOPOEIA, NOOPOEIA, AND MYTHOPOEIA.

Pound, in his **ABC of Reading** wrote, "You still charge
words with meaning mainly in three ways, called
phanopoeia, melopoeia, logopoeia."

I.
(Phanopoeia)

"Throwing the object (fixed or moving)
onto the visual imagination."

II.
(Melopoeia)

> "Inducing emotional correlations by the sound
> and rhythms of the speech."

III.
(Logopoeia)

> "Inducing both of the effects by
> stimulating the associations
> (intellectual emotional)
> that have remained in the
> receiver's consciousness
> in relation to the actual
> word or word groups employed."

To these I have added Tromopoeia, Mythopoeia and, from George
Oppen as suggested by Chuck Pirtle, Noopoeia.

Tromos means trembling in Sappho, and *Tromopoeia*
means the excitation in the reader, in the auditor *and*
in the performer throughout the body, from poetry.
Tromopoeia therefore is the cluster of muse skills that
guides performance, and also the mind as it performs
reading the poem.

NOOPOEIA | George Oppen made a note in his daybook:
"Pound's Melopoeia, etc—Amazing to have forgotten
Noopoeia—revelation. Amazing to have forgotten lucence,
translucence. . . ." Noopoeia covers sudden clarifications, insight
and revelations on a localized, poem-by-poem basis (as opposed
to mythopoeia—the biggest scale) as "The Secret Mind Whispers."
MYTHOPOEIA: | the universal strands that speak to the numinal
and absolute—mythopoeia also covers explanations the mind

reads out after long study and reflection—those sudden clarifications illuminate connections on the grandest scale.

**BOOKS AND ESSAYS
BY CHARLES OLSON:**

A Bibliography on America
Projective Verse
The Special View of History
The Maximus Poems

OTHER BOOKS:

The Oxford Companion to Classical Literature I (ancient
metrics)
Evolution and Lateralization of the Brain I N.Y. Academy of
Sciences, 1977
Physiology of the Human Eye and Visual System I Raymond E.
Records, Harper & Row, 1979. For information on the visual field.
Physiology of the Eye I Irving Fait, Butterworth, 1978
Theory and Practice of Typographic Design I Eric Bain, Hastings
House, 1970
Typography: Design and Practice I John Lewis, Barrie & Jenkins, '77
The Big Jewish Book I put together by Jerome Rothenberg.
Good for examples of shaped verse.
Calligrammes I Guillaume Apollinaire. Good edition with ex-
planatory notes, with original poems and translations by Anne
Hyde Greet—University of California Press, 1980.
"Sappho on East Seventh" I from *Thirsting for Peace in a*
Raging Century Coffee House Press (for poetics section on
Retentia, muse of the Retained Image.)
Investigative Poetry I City Lights Books, out of print, but you can
always photocopy from a friend. Look for new, expanded edition.
The ABC of Reading I by Ezra Pound, New Directions (for
Phanopoeia, Melopoeia and Logopoeia.)
Egyptian Grammar I Alan Gardiner, Oxford University Press; a
good beginning book on hieroglyphics and their implications.

IV

PART FOUR

FILM

VI

FILM

SCREENWRITING AND THE POTENTIALS OF CINEMA

On Techniques of Temporal and Spatial Distortion

Consider a film as a slice of time with which you can do anything you want. You can speed it up, slow it down, run it backwards, flash back, flash forward, scramble, overlay, underexpose, overexpose, and you can also feed in audience reaction. The standard product simply presents a sequential narrative, which is actually an arbitrary form with a beginning, a middle, and an end. It's really as arbitrary a form as the sonnet. But it is what the audience is accustomed to seeing.

Here we have a time segment; say it's five minutes. And I can move around in it. I can smell the flowers, touch the bridge, hear the stream. And I can also randomize it. Now, instead of consciously moving in the time segment, you can simply hold it in your attention. What you have here is a section of film, a piece of time, a five-minute walk. And you can speed it up—you can do five minutes in five seconds, zip around the block; you can slow it down to five hours. So, you can flash back, flash forward, overlay, and super-impose—all by the process of memory. And you can randomize the time segment or split it into fragments.

Now, you can apply contemplation and concentration techniques to this time segment. Let your mind rest on it without effort or direction and see what you actually see, feel, taste, touch; think about your time segment. Don't push at all; just leave your mind on that whole time segment like you were concentrating on a flower or any object. Just let your mind look at it. Now, hold your mind on this time segment, allowing your attention to move away on lines of association but always bringing it back to the time segment. This is more or less the exercise of concentration or one-pointedness: keeping your mind on one point. . . .

Now you can try some more advanced time travel. Go back in your mind seventy-five years ago to June 10, 1900. Now, don't try to decide or improvise what you will see; just go back and look around

WILLIAM S. BURROUGHS

and see what you actually do see. Put your mind back there and look around. A lifetime reporter gave me a hint about time travel: He said you need a peg to hang it on; that is, a coordinate point to line up on, like the sightings you use in flying a light plane. Line up on cobwebs and see the morning dew seventy-five years ago.

You can apply this exercise to writing. Look at your movie sets. You can move your sets and characters around in time, speed up, slow down, etcetera. Try the contemplation exercise on your characters and sets. Let your mind rest there. Don't push; don't improvise; don't put words in your characters' mouths. Let them talk—and act. Just observe and contemplate. The less consciously contrived your characters are, the more real they will be. Now, of course, it is ultimately *you* who are talking; but if you just leave your characters alone and let them talk, you're putting yourself in touch with your own subconscious perception of these characters, and they'll come through a lot clearer.

If you do that—for maybe ten or fifteen minutes—suddenly a character will start talking on its own. You'll find this exercise puts more reality into your characters than if you were to try, consciously, to decide what they were going to say and do, using the very small part of the mind that is the conscious, logical, sequential part.

In 1959 Brion Gysin said that writing was fifty years behind painting. He applied the montage technique to writing, which had already been used for fifty years in painting. As you know, painters had the whole representational position knocked out from under them by photography. There was, in fact, a photography exhibition around the turn of the century entitled "Photography: The Death of Painting." Well, painting didn't die, but it did have to get a new look. I mean, painters couldn't go on painting cows in the grass. So painters turned first to montage. Now, montage is actually much closer to the act of perception—certainly urban perception—than representational painting is. You take a walk down a city street and put what you have just seen down on canvas, whether you've seen a person's form cut in half by a car, bits and pieces of street signs and advertisements, reflections from shop windows. In short, you've seen a montage of fragments. And the same happens, of course, with words. Remember that the written word is an image.

Brion Gysin's cut-up method consists of cutting up pages of text and rearranging them in montage combinations. But if you apply the montage method to writing, you're accused by the critics of promulgating a cult of unintelligibility. Writing is still confined by the sequential, representational straitjacket of the novel, an arbitrary form that's far from the actual facts of human perception and consciousness. Consciousness is a cut-up, and life is a cut-up. Every time you walk down the street or look out the window your stream of consciousness is cut by random factors. Brion Gysin applied this process to text, using a pair of scissors, and provided writers with a new way to touch and handle their medium. These first cut-ups were published in *Minutes to Go* in 1960.

The method had not been used before in writing, but, as I mentioned, montage had been used in painting for about fifty years. It has been used even more extensively in music—John Cage and Earl Brown, for example, applied randomness to their music. Earl Brown would give one of the musicians in his orchestra a choice of three scores, so that every performance was different.

Randomness has also been used quite extensively in military strategy. In fact, what I would call the cut-up method was a basic factor in the strategy of the Air Force during World War II, as explained by John von Neumann in *The Theory of Games and Economic Behavior*.[1] He enunciated the principle of Minimax. That is, you assume that the worst has happened and then act in such a way that it is of minimal assistance to the enemy. Suppose you've got three flight plans. Now, suppose the enemy knows your three flight plans; the worst has happened. But, just before flight you flip a coin or use any random method to decide which flight plan you're going to use. Even if the enemy knows you're going to do this, that knowledge doesn't do them any good because even you don't know beforehand which flight plan you are going to use. Something new is usually the application of something that has already been used, perhaps for some time, in another area.

I've done quite a few experiments in cutting up film with my friend Anthony Balch. In fact, we released a film called *The Cut-Ups* in 1968. It was shown to Nicholas Roeg, who adopted quite a few of the ideas for his film, *Performance* (1970).

Of course, cut-ups have also been used in films. The line between film editing—what goes on in the cutting room—and any random process is a very thin one. So if you consider all film editing to be film cut-up, the method is rather standard in films. However, I consider the two processes to be different.

Any product or invention is standardized by mass production, and this standardization of the product discourages further experimentation. Take, for example, the motor industry. Because it can sell—or rather it could up until a few months ago—as many cars with internal combustion engines as it could produce, it didn't want to know about jet-turbine engines. Of course, the turbine engine is better, more efficient. But why bother with a better product if you can sell what is already in production? This consideration also applies to the film industry: So long as it can sell westerns, gangster movies, spectaculars, musicals, all the standard Hollywood products, why experiment? "What has made money will make money" is a Hollywood axiom. Anything new is a gamble that the big studios don't want to take. In consequence, the surface has barely been scratched with regard to experimentation with the film medium. Now, the flashback, of course, is an old device, but the flashforward is a quite recent device and is still rarely used. Inventiveness, to use B. F. Skinner's phrase, has not been reinforced by the studios.

I've made a number of cut-ups on tape recorders by actually cutting and resplicing tape. This process is laborious and time-consuming if you're working with standard tape; but movie tape, which is much larger, is easier to use. A simpler method than cutting and resplicing is to record for any length of time and then spin the tape backwards and forwards on the recorder, cutting in new phrases at random. Where you cut in, of course, the old words are wiped out and the new words are cut in, seemingly at random. I have experimented with tape recorder cut-ups over a period of years, and I've frequently been surprised at how often the cut-ins fall in appropriate places and how much of the new recording makes perfect sequential sense. So just how random are these cut-ins? Well, consciously, of course, I don't know where in the message already recorded I am stopping the tape to make a cut-in. But because we know so much more than we are aware that we know, on some level I probably do know exactly where in the original recording I am cutting in. The cut-ups put you in touch with what you know and what you don't know you know.

Anthony Balch and I applied the cut-up technique to films by taking a section of film, cutting it into segments, and then rearranging the segments. Now, this process differs from film editing, since you cannot foresee the result, and you will get new images and words and meanings just as you do in cutting up words. This method is simply an extension of the text cut-up. You can cut the film into sections of a minute or you can cut it into one-frame sections. Working with single frames means quite a splicing job, but the results are interesting. We did this once, and the film disintegrated after being run through the projector several times. But I would like to see further experiments in scrambling film in this way.

When working with film cut-ups, you can edit the film and choose the most effective sequences, just as you can with tape and text cut-ups. However, in our film cut-ups, we did not edit the material. We just cut up film sections and rearranged them. When our film cut-ups were shown in London, the manager of the theater said that in all his forty years' experience he had never seen so many people come to the box office furious, demanding a refund of their money, nor so many people express congratulations and approval. After one week, he asked Anthony to withdraw the film, and it hasn't been shown publicly since.

That is one experimental device—cutting and scrambling film segments—but there are many others that you can use in films. And a surprising number of them have not been used. Of course, there are time experiments. You have all seen films sped up, slowed down, and run backwards. But now consider applying these techniques to comparatively immobile subjects. Slowing down the frames of a face that is not moving gives a curious expression of statuesque immobility. This technique could be used to advantage, I think, in science fiction films. Speeding up the frames of a face produces strange seismic twitches, and running the film of an immobile face backwards is quite disorienting. You know that something strange is happening, but you don't know what it is.

Speed-ups, slow motion, and running film backwards have been technically possible since the beginning of motion pictures, and one cannot but marvel at the lack of imagination exhibited by conventional filmmakers. They have had the ability to control time, yet in their films, for the most part, they have turned their backs on slow motion and pratfalls for eighty years.[2]

Methods of Engaging the Audience
There are many simple experiments aimed at capturing the viewer's attention and many variations and extensions that can be derived from each. I suppose some of you must have tried the following experiment; if you haven't, it's quite a lot of fun. You select a film to be shown on a television set, cut the sound track, and substitute a recorded sound track from a similar film if you want. For example, you take one western, cut the sound track, and substitute the recorded sound track from another western. I've seen people watch such an experimental film for five or ten minutes before they realize there's anything amiss with the sound track. The sound track determines for viewers what they're seeing; that is, they mentally alter the image track to fit the sound track. Now, you can do the same thing with your own film images and sound tracks. If you add machine-gun sound effects to a picture of people running to catch a bus, the audience will assume that the people are running from the machine guns. And if one person stumbles and falls in the film, the audience will assume that he has been shot.

Here is another simple experiment that has been performed. I don't recall the director's name.[3] At any rate, he filmed a well-known actor between acts, when his face bore an expression that was quite neutral. The actor wasn't acting; he wasn't doing anything. Then he inserted several scenes in front of the frames showing the empty expression on the actor's face. The first was of a baby in a cradle; then somebody in a coffin; and then an accident victim lying on a street. He showed this sequence to an audience and asked them what the actor's expression meant. Well, they said he was expressing love for the baby, he was feeling sorry for the person in the coffin, and he was horrified at the sight of the accident victim. You see, the viewers supplied the expression. The actor, of course, was not reacting to the scenes in front of him. All of the scenes had been artificially inserted.

This very simple experiment in audience reaction is susceptible to many variations, since you can arrange any context. Precise experiments can easily be carried out with an 8-millimeter camera, a few subjects, some test pictures, and selected audiences. You can show your audience pictures, preferably pictures to which they will have strong and varied reactions. They can be still or moving pictures. For instance, you can photograph an audience and then show the pictures to another audience and ask them to guess what the first group of people were watching. Or you can film an audience's reaction to a disorienting variation of a sound track. For example, the audience may be watching what they think at first is a normal television program, but you've inserted your own prerecorded sound track that you've arranged so that it is progressively more inappropriate and outrageous. In other experiments, you can insert overt sex scenes in a totally different type of film or you can have the schoolteacher in a western lapse into four-letter words. Then, with a video camera, you can capture the moment when your audience finally realizes there's something a bit strange about the film.

Audience reaction to films involves the whole complex mechanism of perception, and, as I pointed out, what viewers see is conditioned by what they expect to see, which in turn is determined by the sound track and by context. Let's go back to the experiment of splicing scenes in front of shots of an actor's face, where the audience supplies the appropriate expression—love, grief, horror—an expression that is not there. You can carry this experiment further. Put your actors in situations in which their faces show very definite expressions. Photograph expressions of people making love.

Photograph expressions of people playing poker, committing a murder, or simply relaxing in a friendly context. Now, shift the scenes around so that the orgasm faces appear at the poker table; the friendly, relaxed faces are murdering someone; and the poker faces are situated in what would normally be a friendly, relaxed context. How far will the audience go in altering the expressions to suit the context? At first, I thought that orgasm faces at the poker table might be carrying the experiment too far; but after looking at the expressions in some photos in sex magazines, I decided that the new context wouldn't be so outrageous after all. Murderous and sexual expressions, of course, are quite interchangeable.

Well, those are some simple experiments in audience interpretation, reaction, and perception. Of course, they could be carried much further with psychogalvanometers or with any reaction detectors. With encephalographic equipment, you could establish an exact correlation between sound and image and the physiological and psychological reactions of the audience.

You can also observe the reactions of subjects who do not know that they are being observed and do not know that they are reacting to an environment you have created. The simplest form of this experiment can be carried out with a tape recorder. You walk down a street and record the street sounds and conversations. Now make the same walk playing back the tape that you have just recorded in the street. What is happening? As long as you adjust the sound level to that of the new street sounds and you move quickly and unobtrusively, adjusting the volume as you go, people hearing the tape will not detect that they are listening to prerecorded sounds. They will think they are hearing actual street sounds and scraps of conversation.

You are throwing a whole, unreal environment around the people you pass, and consciously or unconsciously, they are reacting to this environment. You are tampering with the so-called reality of the people you pass. You are affecting them without their knowledge.

Now, you can also photograph their reactions if you hide the camera and tape recorder. Or you can do a spectacular, using whole truckloads of hidden equipment and covering one street for hours, days, or even months. Then you select the most interesting material from the footage you have taken.

Let's also consider some experiments in deliberately upsetting and deranging the audience. The results could ultimately break down preconceived notions and make way for new film forms. These experiments could take the form of the double bind, as set forth by Gregory Bateson and R. D. Laing. With the double bind, people are subjected to a set of contradictory statements or attitudes expressed by authority figures: "Pay close attention; this is not important." "This is serious; I am joking." And so forth. A simple form of the double bind in film would be friendly and unfriendly words and faces alternating at rapid intervals. If you wanted to make those at one-frame intervals, it would be quite upsetting to watch, I think. "Yes. No. I love you. I hate you." This is basically alternating current. You can carry the experiment much further with friendly faces and unfriendly words; unfriendly faces and friendly words; lynch mobs uttering benedictions and singing lullabies and angelic, kind faces screaming threats and insults. An extreme form of the double bind is the alternation of sex and violence; you soften the audience with pornography and then hit them with a nightstick until they realize there is no sex theme and no theme of violence at all, just images.

Anyone with a movie camera can play God; he can slow time down, speed it up, run it backwards, and he can literally stop the sun in the sky. So he might as well use his prerogative as God to invent, create, and experiment with the film medium.

Devices for Successful Screenwriting

For centuries artists have been asking themselves and have been asked by those who, as they put it, work for a living, "Exactly what are you doing and why?" What socially useful function does art serve? We are not in a position to answer that question and to stop apologizing for our existence or to take refuge in the untenable vacuum of art for art's sake. Recent research into dreams and sleep has demonstrated that dreams are a biological necessity for all warm-blooded animals. Deprived of REM sleep, that is, dream sleep, animals and humans show all the symptoms of sleeplessness, no matter how much dreamless sleep they are allowed. And the relation between dreams and art is very close. In fact, you could say that a dream serves as a model for creativity. So, if art serves somewhat the same biological function as a dream and is equally necessary (and, in fact, no culture has been found, no matter how primitive, that does not have some form of artistic expression)—if it serves a definite purpose—then it can be judged on how well it serves that purpose.

Now, it would seem that the sound film is a relative newcomer to the artistic scene. But this is not so, since the whole concept of the sound film is implicit in painting and picture writing, and before that, way back in the first warm-blooded animals, in the form of dreams, for dreams are in fact, talking films. Now, all warm-blooded animals dream; cold-blooded animals don't dream—at least those that have been tested so far don't dream. Certainly one of the functions of art—and I see this as sort of an evolutionary function—is to objectify some implicit process of perception (in the form of a book, painting, or film) so that we see something that we have been seeing without knowing it; that is, when it's put in front of us, we realize, "Well, I have been seeing this without knowing it."

Yet to call the attention of the public to what they themselves see every day is in some cases to invite the most vindictive and scurrilous hatred. At early exhibitions of abstract art, the viewers would sometimes attack the canvases with their umbrellas. They were so annoyed at having abstract paintings presented as art when they were used to paintings of cows in the grass. In the Middle Ages, people living on the seacoast probably knew that the world was round, but they said they believed the earth was flat. To say or demonstrate, at that time, that the world was round could have resulted in the most drastic penalties, due to the teachings of the Church. That's precisely the function of art, to jar the viewer or reader into awareness of what he is actually aware of already on some level, no matter how uncomfortable the revelation may be. So, science has been acting in concert with art, since the function of both is to make the viewer or the reader more aware of his own perceptions.

WILLIAM S. BURROUGHS

At first, motion pictures were simply something that could be done, a trick; and that was enough in the beginning, since people were impressed just to see this done. The locomotive coming right for the audience made people shriek and shrink away—but not for long. Soon the public became tired of movies being simply demonstrations that people and objects could be made to move on screen, and later actors talked. And they talked too much at first. But long before the advent of the sound film, the public demanded a story in the movies they watched, and the screenwriter came into being—a writer, as we will see, quite different from the novelist. At first, the screenwriter was often the director as well. Some directors required only a few notes on the back of an envelope to shoot a scene. But as time went on, the license of film to present anything on screen, no matter how poor the quality, began to wear out. Take a look at some productions from the 1930s and see what writers and directors could get away with in those days in the way of creaky plots and banal dialogue. The screenwriter has become more and more important; the screenplay is now the first step in making any film. Until the producer has a screenplay—whether it's done by a screenwriter or by the director—the picture cannot be budgeted and cast.

Writing for film is quite different from any other form of writing. It is unlike writing a novel, although at first glance it may seem the same. George Bluestone quoted D. W. Griffith as having said, "The task I'm trying to achieve is above all to make you see."[4] And Joseph Conrad, in the preface to *The Nigger of the Narcissus* (1897), stated, "My task which I am trying to achieve is, by the power of the written word, to make you hear, to make you feel—it is before all to make you *see*."[5] However, it is quite a different kind of seeing. When you read a novel—that is, if the writer is good—you *are* seeing a "film," but you are seeing it in your own mind. There's quite a difference between seeing it on the screen and seeing it in your mind.

When I was teaching creative writing I came to doubt whether any technology of writing could be taught. Perhaps "creative writing" is too vague and too general. But there is a very definite technology for writing filmscripts, and it can be taught. Perhaps attempting to write a filmscript is one of the quickest ways to find out if you are cut out to be a writer, if writing could be your profession, because there are standards by which you can judge your success. The tests of successful novel or poetry writing are not nearly as clear. If a man is called upon to build a bridge and the bridge falls down, there's something wrong with his viewpoint and his blueprint. But if his blueprints are never put to the test of actual construction, he might spend a lifetime doing something that he is not cut out to do.

The test of a successful screenplay is what the film looks like on screen, not what the screenplay looks like on paper. That is, beautifully written sentences don't mean anything so far as a filmscript goes, because the script isn't to be read, it's to be put on the screen. Is it a good film according to the rules of film structure? And if it violates those rules, are the violations justified and valid? Novel and short-story writers may assume that they know how to write filmscripts. But they may find, as I did, that they have to learn how to write filmscripts just as an airplane pilot would have to learn how to fly a helicopter. I found that some of the filmscript ideas I had that I thought were new were not at all new and also were not good. When I wrote *The Last Words of Dutch Schultz* (1970), I knew nothing about writing filmscripts. There are a lot of ideas in that book that are not viable for a film; whatever it may be, it is not a viable filmscript. For example, I thought that mixing black and white and color was a good idea. Well, it's not; it's been tried—in *If . . .* (Lindsay Anderson, 1969), for example—and it doesn't work very well. Now, just because something's been tried and doesn't work doesn't mean that it couldn't work—just that it hasn't worked to date.

Another technique in *The Last Words of Dutch Schultz* (one that I suggested for *Junkie* when I was working with Terry Southern, who's an old hand at writing scripts) was to use the same character playing several different roles. Now, of course, Southern did that himself in *Dr. Strangelove* (Kubrick, 1963), where Peter Sellers played three parts; but I meant the same person who is recognizable as the same person. For example, a snotty doctor who refuses to write a narcotics scrip and calls the police would be played by and recognized as the same actor who plays a narcotics agent. Terry said,

"No, no, no; it's just going to confuse the audience." And you don't want to confuse the audience, not if you're writing a commercial filmscript.

But didn't I just say that the function of art is to increase awareness even if the audience is made to feel uncomfortable? Well, I'm talking now about a commercial script, and before you're really able to jolt the people in an audience you need to know how to please them. Rules are made to be broken, but not to be disregarded.

Now to consider characters further. In a film, you can't describe your characters as you can in a novel. A film doesn't describe; it *is*. You can't say, "George is an old man." You have to show him as an old man. It's a good idea to have a dossier on each of your characters including all of the traits you can think of, even if you don't intend to show all these in the film. That is, you should make a sort of composite picture of each character, his habits, etcetera. It will give you a much clearer idea of your characters and how to handle them.

Here is a scene from *Junkie* that shows the lack of fear in one of the characters. The scene takes place in the Angle Bar, and Whitey, who is six feet, three inches tall and weighs two hundred pounds, all bone and muscle, with nasty, white pig eyes and no more control over his aggression than a baboon, is stomping up and down the bar, sweeping people's change into his big, dirty hand. So all up and down the bar the customers sit hunched over, trying to disappear into their bar seats, as they surreptitiously pocket their change. Only Roy, at the end of the bar, leaves his change on the bar. He's characterized, then, by something he doesn't do—by the fact that he doesn't remove his change. And that establishes Roy's character, that he is the one person in the bar not afraid of Whitey. In other words, you want to establish a character as quickly as possible in terms of something he does or says.

Another example: Here's a fluffy blonde ruffling a boy's hair as she intones, "I love you, anyhoo, but where have you been and stuff?" Well, she's the kind of girl who says "anyhoo" and "and stuff." She's characterized by what she says. Beware, young man, there she is ten years from now fat as a pig, sitting on her chintzy pillows with an asthmatic Pekinese dog, gin bottles hidden all over the house. Supper is canned tuna soufflé; she got the recipe from the evening news. Now, she has served the tuna soufflé, one time too many, and he says, "I'm gonna kill you and stuff." And he starts chasing her around the house with a boning knife.

Now here's another man succinctly defined by one action. He's the real-life proprietor of a bar in Paris, one of the nastiest people in the city. His bar is called Lips, and only certain people can get in. You know the type. The lucky ones are in the front room, and the Americans and the tourists, "the scum of the earth," as he puts it, are upstairs. So here's a young American coming down from the second floor, and the proprietor bars his way to the sanctum of the front room, which is reserved for politicians, journalists, and French writers. So he stands there in front of the guy and just raises an eyebrow—doesn't say a word—and the young American stammers something about going to the toilet. Slowly, like an old dog roused from sleep, the proprietor moves out of the way. You see, it's all in that arched eyebrow. You need his permission to go to the john in his trap. Just that one silent shot shows the whole character of the man. He could be a secret agent in this film, and the gauche young man, who is with the Central Intelligence Agency, will get him back later.

Filmscript writers, with their emphasis on movement, tend to set up some sort of separation between words and action, forgetting that words *are* action, that there's no distinction whatever between action and words. Whether your character is delineated by a raised eyebrow, by leaving his change on the bar, or by saying "anyhoo," the point is that you define the character by something he does or says, something only that character would do or say.

Dialogue is supposed to move, and these days the rules say it's supposed to be short. But these rules are not always valid. When the talkies first came in, characters in them made long speeches. Then the line between plays and films began breaking down. Now the trend is for very short dialogue—the shorter the better.

But whether they give their characters long speeches or short, writers need something called "an ear for dialogue." John O'Hara had it; F. Scott Fitzgerald didn't and neither did Ernest Hemingway.

Having an ear for dialogue simply means that the writer keeps his ears open and derives much of his dialogue from what people actually said at some time in his hearing, maybe years ago. Once you've got a character saying something in his very own words, you can elaborate. As you write dialogue and read it aloud, your ear will tell you whether or not it is right. When I started doing readings and was using mostly dialogue material, I learned that if dialogue doesn't sound right read aloud, it isn't written right. Similarly, if it sounds wrong, then it isn't exactly what your character would say.

List your characters and ask yourself, "What is each character doing at this moment of the picture or what might the characters be doing?" If you're concentrating on the main characters in the scene, you'll tend to forget that other characters could be brought in. What are they doing? Are they just sitting around? You need to think about what will be seen on the screen at all times.

Screenwriters are preoccupied with action—what is being done and said—and I think they fail to realize that what someone does not say or does not do may tell more about his character and advance the action further than what he actually says or does. I gave the example of Roy leaving his change on the bar. Here's another example: The camera picks out a corpse, the face eaten by rats. A man passes with a briefcase. He glances casually at the corpse with a slight purse of his lips, indicating distaste. These shots tell you something about both the character and the setting: that the man has no compassion and that corpses are commonplace at the time the scene unfolds. Then we see an armored band roaming city streets, twenty-dollar bills lying in the gutter, and the people glancing down at the money but walking by. Now, this tells you something more about the setting: that it's some future time when money is worthless.

Look at some of the differences between a novel and a screenplay. There is a different way of seeing and also a different appeal. That is, the filmscript must appeal to a much wider audience than the novel. Also, those people who have bought a novel are already predisposed to be interested. A box-office failure reaches many more people than even a best-selling novel.

Still more important is the gap between the screenplay and

what appears on the screen as a finished film. Now, a writer writes a novel the way he wants it; and there it is; the publisher, in some cases, may want some rewriting, but generally the writer does not have his work heavily edited. But rewriting is almost always required in a filmscript, which brings us to the most important difference between a novel and a screenplay: A screenplay is not a finished product. It is a stage in a process involving many artisans other than the writer. There are as many as thirty stages. When you're writing a filmscript, you have someone looking over your shoulder and saying, "Well, the studio doesn't like that; we don't want it." And you may come back from lunch to find someone else's idea right in the middle of your filmscript. As they say in Hollywood, good filmscripts are not written, they are rewritten, sometimes as often as five or six times.

Kerouac always said that the first version is always the best. I don't find this true in novels, but he did, and that's a perfectly valid way to write a novel. But no one can write a filmscript that way. The first version is usually only to get your ideas out there where you can see them. Then you can stand back and look, and you can see that one of the scenes you liked so much just does not belong in the film, and that certain characters have to be changed or combined with other characters. (This sort of hybrid character, made of two or three characters squashed together, occurs all the time in filmscripts.)

The director may request one kind of a rewrite: "This is a good script, but it simply isn't the type of film I can make." A change of actors may necessitate another kind of rewriting. For example, you may have good dialogue, but if your actor can't say it, what good is it? Or, you may have written a part for a specific actor, and in the middle of the film, or long before your script is finished, a different actor replaces the one you had in mind.

Now let's consider some of the rules for writing screenplays. How do you begin? The first step is to write your film idea in one sentence. It's very important to be able to say in one sentence what the film is about, both when you are writing a so-called original screenplay and when you are doing an adaptation from a novel or a play. What is *The Great Gatsby* (Brenon, 1926, Nugent, 1949, and Clayton, 1974) about? Poor boy, rich girl. *Panic in Needle Park* (Schatzberg, 1971) was described as Romeo and Juliet on junk. Now, this one-sentence rundown can be put in other ways, such as, "What if . . . ?" "What if a Jewish boy married an Irish girl?" That was *Abie's Irish Rose* (Sutherland, 1946). The "what if" always contains the seeds of the difficulties that will animate the film. Remember, when there is no trouble, there's no action; and when there's no action, there's no film. Or you can put it this way: "What is the hero or heroine trying to do, and who or what is keeping him or her from doing it?"

After you have your film idea down to one sentence, you can expand it to three or four pages, giving the barest outline of the film. This is the film idea. The next step is to write a film treatment of thirty pages or so; then a film synopsis; and finally a screenplay. Shooting the script is generally left to the director now, and the director generally doesn't want the writer telling him what camera angles he should use. In fact, after they have the screenplay, most directors prefer not to have the writer on the set at all.

How do you generate a screen story? You use the old Hollywood springboard—the one-sentence summary—and pray there's water in the pool. I learned about Hollywood in just three days. Terry Southern and I had gone there trying to sell the script for *The Naked Lunch* to someone named Chuck Barris, and we were met at the airport by a Daimler and a saluting chauffeur. Two days later the studio's decision about our script was spelled out for us in Hollywood language. When our Daimler shrank down to a two-seater, we knew the studio didn't like this script and it was time to move fast. They'd already frozen our bar bill.

So you run the film backwards to the springboard. Now you pick a topic that interests you. Then you try to view the topic from unique angles.

This one-sentence procedure is even more useful if you're adapting a novel into a film. With an original screenplay, you're already thinking in screen terms, and you will probably have started with a topic and a question. But when you consider a complex novel with a lot of subplots and mysterious, unexplained incidents, it may not be so easy to cook it down to the springboard question.

Many novels are about a number of different things, so you really have to simplify the novel to one sentence or your screenplay will flounder.

The summary is also what sells a film to the viewer, whether on the billboard or by word of mouth. What is this film about? It's about a shark that bites people in two. The movie is all very realistic—and it's enough to scare people out of the water.

A related film device is the running gag. This is a motif that goes through the film to a final payoff. All running gags must pay off. Do you remember the man in *Hellzapoppin* (H. C. Potter, 1941) who kept carrying a plant around, trying to give it to one of the actors? The plant keeps growing; it grows into a tree over the course of the film. Or do you recall the girl nobody knew who kept coming in and out of the party? She's finally revealed to be the assistant producer's girlfriend. Now, running gags are not always comic; they can be simply a recurrent motif, like the tapping of the blind man's cane in *The Informer* (Ford, 1935). Very often the running gag is a mannerism of an actor, like George Raft flipping the coin.

There's an expanded version of the one-sentence summary known as the Weanie or the McGuffin or the Switcheroo. It summarizes the mainspring of the action, the secret formula that everyone is looking for, or the plans. All of Hitchcock's movies are based on Weanies. Here's an example of a Weanie. It's a film idea that I used in a column in *Crawdaddy:* "What if a sure, painless cure for drug addiction were discovered? And then, what if not only the Mafia and the pushers but also the narcotics agents and the Central Intelligence Agency tried to stop this cure?" So you have not only the pusher but the clean-cut agent as well trying to block the cure for addiction, which would put him out of business. Of course, the Weanie is not used for all types of films; it's mostly in serials, mysteries, westerns, and all spy pictures.

Now to consider the plant and payoff. This technique is used in all films and in all novels. Someone said that if you show a dagger on the wall in the first act it should be used for killing somebody in the last act. That's the plant and payoff. The plant is something to which your attention is called, perhaps at the beginning of a film.

The payoff occurs when that thing becomes important later on. The plant should not be telegraphed. That is, when people see the plant, they should not know what is going to happen; they should not know what the payoff is. The running gag, rather similar to the plant, must also have a payoff.

In a film, the camera can zero in on the plant. You can't do that in a play. Of course, you can also zero in on a plant in a novel, but you do it with words. Fake plants are confusing to the audience and will always be resented. That is, if you focus in on something and there's no payoff, the audience is going to feel, quite rightly, that they've been cheated. Your plant cannot be too obvious, but it has to be obvious enough that the audience will remember it. There's a very fine line there. The payoff should always elicit a sense of surprise recognition: "Yes, that's just right, and I see it now at the payoff." If you see a plant before the payoff, you can, of course, avoid the payoff, as when a man remembers the sound of the ticking watch he heard that morning and then realizes there's a time bomb in the room. And, of course, the plant can be verbal. It can be a sound. It doesn't have to be purely visual.

The plant and the payoff also happen all the time in real life. Something you noticed, you don't know quite why, becomes important later. To give an example: I was living in New Orleans about twenty-five years ago. I was thinking about going into raising ramie; that's the hardest fabric known. I went looking for information about ramie, and I happened to walk into the office of a lawyer by mistake. He was the same lawyer my wife hired much later to defend me when I was in jail on narcotics charges. So he was the one I was really looking for, not this lost cause of ramie.

Another example is relayed in a book written about his illness by a man who had leprosy. Before telling you the example, let me say that leprosy is hardly contagious at all. Doctors don't know just how it is transmitted, but it's difficult to catch. Well, years before the man found out he had leprosy, he was riding his horse when it ran away with him on it. It took him to the gates of a leprosarium.

If you learn to recognize and use plants and payoffs in writing and film, you will also learn to recognize and use them in so-called real life. The screenwriter cultivates, as a matter of necessity, marginal thinking, because he's always looking for a new slant on his material. Marginal thinking helps you to solve many problems. If you're just dealing in sequential logical thought, you won't make it as a screenwriter, because you'll never come up with a new angle.

The flashback. Some people feel that the use of flashback destroys the illusion that the characters are real people in the immediate present. However, I don't think films could get along without flashbacks. A purist would say that the less you use flashbacks the better, that flashbacks do not happen in real life. Well, they do.

There are many types of problems in films that have never really properly been solved. One is how to show the passage of time. You know the old techniques of showing calendar leaves blowing off the wall and of showing the seasons changing. Both are very old and not very good, but it's hard to think of new techniques. If time is that which ends, which is my definition of time, then time is always limited. Thus, to show the passage of time, you can show anything running out—water, food, junk, oil, whatever—you need only show the process of running out. For example, say a guy cleans his apartment every two weeks; so you film the apartment dirty, then the apartment clean, and the apartment dirty again.

It is also difficult to show dreams, thoughts, and fantasies. You would think that film could show these abstractions, but they're very hard to convey. I had some experience attempting to do so in the *Junkie* script, and I found that the difficulty is that showing abstractions on film violates reality. A film looks real; to cut in something that isn't real is sort of disturbing, because it's artificial. That is, you're not actually screening a thought or a fantasy, you're constructing it and inserting it.

Climax and relief are very old devices. And films can't do without them. You've got to pick the audience up and let them down. If you hit them with one climax after another, the audiences get bored, and they won't sit still for it. Take the horse's head in *The Godfather* (Coppola, 1972)—you can't have a horse's head on every page in a novel, and you can't do it in every scene in a movie. You remember the scene in *Jaws* (Spielberg, 1975), in which teenagers put a fake fin in the water. Though it's meant as a joke, the people at the beach panic. Well, the teenagers' joke is actually about as funny as talking about a bomb on a plane or about malpractice in a hospital. But it's still a relief in comparison to the real thing. So the audience unwinds and relaxes as a result of that scene.

Now, relief doesn't always follow a climax. The filmmaker can simply shift to a different scene. For example, after a noisy, exciting car chase, the film may cut to birds singing as the hero and heroine wake up in the car in the early morning.

A purely episodic treatment doesn't work very well in films. You need some kind of climax. And there's such a thing as too much tension in the climax. There can also be too much relief if the climactic action goes on too long. You always have to remember that in a commercial film you're dealing with a segment of usually about ninety minutes.

The alternation of tension and release seems to happen in real life, too: A crisis in life is often followed by some sort of relief. Either you've solved the crisis or the whole situation has changed. Once you see this mechanism, it will teach you not to let the release put you too far off guard, since there's always another crisis on the way.

And this brings us to the finale of the film. The important thing about a finale is that it should wind the film up. Ask yourself what you want the audience to carry away from your film. What should the audience feel as they walk out? The finale should be impressive, and it should be positive. A very great error is made when a finale doesn't look like a finale. If the audience isn't quite sure the show is over, there have probably been too many or overemphasized climaxes prior to the finale. I remember an endless Japanese movie. I thought, "This has got to be the finale; he's committing hara-kiri." Then, "This must be it; she's on her deathbed;" and so on. But each time, the film continued. Of course, a conventional finale can be redeemed by a last-minute twist that the audience doesn't expect. Frederick Forsyth is good at that. I just read his novels *The Day of the Jackal* (1971), *Dogs of War* (1974), and *The Odessa File* (1972), and they all had little twists at the end that redeemed rather conventional windups.

Standard Rules and the Potentials of the Medium

Here are some standard rules for screenwriting. A moving film must move. Anything that slows down the action has to be cut. Every scene must either advance the action in some way or tell us something about the characters. Now, let's consider what can and cannot be done in film by differentiating between these rules, which are often put in dogmatic terms, and the devices, or tools, that allow you to use best the potentials of the medium. I'll give you examples of both rules and tools.

Dwight Swain cites a film writer who once told him, "In this business, `Can you do it in a hurry?' counts for a lot more than `Can you do it good?'"[6] That is, the ability to see the film potential in any situation and see it immediately is the scriptwriter's most highly valued skill. Swain also calls creativity "the major tool in (the scriptwriter's) craft-kit."[7] "The creative person," he says, is someone who is "conditioned to make multiple responses to single stimuli."[8] Show him a candlestick and he can come up with ten different ways of murdering someone with it. The creative filmscript writer is always juggling situations, moving them around. Take a newspaper story that has potential as film material: How many different slants can you think of on that particular story? There are exercises, tools, that I think are very useful. One is to leave a film two-thirds of the way through the picture and devise five alternative endings. Then go back and see if the writer has done as well as you have. Of course, you can do the same with novels. If you keep your eyes and your mind open you can come up with two or three film plots every day, actually. Some of them will be good and some of them will be very bad indeed. The source may be newspaper stories, overheard conversations, novels, films, dreams, fantasies.

Now, here's an example of some film ideas I came up with. I was reading a book called *The Ultimate Athlete* (1975), by George Leonard, and he was talking about his experiences with the civil rights movement. He describes a revolutionary technique, which I'd never heard of before, that was devised by a mathematician named Michael Roseman. The technique is, very simply, to use all of the facilities of a university or any other institution to bring it to a grinding halt. For example, everybody takes out all the books they can from the library. Everybody crowds into the study hall; they've got to expand the study hall. Everybody goes into the gymnasium. Leonard says he "can imagine no institution . . . that could survive being used to the full."[9] Now, this could become a film idea with the old "What if?" formula: There are three thousand people in jail in New York on looting charges. What if they all demanded jury trials, a demand that is certainly within their rights? They'd have the courts of New York tied up for twenty years. The whole system finally breaks down, and you have a massive confrontation. It could be a Stanley Kubrick spectacular. It's just a question of keeping your eyes open for ideas. This frame of mind is itself a tool.

"Dreams and memories . . . cannot be adequately represented in spatial terms. . . . (A film's) spatial devices . . . cannot render the conceptual feel of dreams and memories. The realistic tug of the film is too strong. . . . Proust and Joyce would seem as absurd on film as Chaplin would in print."[10] That quote is from George Bluestone. He's got some very sensible things to say in other connections, but this is a dogmatic, purely arbitrary opinion as to what films can and cannot do.

Bluestone also talks about the problems of turning a novel into a film, beginning with the difference between the imaginative seeing that you experience in a novel and the seeing of an actual visual image in a film. As you read a novel and see the action of the novel, you are not in the purely passive position of a viewer. In performing the act of reading, you are also performing the mental act of translating what you read into pictures, words, sounds, and so on. And, of course, different readers will see different pictures and will have different concepts of the characters in the novel. But once the novel is on the screen, whoever the viewers are, they're all seeing the same movie with the same actors. Of course, there'll be some differences in what the viewers notice or what interests them, but they are seeing the same movie. And they do not need to use their imagination to perform any act at all; they need only sit there and watch the screen. So, says Bluestone, the act of reading a novel involves symbolic thinking, which is peculiar to imaginative rather than visual activity.

Now, I would say that, more accurately, reading novels and watching films involve different and incompatible types of visual activity. Some filmscript writers are reluctant to admit that any visual activity exists apart from watching the screen. They are afraid that people will eventually learn how to make their own films in their own heads, just as some doctors are afraid a great cure-all will be discovered and put them out of business.

But the imaginative activity that takes place when you read a novel is certainly visual, in part. You are seeing the scenes and characters of the novel. It would, however, be difficult to carry on such imaginative activity if you were watching a film at the same time. In other words, it's visual activity in both cases, but the two activities are quite incompatible. A film aspires to provide maximum distraction.

Citing Virginia Woolf's statement, "All this, which is accessible to words, and to words alone, the cinema must avoid," Bluestone goes on to claim that "the rendition of mental states cannot be as adequately represented by film as by language."[11] Well, you have to avoid rendering mental states or else find an adequate way of representing them; otherwise, you're going to end up with a debacle like the film version of *The Great Gatsby*.

> Gatsby believed in the green light, the orgiastic future
> that year by year recedes before us. It eluded us then,
> but that's no matter—tomorrow we will run faster, stretch
> out our arms farther. . . . And one fine morning—
>   So we beat on, boats against the current, borne
> back ceaselessly into the past.[12]

The whole charm and point of this novel lies in the prose, which is not really translatable. I don't say it's impossible, but a way hasn't been found to translate passages like the end of *The Great Gatsby* into film terms.

Now, what about the problem of the voice-over? This device violates the dogma that a film has a reality or at least creates the illusion of reality, of real people in real situations in the immediate present. Where is this voice-over coming from? And what is the voice-over doing? In this case, obviously, it's reading a novel. The narrator in a novel from which a film is made is, generally speaking, an unmentionable subject for the film itself. As in *Junkie*: What is Lee doing collecting material for a novel? The novel should not be referred to in the film. So a voice-over is really no solution. And if you try to take those sentences and turn them into little pieces of film, it just doesn't look like anything.

The scriptwriter has to come up with something seemingly new. One way of accomplishing this is with the hook, the striking scene at the beginning of a film that is meant to immediately involve the audience and pull them into the screen. It shouldn't be too striking, unless you're prepared to follow up with things that are even more striking; otherwise the film will never live up to the hook.

Now, crises can be too far apart or close together. Either way is bad. If you get too many crises piling up, people soon get very tired of them. They get apathetic. And if there are not enough crises, then the action drags.

The flashback and flashforward. Consider Lewis Herman. He's pretty hard-core. His rules are hard and dogmatic and apply strictly to commercial films. "Realism is often killed," he says, "with still another popular device, the flashback. . . . The flashback impedes motion. . . . Flashbacks fritter suspense."[13] You see, the audience wants to know what happens next, not what happened before. According to Herman, "It is the motion picture's task to create . . . the illusion . . . that the shadows . . . on the screen are real people undergoing real experiences, *in the immediate present.*"[14] In other words, the audience has to believe what they know to be untrue. They must maintain this illusion to maintain their interest in the film. And the flashback, he adds, does not occur in real life. Well, as I've said, it certainly does occur in real life. Herman doesn't even consider the flashforward, which, I suppose, he would think further violates this illusion of immediacy.

But both flashbacks and flashforwards occur all the time in real life, and it's pretty difficult to write a film without the flashback. I would say that flashbacks actually happen every second. Every time you perform a simple action, say, like drinking water, you're activating a whole network of associations of the millions of times in your life you have performed this action and the contexts in which it was performed. Now, can these associations be represented on screen? Anthony Balch and I did some experiments in which we tried to do exactly that, and I'll discuss them later.

Of all these rules, then, some of them, under the heading of tools (or devices), are valid, and some of them are arbitrary. But you do need to know the rules and the reasons behind them.

Adaptation

No doubt several alternative and successful filmscripts could be based on the same novel. If you took the actual filmscript of *Jaws* and tried to turn it back into a novel, with no reference to the actual novel and just the filmscript as your given material, you would most likely end up with a very dull novel and also quite a short one. In translating a filmscript into a novel, you have to take the same liberties with your material as a scriptwriter takes with a novel. Because there's less to go on, you can write more novels from filmscripts than filmscripts from novels. "Beware of too many characters"—that's one of the rules of scriptwriting. It's a pretty good one, because if you get too many characters, people can't keep track of them. A mistake scriptwriters often make when turning a novel into a filmscript is shoving several often completely incompatible characters into the same persona. Conversely, when turning a filmscript into a novel, you can take a character and split him into two or three characters. You could alter your characters and make them more complex or you could introduce unexplained incidents.

Joseph Wambaugh started out as a cop and ended up a multimillionaire writer of best-selling novels about cops. His novel *The New Centurions* (1970) is written according to the best-seller formula: Write something that people know something about and want to know more about. For some reason, people always want to know about cops. A lot of them are cop lovers, I guess. Well, in the novel the reason for Kilvinsky's suicide is never apparent. He is described as a mysterious and secretive man. But in the film (*The New Centurions*, Richard Fleischer, 1972) he is turned into a very simple character played by George C. Scott, and the reasons for his suicide are as obvious as Hollywood can make them. It's a drastic, surgical simplification of a character. You have only an hour and a half in a film, so every word must count.

There are all sorts of transitions between novels and filmscripts. I wrote a script from a science fiction novel called *Blade Runner* (1982).[15] This novel is set in a future time when medicine has gone underground because some professor or theoretician has demonstrated that medical advances, in the long run, lead to more illness; by saturating the population with antibiotics, their natural resistance is lowered, so that epidemics can break out at any time. So the premise of the book is that no medical service will be extended to anyone who does not first agree to be sterilized. Those who refuse are serviced by underground doctors who are supplied with medicine and instruments by blade runners. Well, I turned this into a filmscript, and Kubrick made it into a spectacular that would be filmed in the ruins of Manhattan devastated by health act riots. (Filming those riots alone would cost five million dollars.) On Rudy Wurlitzer's advice, I dropped the idea of producing this lavish and impractical film. He said, "You've got twenty million dollars to spend already—and you'll have to tear down New York for this film." So I'm now turning the script into a novel with another title.

It often happens, with a science fiction novel or any novel, that the filmscript idea is quickly developed to a point where it has little or nothing to do with the novel. So why bother to keep the original title or pay for the idea? Steal anything in sight. In this case, the novel was simply a springboard. After all, the work of other writers is one of a writer's main sources of input, so don't hesitate to use it; just because somebody else has an idea doesn't mean you can't take that idea and develop a new twist for it. Adaptations may become quite legitimate adoptions.

Short stories are frequently made into films. Take two examples of really horrible adaptations: Hemingway's "The Snows of Kilimanjaro" (1936) and "The Killers" (1927). Just as I blame Christ for the atrocities committed in his name, so I blame Hemingway for letting Hollywood butcher his work so that he could go around shooting animals and catching marlins. Now, "The Snows of Kilimanjaro," to my mind one of the better stories in the language about death, has a great ending: a phantom plane and the pilot pointing toward the snows of Kilimanjaro. And what happens in the film? A real pilot flies in with penicillin. Boy! It was the worst film ever based on one of Hemingway's works. "The Killers" is a beautiful short story but simply is redundant as a film. Exactly enough information is conveyed in the story; in the film, the question of why the killers are after the former prize-fighter is simply not interesting—it's sort of tacked on.

Generally speaking, though not always, good movie adaptations are made from bad books. I think this is partly because screenwriters feel they can take any liberties with second-rate books. The fatal sentiment, "We're gonna make a classic, B. J.," doesn't develop, which is good because such "classics" are, generally speaking, bad films that don't even make money, like *The Great Gatsby*. That's what happens when Hollywood sets out to make a classic.

The Informer is much better on the screen than it is as a novel. The film version is actually, of course, a new creation developed under Ford's direction. The same is true of *The Treasure of the Sierra Madre* (Huston, 1948). After seeing the film, I read the book, and the book just doesn't come up to the film.

Experimentation and Subliminal Perception

How successful has the underground art film been as an alternative to the commercial film? All the rules that I've discussed are aimed at doing a commercially viable film. Experimental films, which presumably are not concerned with commercial viability, have an entirely different set of criteria. For example, in the experimental films that I did with Anthony Balch, we were trying to expand the awareness of the audience by experimenting with the film medium. It's been said that the conscious, logical part of the mind is like the tip of the iceberg that appears above the water. What we were trying to do was jar people into an awareness of the area under the water by actually showing them mechanisms of perception that, of course, go on all the time. And we succeeded to some extent.

By making explicit the fragmentary nature of consciousness, we managed to arouse and upset the audience, just as viewers were upset by the first exhibitions of abstract paintings. I don't think these films shown at the present time would produce such strong reactions because the experiments developed have now been used in commercial films.

In our experimental films, we also went back to the basic premise of film: the retention of the image. Film is based on the fact that you retain an image in your mind for one-tenth of a second, so that images that are actually still, when presented in sequence, will seem to move. And we showed this by having a delayed image. You see someone reaching for a glass, and you also see the one-tenth-of-a-second lag—sort of a shadowy figure—behind that. This is actually what is happening all the time in film.

There's another type of cinema that would seem to offer a possibility for alternative film, so-called cinema verité, where you ignore the process of filming as much as possible. Instead of roping off a street to cut off any random intrusions, you leave the film open to chance encounters.

Cinema verité seems to me to be an ideal testing ground for getting synchronicity into films. It's a very important part of our experience and has not really been shown very precisely in films. Here's an example of an exercise I've given to students. Just take a walk around town, keeping your eyes open, observing what you see. Then come back and write down what you have just seen, paying particular attention to what you were thinking when you saw each thing. These thoughts are intersection points—those points where your stream of consciousness intersects with so-called objective reality. It is at these points of intersection that you will observe the process of synchronicity. Exactly what were you thinking, feeling, remembering when somebody dropped a plate, for example? Very often you'll find yourself saying, "Now, that's something that hasn't been used in films."

The observation of synchronicity, I think, could lead to a whole new film language. For example, in 1968 in Chicago I was asking myself what the role was of a certain cult leader—who shall remain nameless—and just then a police car passed, which told me, in the language of synchronicity, "He's a cop." When people first start noticing synchronous events, they think they're going crazy. I've had people come up to me and say, "Every street sign says something to me." "Of course," I say; "Who else is seeing the signs?" Remember, you don't see everything on the street; you see what you want to see, what means something to you.

However, even if you accept synchronicity as a fact, how can this process be represented on the screen? What actually happens in your mind, and how could this event be effectively transferred to the screen? Take the man walking down the street: How did the cult leader come into his mind? He can't remember exactly. We're in difficulty right away with a script full of holes. Well, you can shoot your film that way, showing a script actually full of holes and whirlwinds of word and image, but that's very hard to do. Or, you can show it as a sort of animation: the music-box routine where tinsel figures revolve in time to the sound track. The cult leader's picture appears on the screen, and then the police car . . .

With cinema verité, you can show the random intrusions as they actually happen. Of course, you're not going to do that unless you can conceal your photographic equipment. I think that cinema verité filmmakers are too eager to work with no script at all. They get to the filming location and then just sort of mill around. If you have a very definite script, but one that is still open enough that you don't rope off the streets, you might get some interesting encounters.

Of course, art films have much less circulation than commercial films. But if they're good, the devices used in them are sooner or later absorbed into commercial films. None of those devices, though, are altogether satisfactory, because we can't as yet photograph thoughts or feelings directly. A film shows surfaces. It doesn't show what people think.

Anthony Balch and I used another device to bring up the whole matter of identity in a film called *Bill and Tony*. We showed Anthony's face projected onto mine and mine onto his. When his face was projected onto my face, the image looked like him. Then we switched the voices around, so that sometimes I had Anthony's face and my voice and sometimes his face and my voice, and so on. It was all done with projections. Now, this technique, which can only be done with color, not black and white, could be used for all kinds of Jekyll-and-Hyde effects, as well as for horror stories.

A lot of what passes for historical fact may be, in fact, distorted. History—a lot of it—is simply rumor and hearsay. You can carry the walk exercise that I mentioned when talking about synchronicity much further with film and sound. Anthony Balch and I got some interesting intersections that way. For example, I was across Piccadilly, and Anthony was filming from the other side of the intersection. I had stopped under one of those news banners, but it was above and behind me, so I couldn't see it. I raised my hat to Anthony just to acknowledge that I saw him; but when the film was projected, just as I raised my hat, the words "Sir William" could be seen on the news banner.

As soon as you start an exercise in synchronicity, even the walk exercise, you'll begin to notice all these intersections. In this instance with Anthony, we had the minimal film context: director, photographer, and actor. Now, what if there's only one person involved and he's director/photographer walking around with his camera? Say, a Coca-Cola truck passes, and that reminds him of a T-shirt with "Cocaine Is The Real Thing" written on it. Now, you could splice in a chorus line of T-shirts to indicate that this association had been made. Of course, you haven't solved the problem of photographing an event that occurs in the brain. You have simply indicated the event with contrived surface images. Unless you have some way of differentiating between the association and the actual event, viewers will get very confused. They will think that people are dancing around in cocaine T-shirts on the street. All devices for indicating mental associations are hard to use; it's hard to make them not seem contrived.

So, with synchronicity we have pinpointed a process that goes on all the time, but we have not found a precise way to indicate it in film terms.

Now, Hollywood has always been a money-making industry dedicated to the proposition that what *has* made money *will* make money. Even if that hasn't always proven true, Hollywood still believes it. So, experiments in film have not been reinforced. When directors have used new techniques, they have tended to keep them to themselves; that is, if a director's got some little trick for doing something, as a rule he doesn't tell people about it. There is a basic incompatibility between experimentation and producing a commercial film. It's hard to stay under budget with a film using conventional techniques; there's simply not enough time or money to try new techniques that might not work out. It isn't the time to get too experimental.

Ideally, an institute for pure cinema research would be set up so that filmmakers and others could perform experiments in film techniques without having to consider immediate uses for the techniques—as has been done with physics and the natural sciences. No doubt, many of the discoveries of such an institute would be counterindicated for public performances, and the institute would have to use volunteer test audiences. The actual performance before an audience is very important, since it's the basic test of any film device. I think one of the important subjects that could be studied is time. Filmmakers still haven't come up with a new way to indicate the passage of time, insisting that the actual experience of time cannot be photographed. Why can't it? I think it can and has been photographed. In the famous massacre scene on the Odessa steps in *Potemkin* (1925), I'm sure Eisenstein was using some of these time tricks.

In *The Writer and the Screen* (1973), W. P. Rilla discusses some of the time tricks that are in use today.[16] Let's say we want to show a man getting dressed. The length of time it takes for him to dress would be, say, ten minutes. Well, that's too long for the film; so we reduce the film segment to three minutes. In other words, we want three minutes that will give the impression of ten minutes. The audience will believe that they've seen everything the man has done getting dressed while we've actually shown only part of the sequence. For instance, a close-up shows his hands putting on the first shoe and beginning to tie its laces. We cut to his face and show its concentrated, immobile expression. In a scene like that, the filmmaker is probably using slow motion on the face; it definitely gives you a sense of more time passing. Now, suppose his face were speeded up. Would the contrary be experienced? We don't know. That film experiment would have to be carried out with test audiences. Would the audiences think the screen time was shorter than it actually was?

The subliminal image, which has been outlawed, could also be reevaluated experimentally. A subliminal image is an image that is on the screen at the borderline of conscious perception. The idea is that any suggestion at that level would act directly on the unconscious, and people would have a tremendous compulsion to go out and buy Coca-Cola or whatever was shown. Well, the question is open. I know that Anthony Balch, who actually ran a theater, tried this, and he said it didn't work at all. The advertising industry was terrified of the whole thing, since it could make them look like sinister manipulators of the public mind. Very bad PR. I don't know if any experiments have ever been carried out to find just how effective subliminal images are.

Say you have a film in which there is no danger on the screen—for instance, some bland documentary about happy peasants; at the same time you show horrible images of death and violence on the subliminal level. Would the subliminal images affect the audience? Would they experience any uneasiness or anxiety? Would they suspect that their feelings were the result of a film trick?[17]

Waking suggestion is a very different thing. That can easily be done on the screen, too. It simply means that while your attention is engaged on one point, a suggestion is made from another. Say I was giving a lecture here, and at the same time voices were coming from microphones positioned in the audience, repeating suggestions at my voice level. If you were paying attention to the lecture, you wouldn't hear those suggestions consciously, though you would immediately hear them if I stopped talking. In other words, they're not at the subliminal level at all; they are simply at a level that is above the noise level around you.

Let's suppose a film does use horrible subliminal images. Would the film continue to produce anxiety on repeated showings? Or suppose the horrible subliminals were shown to the audience at a conscious level. Would doing so completely dispel their subliminal effect? Questions like these can be answered only by experimentation.

I mentioned earlier a recent discovery showing the biological necessity of dreaming for all warm-blooded animals. Dreaming can be seen as a creative act and a talking film. In fact, we can infer that art, in some form, is a necessity for the human, since no tribes seem to exist without some artistic expression.

Some precise experimentation could be carried out on the relationship of dreams to film. Swain writes, "The effective story fools audiences by its use of desire and danger to manipulate tension in the viewers. It poises them for action and then relaxes them according to a preplanned pattern."[18] People attend films, in part, because they find this ebb and flow of tension stimulating and pleasurable. One wonders to what extent this ebb and flow reflects the cycles of sleep and a balance of REM sleep. In fact, during dreams the whole organism is actually poised for action. The brain waves are about the same as in the waking state; blood pressure, heartbeat, and respiration rates go up, just as they would in waking life in response to danger or an interesting situation, even though the body is motionless. I see a parallel between the movie viewer, who is sitting passively in his chair and is stimulated to a not unpleasant extent by his identification with the action and the actors on screen, and the person who is dreaming. Relief is ensured by a change of scene and pace that is relaxing and reassuring, like the cycles of sleep in which there is no awareness of danger. The ebb and flow on the movie screen might actually reflect what happens in sleep. We could also experiment to see the extent to which those deprived of REM sleep could find an acceptable substitute in watching films. And further, we could investigate whether people have recurrent dreams that could be used as models for filmscripts. In other words, could films do your dreaming for you? And to what extent do they do this already?

In view of the fact that films are still the best working model for dreams, it is certainly a cop-out to say that films cannot show us thoughts and feelings directly just because filmmakers haven't been able to do so thus far. No doubt the technical potentials already at the disposal of the film industry have been deliberately neglected, but new technologies could arise in a context of pure experimentation. If we cannot yet photograph experiences, thoughts, fantasies, dreams, it may be that we do not yet have equipment sensitive enough to do so. You see, if we had microphones that could pick up subvocal speech, we could represent at least the sound track of thought. Imagine cameras that could pick up mental images. Innovations of this sort may not be so far away. They get us into a top-secret area that has to do with experiments in behavior modification. Researchers are already capable of stimulating the brain electrically, as shown by José M. R. Delgado in *Physical Control of the Mind* (1969). By stimulating certain areas of the brain, scientists can create anxiety, hatred, pleasure, sexual desire, or what have you.

Now, the reproduction of brain waves is quite within the range of the research that's going on now. The Central Intelligence Agency is said to be developing a brain-reading machine that, so far, can read only reactions but would later be able to read context as well. As with electric brain stimulation, you could produce anxiety but not the context of the anxiety—that is, the actual pictures people see in their minds, which would be different for each person. But with more precise knowledge, that might be possible. For example, I think films could eventually be produced directly in the mind by brain stimulation. Years ago, experiments were conducted in Norway in which researchers conveyed words directly into the brain by an electronic field. By analogy, visual images could be simulated in a test subject's brain, thereby breaking down the line between film and reality. The test subject would be an active participant in what his brain waves told him were real events. William Walters, who wrote *The Living Brain* (1953), told a story years ago about a woman who had an epileptic aura and was visited by a personable young stranger with whom she had sexual relations, which were not only visual but also tactile; in other words, it was a completely real experience produced simply by stimulation of a certain brain area.[19]

Such experiments as I've been discussing would help us to gain more precise knowledge about films and exactly how they work, which would, in turn, give us more knowledge about the process of life. All film techniques do occur in real life. So if, as I've said, the function of art is to increase awareness by showing us what we're doing all the time anyway, then learning more about film processes will teach us more about ourselves. And perhaps we will eventually learn to make up our own movies right in our heads.

NOTES

1 John von Neumann with Oskar Morgenstern, *The Theory of Games* (Princeton: Princeton University Press, 1944).

2 "Pratfalls" is a theatrical term referring to sudden spills (literally, falling on one's buttocks), associated with slapstick comedy.

3 Burroughs is referring to Lev Kuleshov, a Russian director of the 1920s. There are many different accounts of the images Kuleshov actually used in this famous experiment.

4 George Bluestone, *Novels Into Film* (Berkeley: University of California Press, 1961), p. 1.

5 Joseph Conrad, *Three Novels by Joseph Conrad* (New York: Washington Square Press, 1970), p. 7.

6 Dwight V. Swain, *Film Scriptwriting* (New York: Hastings House, 1976), p.3.

7 Ibid., p. 4.

8 Ibid.

9 George Leonard, *The Ultimate Athlete* (New York: Viking, 1975), p. 115.

10 Bluestone, *Novels Into Film,* pp. 47-48, 63.

11 Ibid., pp. 21 and 47.

12 F. Scott Fitzgerald, *The Great Gatsby* (New York: Scribner's, 1925, 1953), p.182.

13 Lewis Herman, *A Practical Manual of Screen Playwriting for Theater and Television* (Cleveland: World Pub. Co., 1963), pp. 66-67.

14 Ibid., p. 67.

15 *Blade Runner: A Movie* (Berkeley: Blue Wind Press, 1979) is a hybrid of novel and filmscript, narrative combined with camera directions. Burroughs's text is not to be confused with *Blade Runner,* a film directed by Ridley Scott in 1982 and based on Philip K. Dick's *Do Androids Dream of Electric Sheep?* (1968), presumably also the novel that Burroughs is referring to. Hampton Fancher and David Peoples wrote the screenplay for Scott's film. Burroughs's work was done before the film was actually made in 1982.

16 Wolf Peter Rilla, *The Writer and the Screen* (New York: W. H. Allen, 1973).

17 Other examples of subliminal suggestion include William Friedkin's alleged attempts in *The Exorcist* (1973) to induce viewers to lean left or right and Hitchcock's use of a red flash-frame just before the murders in *Psycho*. W. B. Key, in *Subliminal Seduction* (New York: New American Library, 1974), considers the uses of subliminal suggestion in advertising, from T-shirts to television commercials.

18 Swain, *Film Scriptwriting*, p. 79.

19 William Walters, *The Living Brain* (New York: Norton, 1953).

This essay is an edited version of five lectures Burroughs delivered June 10 and 12, 1975, and July 20, 22, and 25, 1977, at the Jack Kerouac School of Disembodied Poetics.

V

PART FIVE

ANCESTRAL

PRESENCES

V

PART FIVE

ANCESTRAL
PRESENCES

HE CAPTIVITY AND RESTORATION OF MRS. MARY ROWLANDSON

1

Náwwatuck nôteshem / *I came from farre* (κ 3)

Come, behold the works of the Lord, what dissolations
he has made in the Earth. Of thirty seven persons who
were in this one House, none escaped either present
death, or a bitter captivity, save only one, who might
say as he. *Job* 1. 15. *And I only am escaped alone to*
tell the News. (N4)

The Soveraignty & Goodness of GOD, Together, With the Faith-
fullness of His Promises Displayed; Being a NARRATIVE Of the Cap-
tivity and Restauration of Mrs. Mary Rowlandson, Commended by
her, to all that desires to know the Lords doings to, and dealings with
Her was probably written in 1677 by a Puritan woman "Especially to
her dear Children and Relations" as a reminder of God's Providence. It was printed in Boston in 1682. Avatar of the only literary-
mythological form indigenous to North America, this captivity narrative is both a microcosm of colonial imperialist history, and a
prophesy of our contemporary repudiation of alterity, anonymity,
darkness.

Rowlandson's "True History" was enormously popular at once.
Her captivity narrative ushered in a host of others. Throughout the
eighteenth century, captivity narratives dominated all other North
American forms of frontier literature.

Originally, these narratives were simple first-person accounts of a
real situation. As time went on and their popularity increased, they
were increasingly structured and written down by men, although
generally narrated by women.

SUSAN HOWE

Protestant sermons came to rely heavily on each captive woman's suffering and deliverance as a metaphor for the process of Conversion.

o o o

> Behold the worthies of *Christ,* as they are boldly leading forth his Troopes into these *Westerne* Fields, marke them well Man by Man as they march, terrible as an Army with Banners, croud in all yee that long to see this glorious sight, see ther's their glorious King *Christ* one that white Horse, whose hoofes like flint cast not only sparkes, but flames of fire in his pathes. Behold his Crown beset with Carbunkles, wherein the names of his whole Army are written. Can there be ever night in his Presence, whose eyes are ten thousand times higher than the Sun? Behold his swiftnes, all you that have said, where is the promise of his comming?
> (WWP 23–24)

Early New England rhetoric claimed for every single Christian a particular evangelical and secular use and progress. Individual identity was prophetic and corporate. In the hermeneutics of the Bay Colony every member of the Elect was a figural type on the way of federal eschatology. The break with the Old World was a rupture into contraries.

Split forever in the discontinuous drama of Promised Americanus, God is a thunderer, a clockmaker, a deer tamer. There is always a political message in the language of grace. Progress. Watch democratic King-birds and naked Nature.

A harsh climate, a wilderness, tomahawks, powwows, quickhatch and wampumpeag confronted the immigrant children of the Morning.

Bleak necessity caused millenarian affirmations of destiny to thrive on misery. At Boston in New England, the distinguishing mark of a saint was that he or she could transcend adversity. Extremity was every Puritan's opportunity.

> For *Englands* sake they are going from *England* to pray
> without ceasing for *England, O England!* . . . and for
> this their great enterprise counted as so many crackt-
> braines, but Christ will make all the earth know the wis-
> dome he hath indued them with, shall over-top all the
> humane policy in the World, as the sequell wee hope
> will shew. (WWP 27)

Mary Rowlandson suffered for and was redeemed (ransomed) by
her community. Typology projects theocracy into our fictive future.

o   o   o

While helping the original inhabitants of Earth's millennial fourth corner
to become Christians, members of the moral and profit-seeking Elect
helped themselves to land. As white settlers increasingly encroached
on Native American territory and the precarious food supply was
depleted, hostilities became inevitable. In 1645 the white population was estimated at seventeen thousand. Boston was only forty-
four years old, but already the city was ringed by rapidly growing villages. Dunstable, Groton, Marlborough, Wrentham, and Lancaster
were at the outermost ring from the city center. Beyond Lancaster,
trails of the Nipmunk Indians led away into unsettled wilderness.

In 1675, Metacomet (King Philip), the son of Massasoit and chief sachem of the Wampanoags, formed an alliance between his people
and the powerful Narragansetts and Nipmunks. These tribes were all
part of the loosely connected Algonquian language group. King
Philip's War (as it came to be called by the English) rapidly developed
into an Algonquian assault on colonists everywhere in New England
and was the most serious threat to English interests to date. Contradictory motives, including their own bitter understanding that efforts to
bring the Indians to God had miserably failed, soon had the colonists
fighting a bitter and bloody race war against the forces of "Diabolism."

> I have read of a great City that was destroyed by Ants;
> and of another that was destroyed by Rats, and of
> whole Countreys that have been depopulated by

Frogs, yea by Fleas. Though the Indians are a *Despicable* Enemy, yet the Lord is able to cut us down by a small *Indian axe*. But though I thus speak, I believe that God will reform his people by this Judgment, by this shall the Inquiry of Jacob be purged, and this shall be all the fruit to take away his sin. (BH 175–76)

During the difficult years of Indian wars, frequent epidemics, poor harvests, threats from schismatics, and widespread political and financial insecurity, a written emblematic procession of first-generation founding fathers asserted the sacred and corporate success of their pioneering errand-enterprise. First-generation founding mothers generally went unmentioned. Often they died young, worn out by frequent childbearing.

o o o

It was easie to conjecture that the *Narraganset*, and *Nipmuck* and *Quabaog*, and *River Indians*, being all come together, and the *Army* returned, they would speedily fall upon the *Frontier Towns.* . . . For upon the 10*th* day of *February* some hundreds of the *Indians* fell upon Lancaster. . . . Mr. *Rowlandson* (the faithful Pastor of the Church there) had his House, Goods, Books, all burned; his Wife and all his Children led away Captive before the Enemy. Himself (as God would have it) was not at home, whence his own person was delivered, which otherwise (without a Miracle) would have been endangered. Eight men lost their lives, and were stripped naked by the *Indians,* because they ventured their lives to save Mrs. *Rowlandson.* (BH 110–11)

Increase Mather misrepresented the real event: Mrs. Rowlandson was eager and able to save herself. "*I had often before this said, that if the* Indians *should come, I should chuse rather to be killed by them then taken alive* but when it came to the tryal my mind changed" (N 5).

o o o

Mary White Rowlandson, one of the seven children of John and Joane White, was born in England. The date of her birth is uncertain, but the Whites crossed to Salem, Massachusetts, in 1638, and moved to Lancaster in 1653. John White was the wealthiest member and largest landholder of the small frontier settlement. In 1656, Mary married Joseph Rowlandson, the first minister of Lancaster's parish. The couple had four children. Mary, born in 1657, died before she was a year old. Joseph was born in 1662, another Mary in 1665, and Sarah in 1669. Their house was both a dwelling place for the minister and his family and a fortified garrison for the entire community. Through the marriages of her sisters, Mrs. Rowlandson was connected to many other Lancaster land-owning families. Nineteen relatives were in the Rowlandson garrison on the day it was attacked. She said her life had been easy until that morning.

Joseph Rowlandson was also born in England, probably in 1631. His family emigrated to America during the same year as the Whites; 1638 was one of the great years of migration. Twenty-three ships and three thousand passengers arrived in the Bay Colony during that year alone. The Rowlandsons settled in Ipswich.

In 1651, Joseph, then beginning his senior year at Harvard College, was sentenced to be fined and publicly whipped for the crime of having written a pasquinade in prose and verse that was posted on the door of the Ipswich Courthouse. Later someone said of the accuser who had charged Rowlandson with libel to himself and others: "when he lived in our country, a wet Eeles tayle and his word were something worth ye taking hold of." But the case was tried in Ipswich by John Endicott, Simon Bradstreet, and William Hathorne. The intimidated and chastened sinner produced a penitent obedient retraction beginning: "Forasmuch as I Joseph Rowlandson through the suggestion of Satan, and the evil of my owne heart, by that being strongly attemted, by the depravation of this too facily inclined to the perpetration of a fact whose nature was anomic, and circumstances enormities. . ." (N 155).

Conduct charts are moral thunder in the American creed. Joseph Rowlandson was the only graduate of Harvard's class of 1652.

For the next two years Rowlandson prepared for the ministry, and in 1654 he began preaching in Lancaster. There his mother, father, and brother Thomas soon joined him. He seems to have been well liked by his flock. Twenty years later, when a quarrel arose over the formation of the Old South Church in Boston and the most learned and judicious ministers in Massachusetts were gathered together for advice, he was among the chosen arbiters. When Lancaster was raided and burned and his wife and children carried off, Rowlandson was in or near Boston petitioning colonial officials for troops to guard the village. Lancaster had already been raided once during the previous summer. Later he spent a great deal of time and effort appealing to the Massachusetts Council to arrange for the ransom and release of his family.

Shortly after Mrs. Rowlandson's release, her children were also ransomed. The reunited family lived in and around Boston until 1677, when they moved to Wethersfield, Connecticut, where Joseph Rowlandson had been called as minister. He died at forty-six the following year. Mary Rowlandson's name was listed in the town records of 1679. She had been granted an annual pension of £30. It was never paid.

He holdeth our soul in life, and suffers not our feet to be moved, for thou our God hast proved us, thou hast tryed us, as silver is tryed. (N iv: from Psalm 66:9–10)

Historians assumed, until recently, that because her pension was never collected, Mary died shortly after her husband. In 1985, David Greene, in an article called "New Light on Mary Rowlandson," published in *Early American Literature*, demonstrated that genealogical records of the Talcott family show Mary White Rowlandson married Captain Samuel Talcott on August 6, 1679. Talcott was a prosperous Wethersfield farmer who had been a member of the War Council during King Philip's War. Mary White Rowlandson Talcott outlived her second husband. When she died at Wethersfield, January 5, 1710, she was in her early seventies.

o   o   o

2
COMMUNICATION

Manittóo wússuck-wheke / *God's Booke or Writing* (K 136)

On the tenth of *February* 1675, Came the Indians with
great numbers upon *Lancaster;* Their first coming was
about Sun-rising; hearing the noise of some Guns, we
looked out; several Houses were burning, and the
Smoke ascending to Heaven. (N 1)

On this late winter day the vulnerable village of Lancaster in the
new Jerusalem of New England feels the sword without and terror
within. At sun-rising, on a day of calamity, at the inverted point of
antitypical history, Mary Rowlandson looks out at the absence of
Authority and sees we are all alone. Spite is the direction of creation. In a minute death can and will come. All collectivities will be
scattered to corners.

Epigraph to *The Soveraignty & Goodness of* GOD from the canti-
cle of Moses:

DEUT. 32:29. *See now that I, even I am he, and there is
no God with me: I kill and I make alive, I wound and I
heal neither is there any can deliver out of my hand.*

Near the beginning of redemptive time Moses spoke his savage
song to the disobedient children of Israel. Now the God who has
brought his select nation across an ocean and baptized them in
another wilderness, has rebuked and ensnared them.

In a sermon delivered at the outbreak of King Philip's War,
Increase Mather told his congregation that God decreed their privilege and pattern before the world began. Sanctified affliction must
be every saint's portion.

Increase Mather lived safely in Boston.

Mary Rowlandson is a backwoodswoman, and God's hatred
stretches farther than his love. Her quiet village is now a site of terror.

At this tragic site to what end does the world go on? The Mosaic song is a chant of Combat. The sound is malign.

o   o   o

In the first paragraph of the first published narrative written by an Anglo-American woman, ostensibly to serve as a reminder of God's Providence, guns fire, houses burn, a father, mother, and sucking child are killed by blows to the head. Two children are carried off alive. Two more adults are clubbed to death. Another escapes— another running along is shot. Indians strip him naked then cut his bowels open. Another, venturing out of his barn, is quickly dispatched. Three others are murdered inside their fortification. The victims are nameless. Specificity is unnecessary in whiplash confrontation. Only monotonous enumeration.

In the first chapter of the first published narrative written by an Anglo-American woman, ostensibly to serve as a reminder of God's Providence, twelve Christians are killed by Indians. The author and her youngest daughter are wounded by bullets. The author's brother-in-law is killed while defending her garrison. The author's nephew has his leg broken and is battered to death. The author's eldest sister, seeing "the infidels haling one way and children another, and some wallowing in their own blood," begs these same infidels to kill her, and they do. Finally, the author's two other children (aged fifteen and ten) are pulled away from her sight.

In the first chapter of the first published narrative written by an Anglo-American woman, ostensibly to serve as a reminder of God's Providence, Native Americans are called "murtherous wretches," "bloody heathen," "hell-hounds," "ravenous bears," "wolves."

"There were twenty-four of us taken alive and carried Captive" (N 5).

This is the hasty beginning of Mary Rowlandson's narrative of her sojourn with the Nipmucks and Narragansetts.

She travelled with them as prisoner and slave for eleven weeks and five days.

"I shall particularly speak of the several Removes we had up and down the Wilderness" (N5).

Someone is here. Now away she must go. Invisible to her people. Out in a gap in the shadows.

A far cry from Anne Bradstreet's polished pious verse. But the two women were contemporaries, and their husbands were builders of Sion.

This terse, tense book tells of prefigured force and the dooms of life. For a time its author was elided, tribeless, lost.

o o o

Oh the roaring, and singing and dancing, and yelling of those black creatures in the night, which made the peace a lively resemblance of hell. And as miserable was the wast that was there made, of Horses, Cattle, Sheep, Swine, Calves, Lambs, Roasting Pigs, and Fowl (which they had plundered in the Town) some roasting, some lying and burning, and some boyling to feed our merciless Enemies; who were joyfull enough though we were disconsolate. (N 6)

Pitched into a first night, huddled together at the summit of George Hill, captives from Lancaster look down at their burning village.

They are things; abducted from the structure of experience. Rowlandson wraps herself in separateness for warmth. Tyranny precedes morality. Her little girl was broken in a rift of history.

Somewhere Thoreau says that exaggerated history is poetry.

Now the narrative is divided into chapters called Removes. Each Remove is a forced march away from Western rationalism, deep and deeper into Limitlessness, where all illusion of volition, all individual identity may be transformed—assimilated.

We will read no lovely pictures of the virgin forest; no night fishing, no deer hunting, no wildlife identification, no sunsets, no clouds of pigeons flying. Indian towns are smoky and stinking. It is always either snowing or raining, muddy and dreary. Landscape will never transfix her. The beautiful Connecticut River is just another barrier to get across. Rowlandson's apprehension of nature is an endless ambiguous enclosure.

o o o

Mary Rowlandson has been condemned for her lack of curiosity about the customs of her captors (she was starving, wounded, weary), and her narrative has been blamed for stereotypes of Native Americans as "savages" that later developed in this genre of American fiction. These critics skirt the presence in this same genre of an equally insulting stereotype, that of a white woman as passive cipher in a controlled and circulated idea of Progress at whose zenith rides the hero-hunter (Indian or White) who will always rescue her.

But Rowlandson's presentation of truth severed from Truth is a rude effraction into a familiar American hierarchical discourse of purpose and possession. *The Soveraignty & Goodness of GOD, Together, With the Faithfulness of His Promises Displayed*, composed in a bloody fragment of the world, is a relentless origin.

SUBSTITUTION

A formal ecclesiastical enclosure—God's promise to the elite—confused and assimilated the chaotic genealogy of this colonial archetype. Oh the metempsychosis!

Poor model-muse cut into the cornerstone of New Jerusalem.

You are a passive victim, captured and threatened by a racial enemy until God's providence (later a human hero) can effect your deliverance. You must shelter the masculine covenant as lost lady and lofty idol. You will water the American venture with your tears. "And my knees trembled under me, *And I was walking thorough the valley of the Shadow of Death*" (N 68).

The truth is what you are worth.

o o o

No copy of the first edition of Mary Rowlandson's *Narrative* is known to exist. All the editions we have now depend on the text of a "Second Addition Corrected and Amended" printed during the same year as the first. Future distortions, exaggerations, modifications, corrections and emendations may endow a text with meanings it never formed. Probably Rev. Joseph Rowlandson, who had once been publicly whipped and fined for writing a satirical prose poem, helped his wife to choose scriptural parallels and referents that would support and censor her narrative at the same time that they entwined the telling in a becoming Christological corporate pattern.

In a culture chiefly concerned with relationships of power and production, lip service is a tall tale. An old rule.

In 1863, during the darkest days of the Civil War, Emerson delivered a lecture called "The Fortune of the Republic." In it he said:

> . . . the Genius or Destiny of America is no log or slug-
> gard, but a man incessantly advancing, as the
> shadow on the dial's face, or the heavenly body by
> whose light it is marked.
>
> The flowering of civilization is the finished man, the
> man of sense, of grace, of accomplishment, of social
> power. . . . (CW 537)

A woman is hiking through the Republic's corporate eschatology, carrying her dying daughter Sarah.

She is a mother ensnared in God's plan. She has witnessed the destruction of Lancaster/Sion. She and her children are commodities between two hostile armies. What is their legality? What are they worth?

Other to other we are all functions in a system of War.

o o o

> . . . (by my Master in this writing, must be understood
> *Quanopin,* who was a *Saggamore,* and married King
> *Phillips* wives Sister; not that he first took me, but I was
> sold to him by another *Narrhaganset Indian,* who took
> me when first I came out of the Garison). . . .
>
> I went to see my daughter *Mary,* who was at this
> same *Indian Town* at a *Wigwam* not very far off,
> though we had little liberty or opportunity to see one
> another other: She was about *ten* years old, & taken
> from the door at first by a *Praying Ind* & afterward sold
> for a gun. (N 11–12)

Later, when her captors asked Mrs. Rowlandson to set a price on her own head, she did—£50 in goods, mostly guns. Not long after her release her two surviving children were also ransomed.

"As *Solomon* says, *Mony answers all things*" (N 70).

Sarah was wounded and worthless to her captors. Only her mother remembers.

> . . . down I sat with the picture of death in my lap.
> About two houres in the night, my sweet Babe, like a
> Lambe departed this Life, on *Feb. 18. 1675.* It being
> about *six yeares*, and *five months* old. It was *nine*
> *dayes* from the first wounding, in this miserable condi-
> tion, without any refreshing of one nature or other, ex-
> cept a little cold water. I cannot but take notice, how
> at another time I could not bear to be in the room
> where any dead person was, but now the case is
> changed; I must and could ly down by my dead Babe,
> side by side all the night after. I have thought since of
> the wonderfull goodness of God to me, in preserving
> me in the use of my reason and senses, in that dis-
> tressed time, that I did not use wicked and violent
> means to end my own miserable life. (N 10–11)

God brought Mary Rowlandson into a wood where she lost her children and learned what fear is. Now his trace is peace. She says she
has thought of God's goodness since. Like the aboriginals she assures us she hates (at the same time noting their frequent acts of
kindness to her), Mrs. Rowlandson attributes causation to spiritual
force.

o   o   o

A Sovereign thinks the sun. Form and force begin with Him. If there
is evil in the Universe, it is good and therefore marvelous. Law scans
the grammar of liberty and surrender. Catastrophe is a matter of
fact. Who can open the door of God's face?

Love is a trajectory across the hollow of history.

Captives have been taken for centuries. Some passing matter made it necessary. They stoop sideways far inland; herds of people reentering the Light. What do they want?

I was turning the leaves *of my* Bible, and the Lord
brought me some Scriptures, which did a little revive
me, as that Isai. 55.8. *For my thoughts are not your*
thoughts, neither are your wayes my ways saith the
Lord. And also that, *Psal. 37.5 Commit thy way unto the*
Lord trust also in him, and he shal bring it to pass. About
this time they came yelping from *Hadly.* (N 35)

Sarah's burial in unmarked Christianography reduces the rational *Designe of all Theologie* to gibberish. Good sense got lost during the Third Remove. The text of America bypassed her daughter.

"*Come, behold the works of the Lord, what dissolations he has*
made" (N 4).

Blessed *shall be* thy basket and thy store (Deut. 28:5).
Cursed *shall be* thy basket and thy store (Deut. 28:17).
Here is the way of contradiction.

o   o   o

One of the *Indians* that came from *Medfield* fight, had
brought some plunder, came to me, and asked me, if I
would have a Bible, he had got one in his Basket, I was
glad of it, and asked him, whether he thought the
Indians would let me read? He answered, yes; so I took
the Bible and in that melancholy time, it came into my
mind to read first the 28 *Chap. of Deut.* which I did,
and when I had read it, my dark heart wrought on this
manner, *That there was no mercy for me, that the*
blessings were gone, and the Curses came in their
room, and that I had lost my opportunity. (N 14)

Memory of anonymous thoughtfulness bites the mind that thought it. "Yes" signifying affirmation and permission, must become "No" at once. Her first choice from God's Book of Wonderful Mercy is a vengeful chapter from *Deuteronomy.* "Blessings and curses pronounced." Next she links the curses to her violent self-abhorrence. Each step forward seems mired in the passage for this progress that must always recoil back on herself.

Mary Rowlandson's thoroughly reactionary figuralism requires that she obsessively confirm her orthodoxy to readers at the same time she excavates and subverts her own rhetoric. Positivist systems of psychological protection have disintegrated. Identities and configurations rupture and shift. Her risky retrospective narrative will be safe only if she asserts the permanence of corporate Soveraignty. Each time an errant perception skids loose, she controls her lapse by vehemently invoking biblical authority. "Not what the Selfe will, but what the Lord will," exhorted Thomas Hooker. Joseph Rowlandson warned, "If God be gone, our Guard is gone."

o   o   o

"Thus the Lord carried me along from one time to another" (N 38).

In New England in the 1670s, the beaver and deer population had precipitously declined. Furs and skins the Indians had always used for clothing were becoming hard to obtain, and they were increasingly forced to rely on European fabrics. Mary Rowlandson found that the tribes she travelled with were well supplied with dry goods and needles. Apart from the works she did for her master and mistress, she used her knitting and sewing skills to do many odd jobs for which she was paid. King Philip gave her a shilling when she sewed a shirt for his son. With it she bought a piece of horse flesh. She knit stockings for Wettimore and fixed another pair for a warrior. In return for a piece of beef she made a shirt for a squaw's sannup. For a quart of peas she knit another pair of stockings. Someone asked her to sew a shirt for a papoose in exchange for a "mess of broth, thickened with a meal made from the bark of a Tree."

"Often getting alone: *like a Crane, or a Swallow so did I chatter: I did mourn as a Dove, mine eyes fail with looking upward Oh, Lord I am oppressed undertake for me. Isa. 38:14*" (N 39).

When she was Quannopin's slave, she liked her master, although she despised his wife, her mistress, Wettimore. None of her captors harmed her. Many shared what little they had with her. Although English soldiers had burned their winter supply of corn and driven them from their towns, she never saw a single Native American die from hunger.

Near the end of her narrative, she interrupts the homeward direction of her impending restoration with a list of specific criticisms of colonial policies toward her captors. "Before I go any further, I would take leave to mention. . ."; then she stops her slide into Reason's ruin by pushing her readers back to the imperatives of Wonder-Working Providence. "*Help Lord, or we perish*" (N 59, 63).

THE COPY

John Winthrop kept a journal in three manuscript notebooks. In them he recorded events he considered important from the time he set sail for America on the *Arbella* in 1630 until 1644. The first notebook is untitled. The opening twenty-four manuscript pages make up the author's sea journal, and the rest of the notebook takes up the problems of settlement. Early entries are brief and were probably made on the spot. Political and material changes (Winthrop became governor of the colony in June 1630) altered the author's perception of his role as journalist-historiographer. By 1631 the governor had settled into a more retrospective form of record keeping. The best account of Winthrop's changing purpose is Richard S. Dunn's "John Winthrop Writes His Journal" (*William and Mary Quarterly*, April 1984). Dunn says that after 1632, one of Winthrop's priorities in this account of settlement was to clarify and defend his administration. The first notebook had no title. On the first page of the second notebook the author wrote: "3: vol booke of the Annalls of N: England," and on the following page: "A continuation of the Historye of N: England" (RD 186). After his death the Connecticut Winthrops acquired the volumes. Although early historians of New England—William Hubbard, Cotton Mather, Thomas Prince, Ezra Stiles, Jonathan Trumbull, and Jeremy Belknap—all borrowed them from the Winthrop family for examination, the manuscript books remained untranscribed and unpublished. In the 1780's, when

Governor Trumbull and his secretary, John Porter, finally deciphered and copied the first two volumes, the third had disappeared among Thomas Prince's books. Noah Webster, who later became the author of the first *American Dictionary of the English Language*, saw the transcripts and arranged for them to be printed at Hartford in 1790. Webster wrote an introduction and some notes for that edition titled *A Journal Of the Transactions and Occurences in the settlement of Massachusetts and The Other New-England Colonies, from the Year 1630 to 1644: written by John Winthrop, Esq., First Governor of Massachusetts: And now first published from a correct copy of the original Manuscript.* Richard S. Dunn says the Webster edition was filled with misreadings and omissions. Dunn says that Winthrop's handwriting is "notoriously hard to read, the ink is faded, the paper is often stained, worn or torn, and the text is studded with marginalia, insertions, cancellations, and underscorings" (RD 185).

In the spring of 1816 the third volume was discovered in the tower of the Old South Church in Boston. This was now added to the first two notebooks owned by the Massachusetts Historical Society. James Savage, a descendant of Anne Hutchinson, and the librarian of the Society, collated the former manuscripts with the 1790 edition, usually called *Winthrop's Journal,* and found many errors. As well as transcribing the new manuscript, he revised the other two. He also included copious footnotes. The Massachusetts Historical Society, with the backing of the legislature, financed the project, and in 1825-1826 the two-volume edition called *The History of New England from 1630 to 1649, by John Winthrop, Esq. First Governour of the Colony of the Massachusetts Bay, From His Original Manuscripts* was published in Boston. In his Preface Savage wrote: "Of the title of this work, it may be desirable for the reader to understand, that it is the exact language of the author" (WH I: v). Savage was a sharp reader of Winthrop's hand, and his annotations were extremely thorough. While taking infinite pains with his own marginal annotations, he seems to have considered Winthrop's marginalia, memoranda, and cancellations to be unworthy of transcription. According to Dunn, the editor altered Winthrop's language. Worst of all, Savage borrowed the original notebooks from the Society in order to work on them in his office. There, on November 10, 1825, the second volume, covering the years of the antinomian controversy and the wars against the Pequots and Naragansetts, was destroyed by fire. Fire and burglary have also done away with the original accounts of Anne Hutchinson's two trials.

James Kendall Hosmer, in his re-edited version of Winthrop published by Scribners in 1902, followed Savage in most respects but recalled the word *journal* to its leading position: *Winthrop's Journal: "History of New England, 1630–1649."* He also deleted many of Savage's marginal annotations, divided the narrative into chapters for each year, and cut some "repulsive" passages, including Anne Hutchinson's monstrous birth and William Hatchett's copulation with a cow.

In his introduction, Hosmer wrote: "The *Winthrop* of 1825–1826 took its place at once in the minds of men as the foundation of Massachusetts history, and the importance of the services of Savage was universally recognized: he became a man of mark, attained to the position of president of the Massachusetts Historical Society, and devoted himself to the genealogical and antiquarian work into which he had been led through his labors upon Winthrop" (WJ 17).

In 1931 The Massachusetts Historical Society decided to publish *The Journal of John Winthrop* (their title) in separate installments among the governor's correspondence and other writings in *The Winthrop Papers.* Only one installment was actually published. A new edition of Winthrop's *Journal-History* edited by Laetitia Yeandle and Richard S. Dunn is currently in progress. Dunn says it will draw on the labors of his predecessors. Their edition will be called *The Journal of John Winthrop, 1630–1649.* It will be a compromise, he says.

Meanwhile, although there are now holograph copies of the surviving original manuscripts for scholars to consult, holograph copies cannot be depended upon for accuracy. The Massachusetts Historical Society guards the originals from prying historians and other scholars as if they were guarding the Grail.

THE BROAD TEMPER
OF THE PROPER HISTORIAN

James Kendall Hosmer had a complaint about Savage's footnotes: "As to the annotation . . . the former editor had peculiarities of character making him personally racy and interesting, but impairing the excellence of his commentary. His successor in the presidency of the Massachusetts Historical Society, Mr. Charles Francis Adams, aptly compares him to Dr. Samuel Johnson. Like Johnson, Savage, while most laborious, scrupulously honest, and always resolute and unshrinking, was testy, prejudiced and opinionated; he was prone to measure by small local standards." Hosmer is bothered because sometimes the notes are bulkier than the text. "They are encumbered with genealogies of unimportant people and details as to trivial events and obscure localities. While possessed thus by the spirit of the county antiquary rather than by the broad temper of the proper historian, his hates and loves, equally undiscriminating, are curiously, often amusingly, manifest: he has his *bêtes noires* . . . whom he cannot mention without dealing a stout Johnsonian cuff" (WJ I 18).

James Hosmer assures his readers that notes to the present edition represent the point of view of "a student of history in a large sense. The Anglo-Saxon race is but one of the races of the world" (WJ I 19).

"We want historians to confirm our belief that the present rests upon profound intentions and immutable necessities. But the true historical sense confirms our existence among countless lost events, without a landmark or point of reference," says Michel Foucault in "Nietzsche, Genealogy, History" (LCP 155).

"For the little humanity that adorns the earth, a relaxation of essence to the second degree is needed. . . . This weakness is needed. This relaxation of virility without cowardice is needed for the little cruelty our hands repudiate," writes Emmanuel Levinas in the final chapter of *Otherwise Than Being Or Beyond Essence*, called "Outside" (O 185).

o   o   o

3
FECUNDITY

Néechaw. / *She is in Travell* (K 49)

John Winthrop was the governor of the Bay Colony during most of the years between 1629 and 1649, when he died in office. The austere first president of the Commissioners of the United Colonies of New England had four wives. When he was seventeen, he married Mary Forth, who bore him six children, including John Winthrop Jr. She died in 1625. Later that same year the twenty-seven-year-old widower married Thomasine Cloptin, who died in childbirth in 1616. In 1618, Winthrop married Margaret Tyndal. She followed him to America in 1631, gave birth to eight children, and died in 1647. Several months later the sorrowing fifty-nine-year-old widower and father of seventeen offspring married Mrs. Thomasine Cotymore, a widow. The couple had a son the following year, before Winthrop died, March 26, 1649, at sixty-one.

o   o   o

On March 27, 1638, John Winthrop wrote in his *Journal-History:*

> The wife of one William Dyer, a milliner in the New
> Exchange, a very proper and fair woman, and both of
> them notoriously infected with Mrs Hutchinson's errours,
> and very censorious and troublesome, (she being of a
> very proud spirit, and much addicted to revelations,)
> had been delivered of (a) child some few months be-
> fore, October 17, and the child buried, (being stillborn,)
> and viewed of none but Mrs. Hutchinson and the mid-
> wife, one Hawkins's wife, a rank familist also; and an-
> other woman had a glimpse of it, who, not being able
> to keep counsel, as the other two did, some rumour
> began to spread, that the child was a monster. One of
> the elders, hearing of it, asked Mrs. Hutchinson, when
> she was ready to depart; whereupon she told him how

it was, and said she meant to have it chronicled, but
excused her concealing of it till then, (by advise, as she
said, of Mr. Cotton,) which coming to the governour's
knowledge, he called another of the magistrates and
that elder, and sent for the midwife and examined her
about it. At first she confessed only, that the head was
defective and misplaced, but being told that Mrs.
Hutchinson had revealed all, and that he intended to
have it taken up and viewed, she made this report of
it, viz. It was a woman child, stillborn, about two months
before the just time, having life a few hours before; it
came hiplings till she turned it; it was of ordinary bigness; it had a face, but no head, and the ears stood
upon the shoulders and were like an ape's; it had no
forehead, but over the eyes four horns, hard and
sharp; two of them were above one inch long, the
other two shorter; the eyes standing out, and the
mouth also; the nose hooked upward; all over the
breast and back full of sharp pricks and scales, like
a thornback; the navel and all the belly, with the distinction of the sex, were where the back should be,
and the back and hips before, where the belly should
have been; behind, between the shoulders, it had two
mouths, and in each of them a piece of red flesh sticking out; it had arms and legs as other children; but, instead of toes, it had on each foot three claws, like a
young fowl, with sharp talons. (WH I: 261–2)

He followed this entry almost immediately with another on the following page:

Another thing observable was, the discovery of it,
which was just when Mrs. Hutchinson was cast out
of the church. For Mrs. Dyer going forth with her, a
stranger asked, what young woman it was. The others
answered, it was the woman which had the monster;

SUSAN HOWE

which gave the first occasion to some that heard it to
speak of it. The midwife (Jane Hawkins), presently after
this discovery, went out of this jurisdiction; and indeed
it was good for her to be gone, for it was known, that
she used to give young women oil of mandrakes and
other stuff to cause conception; and she grew into
great suspicion to be a witch, for it was credibly reported, that, when she gave any medicines, (for she
practised physick,) she would ask the party, if she did
believe, she could help her, &c.

Another observable passage was, that the father
of this monster, coming home at this very time, was,
the next Lord's day, by an unexpected providence,
questioned in the church for divers monstruous errours,
as for denying all inherent righteousness, &c. which
he maintained, and was for the same admonished.
(WH I: 263–4)

Within a few pages he reported the premature birth and death of
Anne Hutchinson's "monster," born on the Isle of Aquiday in the
Narragansett Bay shortly after her arrival there. When the event was
announced in open assembly at Boston, Mr. Cotton said it appeared to be "twenty-seven //singula frusta vel globulos seminis
masculini sine ulla mutatione aut mixtura de femina//[1] and thereupon gathered, that it might signify her errour in denying inherent
righteousness, but that all that was Christ in us, and nothing of ours
in our faith, love &c." (WH I: 271).

John Cotton's description failed to satisfy the governor. He demanded a further investigation. Mr. Clarke, a physician and minister
of the island, who had been called in to assist the Hutchinsons and
examine "the issue," was consulted to clear up any doubts. He conveyed further details about the monster—or mass of possible mon-
strosities—to the Massachusetts authorities.

I beheld, first unwashed, (and afterwards in warm
water,) several lumps, every one of them greatly

confused, and if you consider each of them according
to the representation of the whole, they were altogether without form; but if they were considered in
respect of the parts of each lump of flesh, then there
was a representation of innumerable distinct bodies
in the form of a globe, not much unlike the swims of
some fish, so confusedly knit together by so many several strings, (which I conceive were the beginnings of
veins and nerves,) so that it was impossible either to
number the small round pieces in every lump, much
less to discern from whence every string did fetch its
original, they were so snarled one within another. The
small globes I likewise opened, and perceived the matter of them . . . to be partly wind and partly water. . . .
The lumps were twenty-six or twenty-seven, distinct and
not joined together; there came no secundine after
them; six of them were as great as his fist, and one as
great as two fists; the rest each less than another, and
the smallest about the bigness . . . of a small Indian
bean, and like the pearl in a man's eye. . . . Mr. Cotton,
next lecture day, acknowledged his errour, &c. and
that he had his information by a letter from her husband, &c." (WH I: 272-3).

On December 6, 1638 John Winthrop wrote in his *Journal-History:*

Dorothy Talbye was hanged at Boston for murdering
her own daughter, a child of three years old. She had
been a member of the church of Salem, and of good
esteem for godliness, &c.; but, falling at difference with
her husband, through melancholy or spiritual delusions,
she sometimes attempted to kill him, and her children
and herself, by refusing meat, saying it was so revealed
to her, &c. After much patience, and divers admo-
nitions not prevailing, the church cast her out.

Whereupon she grew worse; so as the magistrate caused her to be whipped. Whereupon she was reformed for a time, and carried herself more dutifully to her husband, &c.; but soon after she was so possessed with Satan, that he persuaded her (by his delusions, which she listened to as revelations from God) to break the neck of her own child, that she might free it from further misery. This she confessed upon her apprehension; yet, at her arraignment, she stood mute a good space, till the governour (Winthrop himself) told her she should be pressed to death, and then she confessed the indictment. When she was to receive judgment, she would not uncover her face, nor stand up, but as she was forced, nor give any testimony of her repentance, either then or at her execution. The cloth, which should have covered her face, she plucked off and put between the rope and her neck. She desired to have been beheaded, giving this reason, that it was less painful and less shameful. After a swing or two, she catched at the ladder. Mr. Peter, her late pastor, and Mr. Wilson, went with her to the place of execution, but could do no good with her. Mr. Peter gave an exhortation to the people to take heed of revelations, &c. and of despising the ordinance of excommunication as she had done; for, when it was to have been denounced against her, she turned her back, and would have gone forth, if she had not been stayed by force. (WH I: 279)

Savage's footnote to this passage is worth quoting: "The unfortunate husband, whose life had been attempted by her, was, after her execution, excommunicated 'for much pride and unnaturalness to his wife.' See the letter of Hugh Peter in Hutch. I. 371. The original has been seen by me. Perhaps Peter regretted his treatment of Talby, after his own wife was distracted" (WH I: 279).

On April 13, 1645, John Winthrop wrote in his *Journal-History:*

Mr. Hopkins, the governour of Hartford upon Connecticut, came to Boston, and brought his wife with him, (a godly young woman, and of special parts,) who was fallen into a sad infirmity, the loss of her understanding and reason, which had been growing upon her divers years, by occasion of her giving herself wholly to reading and writing, and had written many books. Her husband, being very loving and tender of her, was loath to grieve her; but he saw his errour, when it was too late. For if she had attended her household affairs, and such things as belong to women, and not gone out of her way and calling to meddle in such things as are proper for men, whose minds are stronger &c. she had kept her wits, and might have improved them usefully and honorably in the place God had set her. He brought her to Boston, and left her with her brother, one Mr. Yale, a merchant, to try what means might be had here for her. But no help could be had.
(WH II: 216–17)

Mrs. Hopkins was Elihu Yale's aunt. Some of the inheritance of this weak-minded woman Winthrop's *Journal-History* certifies as mad, helped to found New England's second college. In a footnote, Savage supplies the male Yale genealogy and tells the reader that David Yale, her brother, may have been from Massachusetts "by the intolerance of the age."

After her husband's death in England, David Yale became the financial guardian of his sister. Mad, bookish Mrs. Hopkins outlived governor Hopkins and governor Winthrop. She died in 1698. "I had intended here to introduced the advice of John Winthrop, jr. on the lady's case, in answer to her husband's application and extracts from two letters of Governour Hopkins in which he mentions it, that were found in Vol. XIX. of the Trumbull MSS. belonging to the Massachusetts Historical Society, but that volume perished, with many other treasures, in the sad conflagration of 10 November last," writes Savage in his footnote to the passage (WH II: 217).

Mrs. Hopkins's books, if they were ever published, are still a blank in American literary history. While Anne Bradstreet gained public acceptance as a writer, her sister, Sarah Dudley Keane, was less fortunate: "My she Cosin Keane (Sarah) is growne a great preacher" (WP V 70).

On March 18, 1646 Benjamin Keayne addressed a letter from London "To the Wor(shipful) my honoured Father Tho: Dudley Esqr: Deb Go(vernou)r of the Matacusetts at his House in Roxburie this present in New England." Thomas Dudley was bookish Anne Bradstreet's father:

> HONOURED SIR, That you, and my selfe, are made sor-
> rie by your Daughters inormous, and continued Crimes,
> is the greatest Cause of griefe that ever befell mee,
> and the moare because her obstinate continuance in
> them, is now to mee by her owne letter made as car-
> taine, as that I am cartaine, I neaver gave her the least
> just Cause or occasion to provoake her to them: But
> most of all it greeves mee, that she has ronne so faste
> from that highth of error in judgment, to that extremitie
> of error in practisse, (both which you may plainely see
> in my other lettre) that shee has not lefte mee any
> roome or way of reconsiliation: And theirefoare as
> you desier, I do plainely declare my resolution, never
> againe to live with her as a Husband: What mainti-
> nance your selfe expects I know not. this I know (to my
> cost, and danger,) shee has unwived her selfe and
> how shee or you can expect a wives-maintinance is to
> mee a wonder. And lastly the breach not being on my
> parte I shall take it as an honour to be known by the
> Neame of Sir Your affectionate Sonne and Sarvant
> BEN: KAYEN (WP 144)

This was endorsed by Robert Keayne: "A letter of my sonnes to my Brother Dudlye per mr. Graues. mo. 4: 14: 1647 sent open for me to pervse and to deliuer or keepe it back as I should thinke meete"

(WP 144). Instead of keeping it back, the senior Keayne, founder and first captain of The Ancient and Honorable Artillery in Boston, handed the letter over to Governor Winthrop. It can now be found in volume V of *The Winthrop Papers.*

The Records of the First Church in Boston, published by the Colonial Society of Massachusetts, show that on the "24th day of the 8th Moneth 1647"

> Our Sister Mrs. Sarah (sometimes the wife of Mr. Ben-
> iamin Keayne but who Devorsed from him) having
> beene formerly Admonished by the Church of her
> Irregular prophecying in mixt Assemblies, and Refusing
> ordinarily to heare in the Churches of Christ, and not
> Answering the Church therein, but falling into odious,
> lewd, and scandalous uncleane behaviour with one
> Nicholas Hart an Exommunicate person of Taunton,
> was by our pastor, in the Name of the Lord Jesus, with
> the Consent of the Church by their silence, and with
> the Power of the Lord Jesus, Excommunicated out of
> the Church. (R 49)

Sarah Dudley Keayne, sister of Anne Bradstreet, lost custody of her daughter and was disinherited by her father. James Savage, in a footnote to another passage in the *History* concerning Robert Keayne, supplies copious information about his complicated busi-ness practices, fines levied against him, a land grant, and his "end-less testament": "Between his only son, Benjamin, and a daughter of Dudley, `an unhappy and uncomfortable match' is spoken of in this will; and that union, perhaps, with other disagreeable circum-stances, compelled the son to return to the land of his fathers, where he died, I presume, in 1668. . . . The male line ended with Benjamin" (WH I: 314–15).

Later Sarah Keayne married Thomas Pacey, a man from the lower classes. Her subsequent history seems to be blank.

o   o   o

Anna Bradestreate.
Deer Neat *An Bartas.*

Anne Bradstreate.
Artes bred neat *An.*
(AB 531)

Anne Dudley Bradstreet, Sarah's older sister, a female member of the "Governor and Company of the Massachusetts Bay in New-England," sailed from England to Salem, Massachusetts, with her husband and other Dudley family members on the *Arbella,* in March 1630. In *An American Tryptych: Ann Bradstreet, Emily Dickinson, Adrienne Rich,* Wendy Martin, whose work on Bradstreet contributes to a deeper understanding of contradictions in her work, falls somewhat short when she describes the poet's father as "a thoughtful and well-informed man who taught his daughter Greek. Latin. French, and Hebrew and encouraged her to read and write poetry" and tells us "she was educated in the Elizabethan tradition that valued female intelligence" (AT 21). Thomas Dudley, one of the most opportunistic and brutal of gentlemen of the first rank in the Bay Colony, was anything but thoughtful at the civil trial of Anne Hutchinson. There he accused her of "venting" her "strange opinions." He said she had "depraved all the ministers" since her arrival in the Bay Colony, and was the "cause of what is fallen out, why we must take away the foundation and the building will fall" (AC 318). Even Cotton Mather remarks in *Magnalia* that Dudley's "*justice* was a perpetual terror to evil-doers." Mather points out and Martin takes note of the fact that poetry was one of Dudley's accomplishments. The patiently meticulous John Savage, in his footnotes to an early passage in Winthrop's journal, supplies a telling epitaph by Gov. Belcher:

Here lies Thomas Dudley, that trusty old stud,
A bargain's a bargain, and must be made good. (WH I 51)

When Bradstreet's father died at seventy-five, July 31, 1653, in Roxbury, Massachusetts one of his poems was found in his pocket. The last lines read: "Let men of God in courts and churches watch/ O'er such as do a *toleration* hatch, / Lest that ill egg bring forth a cockatrice, / To poison all with heresie and vice./ If men be left, and otherwise combine,/ My *Epitaph's* I DY'D NO LIBERTINE" (M I 134).

o   o   o

THE / TENTH MUSE / Lately sprung up in AMERICA. / OR / Severall Poems, compiled / with great variety of Wit / and Learning, full of delight. / Wherein especially is contained a com- / pleat discourse and description of / The Four *Elements*, / *Constitutions*, / *Ages of Man*, / *Seasons of the Year*. / Together with an Exact Epitome of / The Four Monarchies, *viz.* / The *Assyrian*, / *Persian*, / *Grecian*, / *Roman*. / Also a Dialogue between Old *England* and / New, concerning the late troubles. / With divers other pleasant and serious Poems. / By a Gentlewoman in those parts. (AB xl)

Anne Bradstreet's first volume of poetry was published in 1650 in London. The book had been set in type, apparently without the author's consent, from a manuscript her minister brother-in-law, John Woodbridge, carried to England in 1647.

Woodbridge's introduction to the first edition assures the "Kind Reader":

It is the Work of a Woman, honoured, and esteemed where she lives, for her gracious demeanour, her eminent parts, her pious conversation, her courteous disposition, her exact diligence in her place, and discreet mannaging of her family occasions' and more then so, these Poems are the fruit but of some few houres, curtailed from her sleep, and other refreshments . . . and contrary to her expectation I have presumed to bring to publick view what she resolved should never in such a manner see the Sun; but I found that divers had gotten some scattered papers, affected them wel, were likely to have sent forth broken peices to the Authors prejudice. (AB 526)

The first poem in the collection is an abject dedication to Bradstreet's "most Honoured Father, *Thomas Dudley* Esq."

I shall not need my innocence to clear,
These ragged lines, will do't, when they appear.
On what they are, your mild aspect I crave,
Accept my best, my worst vouchsafe a grave.

From her, that to your selfe more duty owes,
Then waters, in the boundlesse Ocean flowes.

—*Anne Bradstreet* (AB 6)

Between "The four Seasons of the Yeare" and "The Foure Monarchies" the author, or her minister-editor-brother-in-law, inserted
another signed filial apology:

My Subjects bare, my Brains are bad.
Or better Lines you should have had:
The first fell in so naturally.
I could not tell how to passe't by:
The last, though bad, I could not mend.
Accept therefore of what is penn'd.
And all the faults which you shall spy.
Shall at your feet for pardon cry.
Your dutifull Daughter.
A.B. (AB 53)

For a woman to break Puritan sanctions against public statements
from her sex was revolution enough in seventeenth century North
America. The madness of Anne Hopkins; the excommunication and
banishment of Anne Hutchinson; the banishment of Mary Dyer; published reports of their "monster" premature babies; the reprimands
or silencing of other women who were midwives, had medical
knowledge, or transgressed the male boundaries of theology by
preaching; the excommunication, divorce, and disinheritance of
her undutiful sister were ominous precedents. Anne Bradstreet was
the daughter of a governor of Massachusetts and the wife of a leading magistrate, both of whom were virulent persecutors of Anne
Hutchinson. Yet she seems to have persisted in her determination to

keep on reading and writing, by carefully controlling the tone of her rebellion.

We can know little about her authorial intentions because original manuscripts for the *Tenth Muse* and almost everything else she wrote have been lost. The surviving copy-texts wear a mask of civility, domesticity, and perfect submission to contemporary dogmatism.

Sometimes Anne Bradstreet's cover slips and a voice of anger breaks out.

In her elegy titled "In honour of that High and Mighty Princess, Queen ELIZABETH, of most happy memory," Bradstreet sharply rebuked the slander, consecrated by Saint Paul and emphasized by Anglicans and Puritans, that man was intellectually pre-eminent over woman.

> Now say, have women worth, or have they none?
> Or had they some, but with our Queen is't gone?
> Nay Masculines, you have thus tax'd us long,
> But she though dead, will vindicate our wrong.
> Let such, as say our sex is void of reason,
> Know 'tis a slander now, but once was treason. (AB 157)

The lapse was covered by John Woodbridge's ministering non-authorial hand. In one of the initialed or unsigned commendatory poems and anagrams attesting to her character and literary achievement appended to the first edition he wrote: "You have acutely in *Eliza's* ditty/ Acquitted women, else I might with pitty./ Have wisht them all to womens Works to look./ And never more to meddle with their book" (AB 528).

Mrs. Bradstreet was usually more discreet.

THE AUTHOR TO HER BOOK.

> Thou ill-form'd offspring of my feeble brain.
> Who after birth did'st by my side remain.
> Till snatcht from thence by friends, less wise then true
> Who thee abroad, expos'd to publick view.

Made thee in raggs, halting to th' press to trudge,
Where errors were not lessened (all may judg).
At thy return my blushing was not small,
My rambling brat (in print) should mother call,
I cast thee by as one unfit for light,
Thy Visage was so irksome in my sight,
Yet being mine own, at length affection would
Thy blemishes amend, if so I could:
I wash'd thy face, but more defects I saw.
And rubbing off a spot, still made a flaw.
I stretcht thy joynts to make thee even feet,
Yet still thou run'st more hobling then is meet:
In better dress to trim thee was my mind.
But nought save home-spun Cloth, i' th' house I find.
In this array, 'mongst Vulgars mayst thou roam,
In Criticks hands, beware thou dost not come:
And take thy way where yet thou art not known.
If for thy Father askt, say, thou hadst none:
And for thy Mother, she alas is poor.
Which caus'd her thus to send thee out of door.
(AB 177–178)

"The Author to her Book" was added to the Bradstreet canon in the posthumous 1678 edition called *Several Poems*, "Corrected by the Author, and enlarged," along with seventeen other previously unpublished works apparently found among her papers after her death. Joel R. McElrath, Jr. and Allan J. Robb, the editors of the *The Complete Works of Anne Bradstreet*, published in 1981, call this poem one of her "truly charming" works.

o o o

To The READER.
Good READER,
As large Gates to small Edifices, so are long Prefaces
to little Bookes, therefore I will breifly informe thee, that
here thou shalt find, the time when, *the manner* how,

the cause why, *and the great successe* which *it hath*
pleased the lord to give, to this handfull of his praysing
saints in N. Eng. *and it will be clearly demonstrated,*
if thou compare them, with any other people, who
have left their Countryes, as the Gothes, Vandals &c.
to possesse a fatter, as Italy, *or warmer, as* Spaine, &c.
(WWP A 2)

Edward Johnson, a woodworker who may at one time have been a shipbuilder, also arrived in Salem in 1630, probably on the *Arbella*. This time he came alone. He was back in England between 1631–35. In 1636 he returned to Boston with his wife and children. Eventually Johnson became one of the founders of Woburn, the town's first "Recorder," a trader, a captain in the militia, and surveyor-general of arms and munition for the colony. In 1654 Johnson was the anonymous author of the first published history of Massachusetts, *Wonder-Working Providence of Sion's Savior in New-England.* This history lavished praises on Anne Bradstreet's illustrious father, Governor Thomas Dudley, and on her husband Simon: "*Now* Simon *yong, step in among, these worthies take thy place: / All day to toile in vinyard, while Christ thee upholds with grace*" (WWP 108). Simon later became governor.

ANNE HUTCHENSON

a non-such (M 2: 517)

"And verily Satans policy here . . . was to keepe men from that one right way. . . . no marvell then if so many Errours arise, like those fained heads of *Hidra* as fast as one is cut off two stand up in the roome, and chiefly about the uniting of the Soule to Christ by Faith" (WWP 93).

    Captain Johnson excoriated Anne Hutchinson in chapter after chapter. She is the Hydra in his Song of America.

Come along with me sayes one of them (Erronists), i'le
bring you to a Woman that Preaches better Gospell

then any of your black-coates that have been at the
Ninneversity, a woman of another kinde of spirit, who
hath had many Revelations of things to come, and for
my part, saith hee, I had rather hear such a one that
speakes from the meere motion of the spirit, without
any study at all, then any of your learned Scollers, although they may be fuller of Scripture (I) and admit
they may speake by the helpe of the spirit, yet the
other goes beyond them . . . the grosse dissimulation of
these erronious persons hath appeared exceedingly,
as for instance first of a Woman, even the grand Mistris
of all the rest, who denied the Resurrection from the
dead, shee and her consorts mightily rayling against
learning, perswading all they could to take heed of
being spoyled by it . . . so that surely had this Sect
gone on awhile, they would have made a new Bible.
(WWP 95–97)

Epigraph to *A History of New-England, From the English planting in
the Yeere 1628, until the Yeere 1652,* declaring the form of their Government, from the Book of Psalms:

> 107.24 *The righteous shall see it and rejoice, and all in-
> iquity shall stop her mouth* (WWP A 1).

o   o   o

After the death of her husband in Rhode Island in 1642, the ban-
ished "nimble-tongued woman" and ten of her children moved to
Long Island Sound near what is present-day Rye, in Westchester
County, New York. Like many other fugitives from the Bay Colony's
theocracy the Hutchinsons moved further away into uncharted
areas to avoid official harassment. When they decided on the
Dutch settlements near New Amsterdam they were probably un-
aware of the brutal attacks Dutch colonists had made on the
Siwanoy Indians during 1643. Anne Hutchinson had experienced
friendly relations with the natives of Rhode Island. As Johnson

scornfully put it in his *History*, "being amongst a multitude of Indians, (they) boasted they were become all one Indian" (WWP 132). A few months after her arrival, John Throckmorton, another dissenter from New England, settled nearby. In August or September, just after the harvest, both settlements were attacked and destroyed as part of a larger Mohegan uprising. Anne Hutchinson, and most of her company were killed. Their house was burned beyond trace.

o   o   o

Edward Johnson, the soon-to-be captain-adventurer-trader and anonymous historian-narrator of *Wonder-Working Providence of Sions Saviour in New-England,* arrived for the second time in the Massachusetts Bay Colony, in 1636, at the height of the antinomian Controversy.

VULNERABILITY AND CONTACT

"Here I am."

Mattacusets These in new England:

"Then my deare friend unfold thy hands, for thou and I have much worke to doe. I and all Christian Souldiers" (WWP 26).

"Now, now: I now in hand for the exalting of his glorious Kingdome" (WWP 117).

Strangers makes signs in a babbling. There is buzzing. Books called *Appeals to the People.* I am no tolerator. Substitution is not an act. Reassemble the subject in bearing it.

Election. Application of the law or precedent. This is the state. Definitive sentence. Immanent. Engender the sense of the term. Passivity is negligent maternity. Not to shut up in it.

These theses drive off skepticism. This ladder-proof account is itself. Errors of which you will further hear: Eros and separation. A woman should love with her children. To them it is not given. Do to them I *Kings* 21.

The author ends Yours to command.

Certaine Indians coming to her house, discoursing with
them, they wished to tye up her doggs, for they much
bit the man, not mistrusting the Indians guile, did so;

the which no sooner done, but they cruelly murthered
her, taking one of their daughters away with them, &
another of them seeking to escape is caught, as she
was getting over a hedge, and they drew her back
againe by the haire of the head to the stump of a tree,
and there cut off her head with a hatchet: the other
that dwelt by them betook them to boat, and fled,
to tell the sad newes; the rest of their companions,
who were rather hardened in their sinfull way, and bla-
phemous opinions, than brought to any sight of their
damnable Errours, as you shall after hear; yet was not
this the first loud speaking hand of God against them;
but before this the Lord had poynted directly to their
(Erronists') sinne by a very fearfull Monster, that another
of these women brought forth they striving to bury it in
oblivion, but the Lord brought it to light, setting forth
the view of their monstrous Errors in this prodigious birth.
(WWP 133)

Between 1651 and 1659, when Captain Johnson was probably writing the twelfth chapter of his history, he combined an earthquake
that "came from the Westerne and uninhabited parts of this Wilder-
nesse"; Mrs. Hutchinson's preaching, civil censure, banishment, and
murder; and the miscarriage of her supporter and fellow midwife,
Mary Dyer, and grouped these signs of creation and conflict with
the "timely death of Mr. John Harvard" who left enough money to
pay for the erection of New England's first college.

This yeare, although the estates of these pilgrim people
were much wasted, yet seeing the benefit that would
accrew to the Churches of Christ and Civil Government, by the Lords blessing, upon learning, they began
to erect a Colledge, the Lord by his provident hand
giving his approbation to the work, in sending over a
faithfull and godly servant of his, the reverend Mr. *John
Harvard*. (WWP 133)

For richest Jems and gainfull things most Merchants wisely venter:/
Deride not then New England men, this Corporation enter" (WWP 14).

Proximity is fraternity in *Wonder-Working Providence of Sions Saviour in New-England*: then who is what to me?

Nettles and brambles feminine.

Colledge is a site of constraint. The system holds together.

o   o   o

> *Of the great Earthquake in* New England, *and of the wofull end*
> of some erronious persons, with the first foundation of
> Harverd *Colledge*. (WWP 131)

> God stamps dominion. Good Reader,
> learn your letters.
> At the margins of the history of the West.

"*If* Harverd *had with riches here been taken. / He need not then through troublous Seas have past*" (WWP 133).

The perils of colonial infancy: Captain Johnson's custom of dropping into poetry. John Winthrop's Journal entering into history.

"The fifth volume of the *Winthrop Papers,* covering the years 1645-1649, marks the end of the first chapter of the history of the Winthrop family in America," writes its editor, Allyn B. Forbes. (WP V) The *Winthrop Papers* is published by the Massachusetts Historical Society. The frontispiece is a portrait of Governor Winthrop now owned by the American Antiquarian Society in Worcester. This portrait may be only a copy, although portions below the head may be original work. Some say the face was painted by Van Dyke before Winthrop left England. Forbes cites Mr. Burroughs, an authority on something from somewhere. Mr. Burroughs supports the originality of the face due to the "freedom and emphasis" of the brush strokes.

The portrait's donor, William Winthrop, was "the Son of John, the Son of Adam, the Son of Adam, the Son of Adam, the Son of John, Governor of Massachusetts" (WP V).

Can the subject escape the concept? John Harvard was a minister: John Harvard, the son of a butcher.

IN THE TRACE OF EXILE

1638: (2.)) The governour, with advice of some other
of the magistrates and of the elders of Boston, caused
the said monster to be taken up, and though it were
much corrupted, yet most of these things were to be
seen, as the horns and claws, the scales &c. When it
died in the mother's body, (which was about two hours
before the birth,) the bed whereon the mother lay did
shake, and withal there was such a noisome savour, as
most of the women were taken with extreme vomiting
and purging, so as they were forced to depart; and
others of them their children were taken with convul-
sions (which they never had before nor after,) and so
were sent for home, so as by these occasions it came
to be conceasled. (WH I: 263)

1638: (3.) 2.) At the court of elections, the former governour, John Winthrop, was chosen again. . . . This court
the name of Newtown was altered, and it was called
Cambridge. (WH 1: 265)

James Savage's footnote to the latter entry reads:

In compliment to the place, where so many of the civil
and clerical fathers of New England had received their
education, this venerable name (may it ever be pre-
served!) was undoubtedly bestowed. There were probably, at that time, forty or fifty sons of the University of
Cambridge in Old England—one for every two villages
of Massachusetts and Connecticut. The sons of Oxford
were not few. (WH I: 265)

RELATION TO SOMETHING

The caress of love. One has just been born. A monist conception. It is
a daughter a monster the other. What verb can deliver consolation?

Go spend your salt plan. Calculation hear me in your name. What is most uncovered? Bury in water and mud. Never enough. Surrender tender face thou I will not be consoled. 49 Isaiah 21 give place to obscurity that I may show.

A little child scrambles out and comes to its mother.

Genesis Exodus Leviticus Kings Chronicles Judges escaping the birth am re-reading chapters. Chapter for child per child.

Awake, awake Deborah; remembering Nebuchadnezzar.

Remembering Nebuchadnezzar go heap coals of fire on chapter.

Interiority of wanton femininity here is the explication I Timothy 12 and the others

Paul to Timothy by the commandment of God:

which is our hope? where are we now?

speck of letter in a sea of silt

Mr. Mather Mr. Hubbard Mr. Prince. Listen to me.

What is finite freedom? Is every founder confounded by error? How is the hammer of the whole earth cut? I hope I will not be un-willing. Always desire to subscribe myself Yours in what I say

Door on the hinge and wheel on the pin I hang and spin and turn again.

Negligence of passivity Love is the interdiction of a history.

o   o   o

In May 1646, John Winthrop noted in his *Journal-History:*

> A daughter of Mrs. Hutchinson was carried away by
> the Indians near the Dutch, when her mother and oth-
> ers were killed by them: and upon the peace con-
> cluded between the Dutch and the same Indians, she
> was returned to the Dutch governour, who restored her
> to her friends here. She was about eight years old,
> when she was taken, and continued with them about
> four years, and she had forgot her own language, and
> all her friends, and was loath to have come from the
> Indians. (WH II: 267)

James Savage, usually so prolific with his footnotes, has no footnote here.

SAVAGE HISTORY GENEALOGY

A meticulous gentleman with the surname Savage is transcribing and editing the *History of New England from 1630 to 1649*, written by a founding gentlemen father.

His marginal notes to the passages in Winthrop's *History* concerning Dyer's monster, the monster's witch-midwife, and the questioning in church of the monster's father "for divers monstruous errours," tell us Dyer's future:

> After long enjoying her revelations, in quiet, at Rhode Island, she was unhappily led . . . again to visit Boston, probably bringing more light, when she was condemned to death as a Quaker. Winthrop, governour of Connecticut, our author's eldest son, inheriting the natural mildness of his father, attempted to save her life; but the bigotry of the age had acquired a severer character, and, for a second return, in June, 1660, she suffered. See Hutchinson, I. 184. (WH I 261. *n*.)

The title page of *The History of New England from 1630 to 1649, by John Winthrop, Esq. First Governour of the Colony of the Massachusetts Bay, From His Original Manuscripts, With Notes to Illustrate the Civil and Ecclesiastical Concerns, the Geography, Settlement and Institutions of the Country, and the Lives and Manners of the Principal Planters*, assures us that James Savage is a Member of the Massachusetts Historical Society. Often the edifying margins of this early Victorian American edition overprint the tumultuous record of Law in early seventeenth century Massachusetts Bay Colony. The Massachusetts Historical Society is an organization of men who are elite.

On June 1st, 1660 Mary Dyer was hanged with two other Quakers on Boston Common.

"She suffered. See Hutchinson, I 184."

Savage says look somewhere else.

Later Savage becomes a genealogist.

During the 1660s, Commissioner Humphrey Atherton was the chief military officer in New England. While he was the governor of Connecticut, John Winthrop, Jr., became a partner in the Atherton Company. Led by Atherton, the Company consisted of a group of land speculators whose double dealings with the Narragansetts made them into wealthy landowners. Rufus Jones, in *The Quakers in the American Colonies,* says that while Mary Dyer's body was swinging in the wind, Humphrey Atherton, who was a witness to the execution, pointed to it and scornfully remarked: "She hangs there as a flag" (QC 89).

Savage's copious footnotes on Humphrey Atherton ("Humphrey Atherton deserves much honor in our early annals") don't cover this incident (WH II: 137).

In the last chapter, called "Friday" of *A Week On The Concord and Merrimack Rivers,* first published in Boston in 1867, Thoreau asks: "But where is the instructed teacher? Where are the *normal* schools?"

o   o   o

Publish in the margin call attention to something.

Letter to the Massachusetts General Court, 28 March, 1659:

> When I heard your last Order read
> it was a disturbance unto me that was
> So freely Offering up my life to him who gave it me
> That was so freely
> Obedience being Presence and Peace and Love in me
> I was so far
> than that.
> Any more the words I should not return to Prison
> I submitted, finding nothing from the Lord to the contrary
> That I may know
> For he is my Life and the length of my Days

I rested I

came at his Command and go at his Command

"Mary Dyer" (MD 92–3)

Who were pledged to loyalty? Unevenness in their course. The violence of ambiguity. Disorder is another order. Now it is *qunnanta-
caun* that is lamentation

my question is: where do we define the
jurisdiction?

Dear sister, I can go no further; a weary body and sleepy eyes
command.

Write to the authorities. Not to be known when I sink down. I have
made your face wrong. Vulnerable as mortal. In the no man's land
I remain Yours forever.

History certifies this.

4
OUTSIDE

Npakénaqun. / *I am put away.* (K 150)

. . .and as for beauty they esteeme black beyond any
colour. Wherefore their *Squawes* use that sinful art of
painting their Faces in the hollows of their Eyes and
Nose, with a shining black, out of which their tip of their
Nose appeares very deformed, and their cheeke
bone, being of a lighter swart black, on which they
have a blew crosse dyed very deepe.

This is the beauty esteemed by them. (WWP 115–16)

For eleven weeks and five days Mary Rowlandson was that "woman
in the Wilderness who may have the vomit of the Dragon cast in her
face." She saw and spoke to King Philip—the Devil. She was the
colonist Sion the outcast.

Returned from daily walking to and fro at the ends of the earth—

with Satan—Reverend Joseph Rowlandson's wife knew that her ordeal might mark her as suspect; vulnerable to ambivalent charges ranging from pride (she had set a high price on her own head) to sexual promiscuity, even to sorcery. Perhaps she told her story to assure herself and her community that she was a woman who feared God and eschewed evil.

One precaution first—rupture erased in a cloud of his Glory in the dust of her text.

> *I have been in the midst of those roaring Lyons, and*
> *Salvage Bears that feared neither God, nor Man, nor*
> *the Devil, by night and day, alone and in company:*
> *sleeping all sorts together, and yet not one of them*
> *ever offered me the least abuse of unchastity to me, in*
> *word or action.* Though some are ready to say, I speak
> it for my own credit; *But I speak it in the presence of*
> *God, and to his Glory.* (N 64)

But her "song of war" tarnishes Captain Edward Johnson's version of the Common-wealth as a figural "refuge" set apart for the encouragement, "cheerfulnesse" and "primitive purity" of these "forerunners of Christs Army."

o   o   o

> Mat pitch cowahick   *The God that made*
> Manit keesiteonckqus I   *you will not know you* (K 192)

> Oh yes! oh yes! oh yes! *All you the people of Christ that*
> *are here Oppressed, Imprisoned and scurrilously de-*
> *rided, gather yourselves together, your Wives and little*
> *ones, and answer to your severall Names as you shall*
> *be shipped for his service, in the Westerne World.*
> (WWP 2)

One of the wives attending to the service of the King of Kings answers to the name of Mary. Mary reapprehends her own story while trapped in New England's use and progress. Sometimes her husband, Joseph, a godly minister of Christ, is left behind in their Westerne Garden.

Away with her by hidden paths into an origin.

There were many hundreds, old and young, some sick,
and some lame many had *Papooses* at their backs,
the greatest number at this time with us, were *Squaws,*
and they travelled with all they had, bag and bag-
gage, and yet they got over this River . . . and on
Munday they set their *Wigwams* on fire, and away
they went: On that very day came the *English* Army
after them to this River, and saw the smoak of their
Wigwams, and yet this River put a stop to them. (N 19)

Here is an amorphous psychic space. Only her retrospective narrative voice can control and connect the twists and turns of time past. *"For a smal moment have I forsaken thee, but with great mercies will I gather thee"* (N 38).

Who has forsaken who? Where are we now? God's text in Rowlandson's text is counterpoint, shelter, threat.

"My Bible: *Which was my Guid by day and my Pillow by night"* (N 38).

Soteriology is a screen against the primal Night. She must come back to that knowing.

But in writing Language advances into remembering that there is no answer imagining Desire. Remembering a wild place there is no forgetting.

"Now must we pack up and be gone from this Thicket. . . . As we went along they killed a *Deer,* with a young one in her, they gave me a piece of the *Fawn,* and it was so young and tender, that one might eat the bones as well as the flesh, and yet I thought it very good" (N 41).

Once Mary Rowlandson was quarry to huntsmen. First she hated them then she joined them now she remembers to hate them again.

She and her children with some nieces, nephews, and neighbors crossed into absence on February 10th, 1675. Out of sight? What of that?

This is a crime story.

Remember, captives and captors are walking together beyond the protective re-duplication of Western culture through another epoch far off. God sent affliction to Lancaster to try Her. Witnesses are all humans linking or heralding truth or transgression in a grammatical irruption of grace abounding.

"The *Indians* were as thick as the trees: it seemd as if there had been a thousand Hatchets going at once" (N 20). "*The* Squaw *laid a skin for me, and bid me sit down, and gave me some Ground-nuts, and bade me come again: and told me they wuld buy me, if they were able, and yet these were strangers to me that I never saw before*" (N 29). "There was here one *Mary Thurston* of *Medfield*, who seeing how it was with me, lent me a Hat to wear" (N 26). "*We took up our packs and along we went*. . . . As we went along I saw an *English-man* stripped naked, and lying dead upon the ground, but knew not who it was" (N 45). "They came home on a Sabbath day, and the *Powaw* that kneeled upon the *Deer-skin* came home (I may say, without abuse) as black as the Devil" (N 52). "*Then came* Tom *and* Peter, *with the second Letter from the Council, about the Captives*. Though they were *Indians*, I gat them by the hand, and burst out into tears" (N 48-49). "There was another Praying *Indian*, so wicked and cruel, as to wear a string about his neck, strung with *Christians* fingers" (N 50). "There was one that kneeled upon a *Deer-skin*, with the company round him in a ring who kneeled, and striking upon the ground with their hands and with sticks; and muttering or humming with their mouths, besides him who kneeled in the ring, there also stood one with a Gun in his hand" (N 51).

o   o   o

This is a crime story in a large and violent place. Too large for subject and object. Only a few of her captors have names. Nearly all of their names are wrong. Anyway, by 1676 most of them are gone.

1677: "*I can remember the time, when I used to sleep quietly without workings in my thoughts, whole nights together, but now it is other wayes with me.* When all are fast about me, and no eye open, but his who ever waketh, my thoughts are upon things past" (N 71).

Carried away unwillingly into the uncharted geography of North America, an author cannot let some definitive version of New England's destiny pull her. Once she senses oscillations of sense close to the face of her hunger, Scripture is a closure. Allegory a grid she can get over.

When Mary Rowlandson can't count sheep she lets counter-memory out.

Clamor in the theater of alienation. Ransom stammers fact of Famine. Divine cruelty and social necessity unleash the dialectical tension between Starvation and Gluttony.

A narrator is narrating something about the recalcitrant beast in Everywoman. In this wild place every human has a bait she must bite.

> There came an Indian to them at that time, with a
> basket of Horse-liver. I asked him to give me a piece:
> *What,* sayes he *can you eat Horse-liver?* I told him, I
> would try, if he would give a piece, which, he did, and
> I laid it on the coals to rost, but before it was half ready
> they got half of it away from me, so that I was fain to
> take the rest and eat it as it was, with the blood about
> my mouth, and yet a savoury bit it was to me: *For to*
> *the hungry Soul every bitter thing is sweet.* (N 21–2)

There she stands, blood about her mouth, savouring the taste of raw horse-liver. God's seal of ratification spills from her lips or from her husband's pen.

o   o   o

"There may be two things spoken to in the management of the Truth" (N 134), wrote Reverend Joseph Rowlandson in his "Last Sermon," preached at Wethersfield, Nov. 21, 1676, on a day of FAST and HU-MILIATION. This is the sermon annexed to most editions of his wife's narrative of her captivity and restoration. A year later he was dead.

The idiosyncratic syntax of Mary Rowlandson's closed structure refuses closure. After the war-whoop terror and the death of her little daughter, a new management of the truth speaks to oppose itself. When the teller skids into schism remembering, she calls on God to keep her ground from shifting. She is a servant of the Lord. Fidelity is her privilege. Faith is a first precaution. Muttering or humming.

—Must rely on God himself—whole dependence must
be upon him—Guns guns—tobacco—he on the *Deer-
skin*—preparation for a great day of Dancing—
Bracelets—handfulls of Neck-laces—Garters hung
round with Shillings—*God show'd his power over the
Heathen in this—there is no thing too hard for God!*
   —nothing to drink but water and green Hurtle-berries
   —nothing over them but the heavens, and nothing
under them but the earth
   —Quonopen fetched me some water himself,
and bid me wash, and gave me a Glas to see how
I looked. I was wonderfully revived by this favor he
showed me—*But to return to my going home—Our
family now being gathered together—*

RHYTHM OF THE OLD WORLD: "Here you have Samson's Riddle exemplified, and that great promise, Rom. 8.28, verified. Out of the eater comes forth meat, and sweetness out of the strong" (N Xiv).

   RHYTHM OF THE NEW: "That night we had a mess of wheat for our supper" (N 22).

   The trick of her text is its mix.

o   o   o

At last, after many weary steps I saw *Wachuset* hills,
but many miles off. Then we came to a great *Swamp,*
through which we travelled up to the knees, in mud
and water, which was very heavy going to one tyred
before. Being almost spent, I thought I should have
sunk down at last, and never gat out, but I may say as

in *Psal.* 94.18, *When my foot slipped, thy mercy, O Lord held me up.* Going along, having indeed my life, but little spirit, *Philip,* who was in the Company, came up and took me by the hand. (N 46–47)

King Philip, Increase Mather's "perfidious and bloody Author of the War," helped Mary Rowlandson climb out of mud and water. When she was an author she remembered to write it.

Her view of King Philip's War and her picture of Metacomet himself is a contradiction of orthodox Puritan history.

One moral sense soon cancels another in a country of progress and force.

Thereupon he (Metacomet/Philip) betook himself to flight, but as he was coming out of the Swamp, an English-man and an Indian endeavored to fire at him, the English-man missed of his aime, but the Indian shot him through the heart, so as that he fell down dead. . . . This Wo was brought upon him that spoyled when he was not spoyled. And in that very place where he first contrived and began his mischief, was he taken and destroyed, and there was he (Like as Agag was hewed in pieces before the Lord) cut into four quarters, and is now hanged up as a monument of revenging Justice, his head being cut off and carried away to Plymouth, his Hands were brought to *Boston.* . . . Thus did God break the head of that Leviathan, and gave it to be meat to the people inhabiting the wilderness, and brought it to the town of *Plimouth* the very day of their solemn Festival. (BH 139–40)

This was in 1676. Wootonokanuske, Philip's wife, had been captured earlier that year with their nine-year old son. They were both sold into slavery and so vanish from history.

On August 6, Weetamoo, sachem of the Pocasset Wampanoags, Quannopin's wife, and Mary Rowlandson's mistress during her captivity, was betrayed by one of her subjects. This deserter led twenty English soldiers to her camp near the Taunton River. Weetamoo was drowned while trying to escape on a raft. Later her body washed up in Metapoiset. The English who found this newly dead body didn't know who it was but cut off the head anyway and stuck it on a pole in Taunton. Some Indian prisoners there "knew it presently, and made a most horrid and diabolical Lamentation, crying out it was their Queens head" (BH 138).

Quannopin was captured August 16, 1676, and taken to Newport, Rhode Island where he was tried by court-martial August 24. The next day the chief war sachem of the Narragansetts and Mary Rowlandson's former master was executed with his brother Sunkeejunasuc.

o o o

"Oh! the wonderful power of God that mine eyes have seen, affording matter enough for my thoughts to run in, that when others are sleeping, mine eyes are weeping.

I *have seen the extrem vanity of this World*" (N 72).

o o o

She came tumbling onto the American trail with the smell of death in her nostrils, and the sound of women wailing for their children.

"Go to Shiloh, and see what I did to it, for the wickedness of my People Israel. Go, and view it" (RS 143-144).

Mary Rowlandson saw what she did not see said what she did not say.

KEY

AB | *The Complete Works of Anne Bradstreet.* McElrath & Robb, eds.

AC | *The Antinomian Controversy, 1636-1638.* David Hall, ed.

AT | *An American Triptych.* Wendy Martin.

BH | *A Brief History.* Increase Mather.

CW | *The Complete works of Ralph Waldo Emmerson.*

K   I   *A Key into the Language of America.* Roger Williams.

LCP   I   *Language, Counter-Memory, Practice.* Michel Foucault.

M   I   *Magnalia Christi Americana.* Cotton Mather.

MD   I   *Mary Dyer of Rhode Island.* Horatio Rogers.

N   I   *The Narrative of Mary Rowlandson.*

O   I   *Otherwise Than Being or Beyond Essence.* Emmanuel Levinas.

QC   I   *The Quakers in the American Colonies.* Rufus Jones.

R   I   *Records of the First Church.* Richard D. Pierce, ed.

RS   I   Rev. Joseph Rowlandson's "Sermon."

WJ   I   *Winthrop's Journal, "History of New England, 1630–1649."* James Hosmer, ed.

WH   I   *"The History of New England from 1630-1649".* John Winthrop; James Savage, ed.

WP   I   *Winthrop Papers.* Vol. 5, 1645–1649. Allyn B. Forbes, ed.

WWP   I   *The Wonder-Working Providence.* Edward Johnson.

SOURCES FOR THE CAPTIVITY AND RESTORATION OF MRS. MARY ROWLANDSON

Bradstreet, Anne. *The Complete Works of Anne Bradstreet.* J. R. McElrath and A. Robb, eds. Boston: Twayne Publishers, 1981.

Dunn, Richard S. "John Winthrop Writes His Journal," *William and Mary Quarterly,* vol. 41, no.2 (April 1984), 185-212.

Emerson, Ralph Waldo. *The Complete Works of R.W. Emerson,* vol. xi (*Miscellanies*). Boston: Houghton Mifflin Co., 1878.

Foucault, Michel. *Language, Counter-Memory, Practice: Selected Essays and Interviews.* Donald F. Bouchard, ed. Ithaca, N.Y.: Cornell University Press, 1977.

Greene, David L. "New Light on Mary Rowlandson," *Early American Literature,* vol. 20 (1985).

Johnson, Edward. *Wonder-Working Providence of Sions Savior In New-England.* London, 1654; Delmar, N.Y.: Scholars Facsimile and Reprints, 1974.

Jones, Rufus. *The Quakers in the American Colonies.* London: Macmillan, 1911.

Levinas, Emanuel. *Otherwise Than Being Or Beyond Essence.* Alphonso Lingis, ed. The Hague: Martinus Nijhoff Philosophy Texts, vol. 3., 1981.

Martin, Wendy. *An American Triptych: Anne Bradstreet, Emily Dickinson, Adrienne Rich*. Chapel Hill: University of North Carolina Press, 1984.

Mather, Cotton. *Magnalia Christi Americana; or, The Ecclesiastical History of New-England From Its First Planting, in the year 1620 unto the year of our Lord 1698*. Hartford: Silas Andrus & Son, 1855.

Mather, Increase. *A Brief History of the Warr with the Indians in New-England . . . Together With a Serious Exhortation To the Inhabitants of that Land*. Reprinted in *So Dreadfull A Judgment: Puritan Responses to King Philip's War, 1676–1677*. Richard Slotkin and James K. Folsom, eds. Middletown: Wesleyan University Press, 1978.

Rogers, Horatio. *Mary Dyer of Rhode Island*, the Quaker Martyr that *was hanged on Boston Common, June 1st, 1660*. Providence: Preston and Rounds, 1896.

Rowlandson, Mary. *The Narrative of the Captivity and Restoration of Mrs. Mary Rowlandson. First Printed in 1682 at Cambridge, Massachusetts, & London, England. Now reprinted in facsimile; Whereunto are annexed a map of her removes, biographical and historical notes, and the last sermon of her husband, Rev. Joseph Rowlandson*. Henry Stedman Nourse and John Eliot Thayer, eds. Lancaster: 1903,

Rowlandson, Joseph. See above.

Slotkin, Richard. *Regeneration Through Violence: The Mythology of the American Frontier, 1600–1860*. Middletown: Wesleyan University Press, 1973.

Thoreau, Henry D. *A Week on the Concord and Merrimack Rivers*. Boston: Riverside Press, Houghton Mifflin Co., 1890.

Williams, Roger. *A Key to the Language of America*. London: Gregory Dextor, 1643; Reprinted for the Rhode Island and Providence Plantations Tercentenary, Committee, Providence: Roger Williams Press, 1936.

Winthrop, John. *The History of New England from 1630-1649*. James Savage, ed. Boston: Phelps and Farnham, 1825.

———. *Winthrop Papers*, vol. V 1645-1649. Allyn B. Forbes, ed. Boston: The Massachusetts Historical Society, 1941.

———. *The Records of the First Church in Boston, 1630-1868*. Richard D. Pierce, ed. *Publications of the Colonial Society of Massachusetts*. Collections, vol. XXXIX. Boston: 1961.

1 Savage claims that "the difference in some particular places, between the correct reading of this edition and the erroneous ones of the former edition, is marked by giving the true word or words in the text between parallel lines before and after, and the word or words of the former edition

between similar lines in the margin below." (WH I: xii) On the following page he substitutes a Latin phrase for an English one. It is therefore here unclear whether the Latin which Savage relegates to the lower margin of the page was in the original manuscript or whether the original was in English because that volume was the one destroyed by fire in his office. The English alternative that Savage inserts into the text reads: "Several lumps of man's seed, without any alteration, or mixture of any thing from the woman."

NEGATIVE CAPABILITY: KEROUAC'S BUDDHIST ETHIC

Jack Kerouac's interest in Buddhism began after he spent some time with Neal Cassady, who had taken on an interest in the local California variety of New Age spiritualism, particularly the work of Edgar Cayce. Kerouac mocked Cassady as a sort of homemade American "Billy Sunday with a suit" for praising Cayce, who went into trance states of sleep and then read what were called the Akashic records, and gave medical advice to the petitioners who came to ask him questions with answers which involve reincarnation. So, Kerouac was interested in going back to the original historic sources. He went to the library in San Jose, California and read a book called *A Buddhist Bible*, edited by Dwight Goddard—a very good anthology of classic Buddhist texts. Kerouac read them very deeply, memorized many of them, and then went on to do other reading and other research and actually became a brilliant intuitive Buddhist scholar. Gary Snyder noted that Kerouac did have an intelligent grasp of Eastern thought, also a learned grasp, and that's something most people don't realize.

He introduced me to it in the form of letters reminding me that suffering was the basis of existence, which is the First Noble Truth in Buddhism. I was at the time a more or less left-wing liberal progressive intellectual, and I was insulted that Kerouac was telling me that the real basis of existence was suffering. I thought this was a personal insult and didn't realize he was simply telling me what he had realized was the basic nature of life.

There is this doctrine in Buddhism of the Three Marks of Existence: first, that existence contains suffering; in Yiddish, existence contains *tsuris,* serious difficulty. Born, as the poet Gregory Corso says, "a hairy bag of water," there's going to be some difficulty before you leave your body, some irritability or discomfort. If you don't like the word "suffering" then you have to accept that existence contains some "discomfort." The traditional definition is that, being

ALLEN GINSBERG

born, the inevitable ultimate consequence is old age, sickness, and death, well described by Kerouac. This is inevitable.

The second characteristic of existence as described in Buddhadharma is Impermanence—the transitoriness of our condition; the fact that what we have here is like a dream, in the sense that it is real while it is here. And so Kerouac would say to me, "Come back in a million years and tell me if this is real." He had the sense of the reality of existence and at the same time the unreality of existence. To Western minds this is a contradiction and an impossibility. But actually, it is not impossible because it is true; this universe is real, and is at the same time unreal. This is known in Buddhism as a co-emergent wisdom, the fact that form and emptiness are identical. These are just basic Buddhist ideas. You'll find the terminology of *sunyata*, emptiness within form, running through all of Kerouac's middle-period writing, especially in *Mexico City Blues*. The idea of transitoriness, of impermanence, is not a Himalayan idea, and not an Oriental idea, it's a classic Western idea. For, as Gregory Corso paraphrases Heraclitus—"You can't step in the same river once." You remember Heraclitus: "You can't step in the same river twice"? So Corso put it one poetic move ahead.

What Kerouac was discovering was not some strange Oriental notion alien to the Western mind. He was exploring the basis of mind itself as it's known in the West as in the East, except that he saw the Buddhist formulations as being perhaps more sophisticated than the monotheistic formulation of the West. Nevertheless there were non-theistic formulations of the same thing in writers that he read like Lucretius and Montaigne.

So, the third aspect of existence or third mark of existence is *anatma—atman* means self; *anatma* is no permanent self. That comes from the second mark, no permanence of any kind. "All the foundations of existence are transitory" or, as Kerouac paraphrased traditional Buddhist terminology, "All the constituents of being are transitory." That being so, there is no permanent self-hood, no permanent me me me me me, and no permanent Great Me in Heaven. There is no reference point at all. There is nothing but open space or, as it is known to existentialists, the Void. *Sunyata* as it is known in the Orient; open and accommodating space. The existentialist sense of "the void" as a claustrophobic bummer is a very Western and theistic notion. In the East, the notion of "open space" or "accommodating space" is considered a liberation from the limitation of horizon or boundary wherein a theistic God image is the ultimate reference point. Or to put it very simply, when Chogyam Trungpa, who appreciated Kerouac's writings a great deal, was asked by his son: "Daddy, is there a God?" Trungpa said: "No." And his son said: "Whew!" That sigh of relief might have solved many of Kerouac's problems.

So, he introduced me to Buddhism in the form of song. As you may know, Kerouac admired Frank Sinatra for his crooning enunciation, for his oratory, for his clarity of speech, for the precision with which he pronounced the affective emotional content of his vowels. And so, like Frank Sinatra, the first direct Buddhist word I heard from Kerouac's mouth after letters, was his singing of the Three Refuges. So, that would be the next step.

This is basic to Kerouac's understanding of Buddhism. It goes: "In Buddha I take my refuge, in Dharma I take my refuge, in Sangha I take my refuge." Buddha may be defined here as wakened mind; clear, not sleeping, not daydreaming but clear, aware of this space. Dharma is the intellectual explanation and exposition of the state of awakeness—historically, through sutra discourses and through understanding of the theory. Sangha is the assembled fellow awakened meditators. So he sang to me in Sanskrit: "*Buddham Saranam Gochamee, Dhammam Saranam Gochamee, Sangham Saranam Gochamee*"; he sang it like Frank Sinatra in 1952. And that first introduced me to the delicacy and softness of his Buddhism aside from the tough truth of suffering, transitoriness, and no permanent Allen Ginsberg, no permanent Kerouac.

Following that are the Four Noble Truths which readers read in his writing without inquiring further about what they are, although in various essays Kerouac expounds them. Have any of his critics read Kerouac closely enough to remember what he said about the Four Noble Truths? We should pay sufficient respect to Kerouac to ask: "What did he mean by the Four Noble Truths? What are these Four

Noble Truths that he speaks of continually?" Perhaps they should be presented here as part of an exposition of Kerouac's ethics, because this refers directly to the central ethics we find in *Dharma Bums*, *Mexico City Blues*, *Some of the Dharma*, *Wake Up*, his unpublished biography of Buddha, *Desolation Angels*, and even in later works more charged with monotheistic Catholic notions of Sacred Heart in relation to suffering.

The Four Noble Truths (based on the Three Marks of Existence) are as follows. First, existence contains suffering. Second, suffering is caused by ignorance of the conditions in which we exist—ignorance of the transitoriness and ignorance of *anatma*, the empty nature of the situation, so that everybody is afraid of a permanent condition of suffering and doesn't realize that suffering itself is transitory, impermanent. There is no permanent Hell, there is no permanent Heaven. Therefore, the suffering that we sense during this transition of life is not a permanent condition that we need to be afraid of. It's not where we're going to end up. We end liberated from the suffering either by death, or in life, by waking up to the nature of our situation and not clinging and grasping, screaming and being angry, resentful, irritable or insulted by our existence.

It is possible to take our existence as a "sacred world," to take this place as open space rather than claustrophobic dark void. It is possible to take a friendly relationship to our ego natures, it is possible to appreciate the aesthetic play of forms in emptiness, and to exist in this place like majestic kings of our own consciousness. But to do that, we would have to give up grasping to make everything come out the way we daydream it should. So, suffering is caused by ignorance, or suffering exaggerated by ignorance or ignorant grasping and clinging to our notion of what we think should be, is what causes the "suffering of suffering." The suffering itself is not so bad, it's the resentment against suffering that is the real pain. This is where I think Kerouac got caught as a Catholic, ultimately, because I don't think he overcame that fear of the First Noble Truth.

The Third Noble Truth says there is an end to suffering, there is a way out of it. And the Fourth Noble Truth is called the Eightfold Path out of our suffering. The Eightfold Path is as follows: first, Right

Understanding, Right View as it is called, Right Perspective on the whole scene of consciousness and space, which is the realization of suffering and the realization of transitoriness and the realization that there is no permanent ego. Right View, then, leads to the Right Aspiration or Right Ambition, or the ambition to overcome the obstacle of ignorance and greed and passion and clinging, and to get out of the fix.

Third after Right Aspiration comes Right Speech, speech that is in line or coordinated with an understanding of the basic situation. This is distinct from, let us say, the problem that Kerouac came to later, within the suffering of grasping for a permanent reference point in a Catholic God, who will save you and take you to Heaven, or who might condemn you to Hell: a sense of permanent doom or a permanent bliss that you are going to come to. So, Right Speech, not creating more mental garbage, not creating more mental fog for others or yourself.

From Right Speech, the fourth step is Right Activity, not messing up the universe with an insistence that other people follow you towards your obsessive wars, either wars against God or for God, or for Hitler or against Hitler, or for your mother or against your mother.

From Right Action comes Right Labor, a right kind of work so you don't get the wrong job in the atom bomb industry and help blow up the world. From Right Labor comes Right Mindfulness, the awareness of what is around you unobstructed by guilt over what are you doing, saying, thinking, and working at.

From Right Mindfulness comes Right Energy, waking up in the morning, happy with what you are going to do, not obstructed by your own garbage. From Right Energy comes Right Samadhi or Right Meditation, basically being here where you are, unchanged, without guilt. Being able to exist without credentials, existing simultaneously with the earth without apology any more than the sun has to apologize.

Here we come to Walt Whitman's original American proclamation of this condition: "not till the sun rejects you do I reject you." This was also in line with Kerouac's understanding. So, from this comes a term which Kerouac pronounces over and over again in his poetry, the "bodhisattva." How many know what a bodhisattva is, and how he's using it? Here's the formula: the bodhisattva makes a very clear set of four simple vows.

First: sentient beings are numberless. I vow to liberate them all (dogs, worms, kitty cats, mommys, myself, Ginsberg). I vow to illuminate all, is the purpose of Kerouac's writing and the ultimate ethic of his writing. Second: obstacles are countless, I vow to cut through them. My own neuroses are countless, my own graspings are countless, one's own aggression is inexhaustible. Yet, one vows to relate to it, to acknowledge it, to work on it, to cut through it and open up and admit the existence of other sentient beings into one's universe and relate to them in an honest way.

Third of the four vows of the bodhisattva: dharma gates are uncountable, I vow to enter every gate. Dharma gates are situations in which to practice wakeful mind, situations to enter into without being afraid, including the situation of birth and death, the situation of writing dharmic works for America as Kerouac did, and the situation of not being afraid to be corny & display Sacred Heart in expounding Kerouac's prose. It's the disposition to allow our own emotion and tears and sense of suffering, to allow mutual confidence in each other with our most sensitive feelings, as Kerouac confided to us his most sensitive feelings: "Gates of dharma are endless, I vow not to boycott anyone." No boycott of any situation, but total openness toward all situations.

And last of all, Buddha path, or path of awakened mind, is infinite, endless, you never can finish with it, it's too long. I vow to follow through anyway. These are the Four Bodhisattva Vows.

Now, when you take the Bodhisattva Vows it doesn't mean you can do it. It only means that this is the direction in which you would like to go. This is your ideal. This is your compass or this is your heart's desire even if you can't accomplish it. You need not be prevented from being a bodhisattva for fear that you'll not be able to accomplish these four vows, because if that's a heart's desire, that's sufficient for you to take that vow. It's a compass point or a direction or an indication of desire, and a vow to go in that direction. No permanent Heaven, no punishment of permanent Hell for that. So, this then leads to the next: Highest Perfect Wisdom, or *Prajna-paramita*, the ultimate philosophical and ethical statement of Zen Buddhism and Tibetan Buddhism, found in a text which Kerouac knew very well, the *Heart Sutra*.

To summarize the gist, *Prajnaparamita*, the *Heart Sutra*, says: "Avalokitesvara (down-glancing-Lord-of-mercy) Bodhisattva dwelled in meditation on Highest Perfect Wisdom when he realized that all the five heaps (*skandas*) of consciousness we have were empty, this relieved every suffering." Then this discourse continues:

> Shariputra (student), form is emptiness, form is no differ-
> ent from emptiness, emptiness no different from form,
> form is the emptiness, emptiness is the form. Sensation,
> recognition, conceptualization, consciousness are also
> like this. Shariputra, this is the original character of
> everything. Not born, not annihilated, not tainted, not
> pure, does not increase, does not decrease. . . . No
> eye, no ear, no nose, no tongue, no body, no mind,
> no color, no sound, no smell, no taste, no touch, no
> object; no eye, no world of eyes until we come to no
> world of consciousness. No ignorance, also no combat
> against ignorance . . . no suffering, no cause of suffer-
> ing, no nirvana, no path, no wisdom, also no attain-
> ment because no non-attainment. Therefore every
> bodhisattva depends on Highest Perfect Wisdom be-
> cause mind is no obstacle, because of no obstacle
> fear does not exist. Go beyond screwy views, attain nir-
> vana. Past, present and future, every Buddha depends
> on this Highest Perfect Wisdom. . . . Therefore, I know
> *Prajnaparamita* is the great holy mantra, the untainted
> mantra, the supreme mantra, the incomparable man-
> tra, is capable of assuaging all suffering. True because
> not false. Therefore he proclaimed *Prajnaparamita*
> mantra, and said mantra goes: *Gate Gate Paragate*
> *Parasamgate Bodhi Svaha!* Gone, gone, gone over

the top, gone all the way over the top to the other
shore, wakened mind. Salutations.

That's a summary of the text of *Prajnaparamita*: "Highest Perfect
Wisdom" *Heart Sutra*. Most of Kerouac's mid-late poetry depends
on some glimpse or some understanding of that statement, as both
an ethic and a philosophical take on reality and appearance. Once
you get that terminology down, you'll be able to read his *Mexico City
Blues* very easily and see how funny they are, what a good representation of the mind they are and how trenchant philosophically.
Few readers have had the inquisitiveness to go into his Buddhism
and learn its basis which can be summarized in one sentence which
Kerouac often quoted from the *Vajracheddika*, or *Diamond Sutra*:

> All conceptions as to the existence of the self, as well as
> conceptions as to the existence of a supreme self, as
> well as all conceptions as to the non-existence of the su-
> preme self, are equally arbitrary, being only conceptions.

It's not very far from the notion that William Burroughs laid on Kerouac in 1945 when he gave him a copy of Alfred Korzybski's *Science
and Sanity,* the basic foundation work in general semantics. The
theme was: don't confuse words (and ideas) with events. The table
is not a table. This is not a finger, it's called a finger but it is what it is.
This leaves the universe open. The slogan is: "Avoid the is of identity."

Unfortunately, Kerouac had no teacher in the lineage of Zen or
classical Buddhism. And so the one thing lacking was the tool, the
instrument to realize the sort of substratum of all this exposition,
namely the sitting practice of meditation—actually to take in his
body the notion of emptiness or examine it as a process of mind,
through the practice of classical meditation as handed down in
immemorial "ear-whispered" tradition.

However, Kerouac was very intelligent and knew that substratum
almost intuitively. You can tell that from his writing, from his poetry
with its metaphors of emptiness and the description of vast spa-
ciousness, which is the same thing as emptiness. You can see it at

the end of *The Town and the City*, the vision of a football field, the sun going down behind the clouds and the vaster spaces beyond in the sky. The sense of "panoramic awareness" runs through all of Kerouac's descriptions of landscape. You always find him focusing on Neal Cassady at the pool table or the snooker table with the camera receding as it does at the end of the movie *Les Enfants du Paradis* when the camera recedes above the buildings, above the Ferris wheel, until we see the vast crowd receding in a much vaster space.

Kerouac, however, lacked specific instruction in the actual method of meditation practice in Zen. This, basically, is to follow the breath and take a friendly attitude toward one's thoughts, but bring the mind back to attention to the breath. Kerouac had worked out his own form of sitting practice which involved squeezing his anus, closing his eyes, and trying to see a golden light.

He had some kind of satori from that. But the instruction one gets in ancient sitting practice is: as soon as you see your thoughts, renounce them, let go. Don't cling to thought, don't try and make it a reference point, keep the space of mind open. As Blake says, "He who binds to himself a joy/does the winged life destroy/He who kisses the joy as it flies/lives in eternity's sunrise."

That's the basis, simply paying attention to the ongoing process of breath while it's proceeding, and taking a friendly attitude towards your thought forms. Not inviting them in, not pushing them away, allowing them to take care of themselves, but keeping your attention on the actual physical space around you, the flow of the outbreath. That's Tibetan style meditation. Gary Snyder never did teach him Zen Buddhist sitting practice style because of some odd miscommunication.

Kerouac's satori was clinging both to despair of suffering, fear of suffering, and permanent Hell, fear of a permanent Heaven: "I am only an Apache/smoking hashi, in old Cabashy/by the lamp," humorously frozen in a kind of horrible hashish Hell. He constantly refers to that image: "Pieces of the Buddha material frozen and sliced microscopically in morgues of the North . . . skeletons of heroes . . . fingers and joints . . . elephants of kindness torn apart by vultures." So obsessed was he with the suffering he encountered that he wasn't able to let go. I think the alcohol amplified that suffering, left him prey to the phantasm of the monotheistic imposition which Blake had denounced as being "six thousand years of sleep" for Western civilization.

So, we have a contrast here, ethically and philosophically, between non-theistic Buddhist space-awareness or awareness practice, and theistic Catholicism's contemplation of or fixation on the Cross of suffering.

As Jack grew older, in despair and lacking the means to calm his mind and let go of the suffering, he tended more and more to grasp at the Cross. And so, in his later years, he made many paintings of the Cross, of cardinals, popes, of Christ crucified, of Mary; seeing himself on the Cross, and finally conceiving of himself as being crucified. He was undergoing crucifixion in the mortification of his body as he drank. Nonetheless, he did have this quality of negative capability, the ability to hold opposite ideas in his mind without "an irritable reaching out after fact and reason," which John Keats proposed as the true mind of the Shakespearian poet.

"I am Canuck, I am from Lowell, I am Jewish, I am Palestinian, I Am, I am the finger, I am the name." Kerouac was not heavily entangled in such fixed identity.

We owe it to Burroughs somewhat for having cut Kerouac loose from that "is of identity" in the mid-1940s so that Kerouac had the ability to empathize with the old transvestite queen and become "one of the world's/great bullshitters,/girls," as he says in his *Mexico City Blues*: "Darling! Red hot/That kind of camping/I don't object to/unless it's kept within reason." He could empathize with the all-American boy, football hero. He could be a sophisticated *littérateur* or an old drunk, alternatively. He could be country bumpkin, he could be as Thomas Wolfe, or he could empathize with William Burroughs as a "non-Wolfian" European sophisticate. So, in the end, his poetry and his prose becomes a perfect manifestation of his mind. That was the whole point of the spontaneous prosody. And the great Tibetan Lama Chogyam Trungpa, examining Kerouac's poetry, said: "It's a perfect manifestation of mind." His work is accepted in the Buddhist community as a great manifestation of poetic mind; true to the nature of mind as understood traditionally by Buddhist theories of spontaneous mind, how to achieve and how to use it.

Kerouac wrote an essay, "Last Words," in January 1967 (published in *Escapade*) quoting the *Surangama Sutra*:

> If you are now desirous of more perfectly understanding Supreme Enlightenment, you must learn to answer spontaneously and with no recourse to discriminate thinking. For the *Tathagatas* (the passers-through) in the ten quarters of the universes, because of the straight-forwardness of their minds and the spontaneity of their mentations, have ever remained, from beginningless time to endless time, of one pure Suchness with the enlightening nature of pure Mind Essence.

Then Kerouac continues:

> . . . which is pretty strange old news. You can also find pretty much the same thing in Mark 13:11. "Take no thought beforehand what ye shall speak, neither do you premeditate: but whatsoever shall be given to you in that hour, that speak ye: for it is not ye that speak but the Holy Ghost!" Mozart and Blake often felt they weren't pushing their own pens it was the "Muse" singing and pushing.
>
> In another sense spontaneous, or ad lib, artistic writing imitates as best it can the flow of the mind as it moves in its space-time continuum, in this sense, it may really be called Space Age Prose someday because when astronauts are flowing through space and time they too have no chance to stop and reconsider and go back. It may be they won't be reading anything else but spontaneous writing when they do get out there, the science of the language to fit their science of movement. . . .

To break through the barrier of language with
WORDS, you have to be in orbit around your mind, and
I may go up again if I regain my strength. It may sound
vain but I've been wrestling with this angelic problem
with at least as much discipline as Jacob.

ADAPTED BY ALLEN GINSBERG FROM AN ESSAY IN *Un Homme*
Grand: Jack Kerouac à la Confluence des Cultures (Carleton
University Press, 1990), edited by Pierre Anctil. Interpretations of
Buddhadharma are modeled after expositions by Chogyam
Trungpa Rinpoche in *Cutting Through Spiritual Materialism*
(Shambhala Publications, 1972) and other discourses. The trans-
lation of *Prajnaparamita Hridaya Sutra* is adapted by the author
and Gelek Rinpoche from Shunryu Suzuki Roshi's.

EROUAC

I thought I'd start out with a sort of two-panel quote from Kerouac to give the range of his language. You might think of these examples as two polar existences of the words in his work. The first:

"Black black black black bling bling bling
bling black black black black
    bling bling bling bling
    black black black black
    bling bling bling

38// Sword etc., flat part of an oar or calamity, sudden vio-dashing young fellow, lent gust of wind; forcible stream of leaf, air, blare of a trumpet or horn, blamable deserving of Explosion as of gunpowder, blame, find fault with Blight; censure, Imputation of a blatant Brawling noisy, Speak ill, blaze, Burn with a blameful meriting flame, send forth a flaming light, less, without blame innocent, torch, firebrand, stream of blamelessly blameless flame of light, bursting out, actness . . ."

And the second one:

"I'm writing this book because we're all going to die—In the loneliness of my life, my father dead, my brother dead, my mother faraway, my sister and my wife far away, nothing here but my own tragic hands that once were guarded by a world, a sweet attention, that now are left to guide and disappear their own way into the common dark of all our death, sleeping in me raw bed, alone and stupid: with just this one pride and consolation: my heart broke in the general despair and opened up inwards to the Lord, I made a supplication in this dream."

CLARK COOLIDGE

Now the first of those is from the novel *Desolation Angels* in the first part of that book where he's in a fire tower in the Cascade Mountains all by himself all summer and obviously he's bored and looking in the dictionary for inspiration or for whatever reason. I looked in the dictionary too and realized that he'd gone from the word "blade" to the word "bleed". Everything in that paragraph comes between those two words: blare, blame and so on. He's working alphabetically through those definitions. I once wrote a whole book using a similar meditation on the dictionary, although I don't think it was inspired by Kerouac. I think I found it or it was an unconscious influence anyway, a book called *The Maintains* which I almost dedicated to this section of *Desolation Angels*.

And the second one is from *Visions of Cody,* so that you can see the vast differences there. From words that are almost totally outside him, he's feeding them back in from an objective source, the dictionary, to what you might call an extreme personal inwards, confessional words, a memory of his own consciousness kind of thing. This might give you some idea of the really quite extraordinary range of his work, which I've always thought of as a lot wider than most impressions would have you think of him.

From there I want to move to what is maybe the key to receiving his work, which is the *sound* of the work, his voice. I know that "voice" has been talked about a lot but I think there are certain writers, and with some of them we have the luck of the recorded evidence of their voices, where what you get is a kind of magic voice. Once you've heard it you can never read those words again without hearing that voice, even if you don't have a very developed sub-vocal ability. Do you know what I mean? I don't know how many of you, when you read silently, hear every word. In my case it's impossible not to do it. I remember one time asking a class here how many people do that, and about half of them did. I was sort of amazed. Somebody like Burroughs, for example, says that he's largely visual but that's a paradox because he's another of those magic voices. You can't forget that Burroughs sound. But Kerouac very definitely. I remember when I was first enthusiastic about his books and I used to lend them to friends, they would take them away and come back and shake their heads and say "I don't know, I just can't read it." And I said "What's the matter?" "Well, the punctuation, I can't . . . I mean, all those dashes, what the hell is that about?" "That's all right. Sit down and listen to this record." And I'd put on one of those three amazing recordings that came out in 1959, and almost every one of them would go away saying "Oh, yeah, I got it. Yeah, right," and then they could read him without any trouble.

So I'm sure that's true, if you have the music of the words to hold in your head. Here's a tiny example, in his vowels, like "gloom dooms", that's a very Kerouac sound. Or with more of the consonants clicking out: "hotshot freight trains," that's the Kerouac sound in micro. And I mean not separate from the sense, although there's an important issue here that I think Susan Howe was touching on in her workshop this morning, which could indicate a whole other pursuit here just parenthetically. What is the relationship for the writer between what he hears of the words and what he sees once they're written down and fed back into the head that's hearing those words? To me there's an incredible generative cycling that's going on, but there's also a problem with the registration, which is always inexact, a bit like the notation of jazz. If you write improvised jazznotes down in classical 4/4 or whatever measure, you're not going to get the nuances of the rhythm unless you divide it into so many micro-moments that it's nearly impossible to then read and play. Which has happened with some so-called modern classical composers. There are Elliott Carter scores, for example, that as a drummer I've tried to read, which are so divided that I don't see how anyone could fluidly do it.

But anyway there is that problem then of registration on the page and also with me the problem of the voice in the head that's never quite the voice that I can speak. And I think maybe that's because there's some of that intellective registrative emphasis on the page mixed with the voice, and all that complex can never really be reproduced as purely voice.

Also, and at any rate, sound is movement. It interests me that the words "momentary" and "moments" come from the same Latin:

"moveo," to move. Every statement exists in time and vanishes in time, like in alto saxophonist Eric Dolphy's famous statement about music: "When you hear music, after it's over it's gone in the air, you can never capture it again." That has gradually become more of a positive value to me, because one of the great things about the moment is that if you were there in that moment, you received that moment and there's an intensity to a moment that can never be gone back to that is somehow more memorable. Like they used to say, "Was you there, Charlie?"

Kerouac said, "Nothing is muddy that *runs in time* and to laws of time." And I can't resist putting next to that my favorite statement by Maurice Blanchot: "One can only write if one arrives at the instant towards which one can only move through space opened up by the movement of writing." And that's not a paradox.

So here's Kerouac whizzing along and picking up and there's something special too about what you pick up when you're moving fast, about the kind of attention that you can develop.

From one of my notebooks: The goo risen up into clacking, statement. States allover always on the rise. You go past poles and hear voices turning like a wrist over what did she talk over what did you hope to do. Writing in the cleft between known-day/memory and the speeding spaces shafting on and out: What will happen?

A matter of momentum. And I get almost a mystical feeling that if you can get to a sort of momentum that works in waves, rhythmic waves, you can pick up things that you might not otherwise even sense. Kerouac in *Old Angel Midnight:*

> "What is this universe
>   but a lot of waves
> And a craving desire
>   is a wave
> Belonging to a wave
>   in a world of waves
> So why put any down,
>   wave?
> Come on wave, WAVE!

The heehaw's dobbin
spring hoho
Is a sad lonely yurk
for your love
Wave lover."

Kerouac, thinking about Shakespeare, claimed: "Shakespeare heard *sound* first then the words were there in his QUICK HEAD." And again, Kerouac: "his handwritten manuscripts were hardly blotted, if at all, as he apparently flowed in his writing and wrote in an inspired hurry what he immediately heard sound-wise while his steel-trap brain kept shutting down on the exigencies of plot and character in that sea of ravening English that came out of him." That's from an article in Show Magazine in 1964 by Kerouac, called "Shakespeare and The Outsider."

After all, Kerouac's first language was not English, it was a kind of Québecois called Joual, which is a totally vocal language. He says he heard it from his mother before he learned English. His mother would tell him tales in this language, and I'm told it's like an ancient French, a pre-Académie Française standardized French, which was a very flowing language that included a lot of other languages. Which in a way is like English, I guess, from the Elizabethan period onward anyway. In Joual, for example, the word for peppermint is "papparmanne".

And then I found this letter from Kerouac to Allen Ginsberg in 1952. I think they'd been arguing about some of Jack's manuscripts and Allen was being a little critical of some of them. Kerouac:

"Literature as you see it, using words like 'verbal' & 'images' etc. & things like that, well all the 'paraphanalia (*sic*) of criticism' etc. is no longer my concern because the thing makes me say 'shitty little beach in the reeds' is Pre-Literary, it happened to me to think that way before I learned the words the litterateurs use to describe what they're doing—At this moment I'm writing directly from the French in my head, Doctor Sax was written high on

tea without pausing to think, sometimes Bill Garver would
come into the room and so the chapter ended there."

Now, inevitably I have to talk about Bop, Bop Prosody and all of
that. It was a music that was very close and dear to Kerouac and I
thought I'd give it a little rundown here. It's a huge subject and impossible to cover in brief. I'm spending my life listening to it and
thinking about it and playing it, but I don't know how many of you
know much about its history. It's beginning to be a bit far back.
We're talking about the '40s now so it's about a half century ago.
Charlie Parker, Dizzy Gillespie, Bud Powell, and I would say Kenny
Clarke, the drummer, probably had the most to do with changing
the music, inventing the bop forms. Also Thelonious Monk. I think the
first Bop recording is considered to be a version of "Groovin' High"
which was made in February 1945, and it still had an older swing-
style rhythm section, with Slam Stewart and Cozy Cole, bass and
drums. Then, by November of 1945, you get the famous "Ko Ko" on
the Savoy label with Bird, Miles, probably Sadik Hakim on piano,
Curly Russell on bass, and Max Roach on drums. Which was a real
Bop group. Now the interesting thing about it is the change in
rhythm from the Swing era (you might think of Benny Goodman,
that kind of thing), from the Swing time to a more evenly divided 4/4
time. Swing time was more like an off-beat oriented time, or um-dah
um-dah um-dah with a 2/4 feel. Bop 4/4 time is a mere even one-
two-three-four, like that. Jo Jones, who was Count Basie's drummer,
one of the great innovators, started playing that shh-ch-ch-shh figure on the highhat cymbals, where the shh was on the one and the
three of the beat, which heads more into a sense of even four,
rather than playing on that off-beat all the time, which was the way
they previously had played. Sid Catlett, a transitional drummer of
this period, used to play every beat of the four on his bass drum fairly
loud. Jo was playing that too but a little softer. The Bop drummers
learned from those guys. In fact Max Roach said a very interesting
thing about how a lot of the things he plays he developed from
hearing Jo Jones on the radio but not seeing him. He had to make
up ways of doing what he heard Jo doing, so when he finally did

get to see Jo Jones play he realized he was doing it all differently. What drummers call "sticking", which means which hand you start a phrase with, the various patterns of the hands in making phrases, he might have gotten wrong, but that's one of the ways that art gets changed and invented.

Now I think that once you get that kind of evened-out 4 beat, you can hear a long line against that a lot easier than you can against a very accented um-dah um-dah um-dah all the time. In Bop there's actually a sort of ghost of an off-beat but it's far less prominent. Charlie Parker began to hear longer lines, and Kerouac obviously did. And what you eventually get to from all that is Ornette Coleman, who was maybe the next great innovator, certainly on the saxophone, by the late '50s, who would sometimes turn the beat around. He wouldn't stay, in other words, with the one-two-three-four and back to one. He wouldn't care. If he got a phrase that took him into the other polarity of that 4 he would just go with it and the rhythm section would go with him. Now this gets into yet another phase which really fascinates me too, what's called Free Jazz which came out of Ornette and Cecil Taylor and Coltrane and so on in the early '60s and died, seems to have hit a wall, or hit freedom?, and recanted. There should be a great history written of this and I haven't seen it yet. But there's a record you can probably still find by the great tenor saxophonist Albert Ayler which was called *Spiritual Unity* and it was a trio with him, Gary Peacock, who has played here at Naropa, on bass, and Sonny Murray on drums, and they got to a kind of time on that session which, if you've been following at all what I've been saying . . . I realize it's hard if you don't have any technical sense of musical metric, but understand that in a 4/4 measure there are always (even to some extent in Bop) strong beats and weak beats, the off-beat or the on-beat, whatever style you're playing. But these guys made a time where there was no strong or weak beat. It was all like one-one-one-one-one-one-one to infinity. In other words, you could play anything at all over that time, you could go anywhere and not worry about how to come back. You still hear this sometimes in some musicians, but I don't know . . . I sometimes think it was a fear there about being so free that became a barrier. The whole universe could be there and you can hear it sometimes in Coltrane's late work, for instance, although he maybe wasn't working specifically with that time.

But anyway, we're talking about an overlay. The more unaccented you have that 4 for an underlying beat, the more you can extend your line over it and I'm sure Kerouac heard something like that. An opening. He was very fond of a lot of those musicians and listened to them a lot.

Now another thing about Bebop is that a lot of what they were playing were existing tunes, which musicians call "standards", like "All the Things You Are." And "I Got Rhythm," the Gershwin tune, was the basis for a lot of them, just taking the chord changes and making your own melodies over the top. Here's a quote from a Kerouac piece called "The Beginning Of Bop" where he's talking about a band he is watching and listening to.

"The tune they were playing was *All the Things You Are* .
. . they slowed it down and dragged behind it at half
tempo dinosaur proportions—changed the placing of
the note in the middle of the harmony to an outer
more precarious position where also its sense of not belonging was enhanced by the general atonality produced with everyone exteriorizing the tune's harmony"

Now I've seen that put down by jazz critics as total idiocy but in fact it is quite close to what Charlie Parker talked about when he broke through, I think in 1939, when he started grabbing notes from the higher intervals of the chord and hearing a possible improvisation there. And there's a wonderful passage, this is one of the greatest descriptions of jazz improvisation I can imagine, from *Visions of Cody*. Kerouac is talking about Lee Konitz, who he said "inspired me in 1951 to write the way he plays." "He can take care of himself even though he goofs and does "April in Paris" from inside out as if the tune was the room he lived in and was going out at midnight with his coat on." Yeah. That has the feeling of improvisation starting at a base and going out and you can get back if you want since you know where that is but you can also go anywhere and take whatever form in the going you want.

There's also a convention in Bop for the quotation of other tunes. Charlie Parker did that a lot, and Dexter Gordon, Sonny Rollins. Which reminds me of Kerouac's inclusion of things that happen to pop out in his memory which maybe didn't have to do directly with what he was describing. Plucked from the great wellspring of forms in his composing head.

Then there's something I like to call Crazy Seriousness. Kerouac used the word "goof" a lot in a very positive way, as when he was describing the Three Stooges in *Visions of Cody*. He was talking about Neal Cassady actually, saying how the free imagination he felt in himself was justified in the world outside and he had nothing therefore to reproach himself for. That sense of goof. Or some funny illuminated moment, which you can hear in some of the few live recordings of Bird and Diz playing together.

Also in Bop you've got extremes of tempo. Particularly very fast tempos, and Kerouac of course, we know, was a master of fast typing, fast writing.

Now here are some examples of what I think of as Bop phrases in Kerouac. Think of it like in this tempo: dah dah dah dah. . . . "Lee, who wouldn't talk to me even if he knew me" dah dah dah dah, one two three four "*Lee*, who wouldn't *talk* to me even if he *knew* me." All right? And then, from *San Francisco Blues*: "The rooftop of the beatup/tenement." Now that's an iambic pentameter line, "The *roof*top *of* the *beat*up *ten*ement," but that's not how it sounds at all. It's this: "The *roof*top of the *beat*up *ten*ement." And we have a recording of him reading that so we know that that's very much the way he heard it. I mean, "tenement" is almost whole-noted out. But it's those phrases: "The rooftop/of the beatup/tenement." I always feel in my own work that I hear that way. I've never heard metrics in terms of feet. You know, on and off, weak and strong, in regulated patterns. I think of a whole phrase, no matter how long. And I think of what they call "tala" in Indian classical music, which may be a sequence of as many as eighteen variously accented beats, which gets repeated as a unit to improvise on.

Here's a great line of Kerouac's for long-line Bop sense: "Lester droopy porkpie hung his horn and blew bop lazy ideas inside jazz had everybody dreaming." It's almost too long for my breath but it's there.

The other thing about the long line, which is terrifying and wonderful, is that you never know where it goes. I mean, you're following it for the sense of where, what's going to drop in, what is that last word, where is it going to take me? Which reminds me of Bernadette Mayer in a letter where she's talking about her writing and I don't think she was thinking specifically of Kerouac but it's apropos. She says

"What I seem to have to do is to have someone to address in order to begin, then lose that, mix it up, get mixed up myself, let the language take over, work out some structures within that, see an ending, bypass it and then see how much longer I can last, having more or less abandoned the addressee, then collapse at some false ending, casting the work aside with the unspoken hope that I may have made some discovery."

That kind of says it all. There's also the sense of you don't want to finish. There's almost a sadness when even the greatest long line you can get to, with something really unexpected at the end, when it's done you don't want to stop. Which reminded me of something else. I have endless, hopeless, jazz references! I hope that those of you who don't have jazz as another language will bear with me. But if anybody knows Woody Herman's early band, and maybe at least Fee (Fielding Dawson) here does, with Davey Tough on drums, one thing they used to do was at the end of a tune, which would often end du-POW, Davey Tough would give about three or five more bassdrum beats, duh-duh-duh-duh-duh. Kind of a stutter on out. And I always wondered what the hell that was all about. Well, finally somebody asked Woody, long after Dave Tough had died, and he said, "Yeah, well, we never could stand to end a number."

So, another aspect of Bop phrasing is a way of ending the

phrase with a kind of Bang, a sudden hard stop sometimes on an unexpected beat. Here's Kerouac from *Book of Dreams,* where he's actually sort of describing the use of this in his own work. "Robert Whitmore my buddy on the SS Carruth is showing me how he describes an apartment building when he writes, 'the wander wada rada rall a gonna gay, *Zack*!' the flow of words and the releasing bop-sound at the end of a prose rhythm paragraph." And here's an example from *Old Angel Midnight.* "He thinks I'm competitive in a long pleasant souse of Wishing all of ye bleed stay meditation everybody martini destroy my black."

Something that also happens with that, in Kerouac, is that I always hear the individual words with an intense physicality of separation. And that previous quote is a good example of that because a lot of the words are not syntactically connected. ". . . bleed stay meditation everybody martini destroy . . ." Whack. As he said in a letter to Don Allen in 1959, "The rhythm of how you decide to *rush your statement* determines the rhythm of the poem." Here's an example of that from *Visions of Cody.* "There and there alone, we'll find our chops and smoky talk of the most important dinner time in Denver." Hear the acceleration in those last six words? Bob Creeley used to talk about how Charlie Parker and Miles Davis were able to give each unit of duration a feeling of longer or shorter, slower or quicker time without it actually being slower or quicker, which is one of the great secrets of jazz movement. And I'll be really specific here, I have to be. There's a record by Sonny Rollins called *Newk's Time,* and there's a tune on there called "Tune Up." Listen to what he plays after he gets through the theme, on the first eight bars of his solo. He plays three phrases, and by the third phrase you would think he was going about three times as fast, that he really had accelerated way beyond the original tempo, but he hasn't. It's all in the genius of his phrasing.

Here's another good one. Kerouac: "Figures crossing the general raily layout in a flat void of activity afternoons." Which reminds me of Ray Bremser, who is another great Bop poet who should be better known. I was once given a manuscript of his by the bass player Buell Neidlinger who used to play with Cecil Taylor's early band. Ray had written this poem called "Drive Suite" sometimes literally *under* Cecil Taylor's piano at the Five Spot. He's a brave man. But "activity afternoons" echoed for me with Ray's phrase in "Drive Suite": "Pituie balloons." Somehow he heard Cecil producing "Pituie balloons."

Here's a bit of a diversion but it's all part of the same fascination. I remember a statement that the composer Arnold Schoenberg made years ago when he was asked "What is the first thing you get in your mind when you start to write a composition?" He said, "an unnameable sense of a sounding & moving space, of a form with characteristic relationships; of moving masses whose shape is unnameable & not amenable to comparison." Well, he couldn't sustain that, it's almost impossible to describe. But there's that sense of a "sounding and moving space." I know that's absolutely indicative of the right direction. I feel that myself. There's a thing there that's got all the outside and it's got the momentum and it's going to move and it's going to demand certain forms and it's totally not embodied at all. There's no material to it yet and you feel absolutely that you're about to embody that, whatever your material is. I think painters feel that too. I remember Philip Guston talking that way. In fact he and I used to talk about paint and words to the extent that we weren't talking about paint and words anymore, we were talking about art, I mean, making that thing where we use all whatever materials we've been given to make it with. I remember some nights talking with him where we felt like it's absolutely up there somewhere and it's not paint and it's not words. I found this echo of the same idea in Nadezhda Mandelstam's book, *Hope Against Hope.* "I imagine that for a poet auditory hallucinations are something in the nature of an occupational disease. As many poets have said—Akhmatova (in *Poem Without a Hero*) and Mandelstam among them—a poem begins with a musical phrase ringing insistently in the ears; at first inchoate, it later takes on a precise form, though still without words. I sometimes saw Mandelstam trying to get rid of this kind of 'hum', to brush it off and escape from it. He would toss his head as though it could be shaken out like a drop of water that gets into your ear while bathing. But it was always louder than any noise, radio or conversation in the same room."

And then I thought of this from Kerouac, talking about another jam session that he saw, talking about these tenor players that he called the "workingman tenors": not the stars but the guys that came to the lesser clubs and blew their hearts out every night to whatever audience, "They seemed to come on in their horns with a will, saying things, a lot to say, talkative horns, you could almost hear the words and better than that the harmony, made you hear the way to fill up blank spaces of time with the tune and consequence of your hands and breath and soul."

So, to kind of pull all this together, I'll show what I see as three aspects of Kerouac's writing. Forgive me for generalizing at all because this is a very particular artist, it's all in the details. But there are three areas of working that you can point to as being different from one another that he would hit into and then move between. The first one is what I call Blowing (as a jazz musician does) on Memory, or on the Subject of Image. As if you could blow present words swinging over key centers of memory. As if words could be the melody of image. Word melody over image chords, that way? What we're really talking about here is improvisation, which is a totally fascinating and endless area. I always look for statements on this from the great musicians. The latest one that intrigues me is Cecil Taylor's "Improvisation is the capability to talk to oneself." That's certainly what a writer does. Kerouac said in "Essentials of Spontaneous Prose," "blowing (as per jazz musician) on subject of image." And on page one of *Doctor Sax*, "and don't stop to think of words when you do stop, just stop to think of the picture better—and let your mind off yourself in this work." Plus the great one in the *Paris Review* interview where he says, "All of it is in my mind, naturally, except that language that is used at the time it is used." All right.

It would be interesting to see the notebooks from his travels Kerouac used when he was writing his novels, because it's almost as if he were using what musicians call Fake Books: those books that have the chords to the tune that you're referring to, and here Kerouac was taking off from what was in his notebooks at every split second. There's a wonderful interview with the poet Philip Whalen, who knew Kerouac very well and watched him writing at one point and described it.

> "He would sit—at a typewriter, and he had all these
> pocket notebooks, and the pocket notebooks would
> be open at his left-hand side on the typing table—and
> he'd be typing. He could type faster than any human
> being you ever saw. The most noise that you heard
> while he was typing was the carriage return, slamming
> back again and again. The little bell would bing-bang,
> bing-bang, bing-bang! Just incredibly fast, faster than
> a teletype. And he'd laugh and say, Look at this! And
> he'd type and he'd laugh. Then he'd make a mistake,
> and this would lead him off into a possible part of a
> new paragraph, into a funny riff of some kind that he'd
> add while he was in the process of copying. Then,
> maybe he'd turn a page of the notebook and he'd
> look at that page and realize it was no good and
> he'd X it out, or maybe part of that page. And then
> he'd type a little bit and turn another page, and type
> the whole thing, and another page, and he'd type
> from that. And then something would—again, he
> would exclaim and laugh and carry on and have a
> big time doing it."

That's something to be aspired to. I think that's the only description, at least that I've found, an actual physical image description of Kerouac writing. Now this might be an example of Kerouac doing that kind of writing, jumping from memory chord to memory chord. From *Old Angel Midnight*.

> "Lou Little explaining to the newsreel audience how
> this football player went mad & shows how on a Co-
> lumbia Practice Hillside it started with father & son, the
> gray reaches of the Eternity Library beyond—I go visit
> my sweet Alene in her subterranean pad near the 3rd

Avenue El & Henry St of old Mike Mike milkcan Lower
Eastside Dreams & pink murders & there she wont ope
the door because I cant get the job I tried so hard to
get & the woman said my form wasnt right but Neal
made it but regretfully it is he's shipping out & I'm on
the ship with him telling him 'If you wash dishes dont
say a word, if you're a yeoman do yr work all well'—
I can see he hates to go without me to this other
Grayshore—Sitting before my stove on a cold gray
Saturday morning with my coffee & my pine, eating
jello—remembering the little jello cartoon that filled me
with such joy as a kid on Sarah Avenue, the little prince
wouldn't take pheasant or delicate birds or celestial
puddings or even Mominuan Icecream but when the
little bird brought his jello inverted in a rill mold cup he
went wild & saved the kingdom, red jello like mine, in
the little dear lovable pages—of long ago—My form is
delight delight delight

> Ring, ring ring—
> Shh, the sky is empty—
> Shh, the earth is empty—
> Look out, look in, shh—
> The essence of jello is the essence of arrangement—
> Be nice to the monster crab, it's only another arrangement
> of that which you are"

Now Kerouac talked about something he called "alluvials," and if
you look that up in the dictionary it says "alluvium, solid material deposited by running water," which you get in a delta at the front of a
river. He said, "Add alluvials to the end of your line when all is exhausted but something has to be said for some specified irrational
reason." Here's a great example, in fact he used it himself in a letter to illustrate just that. Talking about Lester Young, the great tenor
player.

"Lester is like the river, the river starts in near Butte Montana in frozen snow caps (Three Forks) and meanders on down across states and entire territorial areas of dun bleak land with hawthorn crackling in the sleet, picks up rivers at Bismarck, Omaha and St. Louis just north, another at Kay-ro, another in Arkansas, Tennessee, comes deluging on New Orleans with muddy news from the land and a roar of subterranean excitement that is like the vibration of the entire land sucked of its gut in mad midnight, fevered, hot," (and here's the alluvium) "the big mudhole rank clawpole old frogular pawed-soul titanic Mississippi from the North, full of wires, cold wood, and horn."

He got back to Lester. So that's about blowing on memory chords. And then the second aspect of his work I'd like to show is what he called "sketching." In "Essentials of Spontaneous Prose" he said, "Time being of the essence in the purity of speech, sketching language is undisturbed flow from the mind of personal secret ideawords." And, in a letter to Allen Ginsberg from 1952.

"Sketching (Ed White casually mentioned it in 124th Chinese restaurant near Columbia, `Why don't you just sketch in the streets like a painter but with words') which I did . . . everything activates in front of you in myriad profusion, you just have to purify your mind and let it pour the words (which effortless angels of the vision fly when you stand in front of reality) and write with 100% personal honesty both psychic & so on etc. and slap it all down shameless, willynilly, rapidly until sometimes I got so inspired I lost consciousness I was writing. Traditional source: Yeats' trance writing, of course. It's the *only way to write*. I haven't sketched in a long time now & have to start again because you get better with practice. Sometimes it is embarrassing to write in the

street or anywhere outside but it's absolute . . . it never
fails, it's the thing itself natch."

There are great examples of this that I won't quote because they're
long. Like in *Visions of Cody* toward the beginning, his description of
the bakery window, where you know he's standing in front of this
window describing every beautiful little piece of peach and icing
inside and it just drives you crazy with hunger, and horror. And
there's the great sketch of that cafeteria, like a Horn & Hardarts in
New York. Or here's a shorter one from *Old Angel Midnight.*

> "The Mill Valley trees, the pines with green mint look
> and there's a tangled eucalyptus hulk stick fallen thru
> the late sunlight tangle of those needles, hanging
> from it like a live wire connecting it to the ground—just
> below, the notches where little Fred sought to fell sad
> pine—not bleeding much—just a lot of crystal sap the
> ants are mining in, motionless like cows on the grass"

And the third phase or aspect I picked out is what's been called
Babble or Babble Flow: just letting it completely go on. Here's a take
I had on it at one point: Pressure off words so they pile and collide in
and he hears them in mind as if spoken by another. Words, then, are
fresh solids of the just heard. And a line by Kerouac: "infantile pile-
up of scatalogical buildup." Increasing density turns the mind-ear
away from impulse of remembered image toward sound as material for the making. Then Kerouac says, in *Old Angel Midnight*: "The
total turning about & deep revival of world robe-flowing literature till
it shd be something a man'd put his eyes on & continually read for
the sake of reading & for the sake of the Tongue & not just these insipid stories writ in insipid aridities & paranoias bloomin & why yet the
image—let's hear the Sound of the Universe, son."
So, here's a sample of Kerouac's Babble Flow.

> "Aw rust rust rust rust die die die pipe pipe ash ash die
> die ding dong ding ding ding rust cob die pipe ass rust

die words—I'd as rather be permiganted in Rusty's
moonlight Rork as be perdirated in this bile arta pana-
taler where ack the orshy rosh crowshes my tired idiot
hand O Lawd I is coming to you'd soon's you's ready's
as can readies be Mazatlan heroes point out Mexicos
& all ye rhythmic bay fishermen don't hang fish eye
soppy in my Ramadam give-cigarette Sop of Arab
Squat—the Berber types that hang fardels on their
woman back wd as lief Erick some son with blady matter I guess as whup a mule in singsong pathetic mule-
jump field by quiet fluff smoke North Carolina (near
Weldon) (Railroad Bridge) Roanoke millionaire High-
Ridge hi-party Hi-Fi million-dollar findriver skinfish Rod
Tong Apple Finder John Sun Ford goodby Paw mule
America Song—"

I guess you either hear the music of that or you don't.

Now, something that occurred to me out of thinking about
Babble Flow is something that Bernadette and I used to think about
a lot, what we called the Everything Work. It's the incredible ideal
that you could get so practiced in this kind of improvisational quick-
ness of mind and word-dropping-into-the-slot that every single thing
could be included. In fact, Bernadette still has a project called *Mind
of Hour* where she wants to be able to capture/notate everything
her mind possibly touched on in that hour. She tried to teach herself
shorthand, all kinds of hypnosis and still couldn't quite find a way.
But anyway it's an ideal, something to shoot for, and there's a great
feeling of it in Kerouac. The inclusion of everything or the desire to
have everything in there, so you get sections which are catalogues
of things. This is maybe the simplest form of the everything impulse.
Like at the beginning of *Old Angel Midnight*: "Friday afternoon in
the universe, in all directions in & out you got your men women dogs
children horses pones tics perts parts pans pool palls pails partu-
riences and petty Thieveries that turn into heavenly Buddha." Or,
talking about Neal Cassady in *Visions of Cody*: "his whole frame of
clothes capped by those terrible pants with six, seven holes in them

and streaked with baby food, come, ice cream, ashes—I saw his whole life, I saw all the movies we'd ever been in, I saw for some reason he and his father on Larimer Street not caring in May."

So, The Everything Work. And let me bring in a cast of a few outsiders, great artists, to back this. Thomas Bernhard. I don't know if anybody here's read him, a wonderful Austrian novelist, now recently dead, who said: "Unless one is thinking of everything at each moment one is not thinking at all." That's in a book called *Correction*. And Willem deKooning, this in a *New York Times* story about him in 1983. He's talking about his painting: "It's never right, you know, because it doesn't have everything in it. So you keep going until you've put everything you can into it. Then you go on to the next one." You only go on to the next work after you've put everything in it that you can. I mean, dig that as a statement about composition. And then I found this from John Berger in his book called *And Our Faces, My Heart, Brief As Photos:* "Once one lived in a seamless experience of wordlessness." He's probably thinking about Paleolithic man here. "Wordlessness means that everything is continuous. The later dream of an ideal language, a language which says all simultaneously, perhaps begins with the memory of this state without memories." That's an interesting riff, if you think about it in connection with what I've been talking about. And then this just cracked me up. Do you know the stand-up comic Steven Wright, who has these great one-liners? He said: "When I first read the dictionary I thought it was a poem about everything." Which it is, if you can dig it that way.

Okay. Now, the opposite of everything, you might say, is ignorance or the breakdown of recall, which I think is happening to me more and more and I'm trying to make it into a positive aspect of the work. Kerouac says, in an *Escapade* magazine article in 1961: "in describing the stormy sea in *Desolation Angels* I heard the sound 'Peligroso' for 'Peligroso Roar' without knowing what it meant, wrote it down involuntarily, later found out it means 'dangerous' in Spanish." I one time wrote down in a notebook: You enter meaninglessness every time you reach for a word. I think poets all know the feeling of grabbing a word and you really don't know what the hell it means but you put it in and you know it's right, and you always find out somehow, or maybe you find a way of finding out it's right, but anyway it goes in and has to go in.

And then there's pure forgetting: Not being able to think of something and using that as part of the structure of the writing itself. This from *Midnight* again:

"Ah Angel Midnightmare—
Ah Crack Jabberwack, play piano, paint, pop your
pile anum coitus semenized olium o hell what's his biblical name, the pot that spilt in the room ere Sarad had
hers, ad her share, the name, the word, for masturba-
tors, the Neptune O YA you know the name, the Bible
Keen Mexican yowl that old tree still hangs in the same
moonlight—Ilium, Anum, Ard Bar, Arnum, Odium,
Odious, *ONAN*! ONAN KERAQUACK go heal yr own
toiletbowl, stop dropping shavings in mine, & leave my
grave unsung, my death unlearn, my qualities you can
have, but onanist no quarter given you Angel Midnight
by in that holy gallows of the moon!"

So, finally, I was thinking about Kerouac's work as being in motion in a cycle between these aspects of the work: Sketching, he's right in front of the things, leading to the Memory Blowing, writing the words coming off the memory or the notebooks from the experience, per- haps leading then on to the BabbleFlow, which in some cases leads to a feeling of a sort of emptiness and almost, in a Buddhist sense, that he was aware of that emptiness in which the world images begin to appear again, and the cycle goes around. As maybe an example of that cycling in miniature, this section from *Midnight* again. I'm using *Old Angel Midnight* a lot because it's almost a Kerouac-in-small, al- most condensed. He's so vast and to give you quotes to get all these elements in would take hours. It would be wonderful to hear, it would be incredible, but we can't so I'm using here these short prose para- graphs of *Old Angel Midnight*. And I'll end with one from towards the end of that work which shows the whole cycle coming around again.

"The wush of trees on yonder eastern nabathaque
Latin Walden axe-haiku of hill where woodsman
Mahomet perceives will soon adown the morning
drear to pail the bringup well suspender farmer trap
moon so's cock go Bloody yurgle in the distance
where Timmy hides, flat, looking with his eyes for purr
me—O Angel, now is the time for all good men to
come to the aid of their party, & ah Angel dont paper-
party me, but make me honified in silken Honen honey-
rubbed Oxen tongue of Cow Kiss, Ant Mat, silk girl ran,
all the monkey-better-than secondary women of Sam
Sarah the Sang of Blood this earth, this tool, this fool,
look with your eyes, I'm tired of fooling O Angel bring it
to me THE MAGIC SOUND OF SILENCE broken by first-
bird's teepaleep—"

Naropa Institute

July 8, 1991

HINKING SERIALLY"
IN *FOR LOVE, WORDS*
AND *PIECES*

The social conditions in which the courtly love poem arose were such that relations between people are convention. If one is looking at relations between people in their writing, that is convention—as the writing's form.

Creeley uses the form as inherent conflict by its being (only) present time.

His particular circumstance or place (in the poem), the factor of being in it, does not allow convention. "One's" only existence is in conflict *per se*.

The being of "one" is conflict. He sees the real as only the present.

Poems in *For Love* use the convention of Elizabethan love poem or quality of medieval courtly love tradition, written as Creeley's present time: as that is what is actually occurring (in the conception of marriage; or the courtly conception of the idealized love, which is outside of marriage)—the two continually separate. *For Love* is a serial work because it is inherently conflict which starts again and again: it has the quality of being precisely that which is its form; so the "theme" of the poems is its form.

> Moving in the mind's
> patterns, recognized
> because there is where
> they happen.[1]

Creeley's "two" who are separate are sometimes the lover and his lady, or two ladies, one in the lover's mind and one in reality; or the lover himself who is double split internally as being both the lady and himself.

> I know two women
> and the one

LESLIE SCALAPINO

    is tangible substance,
        flesh and bone.

The other in my mind
        occurs.
She keeps her strict
        proportion there. ("The Wife," CP 252)

Delineation of the conflict is the form of the poem.

    In the dream
    I see
    two faces turned,

    one of which
    I assume mine, one
    of which I assume

    . . . . .
    If all women are
    mothers, what
    are men

    standing
    in dreams, mine
    or theirs,

    empty of
    all but themselves.
    They are so

    lonely, unknown
    there, I run
    for whatever

    is not
    them, turning
    into that consequence

    makes me
    my mother hating
    myself. ("The Dream," CP 298)

The only description is the weight of the measure itself, the tracking that is the poem. The poem is serial because it is separate, because it is its measure. The poems are a series because they are separate and continuous. There may be a reversal of what's actually being said, the form of experience:

> I will never get there.
> Oh Lady, remember me
> who in Your service grows older
> not wiser, no more than before.
>
> How can I die alone.
> Where will I be then who am now alone,
> what groans so pathetically
> in this room where I am alone? ("The Door," CP 201)

Position in ordering (from the reader's perspective, or writer's, of the serial collection) is arbitrary; perspective is no ordering. "Position is where you / put it, where it is" ("Window," CP 284). That's why he would die alone: the shapes that one creates do not mimic reality, but appear with reality, are part of it. One can't be united with one. (I'm reading For Love, Words, and Pieces as chronological collection, not considering these as separate "books.")

If perspective is no ordering, the chronologically ordered Collected is a range and configuration of potential, infinite actions which are on the edge-of-seeing their actual occurring (by being chronological). The shape and movement of the real past event—which was as that time's present—is activated in configurations continuously.

The senses recreate the particular place which is then closure of that place ("Variations," CP 288). The individual component of the series is not description ("I do not feel / what it was I was feeling"); and therefore the "place" does not exist once it is over and the writing must begin again. Unlike the courtly love poem, serial thinking is what Creeley's poem is beginning in For Love. It's articulated as the "two" which are separate, and a series: "in its feeling, / two things, / one and one" ("Song," CP 319). (I'm considering the numbers "two." A series of numbers, moving the center off "two," occurs in *Pieces*.)

The terms that courtly love convention posits are that one's being is possible only within those courtly terms: in impossible union. For Creeley, one can never equal one. Being absolutely in the present and absolutely separate from it at the same time:

THE WINDOW

There will be no simple
way to avoid what
confronts me. Again and
again I know it, but

take heart, hopefully,
in the world unavoidably
present. Here, I think,
is a day, not *a*
but *the*. My hands are

shaking, there is
an insistent tremble
from the night's
drinking. But what

was I after, you
were surely open to me.
Out the far window
there was such intensity

of yellow light. But love,
love I so wanted I
got, didn't I, and then
fell senseless, with relief. (CP 336)

The mystery of that being (it being that form) is union.

The union isn't the love.

It's a space or "inner" configuration that's unknown and to which the love is articulated.

Creeley's writing in these works is in continual conflict between an over-riding conception, and the process which is being within the series and not seeing what's ahead: "is an event only / for the observer? / No one / there" (CP 379). Creeley, in *Pieces*, is moving around in what he characterizes as an American quality of event or mind: having no over-riding conception, continually resisting such, which itself creates it.

> Americans have a funny way—
> somebody wrote a poem about it—
> of "doing nothing"—What else
> should, *can*, they do?

o   o   o

> What
> by being not
> is—is not
> by being. (CP 406)

That hole ("When holes taste good / we'll put them in our bread") is merely a component of that place (of or in the series). The theme of hole or circle, sometimes delineating seeing only within the mind's own forms repetitively, or an emptiness (*not* repetitive) that is joy (*Words:* "The Circle," CP 343; "The Hole," CP 344; "Joy," CP 350) is only the particular articulation of those spaces there (in the series) as the number zero.

The fixed place or the place which is recreated by the senses and thus closed, is the point of being separated from the present. It is where: *They* were imagination, and the *world* also; the rules known prior to be wrong—then the mind followed and I also as it was true. Phenomena has to be ahead of mind. It is the "ground of people," the place or relation between people as the form of the writing, the converse of definition *by* place (as in "The Puritan Ethos," CP 414, the geographical mind space which displaces the "other space" that is "several / dimensioned locus").

The "several dimensioned locus" is the serial work that is really all over, multiple. It occurs in the ground that has been excluded by the conception of "higher authority"/Puritan Ethos (our *actual* social construction) for which work, the visible result and activity, *not* the relationship between people, exists. These "relations" as such (as *private* mind) aren't hierarchical, except when interpreted through convention of that hierarchy. So they don't exist except outside it.

If erotic love is knowledge to be tracted occurrence isn't ever seen.

As in the courtly love tradition, the dual consciousness of the "Puritan heritage" is to be transcended. The autobiography, the "life," in this society is to be obliterated. The "confessional self" of writing is a format, so it obliterates the "real." Creeley is obliterating literary "confessional self" by the "life" being.

In the poem "The Window," "reaching" (or being in) love is being in *the* day, the unavoidable single present world. If "They"/American/or Puritan Ethos are imagination and the *world* also, they are constituting a geographical mind space that excludes the possibility of that relation with people (i.e., that of being in the unavoidable single present *world*).

The American's funny way of "doing nothing" is such being in the single present world. The "several dimensioned locus" of the serial writing is not planned, or composed which is ordered in advance. The components/individual poems of the "series" (the three works read as chronological collection) are delineations of that mind space of that particular poem as it occurs.[2] In-so-far as a poem delineates the conflict of "convention"/of "love," for example, the poem is literally the presentation of the "mind's patterns" rather than a hierarchical imposition on that mind space substituting social convention as the point of view ("The Dream," CP 298). Poems in *For Love* and *Words* using courtly love conventions/as reflection of American/or Puritan Ethos space, as serial thinking are "doing nothing" in the sense of being in the single present world only where that very *convention*/of love is not taking place. (Creeley's intention is not to be in convention.)

The mind's patterns contain convention and repeat it but do not remain in it in the serial writing, though it is a race to continually move off of the dead center which is its formation:

Quicker
than that, can't
get off "the
dead center of"

myself. *He/I*
were walking. Then
the place *is/was*
not ever enough. ("A Sight," CP 340)

The mind space that is "created" which is the form of these poems
is the geographical space of that love; where one is most oneself,
and thus alone in the heretical sense/of our Puritan Ethos.

It is actually where relationship between people can occur,
heretical for that reason; in that that specificity is the *world* ("The
Providence," CP 415) unraveled from "that" mind imposition.

It is ahead of the dissolution of the self as "real."

The form of the *Collected* can be a being in "history" by virtue of
its ground/the individual poem (i.e., the particular configuration/
form of a conflict as a component in a series of such) *not* mirroring
that which is outside. It is to be the opening of a space (that of
American "doing nothing") which is what is really outside — i.e., outside of the mind's continual imposition of the/its own form. Resisting
one's/and *their* ("They," CP 417) "formation" I think is the meaning
of Creeley's comment:

I've always been embarrassed for a so-called larger
view. I've been given to write about that which has
the most intimate presence for me . . . I think, for myself
at least, the world is most evident and most intense in
those relationships. Therefore they are the materials out
of which my work is made. (*Contexts* 97)

Creeley's use of autobiographical reference, is following the movement of itself in time (watching the mind)—rather than the expression of "creation" of a personality. Its mirroring of its own mind

formation and its race to out-run that as "serial thinking" is not static personality creation *because* it is only that movement.

This internally produced "argument" (the mind watching itself and trying to outrace its own closure, as a "particular" form in this time) rather than being a trap that ultimately enshrines the self, are pieces in the collection of writing which by the very fact of occurring as "merely" components repeating a conflict, as it shows up, *without* essential change, are not "that" (fixed) psychology.

The central fear of the Puritan Ethos is that which is "internally produced"—heretical precisely because it is the American "doing nothing," what Creeley identifies in Williams: "He knew that you change your mind every time you see something, and—what is it he says?—'A new world is only a new mind.' So the context is continually what you can feel and where you are" (*Contexts* 17).

The grounds for our elimination of eroticism (as the extension of the terms of Puritan heritage) is the contention that it is the area quintessentially subjective and egoistic; the assumption "now" is even that eroticism itself is inherently sexist. That's what *social context* may reflect.

If eroticism is eliminated in the sense of not seeing it in or as being the occurrence, that leaves only that social context; there is then no area existing for apprehension or change. We are split from ourselves, and therefore are *not* articulated. This occurs as the conditions of writing then.

The corollary of the dual strand (of Puritan Ethos) is that subjectivity is regarded as inherently contaminated, not only because it is ego *per se*; but also because as such it becomes a literary commodity *either* as confessional writing *or* the process of the unraveling and examination of the personality as the writing's form.

H.D.'s bitter jewel/worm-cycle is seen as the self, which when the *world* allows only itself, isn't of the "real." Creeley's saying self is only being the "real."

Robert Wilson's form of theater presentation is many scenes unfolding beside or out of each other which therefore seemingly take place within a limitless context. The quality of it not being in a "box" derives from it emanating from the viewer, by the viewer seeing it.

Similarly, Creeley's *Collected* has the quality that "you" are creating it.

Wilson's visual spectacle unfolding unmediated by language (in the unfolding not being formed seemingly by language our impression is not "informed" by it) creates a sense of sites/sights essentially not changed from their "original."

One/the viewer is seeing them and ordering them as a "history." Creeley's *Collected* maintains its "original seeing" repeating it as oneself seeing it.

NOTES

1 Robert Creeley, *The Collected Poems* (Berkeley Univ. California Press, 1982), p. 437. cited hereafter in text as *Collected*.

2 Robert Creeley, *Contexts of Poetry: Interviews 1961–1971* (Bolinas, Ca: Four Seasons Foundation, 1973), p. 101. Cited hereafter in text as *Contexts*.

TRANSLATION/ ANTITRANSLATION/ CULTURE/MULTICULTURE SOME CONTRADICTIONS?

I would like to lead into this talk with a few personal notes.

First. I must admit that, for many years now, I have avoided paying great attention to writing about translation. This was because I was under the strong impression that very little new was being said and, perhaps, *could* be said about translation as a *craft*. It seemed to me that conferences on translation had to do with academic self-perpetuation and no more. I felt strongly that translation should be *done* as opposed to being talked about. As a result of this misapprehension, I have missed some new information about the field.

But books about translation are not all that easy to get hold of. When I tried to get some ten recent books on translation out of a provincial university library near my home recently, I could not find a single one.

Second, I have felt a connection between my lack of interest in translation theory and my waning interest in anthropological theory itself, a waning which, of course, went with the waning of any desire to do anthropology. Perhaps the turning point came when I interviewed Gary Snyder at Princeton in the early seventies. It was much more of a conversation than an interview but, for publication purposes, in *Alcheringa*, I erased my own contribution. It was Gary I believe who chose the title: *From Anthropologist to Informant*, but this title corresponded very strongly to a deep longing of mine: that is no longer to ask questions but to put myself into an activity in which there was an opportunity of giving *answers*. This activity would be the constantly sought, ever receding possibility of being a poet and nothing but a poet.[1] In case you ask why that was tough, let me just say that, in my youth, you could not earn a living as a poet—something most people do today as "creative

NATHANIEL TARN

writing" teachers. I mention all this here because it is going to have something to do with what I have to say about Antitranslation.

A couple of other points which may be related. The first (to be taken somewhat tongue in cheek) is that I have had growing doubts over the years about the advisability of any poet—young poets especially—taking on translation jobs on *major* authors if their own intent is firmly to be totally married to poetry.

This is because, quite simply, in this society, if you translate a major poet—perhaps a Nobel prize winner or one in the running for such—you run the danger of being held all your life as married to the work of that poet rather than to your own. The "work of yours" which others may want to discuss with you is nine times out of ten your version of the work of that poet and, whatever merits your own work may have, an infinitesimally small number of people will actually think of looking at it, even after having admired the work you did on *that* poet.

Now, it goes without saying that the work of that poet (being a Nobel) is believed to be more important than yours and that is o.k. What may be less o.k. is that it frequently negates, erases or totally obscures yours—indicating something about the sociological standing of poetry on the one hand and translation (even of poetry) on the other. We have come a long way from someone like Novalis being able to say "there is hardly a German writer of importance who has not translated, and who does not take as much pride in his translations as he does in his original works."[2] The difference may well have to do with our American habit of fawning on foreign poets in order the better to ignore our own. In any event, I would advise young poets to consult older poets they wish to translate and ask them if they are considering winning the Nobel prize. If they are, turn around and run for it.

The final point: while everyone today in the academy pays lip service to interdisciplinary work, such work only has to appear on the scene for it to face almost insuperable difficulties in being consumed, respected, taught, and published. Our specializationism—to coin an awful word meant to double-underline the depth of our classificatory dis-ease—is that strong. As a personal example I will say that, but for the insight of one particular editor with what amounted to an imprint of his own, Lee Bartlett of the University of New Mexico, my selected essays in poetics and anthropology[3] could never have been published without very considerable mutilation. Another work, deliberately designed as an interdisciplinary project in literature and anthropology and financed as such by a major foundation for anthropological research will probably remain on the shelf because it is "too literary for the anthros," "too anthro for the literary."

Footnote: the absurdity of the situation is underlined when you realize that any amount of interference with linear narrative—to take one instance of complaint—can be published in a work of fiction nowadays (and earn big bucks) and the difficult poetry of many avant garde communities of poets can get published but God forbid there should be any such thing in Holy Science: the public—intone the suddenly all-wise publishers—would not stand for it a single instant! This too is not unconnected to the subject of translation.

2

So much for the personal.

In what follows, I will be coming from at least two major innovative stances. The first is George Steiner's. In his *After Babel,* he shows with massively erudite deployment of phenomenal fans of encyclopedic knowledge (I guess such has to be his poetry) that virtually all acts of cultural communication, whether in time (usually the dimension of one's own culture) or in space (the dimension of interculturality) involve a transformative activity which in essence is what we mean by Translation.[4] The second is that of Edward Said who, following Gramsci, Foucault, and Schwab, demonstrates in his masterly *Orientalism* the extent to which the construction of apparently apolitical systems of representations in all our disciplines in fact constitutes cultural hegemonic mechanisms which inform, strengthen and perpetuate the political control of whomever is studied by whoever studies.[5] Both Steiner and Said lift discussion of Translation into an altogether different realm from that in which it is usually carried on. What we have now is a dawning Sociology of Translation rather than the old stuff about Translation as a Craft.

I am not here going to a critique such major works. I note in passing that, as of this moment, I cannot see much attention to translation as a craft—rather than as a category of political action—paid by Said: o.k., that may have to be given up at this time. More importantly, I do not hear him suggesting that, given all the years in which Islam had some hegemony over parts of Europe, we should at some time have a study of how Islam interpreted the Occident.

Is it not the case, however, that all communication is political in any direction whatsoever and that its passing from a sender to a receiver—whoever they may be at any moment, constitutes every single time a translation? If so, would this not imply, for one thing, that the study of a hegemony of x over y can never be separated from the study of the reaction of y to x's hegemony: i.e. there should, ideally, be no privileging of x or y because of a temporary, however long, situation of dominance of one over another? If the answer is yes, then, clearly, we need a discipline which would study the code of hegemony (or of anti-hegemony) in the very stuff or matter of the translational process itself, thus reinvigorating the central branch of our study as translators: translation as activity, as politico-cultural action. Whether this is covered in such proposals as James S. Holmes's call for a "sociology" of translation or not, I have not yet been able to find out.[6] Lawrence Venuti's work on "resistancy" versus "domestication" certainly seems to be a major step in getting "to that very stuff," raising a host of questions I am not dealing with here.[7]

Hegemony and anti-hegemony, then, may be the two dimensions or facets of translation which should interest us most: especially at this moment when power in the world is re-organizing itself to an astounding, almost hallucinatory degree. This brings me to trying to explain why Translation / Antitranslation figure in my title as they do. What I am trying to say is that there are forces which resist translation as much as there are others which elicit, require, or demand it and that these, perhaps apparently negative, forces—which I am calling those of Antitranslation—should be of as great interest to us as those, apparently more positive, of Translation itself.

By association, you will have guessed that I am asking whether we can associate Translation with Culture and Antitranslation, not with Anti-Culture, of course, but with something I'll here call Multiculture. Multiculture would be a neutral transform of what we all discuss nowadays—sometimes appreciatively, often pejoratively—as Multiculturalism.

To an anthropologist, the study of translation is not new. It was what appeared on the syllabus in my student days—some forty years ago—under such headings as acculturation, transculturation, crossculturation and so forth. Power, to anthropologists, was not something discovered during the sixties (though, of course, anthropology as "daughter of imperialism" revealed her full dance of Salome at that time). It was understood, for instance, that Mesoamerican Indians would be directed and constrained in their behavior by subordination to Spain; Native North Americans by subordination to the United States; many Africans, Asians or Australasians by subordination to France, Germany or England, etc.

Of course, in most instances studied, it was also understood that conquered Y would have to accept and adapt to the culture of conqueror X. But, whether because of cultural relativism (i.e that all cultures are valuable to their owners and should not be moralized about by us), then instilled as a virtue and guiding light in all students, or because of inherent sympathy with the Ys—whatever later critics have said—anthropologists quickly understood that such acceptance and adaptation was never completely one-sided. Many, if not all, Ys would accept only to some extent and would adapt what they accepted to their specifications. Syncretism of one sort or another—the religion of the great masses, for only elites can ever afford "pure" religions—was almost always to be found.

And in many cases, anthropologists came to have great admiration for the brilliance of these adaptive mechanisms. I have come to believe over the years, for example, that what the Highland Maya peasant of Guatemala and Chiapas has done with Christianity actually gave richer tints to that religion in its folk manifestations than the Mayas had originally received from the first Spanish Catholic priests at the time of Conquest. There had been a retroactive translation, as it were, a translation into Maya which has enriched or bettered the Spanish original—if, that is, one may be so unrelativistic for a moment as to risk such a value judgement.

From this, it should not be many steps to another statement. The path is facilitated by the adversarial stance which Native Peoples as well as many other "Liberation groups" have taken in the last forty years, realizing that now the question is one of sheer biological (anti-genocidal) as well as cultural (anti-ethnocidal) survival. For them, an Antitranslational stance is a perfectly valid antithesis to a Translational one and it is in fact manifested—empirically verifiable I suppose we would have said in those days—by a great many human groups today. Further, it is a striking facet of the ideology of many "minority" groups in what I have come to call the Internal Empire of this country, a facet which may be more covert and implied than overt and bluntly stated but nevertheless massively powerful. For the subjects of the Internal Empire are now flying the banner of something called "Multiculturalism" and the whole cultural world in this Republic is in turmoil over that term. If, instead of the old banner of "Don't tread on me," we were now seeing one proclaiming "Don't translate me," the case could hardly be clearer once it is formulated.

3

I believe I am going to say more about Antitranslation than about Translation, but let's start with the latter. Translation occurs, at its simplest, when a culture is built on a society with the material strength and extension to acquire, almost interminably and without limits, the cultural products of other societies. A culture has to feel very secure about itself before venturing into the luxurious course of taking an interest in other cultures. Learning other languages is not something most people can afford the time for, before backing this interest by bringing the products, say here texts, of those other cultures into its own sphere of discourse, say here language.[8]

Another point which is being made more and more by translation theorists—see, for instance, Tejaswini Niranjana's *Citing Translation*—is that translation into the subordinate language is usually controlled by the dominant. An obvious major example would be the translation of the Judaeo-Christian Bible into indigenous languages: but the situation is actually all-pervasive. For Niranjana, our whole traditional view of India's culture is constructed by British Imperialist translation programmes in such a way that British rule is justified.[9]

I stress text and language here because of our own primary topical interests but much the same could be said of other items of culture—say cooking to take an obvious one. You'll say "but cooking is not translated!" I'll say "Watch what becomes of French, Spanish or Italian cooking in this country. Or, in more detail, watch what becomes of *tapas*, for instance: in Spain, very small mouthfuls of fish usually— to go with aperitifs; in the U.S. invariably full-scale dinners."

It should follow that small and weak societies would not have such resources and would not, therefore, translate much into their own language. But, you'll say, it is very precisely small societies that do! Think of the Icelanders; the Dutch; the Hungarians. Well, first, I would answer, I was thinking of the *really* small and weak: the Papuans, the Pygmies, or the Highland Maya for instance. The smaller European societies are not "small" and especially not "weak" in *that* sense. Imbricated into an areal Western economy of huge proportions, they cannot afford not to translate and you will find that such small European societies actually spend a great deal on translation into their own language with much governmental support.

The other side of the medal—which is the most revealing—is the extreme anxiety of such societies in the matter of having themselves translated into the language of dominant partners. I have heard Hungarian, Dutch, and Icelandic poets, for instance, speak of the feeling of extreme constraint they experience when living solely within their own language and how they consider translation into the "great" languages a matter of sheer survival. And you can bet that there is a hierarchy here: most make it clear, to take the most obvious instance, that it is nowadays more important to be translated into English than into any other language. I am willing to bet that other (secondary) preferences would reveal much that is not immediately obvious—a whole aspect of sociology at present submerged. The question of size alone then is not necessarily a pointer to subordination. And if you are a willing partner in Empire, what is happening should perhaps not even be called subordination.

It is not only a matter of our own time and circumstance. India, China, Japan, at various times in their histories, virtually made culture-heroes of translators by sending them out, often at great danger to themselves, on immensely long missions to acquire texts for translation. That these were religious or spiritual texts, rather than technological ones, need not concern us overmuch when we note that religion can be an instrument of political power (think of Asoka in India) or even, very directly, techno-economic development: Jacques Gernet has shown how Buddhist monasteries were at the root of banking in China during the T'ang Dynasty.[10] Certain other figures are worth remembering. Think of the Egyptian Pharaoh Akhnaton's translations of doctrine into his own system, or the great Mughal Emperor Akbar's search among religious systems to find a synthesis, having Jewish, Christian, Hindu, Buddhist and other texts translated into the language of his own Empire when he himself was actually illiterate! Throughout history, there are many fascinating examples of such encyclopedic reaches for bodies of knowledge commensurate with the sublime political role a society saw itself as playing. Again, on Venuti's wavelength: might it be that India translated domesticatingly whereas China translated resistantly? Much in the varying welcomes accorded Buddhism might have been thus determined.

If this is Translation, what would Antitranslation be? It is tempting to pass straight from Translation as just described to Antitranslation as sheer political resistance: what I described above as "Don't translate me!" This would leave out a vital consideration about those I've described as truly poor—the Aborigines of the Third World. We must not forget that if those Natives are too small and poor to translate other cultures into their own, it is probably as much as anything because, in so many cases, they themselves have been already translated. Most of Latin America is already, as it were, *in* Spanish or Portuguese; most of Africa and Australasia and much of Asia is already *in* English or French. And, of course, what I have called the Inner Empire—in this country the ethnic minorities: Black,

Hispanic, Native American mainly—have been already translated. Does this exclude them from Antitranslation? I think not.

Steiner, in his very first chapter, points out that "the agonistic functions of speech inside an economically and socially divided community possibly outweigh functions of genuine communication" and goes on to list a number of ways in which subordinates will resist, actively or passively, the linguistic onslaughts of the dominant.[11] He talks of the way in which language events assume the nature of a duel—with incommunicativeness; apparent misunderstanding; thickening, blurring, or other distortion of speech; confusion by slowness or rapidity; false obsequiousness; resort to dialect and many more such methods being the modes of resistance on the part of the subordinate faced with the ever more exasperated "clarifications" of the dominant. I remember a Kipling quote very current among Europeans during my study time in Burma: "The Christian swears and swears and swears; the Buddhist smiles and smiles."

Gender definition resistances are not as clear-cut as those of ethnic groups. However, gender definition groups and their texts have to be included in the Inner Empire in that they share with ethnic groups the status of being oppressed by the dominant culture. It would probably be possible to demonstrate that there are, as it were, women's dialects, gays' dialects, or, say, children's dialects, which resist the dominant culture's attempt to translate them. Much of the fiction concerning what used to be known as the war of the sexes reveals the history of these evolving and ever changing resistances.

And there is, of course, an extreme form of translation, especially in sexual matters (but not exclusively—cf. the recent history of certain rap groups), that is the absolute negative, or nadir, of Translation—when you bring a subordinate group totally under your control by absolute suppression. The name of that one is censorship, pure and simple when dominant, manifesting as self-censorship when subordinate.

We should note that "subordinate" does not necessarily imply politically laudable, embraceable, or correct. In fact, perhaps, it may also englobe just the opposite. At the time of writing, I have just watched a two-and-a-half-hour trial in video transcription: the case of two Human Rights' groups in Portland, Oregon, against the

Metzgers, father and son, leaders of WAR, the White Aryan Resistance. In this case, I am thinking of the doublespeak which characterizes such subordinates. When seemingly free and unfettered, their racialist discourse is brutal to the point of incitement to murder. When under any form of constraint or examination, Antitranslation here manifests as a purified language in which violence, for instance, becomes "violence-only-as-self-defense"; "all Xs are mud" becomes "some Xs are mud"; a racist murder becomes a "tragic-event-brought-on-by-two-people-fighting-in-the-street" and so forth.

The doublespeak of a David Duke was widely noted when Duke ran for governor of Louisiana. No doubt such processes stretch back into the history of the Ku Klux Klan, America First, and many other organizations, back to the first immigrations into this republic, all demonstrating censorship and self-censorship in plenty. In the case of "decent people"—I happen to be thinking of certain private diaries written in controversial times as an example—self-censorship attains such degrees of subtlety that it strains our analytical talents to the highest degree and we despair of ever being able to uncover the exact dimensions of the opinions held.

Other examples of resistance: Anthropological cases in which a tribe or other sub-group of a society—a religious sodality, say— refuse to act as informants to anthropologists are very frequent. There are many groups among the Eastern Pueblos right around my present home in New Mexico which so refuse. I read this as Antitranslation, stating "I will not let you translate this sacred information into your empirical, statistifiable, so-called scientific language." The case of such groups who, after a certain time, seem to break down completely and, against all precedent, seek out those who would so translate their secrets parallels the case of the Dutch, Danes, and Hungarians I spoke of before: such seeking out occurs when the fear of extinction occurs: "better these survive in translation than not at all; better we give up on autonomy and merge into Empire rather than disappear altogether" seems to be the message.

I read another example of Antitranslation in the behavior of some minority artists who exemplify in their attitudes the maximal contempt for would-be translators (and actual translators in the case of, say, white rip-offs of black music). I think of Miles in music or, more subtly but just as directly, of Gwendolyn Brooks in poetry. After decades of publishing with Harper & Row, Brooks, as I understand it, deliberately turned her back on the world of dominant publishing in order to give all her books to small black publishers mainly in Chicago. A variant of this, it seems to me, is the belligerent attitude taken by some Chicano poets I once heard state to a dominant audience "stop paying attention and lip-service to poets like Paz, Neruda and Vallejo and listen to us for a change." While this would seem to be saying "Translate me!" rather than "Do not translate me!," I think it says primarily "Stop translating those you think to be, rightly or wrongly, at your level and pay attention to *our* uniqueness for a change! . . . but, incidentally, that uniqueness is not available to be co-opted or taken over by you!"

In the June 1992 *Art in America* there is a fascinating piece on recent conflict in Los Angeles between a Mexican Government series of art offerings and local Chicano art offerings. Another example: Years ago, I pointed out how English poets in the dominant schools translated other poets whose parameters seemed to equal their own.[12] Other poets, both English and foreign, whose parameters were different—usually far more experimental and exciting—were marginalized if English, ignored and not translated if foreign. Similar phenomena occur right now among us. But, watch it! a marginalized poet of only yesterday has a text from Harvard and a named chair today. Things move fast and furious in this field!

This, I trust you understand, is also a response to a situation in this country in which the dominant Anglo/white poetry community (however much itself divided) knows virtually nothing about the black or Hispanic poetry communities and cares still less: a radically scandalous situation which cannot be allowed and will not be allowed to continue—if only because the ever-increasing specialization of the Anglo/white elite's products may well ensure dinosaurial disappearance and the triumph of the non-Anglo/white poetries is virtually a foregone conclusion if any kind of genuinely popular support for poetry continues to be part of a desirable landscape.

These are obviously variant facets of the huge debate going on at present in this republic. Are we far wrong if we say that Translation, as read here, is equivalent to Culture if we take the latter as an imperial, hegemonic, dominant entity confident that its traditions, canons, and values are *the* traditions, canons, and values that count and that none other can be held to be at that level—the level of God-Almighty Western Culture itself? And that Antitranslation would then have to be the transform of, not Anti-Culture, definitely not that, but of Multiculture defined as (since we are talking here in this republic) the culture of these United Mistakes seen, no longer as the melting pot transforming all ingredients into one soup, but as an aggregate of the cultures which have entered into this land and now compose what, for better or for worse, has become the eternally invoked "American People"? Which would then leave Multiculturalism for that body of socio-cultural policy which respects, honors, validates, defends, and puts into action such policies as will uphold Multiculture instead of Culture.

In the last few years, just as we have heard the white racist arguments—both overt and, alas far more extensively, covert—that invading colored hordes are taking over white jobs and white country, we have heard the arguments opposing the defenders of Culture to the defenders of Multiculture and, knowing Acanaemic Burrocrassy as I do, I have been scarcely surprised to hear that Multiculturalism is being decreed by dominant Administration down to subordinate Professorate very burrocrasstically indeed, which helps no one to understand or be sympathetic to anything ongoing. Obviously, very little is going to be achieved if quotas are the name of the game—if every time you mention Plato you have to mention Confucius or Ogotemmeli; if every time you talk Joyce and Kafka you have to bring in Soyinka or Achebe. That is mere tinkering. What the situation is asking us to achieve—and not being in the academy at present, I find it hard to say how much *genuine* response there is, or not—is a re-evaluation greater than ever before in our constantly re-evaluating history, a re-evaluation that amounts to a philosophical earthquake of mega-ten on the Richter scale.

A major question remains in my mind: does Culture have to be given up if we want or require Multiculture? I always seem to come up in theory with *both/and* answers rather than *either/or* answers. It looks like I'm going to do the same again and do it with the aid of a model of the poetic self that I've used before in other contexts.

The model of poetic activity I refer to has three levels: that of the vocal on top, the silence in between, and the choral at the bottom. I won't apologize for the hierarchical look of that any more than I'll apologize for the relative positions of my—and your—heads, navels, and feet.

First. By *vocal*, I mean what appears to be our normal everyday state of poetic activity in which any given poet is competing with other poets to find, in language, something so unique to him/herself (a voice, a trace, a style, a signature, whatever) that her/his writing cannot possibly ever be mistaken for that of anyone else. The extremist possible individualism and originality is the name of this game. The player is an aspect of self or ego, and the social situation is one of self-other reciprocity since the ratio between competition and co-operation is the guiding principle of this state. Most times (exceptions are usually momentary and tactical), the worst thing that can possibly happen to a poet in the *vocal* is to be told that s/he has been influenced by other poet x or y (i.e. is part of a lineage); or forms part of a school x or y (i.e. is part of a community of poets); or even reminds a given reader of x or y (i.e. has been subconsciously influenced by another).

This is the poet as Arch-Informant and Antitranslator *par excellence.* This is poetry in its purest possible state, something so unique it might as well be music—often regarded (illusorily) as the purest of the arts and . . . just as untranslatable. The poet's stance here is that of the Arch-Informant—in Snyder's terms—and is Antitranslational in its most rigorous form: s/he is saying in effect: "I am not even telling you 'Don't translate me' for you could not if you tried: it is quite simply and purely impossible."

Again with George Steiner *inter alia,* you are familiar with silence as the state out of which poetry issues and to which it returns—something as binary as our binary of binaries, the couple life/death. A great deal of fine writing—poetry, fiction, nonfiction, sheer mysticism—has issued for ages from the dialectic of silence and non-silence, i.e. the *vocal.* I was long satisfied with this as the complete picture. Lately, I have realized that something is called for to be under the silence if the model is to be complete. And if that something exists, then silence changes from being an oceanic absolute to being a category, *the silence.* I will eventually suggest that it is the only category of my three which can be ascribed to the real.

The silence, then, is that place where poetry passes from what is under the silence to the vocal and back again; that place where, sociologically, the situation is one of self-self reciprocity. It is the place in which the poet, in communal conversation with her/himself, determines the situation of the presently birthing poem, its relation to *information,* its relation to *opus,* i.e. all the poems written by that poet from birth to death and its relation to text/page, i.e. the possibilities of poetry in the totality of space/time. It is the place, the only place where, mystery of mysteries, tautology of tautologies, poetry takes place.

I call *choral* that which is under the silence. Choral because, however many parts a chorus may have (think of, say: soprano, alto, tenor and base) the essence here is unity, homogeneity, the drowning of individual "purity" into the commonality of a whole more extensive than itself, the realization on the part of part that it is not purely and simply whole of itself—but part of something altogether greater and other. Sociologically, the situation is one of no reciprocity. That is: if x is already wholly y, there is nothing x can give to y and vice versa. In regard to our topic, there is something ecstatic about the choral. You can think of everyone and everything in it as singing "Yes, translate me! translate me!" or you can think of it as already such a great white rose that the song you hear is "Why even think of translating me when I am so wholly yours, and your song, and you are so wholly mine, and my song?"

Here one can think of it in the terms of *Guardame ben, ben son, ben son Beatrice!*—to me the recognition of all recognitions in all literature or, perhaps, as the figures stretching out their arms in the *Paradiso* of Giovanni di Paolo, ready it seems to pass through each other, so much are they already part of each other by the very determination of the paradisal state.

Now, why do I take the silence in this model as the only reality?

It is because the vocal and the choral both seem to me so clearly to be illusions of each other—reciprocal illusions of the two extreme possible sociologies if you wish. A poet, in the vocal state, massively impressed by the statistical enormity of what and whom has to be gotten through before "pure" individuality is reached, can only laugh at the very notion of choral: empirically speaking the whole matter is absurd. Likewise, what on earth can become of something as insane as a desire for originality in the choral ???!!!

Does this mean that the vocal and the choral are not real, do not exist? No way! They exist as much as Samsara and Nirvana exist, for instance, in Buddhist philosophy—and they are part of one and the same existence in the same way as, at the extreme, Samsara *is* Nirvana or Nirvana *is* Samsara. They exist as much as the two faces of Janus exist, on the one body of a Roman deity, or on a coin so thin its two sides would be one—a one-sided coin.

And they exist also in another seeming contradiction. In what I've said about Translation and Antitranslation, Culture and Multiculture, you may have detected a suggestion of villainy attached to Translation and Culture, a suggestion of politically praiseworthy correctness attached to Antitranslation and Multiculture. Likewise, you might have felt a breath of disdain for the struggling vocal in contrast to a bias in favor of the seemingly paradisal choral. How logical it would be, then, to have Translation and Culture as part of the same "baddy" classification as the vocal (—under the same totem, to speak Lévi-Strauss if you wish—) while Antitranslation and Multiculture would fit in on the "goody" side with the choral. However: that is not the way it goes!

The world of Multiculture is—we see this every day—a world of intense competition, heterogeneity, antithesis: it is very clearly the world of the vocal. The world of Culture, however, is just as intensely non-adversarial and homogeneous and so, we might think, choral. This is not entirely what we might have expected.

We can all relax, however, in reminding ourselves of the illusory character of the vocal and the choral. Or rather, we must recall to mind that they are reciprocal illusions: they are both as important as each other in the overall process: it is simply impossible, in fact, to have the one without the other. The situation is a *both/and* one by nature, not an *either/or* one. This is comforting for one major reason. It seems to me that the whole weight of our cultural scene and the media which carry it favor—and for obvious political reasons (Divide and Rule!)—*either/or* positions over *both/and* positions. We are constantly presented, it seems to me, with the relation of Culture to Multiculture as an *agon*, as a struggle. We are told that we are in the profoundest of troubles because we must decide and decide quickly, critically, between the "tradition" of Culture and the "new" of Multiculture.

I see no such *agon*. It is clear that we must have *both* Culture and Multiculture and very seriously work toward that earthquake measuring ten. It was being said in the sixties that anthropology had to go all the way from the Self to the Other only to find, as it got closer and closer to the Other, that the Other had the same face as the Self. Similarly, we have to go to the extremes of each cultural Other and accept the extremist implications of Antitranslation in Multiculture if we are to measure the full extent of human possibility. Without measuring that full extent, we measure very precisely nothing *at all*. We put ourselves on the socio-cultural level at the same point in which we are putting ourselves biologically by allowing the atrocious diminution taking place every day in the extinction of species after species.

Multiculture is as important as that. As I tried to put it years ago in *The Beautiful Contradictions*, the daughter remains blind before and until we fully know the mother.[13] I am of course, talking of the ancient ideal of HUMAN-UNITY-IN-DIVERSITY—one without which humanity will not be saved and this planet will not be saved. The choral, which may be a transform of Benjamin's "true language," however illusory, is as important as that.[14] Culture is as important as that. There are no contradictions. It is as stark as that.

In practice, of course, it is easier to say this than to see it done. Can the equality implied by Multiculture ever become a reality when social inequality remains as blatant as it does today? Can Culture, which has not yet been divorced for its salvation from nation and polity, ever be purged of its appalling weight of guilt when social inequality remains as blatant as it does today? We are all in the furnace on those questions. Perhaps a beginning can be made if we can persuade ourselves that we have, quite literally, no alternative. Perhaps we can begin if we understand that.

As I have often claimed before, Poets' Liberation is the most primal and profound of all liberation movements. I urge those who are out of the movement to join it. Those on the inside never will.

June 1992

NOTES

1 See "Child as Father to Man in the American Uni-verse" in N. Tarn, *Views from the Weaving Mountain: Selected Essays in Poetics and Anthropology,* An American Poetry Book (Albuquerque: University of New Mexico College of Arts and Sciences).

2 As quoted in Andre Lefevere: *Translating Literature: the German Tradition* (Assen/Amsterdam: Van Gorcum, 1977), p. ix.

3 *Views from the Weaving Mountain.*

4 *After Babel* (London: Oxford University Press, 1975).

5 *Orientalism* (New York: Pantheon, 1978).

6 See *Translation Theories, Translation Studies and the Translator,* paper presented at the VIIth World Congress of the International Federation of Translators, Montreal, 1977. (R. Kelly position paper note 20)

7 See, *inter alia, Simpatico,* in *Sub-Stance,* no. 65 (1991), pp. 3–20, Milwaukee, Wisconsin.

8 I should insert here a note from Dennis Tedlock to the effect that the Zuni and Hopi are interested in telling *other peoples' stories.* He argues from this that it does not take a very large society to be interested in translation. I stand contradicted to some extent—though I doubt Zuni or Hopi telling is appropriative in the same way our translations are.

9 Tejaswini Niranjana: *Siting Translation: History, Poststructuralism, and the Colonial Context* (Berkeley: University of California Press, 1992).

10 *Les aspects économiques du bouddhisme dans la société chinoise du v au xème siècle* (Saigon: Ecole Française d'Extreme-Orient, 1956).

11 Steiner, op. cit., p. 32.

12 "The World Wide Open" in *Views from the Weaving Mountain,* p. 32.

13 *The Beautiful Contradictions* (New York: Random House, 1970); reprinted in *Atitlan/Alashka* (Boulder, Colorado: Brillig Works Press, 1979).

14 See "The Task of the Translator" in *Illuminations* (New York: Schocken Books, 1969), pp. 69–82, and Lefevere, op. cit, p.102.

LPHABETS AND EMPERORS

REFLECTIONS ON KAFKA AND BORGES

Borges was a young man when he translated Kafka, and one imagines that he must have been profoundly haunted. Indeed, the translator, if haunted, is himself a ghost ambulating unseen and unheard in another's *Mundus Imaginalis* which—by the time he is done—has revealed its secrets. The act of translation is of cabalistic nature; manipulating alphabets—those living bones of language—the object is transcendence: to recreate the luminous complexity of original speech in an alien tongue. The finished work, conjured by a new arrangement of letters, is a vital thing: an old snake in a new skin.

o   o   o

It is Christmas Eve, and very late. The year is 1930, and Borges' translations of Kafka have only just appeared. The moon, Borges' favorite planet, its name *different in different languages and variously lovely (Seven Nights)* is not visible. In the acute darkness, Borges bounds up stairs which are profoundly familiar, yet slams his skull against the cruel edge of an open window. Suspended in delirium, he is for many weeks seized by hallucinatory fevers and incapable of speaking. When, at last, he is able to return to his writing, he sets himself the task to do what he has never done before: to write a piece of `fantastic' fiction. He writes "Pierre Menard, Author of the Quixote"—the story of a man who has so *totally identified* himself with Cervantes and his world, that he is able to produce several chapters of *Don Quixote* which are, in every way, *exactly like the original.* And this is what we ask of a translation: a complicity so entire, and of such potent wizardry, as to lay that living snake at our feet—and its apple—as green as original sin.

I propose that by translating Kafka into Spanish, Borges was himself transformed; that a mysterious operation which combined Kafka, an open window and a moonless night gave us `our' Borges. And that Kafka's story *The Great Wall of China* may be seen as that *small iridescent sphere of almost unbearable brilliance*—the

RIKKI DUCORNET

Aleph—in which the future itineraries of Borges' own labyrinths are mirrored.

o   o   o

Before I begin my brief if amorous scrutiny of Borges' debt to Kafka, I would like to open two more windows—of glass weirdly fractured—which reveal elements essential to the fictive landscapes of both authors; one window is called Cabala, the other Gnosticism.

The Cabala proposes the peculiar idea that the corporal universe is that portion of Yahweh's footstool which, thrust from Him and anchored in chaos, emerges from the abysmal waters. Yahweh's configurations—issued from a void he has knowingly created, and which animate His footstool world—are the reflections of dreamed archetypes. All things visible and tangible, from gnats to walruses and carpenters, are but flickerings in the mirror of Yahweh's *whereness*. We enter here into Lands of Looking Glass; as much as he loved the Cabala and Kafka, Borges loved Alice.

Everything happens, Borges writes (in his book titled *Mirrors*), *everything happens and nothing is recorded in these rooms of the looking glass, where magicked into rabbis, we now read the books from right to left.*

Yet, if all the world is semblance, still it is a mirror of sorts, for according to the Cabala, each thing perceived is the fruit, however volatile, of Divine Intention—a shadow of the sublime original. (Which recalls Kafka's complaint that all human language is but a poor *translation*.)

And, in that heretical library of gnostic books discovered in Fayoum by *fellaheen* looking for bird manure, we read that the visible universe was created by an aborted monster—a hideous chimera with the face of a lion and the body of a snake—which, abandoned by Pistis Sophia—its horrified mother—to a distant corner of the universe where he could not be seen, set about to steal his mother's light. Cementing it with darkness, he created a world—our world.

Both these visions of the planet—submerged footstool and the toy of a bitter demon—admit to the possibility of transcendence. Because the world contains particles of discarded or stolen light, a memory, however faint, of *home*—immaterial and incandescent—nettles the searching mind as a chance for liberation. A possibility invoked by Borges in his short story *The Approach to al-Mu'tasim*: "*Rethinking the problem (the student) arrives at the mysterious conclusion that 'somewhere on the face of the earth is a man from whom this light has emanated; somewhere on the face of the earth there exists a man who is equal to this light.' The student decides to spend his life in search of him.*"

And echoed in this passage from "The Library of Babel": "*Let heaven exist, though my place be in hell. Let me be outraged and annihilated, but for one instant, in one being, let Your enormous library be justified.*"

However, in the darkling worlds of both Borges and Kafka, the light is so very dissipated that were we given the Book of Knowledge by Pistis Sophia Herself, we would not find sufficient light to read by. This is Borges' message to us when he describes those library lamps of Babel in the shape of *spherical fruit; the light they emit is insufficient, incessant.* And surely, the most startling metaphor for the spark imprisoned in the cage of corporality is Kafka's portrait of Gregor Samsa waking in the body of a *monstrous vermin.*

For the Gnostic, the body and its hungers are seen as a species of demonic joke; we are, each and everyone of us, a Gregor Samsa left to perish in a room cluttered with the archetypes of nightmares, an apple festering in our ribs. Time, Space, and Gravity are the implacable enemies of Spirit; the planet is a malignancy, and the reeling zodiac—the crushing gears and pinions of a mad machine performing without rhyme or reason: *The Penal Colony* on a cosmic scale.

According to the Cabala, Satan rules the world of form and matter—and here the implication is that it is the world's *transience* which is satanic: the very fact that the world of things is in a continuous state of flux. (Abulafia on the *Sefer Yezirah*)

o   o   o

Now we are ready to investigate *The Great Wall* itself. The wall (and the word, held to a mirror, spells *Llaw*) is a species of *horizontal* tower of Babel, and like the tower, an attempt to reach a god who *refuses to be reached*. Just as in Eden, the god of Babel will not be known, nor named. (In traditional Judaism, YHWH'S name must never be pronounced with its correct vowels; *letters*, which are divine potencies, both activated and participated in the creation of the world. Letters are so potent that a scribe's mistake, as he copies a sacred text, could lead to a cosmic disaster.) The Wall, the confounded Tower and the Forbidden Fruit form a diabolic Trinity: a Trinity of Denial.

The failure of Babel and the loss of a universal language has imposed upon humankind *translation as a way of life*. Here I cannot help but pause to remember Kafka's account of 'sea-sickness' on *terra firma*—an amnesic state in which the names of things are lost, when *the poplar in the fields which you have named 'the tower of Babel' . . . sways again namelessly. . . .*

Language, the vehicle of messages and meanings, is central to Kafka's tale. The wall percolates beneath the eye of heaven like a dispatch in Morse code; it is atomized, its syntax riddled with gaps. If, as claims a scholar, the wall is intended as a foundation for a future *tower*, it is a foundation full of holes: Holy Dogma.

Rumors are everywhere—in the air, on every tongue—as is aborted information. A first messenger is ignored and beaten; his message, written in an archaic dialect, is incomprehensible. A second cannot reach us; between the yawning mouth of a moribund emperor and our own finite ear stretches an infinite[1] obstacle course: *So vast is our land that no fable could do justice to its vastness, the heavens can scarcely span it. . . .*

In other words, the Empire cannot be circumscribed and so cannot be conceived in space; nor can it be mapped and therefore it cannot be found. Unfound, unmapped—can it be said to *exist*? Just as the Emperor's elusive message, the Empire itself is a fiction. The risks of such speculation are so great that the narrator must leave off the telling of his tale, else find himself—a Babel tower of flesh and bone—tumbling from his own faulty foundations: *To set about establishing a fundamental defect here would mean undermining not only our consciences, but, what is worse, our feet.*

The frontiers of such an illusory world, created—as Kafka said to

Max Brod *at the instant God looked away*—upon a foundation as porous as lunar cheese, is extended by Borges in his own cruel Babylon. If the destiny of the Emperor of China, sprawling on a shrinking couch,[2] is as tenuous as the wind, and the rumors about him as variable as the weather, *There is nothing so contaminated with fiction as the history of the Company whose orders, issued continuously (perhaps incessantly) do not differ from those lavished by imposters.* ("The Lottery of Babylon") Just as long dead emperors are set on the throne in Kafka's China, *someone abominably insinuates the Company has not existed for centuries. . . .*

Kafka's China and the Babylon of Borges are, like the windowless and mirror-glazed rooms of a fun house, ruled by willed distortions, cruel illusions, false leads, a *divinity in delirium* ("Library of Babel"); the cosmos *magicked by rabbis,* is a hoax. God is a defrauder, Divine Order is reduced to rumor, a game of craps played out by old men in a latrine. It is no accident that in Babylon, there is a sacred latrine named QAPHQA (Kafka) Or that in "The Approach to al-Mu'tasim" (and its subtitle is: *A Game With Shifting Mirrors*) a law student's first step towards transcendence is initiated by the sight of a beggar urinating in a disordered garden. Fecal necessity exemplifies the absurd and its incontournable determinism: each time we shit we know we are doomed to die. A cognizant vermin, riddled by pride and an enfeebling awareness of his own finitude and deluded by capacity to create myths and to succumb to them, man—proconsul, librarian, emperor, or slave—rolls the shit-ball of God's possibility up and down the corridors of a maze of shifting mirrors; in the Library of Babel, *there is a mirror which faithfully duplicates all appearances.*

I always dream of labyrinths or of mirrors, Borges writes (in *Seven Nights*) . . . *the two are not distinct, as it only takes two facing mirrors to construct a labyrinth.*

Yet, even as two facing mirrors offer us an intimation of infinity, and although our spirits reel, we know that we are being deceived; the dung-beetle is being toyed with; what he calls his `perceptions' are a joke.

o   o   o

I recall being deeply perturbed when, as a child of ten, I stepped into an elevator in Cairo, the walls of which were made of mirrors; the elevator's vertical function—if real—was finite, and the horizontal capacity—if illusory—was (to use a favorite word of Borges) *interminable*. Years later when I took that Borgesian stairway which *sinks abysmally and soars upwards to remote distances*, I recognized my vertiginous Egyptian elevator.

"*But oh, Kitty!*" says Alice, as she is about to step into the land of Looking-Glass, "*Now we come to a passage. You can see a little peep of (it) in Looking-glass House, if you leave the door of our drawing-room wide open: and it's very like our passage as far as you can see, only you know it may be quite different on beyond.*"

o   o   o

There is a cabalistic parable in which the mutable world is likened to an infinite set of windows of colored glass which change aspect as the sun passes before them. These windows exemplify the transient aspect of *Mundus Imaginalis*—the unfixed world which is illusion. The sun exemplifies the immutable nature of God.

A number of years ago, I visited the Museum of Science in London and stumbled into a series of darkened rooms in which holograms were on view. The first image I encountered was that of a woman's severed head which hung suspended in the artificial dusk like the head of an astrological dragon. As I approached, her eyes sparkled with recognition and she flashed me a smile. When at last I could tear myself away from this exemplary encounter, I turned and was greeted by a startling series of spheres about the size of billiard balls. Brightly colored in the classic hues of holography (and, coincidentally, those of a High Priest's breast plate!): carnelian, lapis lazuli, topaz, green jasper—they appeared to spin in deepest space, contained within a phantom grid in an ordered configuration. Because I had been reading Borges at the time—*The library is a sphere whose exact center is any one of its hexagons, and whose circumference is inaccessible*—I played a little game with myself, pretended that I was in the presence of a mockup of the universe, a master plan of divine intention, or—as from some impossible distance—seeing the universe itself, seized in the void and as ordered as an alphabet. For several long minutes I imagined that the cosmos *was* an alphabet, a set of potencies, seed syllables in the shape of palpitating moons; Borgesian Alephs encompassing all possible worlds simultaneously. But then, shifting my weight from one foot to the other, the spheres dissolved and instantaneously reappeared metamorphosed *into cubes*.

At that moment I recalled that blasphemous sect of librarians which *suggested that the searches* (for the One Book) *should cease and that all men should juggle letters and symbols, until they constructed by chance the Canonical books* ("Library of Babel"). And it seemed to me that the whole Qaphqa-Borgesian problem of the impossibility of ever perceiving the Emperor's new clothes had been offered me in a most unsettling and unforgettable manner. As in that mirrored elevator, I was seized with vertigo.

To end, I will read to you the parable of the Emperor's message from *The Great Wall of China* which is about the delusion called Faith and the illusion called God:

> There is a parable . . . The Emperor, so it runs, has sent a message to you, the humble subject, the insignificant shadow cowering in the remotest distance before the imperial sun; the Emperor from his deathbed has sent a message to you alone. He has commanded the messenger to kneel down by the bed, and has whispered the message to him; so much store did he lay on it that he ordered the messenger to whisper it back into his ear again. Then by a nod of the head he has confirmed that it is right. Yes, before the assembled spectators of his death—all the obstructing walls have been broken down, and on the spacious and loftily mounting open staircases stand in a ring the great princes of the Empire—before all these he has delivered his message. The messenger immediately sets out on his journey; a powerful, an indefatigable man; now pushing with his right arm, now with his left, he cleaves a way

for himself through the throng; if he encounters resistance he points to his breast, where the symbol of the sun glitters; the way is made easier for him than it would be for any other man. But the multitudes are so vast; their numbers have no end. If he could reach the open fields how fast he would fly, and soon doubtless you would hear the welcome hammering of his fists on your door. But instead how vainly does he wear out his strength; till he is only making his way through the chambers of the innermost palace; never will he get to the end of them; and if he succeeded in that nothing would be gained; he must next fight his way down the stair; and if he succeeded in that nothing would be gained; the courts would still have to be crossed; and after the courts the second outer palace; and once more stairs and courts; and once more another palace; and so on for thousands of years; and if at last he should burst through the outermost gate—but never, never can that happen—the imperial capital would lie before him, the center of the world, crammed to bursting with its own sediment. Nobody could fight his way through here even with a message from a dead man. But you sit at your window when evening falls and dream it to yourself.

NOTES

1 For Borges, the idea of an infinite universe has its seductions because it contains all virtualities *including free will*. If infinity is an illusion, then so is freedom. Yet, paradoxically, *the certitude that everything has been written . . . turns us into phantoms* ("The Library of Babel") and dissolves the difference between good and evil ("The Garden of Forking Paths").

2 This diminishing Emperor is unintentionally invoked in the *Zohar* where it is a question of God's beard:

The beard is the essence of the whole body; all the splendor of the body follows behind the beard. Thus all is dependent upon the beard (The Book of Concealment).

ALPHABETS AND EMPERORS
SELECTED BIBLIOGRAPHY

Jorge Luis Borges, *Seven Nights* (*New York:* New Directions, 1980).

Jorge Luis Borges, *Labyrinths* (*New York:* New Directions, 1962).

Franz Kafka, *The Complete Stories* (*New York:* Schocken Books, 1971).

E. Rodriguez Monegal, *Borges* (*Seville:* Ecrivains de toujours, 1970).

Abraham ben Samuel Abulafia, *The Path of the Names* (Trigam, 1976).

Gershom G. Scholem, *On the Kabbalah and Its Symbolism* (*New York:* Schocken, 1965).

Max Brod, *Franz Kafka: A Biography* (*New York:* Schocken, 1963).

Lewis Carroll, *Alice's Adventures in Wonderland* (*New York:* Bantam Books, 1981).

Hans Jonas, *The Gnostic Religion* (*Boston:* Beacon Press, 1958).

THE BLUES AND THE KING'S ENGLISH

There were some things I heard at the colloquium on Saturday morning that I think might be a focus for today's discussion, that is, What is the function of the word? I heard people saying "No one seems to read poetry anymore," and the comment was made, "Well, we have our community here of poets and we listen to each other and eventually, perhaps, if we keep the flame alive, there will come a moment in time when it will spill over into the rest of the traffic out there."

That started me to thinking about the concept of public versus private poetry. This is, I think, a major issue that has always confronted American letters because it is deeply entangled in those traditions that present the models of literature in the English language. I don't think that the real problem of the lyric poet in America today is expressed by standing up and complaining, "Gee, I have this poem and I cannot get the people standing around on the mall downtown to listen to me." You're not supposed to! That's part of the tradition of lyric poetry in the English language. We have to accept that. It is built in. If we go back to one of the sources of the place where we are now—I'm talking about England, Europe— we find that much of the poetry we are taught comes out of a tradition of a literate nobility, the owner class of people. Such poetry is a very special form of intellectual exercise and amusement. It takes place in the royal court, and we can imagine that one literate knight with a modicum of wit stands up and addresses the rest, and the contest then becomes for someone else in the company to match or surpass that witticism. Later on the contest gets structured so that you have specific rules: rhymes, meters, stanza forms that have to be mastered. Like any other contest there are rules to the game. Certainly what is being expressed here is something for the amusement of a small crowd of people, and expressed within terms that are appropriate to that group of people. To try and carry that tradition into a country of some 200 million folk who,

LORENZO THOMAS

functionally, are all literate is impossible. We know that from experience; it's not possible.

There is another part of that courtly tradition which also has to do with the question of amusing oneself. And of course the word *amusement* means just what it says: being touched by the muses, you know, just like *amazement* means being lost in a maze. But that aspect of the courtly poem involves taking all of one's musical and linguistic skill and turning it into a little song. The word *sonnet* is just that: it means *little song* in Italian. Sir Philip Sydney recognized this and brilliantly translated the Italian convention into the English of his day, and stunned everybody at court, amused them, amazed them.

The convention of the "little song" is the convention of the distant lover who sings out his desperation to his beloved afar, who may or may not respond, who may or may not ever hear the little song. That's part of the convention. So on one level we're talking about poetry meant for select company and the courtly verbal duels; or in terms of the love-poetry traditions, we're talking about poetry meant for an even more select audience: one other individual. Often a person who is not even privileged to hear the song—but that's part of the beauty of the song in our conception of it. The beloved doesn't even have to be a human being. And frequently, in the history of English language poetry, is not. The beloved is someone distanced by dimension. That is, one thinks of God—in whatever conception you have of him or her—as the beloved, and the poems therefore are addressed to God. But again, that's a private conversation.

The traditions that English-speaking people bring to the shores of this continent, as far as poetry is concerned, are partly those traditions. The result is a marvelous poet like Anne Bradstreet who is not part of the courtly tradition—she's just a housewife; her poems are about God; they are meditations and contemplations on the meaning of the universe and the relationship of us to the creator. Anne Bradstreet is embarrassed when her poems are surreptitiously sent off to England to be published and she writes poems about her embarrassment. Again, that's also conventional: a kind of required modesty. But the whole concept of poetry there is that one sits down and writes conversations with God, or she (Anne Bradstreet) writes letters to her husband upon his being absent, telling him how much she misses him or how the household is faring in his absence and these, the theory goes, are not intended to be published for us to read. They are private communications.

So poetry is a private thing. This notion lasts as long as Emily Dickinson, who writes poems for some kind of communion between herself and God, or herself and her spirit, or herself and her intellect or whatever it is. And she makes little books out of them, but they're not for you or me. It's a private matter. So if that's our tradition, we have no right to complain that the people in the mall aren't interested in what we do—that's not part of the business.

There is, of course, another poetic tradition and that is a public type of poetry, and it has many different aspects to it as well. We are, I think, erroneously taught that there is such a thing as anonymous folk creation—a kind of collective and communal creation of something. And so we are taught ballads and songs and poems and we're told, "Well, no one actually wrote these, you see, they developed over the space of some period of time, the folk contributed to this and there are no authors, the community created this and has handed it down to us by word of mouth" . . . until it fell into the hands of some English professor who printed a book of it and now you've got it.

I don't believe that any such thing happens. I believe that all poems are produced by some force out there which then focuses on some individual to collect the sounds and words. And it happens with these poems whose authors have been forgotten. But the difference there, when we're looking at that kind of poetry, is that it doesn't share the kind of private concerns that the court poetry for a select audience of peers has attached to it, or the fiction of the one perfect reader or listener of love poetry or contemplative poetry. It seems to address a much larger audience: all of the people in some way.

So we accept that as a kind of a public poetry—dealing with public issues, public affairs, public knowledge, common knowledge. What happens then is we come to a kind of a dilemma about what that public type of poetry is. Leaving aside the fact that some individual actually put the words together, does that then represent a consensus of what everybody in the public thinks and believes? That's one possibility. That is, public poetry is appreciated because it's telling you and me exactly what we agree to and understand and know. Fine, we agree on that. It's something that binds us together. Or is it a public poetry that expresses an opinion of a group of us that the rest of us then need to act upon in some way? There seems to be lots of evidence for that kind of operation as well—that one group will create some songs to express its perception of life and they will sing it to the rest of us and we will be persuaded to, perhaps, see things that way.

Finally, you get to a level of public poetry where you give it back to an individual author, but now you're talking about that individual having some right to present the song from her point of view that is intended for all of us to pay attention to, to attend, to audit. It is going to tell us something that, hopefully, changes our view of the world. Most generally that becomes protest poetry of some kind and we do have certain traditions of that in the English language. Again, these are traditions coming from different places, and we have to be clear about that.

I would like to particularly talk about one such tradition in American English, and that is the African-American oral tradition, later turned into a literary tradition. There are a couple of keys to understanding this. One thing to understand about African-American poetic traditions is that the traditions of the European court never took hold there. There is courtly poetry in Africa, in African languages, but it didn't travel across the middle passage with the slaves, it stayed there. Maybe because the courts didn't travel either. No need for courtly poetry if you have no court, right? So that tradition doesn't apply to African-American poetry or literature, the courtly tradition.

The other tradition, of the contemplative poem or the poem addressed to the beloved, holy or mundane, exists to some extent. Most of the African-American poetry that we have today is sort of a reaction to the Euro-American poetic traditions that I just talked about. We do after all have the same language in common, so we share some of the same approaches to that language. But the largest part of the tradition is a public type of utterance that directly addresses an entire community and is directly concerned not with protest or offering alternative opinions. It is directly concerned with creating and maintaining normative values in that community. What has happened is that in the United States, because the African-American people have been in a peculiar social and political situation vis-à-vis our non-African neighbors, is that the normative structures of the black community have, by definition, been in contradiction and protest to the normative values of much of the rest of the community at various times and to varying degrees. So that what is a normative function within a black community can, from the outside, appear to be social comment or protest, and has to be, if the normative values means the community's survival, right? Then poems by that community about lynching are going to be a protest to the community that sponsors lynching or supports it—it's necessary.

In looking at this kind of tradition the first thing you come across is this anonymous folklore. I've been doing some studying of that in recent years and it is fascinating. The first body of it, of course, are fables that feature animals who talk, wear clothes, and misbehave like people. These stories are traceable directly to African peoples and African languages and I just got a copy yesterday of a magazine called "The Underground Forest" which has an interesting article tracing the Anansi Stories, which are about the "clever spider," that come from West Africa. These stories are found all over the Caribbean and in some parts of North America and South America. In some places the animal changes—it's still a spider in the West Indies. In some cases it changes to another animal, in North America—but the stories can be traced back to West African originals.

Brer Rabbit stories are the most widely known in this country because they were recorded by Joel Chandler Harris back in the 1890s. All of those stories have morals to them and they're meant to teach the listener something about life and the proper way of doing things and, of course, the improper way of doing things, by seeing what happens to the critters that do things the wrong way. You know, the message is always "do the right thing." It still is—that's the message of African-American literary art: "do the right thing!" Spike Lee is in the tradition and very carefully so, he knows exactly what he's doing and why. He's just using a different set of images to tell the same story, again.

Those tales are very entertaining and marvelous and everybody, I think, knows the most famous one, of Brer Rabbit and the tar baby, where one of his animal enemies, Brer Fox, makes a little creature out of tar, puts it in the road, Brer Rabbit comes along and says "good mornin," little tar baby don't say nothin, the rabbit's taken aback, he says well "I think ya did hear me, I said, mornin." Tar baby don't say nothin, little Brer Rabbit says, well I think I'll teach this tar baby some manners. "Didn't you hear me when I say good mornin?" Tar baby don't say nothin, "I think I'll go upside yo head," (smack), course his hand, it stuck there, Brer Fox laughed low, Brer Rabbit said "well, still wont say nothin, huh?, 'fore God I'll teach you some manners!" (smack), his hand stuck there. Brer Fox, he laugh low. By this time Brer Rabbit got so mad he reach back and kick him, (pop), his foot just stuck there. Brer Fox he laugh low. Now what you gonna do when you got one hand there and a foot . . . he does exactly . . . well the hell with this! Foot . . . stuck there, right, and Brer Fox, he laugh low.

That's what comes about trying to teach manners to people that don't respect you. And it's a game within a game because Brer Fox fixed this whole tar baby stunt up to trap Brer Rabbit. And of course you can read that allegorically on any level you want to because it's told to you by people, it's a story told among people who are officially not considered people and who certainly are not given the time of day in the place they live.

But taken outside the slavery situation and put in the context of any small community, of any children listening, it tells the story, "yeah, you give people the time of day, you be polite, and certainly you don't act the fool when you see a situation you can't fix." It's got a lot of different messages to it that are all, of necessity, normative information; this is how you act, this is how you look at the world, this is how the world operates. Listen and learn and "do the right thing."

After slavery and all these animal stories there is another great cycle of black folklore stories which are called the "John Cycle," sometimes referred to as "John and Ol' Masa." The black Texas folklorist J. Mason Brewer, who I spent the last couple of years studying, collected these tales back in the 1930s in rural Texas and he presents them in a different way. Zora Neale Hurston collected these tales also and includes them in *Mules and Men*. These stories don't have animals as characters—they have people, humans. And they have John, who is a kind of a trickster. In some collections they have Ol' Masa, and the contest is always between John and Ol' Masa. Brewer makes the point that not all the stories concern Ol' Masa, but they usually do concern John and his boss man. Brewer makes the very convincing point that these are not slavery tales at all but are tales that come about in Reconstruction days, after slavery, and these human characters replace the animal characters. From what I've read, I tend to agree with Brewer. Even when it's John and Ol' Masa, they are stories of "once upon a time, in slavery days, John and Ol' Masa. . . ." And they are, again, pointedly didactic, with lessons to be learned about how one relates to the rest of the world. John sometimes wins and he sometimes loses.

There's a great story collected by J. Mason Brewer: John and the two white men in court. It seems that it's a particularly hard season, nobody's made a good crop and it's been bad, been a lot of robbery and thievery around the county, and it just so happens John shows up in court, arrested, and two white men are in court the same day. John, never having ever been in trouble before, decides he's gonna watch to see what happens so he'll know what to do when he gets up before the judge. The first white man is called up before the judge and the bailiff reads off the charges—says this man here has been accused of stealin' a horse. Judge says, well how do you plead? Man says, well your honor I must plead not guilty, you see I've had this horse ever since it was a foal. Judge says, well sounds good to me, case dismissed. While John's lookin' on, next white man comes up before the judge and the bailiff reads off the charges, this man here has been accused of stealin' a cow. Judge says, well how do you plead? Man comes up and says, well your honor sir, I must plead not guilty, you see, I've had this here cow ever since it was a calf. Judge says, sounds good to me, case dismissed. So John gets up, it's his turn, bailiff reads off, says, well, judge, this Negro here has been accused of stealin' Ms. Brown's wagon. Judge says, how do you plead boy? John says, well your honor, sir, I must plead not guilty, you see I've had this wagon ever since it was a wheelbarrow. It's a very interesting story. If things went logically, why not? Of course, we all know better than that, right? In any case, those John stories again have that same didactic theme to them, they support ideas that are important to the community, they tell the community how to look at life in the situations that they're in, that particular one being a ludicrous example. It tells you, yeah, if you expect logic to work in your dealings with the judge, like these two white men, forget it, it's not gonna happen! The other message is how ridiculous can John be in attempting to get away with something quite so foolish.

So, there's always more than one level of message in these folktales, which is one of the things I find fascinating about them.

There's another set of tales from about the same time that deal with how the black community relates to the standards of the white community. There's a story about the two old women who are going to Dallas from down in Brazos County to a funeral for their sister. One is promptly at the station to catch the train, the other is busy as usual, dilly-dallying. And the one sister has to wait for her sister to come there, and she gets on the train, she's got the tickets and everything and she says to the conductor, mister can you please hold the train, my sister Viola is comin'; we've got to go to Dallas for my sister Emma's funeral. And the conductor says, this train don't be held back for nobody, train always on time. Ol' sister says well, we'll see about that, and she gets down on her knees on the edge of the station by the little stairs that go to the train, she puts her hands together and says, dear Lord our father in heaven, you know me, my sister Emma died in Dallas and we're waitin' for Viola to get here so we can go to the funeral. This is the only train to get there, man says he won't hold the train for nobody, please do somethin' to help us. Well, they start tryin' to start the train up, the conductor blows the whistle, all aboard, nothin' happens, they can't get the train started, they try again, people come out and look at the hot box and this that and the other thing, can't get the thing started. Finally around the corner, here comes Viola, huffin' and puffin', late as usual, runnin' up here with her bag, gets on the train, sits down next to her sister, conductor comes by, train suddenly starts up, conductor comes by pickin' up tickets. He says, huh, yo sister got on the train, don't matter all those tricks you gonna pull, cause by the time we get to Longview, we so late already, that train you gotta connect to Dallas already be gone and you'll have to spend all night in Longview. Sister says, I ain't worried about that. God who stopped this train down here in Temple gonna hold that one in Longview till we get there.

Again, it's the community making fun of itself in many different ways: tardiness, ignorance, old-fashioned fundamentalism that doesn't match with the twentieth century at all. Also showing some things about the twentieth century and the ways that it operates according to the railroad clock, which quite obviously is amiss because it doesn't take into account the real needs of anybody. Like the man says "This train don't be held back for nobody." That's the attitude that's being characterized. So, if you look at that kind of literature as a literature that is public, what you find in Black poetry of the literary tradition is that it is based on exactly that heritage. It is intended to speak to people in exactly those terms. Very often it borrows the techniques of English language poetry, but uses them to these ends.

To look at the history of how that comes about, there is a fascinating book, *The Line in Modern Poetry,* by Robert Frank and Henry Sayre. It has different poets and critics discussing the poetic line, how it's written, and how it comes about. Stephen Henderson from Howard University, who is a marvelous critic on Black-American poetry, particularly the sixties and seventies, the poetry of the Black Arts Movement, has an important essay here. He goes back to show that the Harlem Renaissance writers of the twenties, writers like Langston Hughes, Frank Marshall Davis, Sterling Brown—encouraged by the example of the little magazines like *Poetry* (Chicago), people in the teens like Sandburg and others—explored the verbal dynamics of African-American culture itself, not some fancy version of it. These poets probed deeper into the language than Paul Laurence Dunbar or James Weldon Johnson did as they realized that black spoken English was not the same thing as Negro dialect and indeed was capable of a full range of expressive possibilities, some of which were unattainable in standard English.

That's one level of what they did. Another level is the fact that they carried over the concept of the oral stories having a communal audience and providing a normative function. This was carried over to poetry in the literary mode, and again, the people working at *Poetry* magazine, the Imagists, etc., were working in similar directions, trying to understand the American vernacular. And that mode certainly suited the Harlem Renaissance writers, who were looking at this same body of folklore that I'm talking about, of the African-American community, and translating it into literary terms, that is, poetry on paper. One aspect of what happened with the Harlem Renaissance and that approach is that it further goes on to take the image of the blues singer, the gospel choir, the backwoods country preacher, the illiterate preacher who works entirely with the oral figures, and it engages these as part of the poetry. So that the poet stands in as those voices and presents those words in much the same way. The Harlem Renaissance poets were influential enough so that the Negritude poets, poets who write in French from the West Indies and Africa, people like Aimé Cesaire, Leopold Senghor, and Leon Damas began writing poetry in the 1930s when they came across *The New Negro* and other books from the Harlem Renaissance. Senghor has said, "We were sitting in Paris at the Sorbonne, these African and West Indian students, and we read Langston Hughes and Countee Cullen, and we realized that a black man can write poetry about black people, in the tradition." And so they did the same in French. That becomes part of the Third World literature that we can look at today.

One of the other things that happens with this branch of poetry, this poetry that is tied very carefully to that oral tradition, comes up again I think in the 1950s, with the so-called Beat poets who respond—Allen is here, he could tell us—not directly to Langston Hughes and Sterling Brown and what those Harlem Renaissance poets were trying to do with that body of music and folklore, but who in fact respond directly to the musical and folkloric elements they're finding in jazz, which is an art form created by sophisticated musicians using that African-American folk heritage, just as Hughes and others are sophisticated poets using some of that oral tradition heritage. The Beats are poets who touch that same oral tradition, that same concept of a public poetry, because they are in contact with some of the same forces that the Harlem Renaissance poets were dealing with. The Black Arts Movement of the 1960s and 70s, people like Larry Neal and Askia Muhammad Touré, Ishmael Reed, David Henderson, Amiri Baraka, all of those people, again, are deeply knowledgeable about the Harlem Renaissance, about the Imagists, about the Beats, and about the current extensions of that same body of original African-American communal lore in music, and the preacher and the tales and jokes.

The Black Arts poets present themselves as public poets, they talk to the public, they talk on the street corner and the people on the street corner do listen, because that is the tradition that these poets are working in. If the people don't listen, those poets then have a right to complain, or go back to the woodshed, if in fact they didn't do the thing right. But that is the tradition of public poetry. It is public and does in fact express the community's ideas. It can be protest poetry, but its real foundation is that it expresses the community's ideas. So the poet is in a somewhat different relationship to the community than Sir Philip Sydney at court or Sir Philip writing a little song to Stella. Here the poet is more in the condition of the preacher, the story teller, the session leader, and each one of us gets to be leader in turn as we go around the story-telling circle.

I think that if we today want to aspire to that kind of an impact, of a public poetry, we cannot do it unless we are very clear about which traditions we are working out of. We cannot do it working out of the English courtly tradition, and we can't do it writing out of the "addressed to one's beloved," be that beloved here on Earth or beyond in another dimension. It has to be done working from a tradition of public voice, which means you can challenge some of these prevailing opinions as I've tried to demonstrate in a couple of stories from the folktales. There's not just one narrow message in these things. You can, in fact, comment on and challenge some of the prevailing opinions, but it has to work from within that focus.

One thing I've been looking at with the blues is trying to figure out how the blues fits into that specific type of public poetic tradition, particularly since the subject matter of the blues seems, to many people, bizarre. Langston Hughes has a poem, that attempts to deal with both of these problems. It's called "Same in Blues." It's written in alternating stanzas—the first stanza's a blues stanza, or blues-feeling stanza, the second stanza is in a different language.

SAME IN BLUES

I said to my baby,
Baby take it slow.
I can't, she said, I can't
I got to go!

> There's a certain
> amount of traveling
> in a dream deferred.

Lulu said to Leonard,
I want a diamond ring.
Leonard said to Lulu,
You won't get a goddamn thing!

> A certain
> amount of nothing
> in a dream deferred.

Daddy, daddy, daddy,
All I want is you.

You can have me, baby—
but my lovin' days is through.

> *A certain*
> *amount of impotence*
> *in a dream deferred.*

Three parties
On my party line—
But that third party,
Lord, ain't mine!

> *There's liable*
> *to be confusion*
> *in a dream deferred.*

From river to river,
Uptown and down,
There's liable to be confusion
when a dream gets kicked around.

Of course the play in the poem is on the language of the people, which is the blues lyrics, and our other inherited tradition of the English language—the "King's English"—which Hughes uses to translate and explain what happened between Lulu and her daddy. And of course Hughes manages to make the explanations ludicrous:

> A certain
> amount of impotence

Something's lost in the translation; so Hughes plays with the tensions of those who live in want, using both vocabularies of our heritage. This poem can be found in *Black Voices*, edited by Abraham Chapman, which is a marvelous anthology of Black writing going back to the nineteenth century, up to the 1950s. There is a companion volume called *New Black Voices* which goes from the fifties into the sixties and seventies. But people like Richard Wright, James Baldwin, Malcolm X, LeRoi Jones, Langston Hughes, Ralph Ellison,

W. E. B. Du Bois, Gwendolyn Brooks, they're all in here. The poem "Same in Blues" is from about 1950, *Montage of a Dream Deferred,* the same collection that gives us the title "A Raisin in the Sun" from Langston's poem "Harlem":

> What happens to a dream deferred?
>
> Does it dry up
> like a raisin in the sun?
> or fester like a sore—
> And then run?

Again, Hughes plays with both of our poetic traditions. To me, how all of this works for us as practicing poets is to remind us to be very careful about the traditions we find ourselves working in; understanding those traditions, and not demanding something of a tradition that's not in it.

Claude McKay managed to do some interesting things. He, like Countee Cullen, was very enamored of the English language literary tradition. They both loved Keats, Byron and Shelley, Sydney, and they wrote in that form. Except for McKay's earliest work, they didn't try to write in Black dialect. They wrote in standard English language poetic forms. But they addressed themselves to the content, the concerns of African-American poetry, which is this public type of poetry. They simply borrowed the English language forms and cast their words in that. Let me just take a little bit more of your time and read you Claude McKay's poem in protest of lynching:

IF WE MUST DIE

> If we must die, let it not be like hogs
> Hunted and penned in an inglorious spot,
> While round us bark the mad and hungry dogs,
> Making their mock at our accursed lot.
> If we must die, O let us nobly die,
> So that our precious blood may not be shed
> In vain; then even the monsters we defy

Shall be constrained to honor us though dead!
O kinsmen! we must meet the common foe!
Though far outnumbered let us show us brave,
And for their thousand blows deal one deathblow!
What though before us lies the open grave?
Like men we'll face the murderous, cowardly pack,
Pressed to the wall, dying, but fighting back!

Marvelous poem, certainly. Because of the sonnet form it would have been at home at the European court, as the knights among themselves decided that they would in fact stand shoulder to shoulder against the foe of the week. What happened to this poem is so very interesting. It is written from McKay's sense of a community purpose, but using the courtly English form. The poem was written in 1919 to protest the lynching of Black Americans in the southern states in this country. 1919 was known as the Red Summer. It was so bad that American GI's, black men coming back from France, in uniform, were lynched on the streets in the South, because *in uniform* they refused to get off the sidewalk, or they refused to take off their hats and say "Good morning" to white people. So the white people "taught 'em some manners." Remember that first story? Except—this time—it was tar and feathers, and fire.

So McKay wrote this poem in protest, and to awaken the black community, and to point a direction for the black community. The poem appears again in the 1940s, during the Battle of Britain. The Luftwaffe was shooting their missiles into London . . . my brother always said . . . Wernher von Braun's autobiography, *I Aim For the Stars* was what it was called . . . Von Braun was a great rocket scientist. My brother always said the book should have had a subtitle: I aim for the stars, but I keep hitting London. Anyhow, Winston Churchill found the poem. Churchill being a student of the English-speaking peoples, you can imagine his thoughts: "Ah yes, Claude McKay is from Jamaica, a British subject. Afro-American? None-the-less, perfect poem in OUR tradition, the English sonnet." Winston Churchill got on the BBC and he read the poem, to tell the people of England that Wernher von Braun and the Luftwaffe would not defeat us.

Everyone accepted that. It was in the tradition and it spoke to the community. It is public poetry.

The poem surfaced again in the 1960s. There was a riot at Attica State Prison in New York. The prisoners barricaded themselves into the complex, they had hostages and they had lists of demands; and the governor, Nelson Rockefeller, was outside the walls negotiating back and forth. Finally, the governor gave the word and the crack troops stormed the cell blocks, and, well, go back and look up Attica. It was horrible. In any event, among the debris was found a scrap of paper, and on that paper was written, "If we must die, let it not be like hogs / Hunted and penned and in an inglorious spot." And *Time* magazine reprinted the poem and said, "To show the raising of consciousness among the blacks, and having to do with this militant blackness and revolution as in the mouths of people like LeRoi Jones and all the others, here is this little bit of found doggerel that was written by one of the desperate prisoners in his cell." The Time-Life research department was on vacation that week. As soon as it came out, nineteen professors wrote back saying, "Listen people, this is Claude McKay . . . 'If we Must Die'."

But again, why is it public poetry? Because it serves a public purpose, it has a function. In the case of this particular poem, it had a function in 1919 for its community. If you indeed think that the English-speaking world is a community, as Winston Churchill at least did insofar as selling books, it served a purpose in the 1940s to *that* community. If, in fact, you were a prisoner, black or white, in Attica in the rebellion, then that was a community that this poem also served a public purpose to, same poem speaking to the community. I guess what I'm trying to say is that unless we are creating poetry out of that tradition, with that purpose, then it is not our place to complain—if we are not writing a poetry intended to fulfill the destiny of that particular tradition.

24 July 1989

THE POETICS OF INSTRUCTION: ROBERT DUNCAN TEACHING

> Yes, there is a teaching that I know.
>
> Slow, slow, even as time alone erodes the matter,
> I turn and turn upon my life.
> Tho I resist the learning,   the drive to study it out
>   returns.
>   I hold to this and this,
> and *this* holds me.
>   And there is freedom in so taking hold
>
>   each time
>
> —Robert Duncan, "A Seventeenth Century Suite"

I first heard of a projected "Poetics Program" in Diane di Prima's kitchen in, I think, 1979. When Robert Duncan returned from Europe, I attended his lectures on Browning's *Sordello* at the San Francisco Zen Center in March, April, and May of 1980. At that time, rumors were circulating about Duncan teaching in a poetics program with other poets, including Diane di Prima, David Meltzer, Michael Palmer, Duncan McNaughton, and Louis Patler. I believe the first students were John Thorpe and Bobbie Louise Hawkins, alerted by McNaughton and Patler, then Aaron Shurin and myself, alerted by Diane and Duncan. Duncan agreed to teach for five years, and classes began on September 22, 1980 at New College of California.

I studied in the Poetics Program from 1980 to 1983, and I realize now that everything I've written in the ten years since then has come out of that instruction in poetics: the study of how things are made. Though we concentrated in the Poetics Program on the *poem*, our investigations (certainly Duncan's investigations) were not limited to that. As Duncan said, "the seriousness of the study of

DAVID LEVI STRAUSS

Poetics we intend is the seriousness of the study of creative events."
I've had no trouble extending these principles into the study of photography, film, television, sculpture, painting, performance, propa-
ganda, ethnography, tattooing and body modification, pranks,
drugs, war, and virtual reality.

Duncan took these years of teaching very seriously, as a particular kind of work. He came to it as a lore-father, someone who had
been poetically obsessed for forty-five years ("Everything I've done
since age 16 has been *the poem*. I don't think but that it borders on
the poem. That's embarrassing when you're in the company of
people who couldn't give a *fuck* about the poem."), and now
wanted to pass on as much of it as he could, orally, mouth-to-ear.
It's clear that he had a premonition of his coming debilitation and
death (in 1988, one month before his sixty-ninth birthday), and that
the teaching came at precisely the right time. When he began, he
was the youngest sixty-one-year-old any of us had ever known.

In his introduction to the program (speaking in an open meeting
of all involved), Duncan said that poetics is to poetry as medicine is
to the body or as botany is to flowers, and that real information was
equally as scanty in those other disciplines, as needful of inquiry. He
proposed the possibility of a *discipline* of poetics.

He also expressed his own doubts and fears going into this teaching. He described waking up the night before in a cold sweat from
a dream that his teaching would fall on deaf ears and fail completely. He said it was only the recent "observable collapse of craft"
that had brought him back to teach, that it was like when dangerous machines break down (a car with a leaky exhaust, or a poorly
constructed bookshelf that falls on someone's head), and all of the
people who make these things feel responsible. He proposed to give
us better tools to work with (and to pass on a great deal of lore).

The intent of Duncan's last teachings was to show the way to the
Sources, and how to derive from them what could feed us. One
needn't accept Duncan's particular sources to benefit from the
teaching, only observe the way to the sources. The teaching was
about relation, not about absolutes. In a 1985 *Sagetrieb* interview,
Duncan said, "I still respond to poetry as if it too were, as the

hermetic world is, a series of epiphanies that are then discovered, and so a way is discovered—that is, a Blake *is* going to find a Swedenborg, *is* going to find a Paracelsus, and so on. Which is the background of our Poetics Program."

Using the sources involved a kind of radical derivation. All of the earlier senses of the word *derivation* have to do with the motion of water over land, "the action or process of leading or carrying a current of water, or the like, *from* a source, *to* another part," referring originally to the branches of a river, by which such a draw-off is effected. You *derive* by branching out. Duncan could still see the "river" in the French, *dériver*, which also has the sense of causing a river to overflow its banks. So, it has to do with Source, origin, branching, flow, and overflow. In my copy of *Groundwork I*, Duncan wrote, "For Levi, adhering to his source!"

Luckily, most of Duncan's lectures at New College were taped, and students kept copious notes, so it is possible to research these teachings even if you weren't in San Francisco in the eighties. I've been trying to find a way to present this material in a way that makes sense. Direct transcription wouldn't work at all. I suspect the way to do it is to build something out of students' notes. Duncan hated the idea of publishing speech—transcribed interviews or whatever—but he did approve of reconstituting a teacher's lectures for use, as was done by students of Saussure, Wittgenstein, Olson, and many others.

Doing this with Duncan's teaching presents special problems, of course, because of the way he spoke. His lectures had little in common with university lectures or the "talks" being given by other poets. They were *psychedelic,* in the sense of "mind-manifesting." I would also describe the method as *catastrophic.* In the beginning, the teaching was overwhelming in its *influence,* and students did get sick with it. Most of these reactive illnesses were either respiratory or circulatory—students tended to have trouble with breath and teachers with blood. Aaron went through a period where he'd wake up in the middle of the night gasping for air, unable to breathe. I suddenly lost all vitality, as if a reservoir had been drained, and was left physically and mentally exhausted for months. Others had allergic reactions. Emotional breakdowns and blow-ups among students were common during this period. There was at least one full-blown psychotic break and a number of lesser episodes. We were pushed to the limits of our capabilities. Duncan's poetics had an open architecture. He worked by opening into the field, being energized by letting it all come into him, through him, and this was a singularly dangerous method to emulate.

We variously discovered ways to protect ourselves from Duncan's torrential polymathic fluency. Many of us found that the best defense was writing. As soon as the lecture began, we began to write furiously—notes, observations, direct dictation, poems, incoherent ramblings and scribblings, vehement disclaimers and aggressive arguments against the teaching. In this way, the torrent was diverted, and the force grounded: in the ear, through the body, into the hand, and out onto the page.

Duncan's method was πολύμιτοσ, πολύμυθοσ, πολύσημοσ (many-threaded, many-worded, many-signifying or many-meaninged). In going back to my notebooks, I can pick up one thread and follow it through three years of lectures, but within individual lectures that thread would be surrounded by hundreds of others. Part of the teaching was this "art of weaving," ἡ πολύμιτκή. Its effect was to keep the listener always off-balance, never able to actually sit down on a particular fact or idea, but forced to make connections over time. "Context" was woven (textus) together (con) into a complex fabric that was constitutive.*

The first class Duncan taught was called "Basic Elements." In a catalog essay Duncan wrote, "It's at the level of the basic elements: in oral and written poetry alike the sounds and silences of language, telling patternings and depatternings of consonants and vowels, the articulation of syllables in measures and utterances toward and from sentences, lines, stanzas—where rime, rhythm, and

o o o

* I'm thinking here of Christa Wolf's description in the Frankfurt Lectures on Poetics of the intricately woven fabric of her *Cassandra*: "There are wefts which stand out like foreign bodies, repetitions, material that has not been worked out to its conclusion" (Christa Wolf, *Cassandra: A Novel and Four Essays*, New York: Farrar, Straus & Giroux, 1984, p. 142).

ratio originate—that creativity in language works. And it is here that poetics must begin." Rather than an introduction or a survey, this was to be an *inquiry*, so Duncan began by asking the question: what *are* the basic elements of poetry and of language? and we began to make a map:

mode & mood	series & sets
juncture & boundary	open & closed forms
rime & reason	letter/word/sound/number
vowel & consonant	sound-letter-syllable-word-
sound & silence	sentence
phonation & audition	line-syntax-stanza-page-
phoneme & morpheme	text
seme & hyposeme	segmentations &
metaphor & metonymy	coordinations
speech & writing	writing/conditions
pronouns & persons	topos/trope/type

As we went along, "Basic Elements" became an increasingly focused inquiry into the structure of language. Duncan saw the impact of recent continental theory—structuralist, post-structuralist, and beyond—as something we must deal with in order to get *past* it. The scientific approach to language certainly intrigued him, and he seemed to be a tireless reader of linguistics (much of it in the original French), but he did all this in order to get *through* it, *to* something beyond linguistic materialism. "This structuralist approach to poetics is, I think, capable of going all the way through—it just hasn't been *pushed* yet." "Deconstruction," he once said, "is not done with any idea of *building* on the lot. If you did, that would be *exploitation*. That's *me*."

But before deconstruction, we painstakingly dissected Saussure, Hjelmslev, Eco, Barthes, Jespersen, Piaget, Lévi-Strauss, Jakobson, Jameson, Kristeva, etc., etc. When we balked and complained, Duncan would say "A historian is not a judge, she's a detective." But at another time he allowed that "I'm glad I didn't have to deal with all this when I was in my twenties, but I did have to deal with Marxist terms then in one way or another," to get through that reduction.

At the beginning of the "Basic Elements" class, Duncan revealed another possible motivation for going so far into this material when he claimed that Olson was totally antagonistic to linguistic study, wouldn't read it at all. Duncan's early influence in this direction came from Jaime de Angulo (in America, "descriptive linguistics" (structuralism) arose out of a concern for accurate treatment of native Indian languages in the work of Boas, Sapir, Whorf, de Angulo, later Bloomfield), and Jack Spicer. At one point Duncan cited Spicer's view that there were diseases of language that could come in and concentrate in poetry, and destroy poetry for entire periods.

One tool he embraced with a passion was the International Phonetic Alphabet (IPA). He insisted that we all learn the IPA and then translate poem after poem into it. Trager and Smith became our constant companions. Duncan was convinced the IPA was a real breakthrough in comparative poetics and translation, allowing one to move around from one language to another, recognizing rime. At one point he said "The IPA makes Babel obsolete." We applied the IPA broadly, for analysis, and narrowly, for recording how someone is speaking. This also Duncan got from de Angulo, who had invented a system of transcription of the IPA on a regular typewriter and written entire books in IPA.

Duncan worked closely with the other core faculty to develop an integrated curriculum. "Basic Elements" was the foundation of the program, and was team-taught after the first three years. In 1984, Michael Palmer taught "Sound: Phoneme & Silence," Diane di Prima taught "Letter," Duncan McNaughton taught "Number," Duncan taught "Word," David Meltzer taught "Rhythm," and Louis Patler taught "Line." In the Spring semester of 1985, they divided things up in even larger chunks:

Patler | "Speaking"
Duncan | "Writing"
Palmer | "Reading"
McNaughton | "Source(s)"
di Prima | "Memory"
Meltzer | "Book"

In the Fall, the assignments were:

Meltzer | "Coding"
di Prima | "Source"
Palmer | "Imagination"
Duncan | "Hand Writing"
Patler | "Sound"
McNaughton | "Rhythm"

and in the Spring of 1986, it was:

Palmer | "Symbol"
Duncan | "Form(s)"
McNaughton | "Body"
Patler | "Metaphor"
Meltzer | "Decoding"
di Prima | "Process"

One part of "Basic Elements" became a course Duncan taught called "Linguistic Approaches to Poetics: an introduction to Saussurean problems: metaphor, metonymy, person, semiotic analysis," and two other courses—"The Articulation of the Poem: Segmentations and Coordinations," and "Temporal and Spatial Propositions of the Poem"—were team-taught by Duncan and Palmer.

Duncan's other classes included "What Is at Issue in Poetics: Baudelaire, Dickinson, and Whitman," "Political Vision in Poetry: A Study in the Poetics of Politics (Dante, Milton, Blake, and Whitman)," "The Poet, the Ruler, and the Saint: Studies in Medieval and Renaissance Poetics," and "The Later Poetry of H.D." In the Summer of 1982, Duncan, di Prima, and Meltzer put together a symposium on *Poetry & Occult Tradition,* at which Duncan lectured on Swedenborg and "Ideas of Electricity, Forces, and Energies."

Duncan and the other poets on the faculty worked together to design a more or less integrated curriculum that did not regard explorations of the mysteries in western mystical and philosophical traditions and analyses of the most recent poetic innovations and linguistic theory as separate itineraries. Diane di Prima taught courses like "Hidden Religion in the Poetry of Europe," "Poetry & Magic," "Vision and the Visionary Poem: Blake, Coleridge, Keats, Nerval, Paracelsus, Rumi, Shelley, Yeats," "The Grail," "Paracelsus, Dee, and Bruno," and "Texts of Alchemy"; David Meltzer taught the Kabbalah and "Letter, Word, Sound, Number"; Michael Palmer and Robert Grenier taught Prosody; Anselm Hollo taught Translation; Duncan McNaughton taught Shakespeare and Plutarch, "Muslim Sources: The Sufis," "Preclassical & Classical Sources: Eurydice & Hermes," among many other things; and Louis Patler taught reading courses on Duncan, Olson, Creeley, John Weiners, and others. Seminars by visiting poets included Robert Creeley, Susan Howe, and Bev Dahlen on Emily Dickinson; Nate Mackey, Ken Irby, and Bernadette Mayer on Walt Whitman; Jack Clarke (the lectures eventually resulting in *From Feathers to Iron*); Anne Waldman on Gertrude Stein, Bill Berkson on Vernacular Poetics, Judy Grahn, Joanne Kyger, Leslie Scalapino, and many others.

Duncan talked a lot about the recent impoverishment of poetry: "Young poets don't hear themselves in the presence of anything," he'd say. But he also cautioned us against himself, saying "I preach dispersion," "perhaps I need to lose some energy." And he often repeated the prophetic "I don't know how I'm going to notice senility when it comes," which haunted me as I sat at his bedside in Seton Hospital five years later, taking dictation out of his magnificent delirium.

The "Basic Elements" class was originally titled "Structure of Rime I," and another course, "Persons in the Poem," was "Structure of Rime II." At the same time, Duncan taught a complementary course called "Ideas of Meaning in Poetry," described as "a series of lectures on the idea of revelation of meaning in poetry," from Homer, Hesiod, and Parmenides to Pound and Williams. This was almost broad enough to allow Duncan free rein. He came out of the gate flying and did not touch the ground until his illness forced him to.

In the first session of "Ideas of Meaning in Poetry," on September 24, 1980, Duncan covered the following topics. This was a two-hour class. I'm just going to list the topics, on many of which Duncan expounded at length:

The Pearl, back of Langland

Pound's "The Serious Artist"

Coleridge's *Biographia Literaria* (fantasy & imagination)

Plato, Bk 10 of the *Republic, Phaedrus*

Hesiod, Homer, Parmenides—trance poems, poetic seizure

Freud, Chap. 6 in *Interpretation of Dreams,* poem is a rebus
    and the perfect rebus-reader is Joyce

Longinus, *On the Sublime*

Aristotle, *On Poetry & Style*

Jung's specious division between imaginal and imaginary

Gate of Horn

Shakespeare, mystery plays

Wieners, Whalen, di Prima

Pound & Shelley

Williams & Keats

Wordsworth, *The Prelude,* nature of passion in poetry

Marlowe

Frances Yates (Dr. Faustus was an attack on John Dee)

Hermetic/Kabbalah

Edward II, Tamburlaine "Every young queer should see this"

Dante, *De Vulgaria Eloquentia, Convivio, Tenth Epistle*

Shekinah

Corbin, Dante's base in Islam

Alchemy & Poetry

Blindness of Homer

Memory

Nietzsche (the child must work to become the Child)

Chaucer

Herbert

Milton

Blake

Emerson & Carlyle

Whitman

Dickinson

Chomsky (against the creative minds of Sapir & Whorf)

John Stuart Mill and liberalism

Abraham, Jacob & Issac

Zohar

Solomon erecting altars to Ishtar

Midrash

Frank O'Hara

How the Virus changes all that stuff about "species purity"

Miscegenation

Germans, Scythians, Eurasians

Disease

Deceit (as integral to mind, "How do we take deceit into the
New City of Truth?")

Have you ever been so in love that you didn't know if the Other
was angel or human?

Pain

Sappho

Craft

Lore

That was the first lecture. He started precisely on time and quit on time and left. We all just sat there, stunned, drifting into despair. I think someone eventually came in and told us to leave.

So the beginning of the teaching, the first three years, was like this, like an avalanche. It overflowed into the Homer Group, where a small group of us met every week for seven years, reading the *Iliad* in Greek, translating each word, singing the last lines just before Duncan's death. Duncan's teaching continued in this group, but it was very different, more informal. He said we were married to Homer's poem. Then, as Duncan's illness progressed, the teaching changed again, as he opened his heart and his home to us, letting us in. For some of us, this was the most difficult teaching of all at first, to accept the man Duncan's mortality. But the dying was an important part of the teaching, and those of us who attended the dying understood, finally, that this was a teaching without an end.

In the old stories, the protagonist learns
what Time has to do with him.   And in his true
identity burns within the learning.
He serves the years.

VI

DOCUMENTS

VI

PART SIX

DOCUMENTS

OUNTERPOETICS STATEMENT

PREAMBLE & STATEMENT FOR A COUNCIL ON COUNTERPOETICS

On the weekend of September 16, 1989, the undersigned group of poets, artists, environmentalists, and scholars met together under the auspices of the Telluride Institute in Telluride, Colorado.

Our purpose was to discuss the relationship of ethnopoetics— the poetry-and-culture nexus over diverse space-and-time—to the contemporary crises (ecological, political, ethnic, and spiritual) that continue to confront us as a single but divided species on a single but divided planet.

In the light of that meeting it became clear that what we were seeking in common was an activist poetics that would expand from an ethnopoetic base to incorporate concerns with ecology, language, polis, tradition, and those alternative human models—cognitive, social, and spiritual—that have always been the foundations of what we take to be a true and germinal ethnopoetics.

A poetry so centered in its mission, we felt, was suffering today from a sense of fragmentation and alienation—from the segregation of individuals and groups that, taken all together, might exercise a force larger than any of its particular manifestations. And we recognized further that what was true for poets was also true for other artists and for those whose humane practices lay outside the arts as such.

It is our firm belief that what we are setting out here is not a minority poetics but one that represents the true mainstream of the world's poetries (both deeply traditional and militantly avant-garde), wrongly seen as marginalized from the still dominant western perspective.

With that much as preamble, we offer the following statement of our concern for what a truly contemporary poetics might include, along with our proposals for a loose alliance and interchange between poets and other cultural workers in the various worlds, local and specific, that comprise our global system.

o   o   o

STATEMENT. There exist today, as there have throughout this century, poets and groups of poets and cultural activists driven by a sense of planetary urgency toward the exploration and enhancement of a deeply-rooted human and natural potential. While this takes different forms, dependent on the needs and views of individuals and groups and regions, we feel that there is a widespread desire today to accomplish the following:

1. to encourage local forms of expression within a global perspective—both multicultural and intercultural in intention;
2. to remember the sources of poetry in an earth consciousness ("earth as a religious form"—Eliade), thus to support moves toward an enlightened relation to the natural world in which we live and to those fellow species with whom we share the planet;
3. to recognize that advances in technology are not merely a danger to be resisted but an opportunity to advance those principles of interpenetration and communication on which these proposals rest—not least for those of us for whom language is our "proudest tool";
4. to encourage the recovery and expansion of our pre-technological repertoire of powers: of body, of voice, of performance, of deeply-rooted ritual acts, of private and interconnected dreams and dreamworks;
5. to avoid ethnocentrism and a naive provincialism by setting song and speech, spoken and written forms of language, performance and text, on an equal footing, and by recognizing and fostering common goals across the range of human arts and sciences;
6. to oppose with an awakened heart all forms of racism, sexism, and cultural chauvinism, and to encourage an active

interchange with third and fourth world peoples on terms of mutual assistance and respect;

7 to resist all forms of repression and censorship, and to defend thereby the acts of the individual (that most local and most threatened form of human life) against the restrictive pressures of the state, of organized religion, and of the vigilante actions of those who live in fear among us;

8 to revitalize a view of artistic experiment as a form of political and social action, and to move beyond that to break down the barriers between art and other forms of human enterprise;

9 to foster alliances between poets, artists, and other cultural and intellectual workers, by reinforcing and creating networks of cultural activists toward an exchange of ideas, information, and projects in common;

10 to transmit to the century ahead of us that sense of mission that has invigorated and justified the formal experiments of our own time, and to bring the work of poets and artists so committed once more into the public sphere.

o   o   o

Constituting ourselves therefore as a preliminary council for the furtherance of such a counterpoetics, we are committing ourselves immediately to the following steps and are inviting all in basic agreement with us to join in their fulfillment and expansion:

1 we are establishing a newsletter as a platform for making the ideas and activities described above available and visible both to those now engaged with them and, by "interventions" in the public arena, to those who may later come to share in our concerns;

2 we are soliciting brief contributions of an informational and ideological nature and assistance in the compilation of an international mailing list, focusing on individuals and groups committed to the range of goals we have heretofore projected;

3 we are actively planning a series of further conferences and gatherings to focus on specific aspects of the sort we have outlined in our preceding statement;

4 we are hoping to develop from these beginnings an ongoing organization of cultural activists and to connect, for purposes of assistance and exchange, with already existing organizations, including those outside the poetry nexus as such;

5 with recognition that many of us—American poets and artists in particular—are engaged in the profession of teaching, we are inviting a continuing dialogue, to supply models for new approaches to curricular revitalization consonant with the principles and goals set forth herein;

6 we will be looking for ways to encourage and promote the arts of translation, both written and oral, and to recognize that the ways in which we translate each other are keys to how we learn to live together on this planet;

7 we will begin to take steps toward the establishment of an archival repository of documentations (tapes, videos, newsletters, magazines, etc.) that can serve as a resource for those involved in the kinds of poetics we are proposing to support and reinforce.

Our home base for the time being will be the Telluride Institute in Telluride, Colorado, which has generously offered to coordinate our first activities as a poetics institute. We ask those whose concerns parallel ours to join us in this enterprise, with the awareness that what we have set forth here is only an attempt at a beginning, the later form of which will be the joint work of all who come together in these acts of sighting and of transformation.

Pamela Zoline, Director l Telluride Institute, Telluride, Co.
Anne Waldman l Director, The Jack Kerouac School of Disembodied Poetics, The Naropa Institute, Boulder, Co.
Nathaniel Tarn l Santa Fe, New Mexico
Ines Talamantez l Religious Studies, University of California, Santa Barbara, Ca.

Jerome Rothenberg | Visual Arts & Literature, University of
California, San Diego, Ca.
Diane Rothenberg | Anthropology, University of California,
San Diego, Ca.
Janet Rodney | Santa Fe, New Mexico
John Lifton | Director, Telluride Institute, Telluride, Co.
Pierre Joris | State University of New York at Binghamton
Anselm Hollo | The Jack Kerouac School of Disembodied
Poetics, The Naropa Institute, Boulder, Co.
Mary Crow | Colorado State University, Fort Collins, Co.

NOTE

This is a document of aspiration. Many of these initiatives have been put into practice at various locations, including the Jack Kerouac School which regularly holds classes and forums on ethnopoetics and related concerns. The newsletter and archives have not yet come into existence—a task of the future for poets and cultural workers.

—Editors

A DECLARATION OF INTERDEPENDENCE

PREFACE

Events of recent decades have shown that the planet now faces an immense threat to its health and future as a life-sustaining celestial body. Evidence of global warming, destruction of the ozone layer, pollution of soils, air, and water, deforestation of tropical and temperate forests—all derived from human activities—have provided this species with ample warnings to change its ways or risk the possible loss of the planet within the next hundred years. Our planet is an organism existing as a series of interdependencies and interpenetrations; what all people do now and in the coming years will determine the fate of the Earth.

We believe acceptable human behavior now and in the future should harmonize with the law of interdependence (which includes all living creatures), recognizing that what we do will come back to us or to our descendants, as well as to all other beings on the planet.

We believe all beings on this planet have a perfect, inherent, and natural right to clean Earth, Air, and Water; this right is sacred and inviolable.

These principles should be the working premises for any future human activities. We call for an ecological reconstruction involving community action in which every person contributes his or her part in maintaining ecological equilibrium in their location.

THE REAL WORK
MILITARY & INDUSTRY

We citizens, men and women, encourage Congresses of all nations to continue negotiation to end the arms race. We recognize the right of nations to self-defense, but conclude that true arms reductions, reconciliation between hostile nations, treaties and further development of economic connections between nations will result in less of a need for weapons and defense systems. As military resources are progressively freed from the labor of arms, Congresses can retrain persons currently serving in the armed forces. Some may serve as guardians, to maintain a vigilant watch over waste materials that at present cannot be disposed of; some may serve as corps of planters and nurturers, supervising urban and future wilderness areas. Military vendors and suppliers could serve as sources for research and development for cleaner technologies, for discovering commercial uses for recycled products, and for discovering how we might break down and recycle components of hazardous waste products.

This would maintain jobs for some of the people currently serving in armed forces, continue government involvement with companies whose business is connected with the military, and redirect R & D efforts away from harmful and wasteful expenditures toward an economy that benefits all beings.

FORESTS

We call for the cessation of all logging in ancient forests immediately.

We support diverse reforestation on public lands with all-age management and local varieties.

We call for a halt to federally subsidized grazing on public lands, or if this is impossible, for ranchers to pay royalties on profits from grazing on these lands.

Nations must find alternatives to clear-cutting, and to the wasteful practices now destroying the rainforests and temperate forests of the world.

Congressional Bill HR 4492 provides for the protection of the remaining ancient forests on the federal lands of the states of California, Oregon, and Washington, and is legislation worthy of support.

CLEAN AIR

We support the Clean Air Act in its strongest possible form.

This includes:

1 Maintenance of the Clean Car Amendment, which promotes clean alternative fuels and extends warranties on pollution control equipment. The subsidy on alternative fuels should be equitable until we know which approach is best. Fuels should be tailored to individual airsheds.

2 Maintenance of the Toxic Accident Prevention Amendment, which creates stronger standards and an effective Chemical Safety Board to investigate toxic-releasing accidents.

3 Maintenance of the National Parks Protection Amendment.

4 Maintenance of the Stop Ozone Depletion Amendment, which phases out the production of ozone-depleting chemicals.

In states where there are retrofit standards for pollution control equipment, we request subsidies for poor people so they may comply with the new standards.

Other important Congressional legislation includes:

(a) S 324, which establishes a national energy policy to reduce greenhouse gas emissions through conservation.

(b) HR 3299 and S 1750, budget reconciliation bills which also levy an excise tax on ozone depleting chemicals.

(c) S 1224, which requires new CAFE standards to reduce carbon dioxide emissions.

MINING

We call for the abrogation of the Mining Law of 1872. There should be stricter regulation for mineral entry. Operating mines should pay royalties on profits made on public lands, and set aside trust funds for the restoration of these lands.

FARMING

The Organic Farming Bills (HR 4156 and S 2108) are examples of good farming legislation. These bills establish national standards for and promote and strengthen the organic and sustainable farming industries.

SOLID WASTE & RECYCLING

We support a massive effort on the part of government and industry to develop clean technologies and to solve the immense problems of waste cleanup.

This should include zero-discharge recycling systems. These systems should maintain greenbelt, restored lakes, and grazing land. The funds to develop them should not be used as an excuse to suburbanize rural areas around cities.

In addition, we announce our support for building a comprehensive recycling infrastructure, and for the passage of laws requiring individuals and corporations to comply. We support grants and tax incentives for responsible corporations, and laws that punish behaviors not in harmony with the principle of interdependence.

We request immediate action on the CSO city sewers issue; of 1200 CSO systems in the nation, EPA has documented the need to fix or replace 328 of them at an estimated cost of $16.4 billion, with a total estimated cost for all 1200 being around $80 billion. These aging systems spread countless gallons of waste and sewage into our streams every time it rains; they increase cleanup and purification costs and are harmful to the streams, lakes, oceans and their inhabitants; it is time that we begin to address the problem.

BIODIVERSITY

We support the strengthening and strict enforcement of the protection provisions of the Endangered Species Act.

Specifically, we call for the protection of this nation's sky islands and unique gene pool areas. The Congress of the United States must protect the grizzlies of Yellowstone, the spotted owl of the Pacific Northwest, the Mount Graham red squirrel, the red cockaded woodpecker, and other threatened species. The ancient habitats that make their lives possible are equally important.

We acknowledge and appreciate the efforts of Starkist, Chicken-of-the-Sea, and Bumblebee Corporations for promising not to can tuna caught by methods that endanger dolphins.

We support Congressional Bill HR 1268, which establishes

biodiversity as a national goal and begins the process of implementing this goal.

POPULATION

We believe that the global carrying capacity—in terms of human numbers—has been reached. We support non-totalitarian encouragement of voluntary limitation of population growth. We support the right of abortion for women, seeing that this right is, in an ecological sense, truly pro-life.

EDUCATION

We urge a thorough course of environmental education for all grade levels to make new generations aware of their relationship with other beings on the planet.

OTHER AGENDA

We support the continuation of the moratorium on the killing of whales, new oil spill legislation, wilderness designation, toxic cleanup and coastal marine bills, restoration of wetlands and the establishment of marine sanctuaries such as in the Florida Keys.

CONCLUSION

We signatories, men and women, use our skills as writers and thinkers to awaken and arouse ourselves to the common peril we and all other sentient beings on the planet face. We invite citizens and workers in all fields to join in the common endeavor; whatever our visions of the future, our democracy and the nations of Earth should be steadfast and fierce in the quest to establish sustainable culture on this planet.

> July, 1990
> The Jack Kerouac School of Disembodied Poetics
> Boulder, Colorado

- ○ Antler
- ○ Jack Collom

- David Cope
- Victor Hernandez Cruz
- Rick Fields
- Lawrence Ferlinghetti
- Christopher Funkhouser
- Allen Ginsberg
- Eliot Greenspan
- Miguel Grinberg
- Anselm Hollo
- Mary Kean
- Joanne Kyger
- Lewis MacAdams
- Christina Nealson
- Jeff Poniewaz
- Joseph Richey
- Ed Sanders
- Andrew Schelling
- Gary Snyder
- Anne Waldman
- Peter Warshall

LETTER FROM ROBIN BLASER

21 August 1992

Dear Anne and Andrew,

I've failed to pull that twenty pages together in time for your purposes. I assure you I've tried—working, distractedly, a part of each day to shape that twenty from what was, as both of you noticed, a large work. No doubt, overprepared for those lectures there. My effort has been to draw together in those pages a persuasive, honest narrative of the cosmos I *called* for at the end of my last lecture, proposing a passage from Michael Serres—a cosmology to think of, as cosmogeny to stand in—among things. A thing—whatever that is—among things. (Anne, you and I spoke of the "call" in the work I did there.) This, for me, cannot be mere rhetoric, but may be imagined—as in historical consciousness *(poesis)* and our relations to it. And in this, my Naropa visit seemed wonderfully creative—and, in a complex way, decisive—as each day there—you may have noticed—I rewrote what I was *writing* for you. "By the seat of my pants," as Clayton delighted me in so describing my method (his strikes me as sure-footed—brilliant—in risky terrain—I hope those who attended think over those *first steps* beyond our animal selves, recorded in the depths of caves—uncomfortable imagination—and Artaud—recently in our midst—angel of extremities— "low-ghosts"—which are ours). *I do not like disappointing you,* and, so, write to ask if you could use something from me in a later issue?

I confess that I must stop now for a while. I returned from Boulder exhausted, yet carrying in my beautiful Naropa tote bag, so to speak, the good presence of having been there—rich in recognitions. *Exhaustion*—what is it? That may be explained to both of you? I worked to deadlines since last November: a long essay for the catalog of the Duncan exhibition at Berkeley U.C. Art Gallery, just published, handsomely; a public lecture on and reading of Duncan's work in Berkeley with much loved companion of these woods, Robert Creeley—in late February—a huge audience from the 1940's, joined by later, new readers and guardians; in the midst of this, my mother died, grief and stress, for me, clouding the occasion—from which I flew to family concerns in Twin Falls, Idaho, to be tolerated by the priests of the Requiem Mass and to stand there reading from a lectern assigned passages from Ezekiel and Timothy, the first a poet, both of them selected by *Christianism* to read as supernaturally moral—this stressed me out—in my distance; wrote, while still trying to shape my material for Naropa, a preface for the first volume of Duncan's *Collected* in seven volumes (U.C. Press)—stress that it would usefully lead from the works of 1946–1956 (Vol. I) towards the works of later volumes—Creeley has responded marvelously to what I tried to accomplish—haven't heard from Bertholf or McClung yet, so . . . ; and then, still working, I arrived among you—pushing my mind around the "stuff" I wanted to give Naropa—and, simultaneously, searching out a final form for *Bach's belief*, a piece for Olson's *Curriculum of the Soul*—to get it to Jack Clarke before he died—wherein I sadly failed—now, thinking daily of his companionship—

So, dear, dear Anne and Andrew, put simply, I must stop a bit—be silent and curious—thus I ask your forbearance in this matter—

How rich my return from Boulder was—weighted

with books by both of you—by Bobbie, Jerome, Diane, Kelly, Tarn,—mss. by David L-S—letters in the mail from Nathaniel and Rachel—important! for me—To which I'll now take time to turn—But how complex things be-came: the tape in my answering machine had run out, David having been in New Brunswick for his mother's 80th birthday—among those voices, one that said Jack Clarke was dead—Thus, a missing I must find a way to say—my letter couriered to Cass is not enough; requests from graduate students for letters as they hope to land rare jobs. . . . At the door, as I came up the steps, a huge box of Duncan's catalogues to sign and send—Rush!—to Virginia Admiral in New York; a courier envelope of contracts from Paris for Jack Spicer's *Billy the Kid*—a fine rock-n-roll performance by *Kat Onoma*—concerts, cassettes, and CD—many pages in tight legal French to be studied and signed in triplicate—the translation to be checked for quality of mind—all *Rush!*, of course. And the energy of my mind when John Cage died—wandering my city to find the day-old *New York Times* obituary. Did I mention to you while I was there that Olson's *Bach's belief* comes round to the supposition of Cage and Boulez?—for Olson, dating from August, 1951—an astonishing quar-rel over cosmogeny in musical language, which Olson, so to speak, stepped into—and I wind up writing of—ultimately for Jack Clarke—

I'll try to rest—before I become a scrambled egg—

Speaking of which, you could guess, though I was taken off guard, that the Republican convention—not mindless, but certainly vicious of mind—would become percussive in my mind's belief—embodied, as it must be, if we are to understand this empowerment of this most vicious Christianism—loose, many-headed, American horror that it is. Watch democracy become the shadow of our concern. And this, during the few days I'm trying to explain in terms of exhaustion, is joined by the Vatican advisory that it is acceptable to "discriminate" against homosexuals—in acceptance—in living quarters, in professions. What is *existentially given* is once again viciously attacked (just as I read it there in "Even on Sunday"). Now, you may well recognize another reason I have, especially, had to stop—in order to find my way. I *rage*. I sit here, writing you, fighting my rage. I wish to throw the trash of this tradition out. We've long stood in the empowerment of this anthropological fear and ignorance, which attracts all definitions of outsiders and outsidence. We've also lived long inside the humiliation of that tradition which merely transmogrifies—that is, becomes monstrous. The Arts have long been at the work of *transformation* within the *world explanation* that we had hoped was passing away—knew to be—.

I comfort myself, thinking of Montaigne—as I did there; *Embraces remembered (or still vaguely hoped for) are 'our final accolades.'* Studious walls surround the culturally broken heart of most things—given the work of—the writing of—the *alarum*. I open a letter from Rachel DuPlessis for the pleasure of companionship with her lovely mind—and find she's been reading *Pell Mell* most generously—to speak of the poetics there, so carefully recognized, "the practice of exact *coupure*"—"the wonder is like prayer." I'll begin there, again—

So, whatever, I'll send you something—a nevertheless, if you will have it—little late—that is, too late—

Love, Robin

P.S.

In the midst of this, a couple of goodnesses that might amuse you both—I explain to myself these gifts are due to something I carried back from our effort, Anne, to visit the Buddha's rooms and the temple downtown:

A former student stopped me on 4th Avenue and gave me a set of Tibetan prayer flags in each of the five colors we spoke of. He said, "You must promise to hang these outside—they'll bless the neighborhood." David and I searched for red silk rope, found some, and prayers are blowing in the wind—

The snow lion: I searched out the man it came from. He'd got TWO of them from an old Tibetan man and his wife. As he described this couple to me, they seemed to appear beside us. Their snow lions should not have been separated, they seemed to say. I gave the second one to David. They differ only in the symbols on the bottom-side of their bases. This difference I'll go about understanding. Now, they are side-by-side—large as three mountains, *as* Robert Kelly said—and so I greet them, *as* you taught me, Anne. *As* I continue—

Note: My hand and mind become nervous.

IND WRITING SLOGANS

"First thought is best in Art, second in other matters."

—William Blake

I GROUND (SITUATION, OR PRIMARY PERCEPTION)

1 "First Thought, Best Thought" —Chögyam Trungpa, Rinpoche
2 "Take a friendly attitude toward your thoughts." —Chögyam Trungpa, Rinpoche
3 "The Mind must be loose." —John Adams
4 "One perception must immediately and directly lead to a further perception." —Charles Olson, "Projective Verse"
5 "My writing is a picture of the mind moving." —Philip Whalen
6 Surprise Mind —Allen Ginsberg
7 "The Old pond, a frog jumps in, Kerplunk!" —Basho
8 "Magic is the total delight (appreciation) of chance."
   —Chögyam Trungpa, Rinpoche
9 "Do I contradict myself?
   Very well, I contradict myself.
   I am large. I contain multitudes."
   —Walt Whitman
10 ". . . What quality went to form a man of achievement, especially in literature? . . . Negative capability, that is, when a man is capable of being in uncertainties, mysteries, doubts, without any irritable reaching after fact & reason."
   —John Keats
11 "Form is never more than an extension of content."
   —Robert Creeley to Charles Olson
12 "Form follows function." —Frank Lloyd Wright
13 Ordinary Mind includes eternal perceptions. —A.G.
14 "Nothing is better for being Eternal
   Nor so white as the white that dies of a day."
   —Louis Zukofsky

15 Notice what you notice.—*A.G.*

16 Catch yourself thinking.—*A.G.*

17 Observe what's vivid.—*A.G.*

18 Vividness is self-selecting.—*A.G.*

19 "Spots of Time"—*William Wordsworth*

20 If we don't show anyone we're free to write anything.—*A.G.*

21 "My mind is open to itself."—*Gelek Rinpoche*

22 "Each on his bed spoke to himself alone, making no sound."—*Charles Reznikoff*

II PATH (METHOD OR RECOGNITION)

23 "No ideas but in things." ". . . No ideas but in the Facts."
—*William Carlos Williams*

24 "Close to the nose."—*W.C.Williams*

25 "Sight is where the eye hits."—*Louis Zukofsky*

26 "Clamp the mind down on objects."—*W.C.Williams*

27 "Direct treatment of the thing . . . (or object.)"
—*Ezra Pound, 1912*

28 "Presentation, not reference."—*Ezra Pound*

29 "Give me a for instance."—*Vernacular*

30 "Show not tell."—*Vernacular*

31 "The natural object is always the adequate symbol."
—*Ezra Pound*

32 "Things are symbols of themselves."—*Chögyam Trungpa, Rinpoche*

33 "Labor well the minute particulars, take care of the little
ones

He who would do good for another must do it in minute
particulars

General Good is the plea of the Scoundrel Hypocrite and
Flatterer

For Art & Science cannot exist but in minutely organized
particulars"
—*William Blake*

34 "And being old she put a skin/ on everything she said."
—*W.B. Yeats*

35 "Don't think of words when you stop but to see the picture
better."—*Jack Kerouac*

36 "Details are the Life of Prose."—*Jack Kerouac*

37 Intense fragments of spoken idiom, best.—*A.G.*

38 "Economy of Words"—*Ezra Pound*

39 "Tailoring"—*Gregory Corso*

40 Maximum information, minimum number of syllables.
—*A.G.*

41 Syntax condensed, sound is solid.—*A.G.*

42 Savor vowels, appreciate consonants.—*A.G.*

43 "Compose in the sequence of musical phrase, not in sequence of a metronome"—*Ezra Pound*

44 ". . . awareness . . . of the tone leading of the vowels."
—*Ezra Pound*

45 ". . . an attempt to approximate classical quantitative
meters . . ."—*Ezra Pound*

46 "Lower limit speech, upper limit song"—*Louis Zukofsky*

47 "Phanopoeia, Melopoeia, Logopoeia."—*Ezra Pound*

48 "Sight, Sound & Intellect."—*Louis Zukofsky*

49 "Only emotion objectified endures."—*Louis Zukofsky*

III FRUITION (RESULT OR APPRECIATION)

50 Spiritus = Breathing = Inspiration = Unobstructed Breath

51 "Alone with the Alone"—*Plotinus*

52 Sunyata (Skt.) = Ku (Japanese) = Emptiness

53 "What's the sound of one hand clapping?"—*Zen Koan*

54 "What's the face you had before you were born?"
—*Zen Koan*

55 Vipassana (Skt.) = Clear Seeing

56 "Stop the world"—*Carlos Casteneda*

57 "The purpose of art is to stop time."—*Bob Dylan*

58 "The unspeakable visions of the individual."—*J.K.*

59 "I'm going to try speaking some reckless words, and I want you to try to listen recklessly." —*Chuang Tzu, (Tr. Burton Watson)*

60 "Candor" —*Whitman*

61 "One touch of nature makes the whole world kin." —*W. Shakespeare*

62 "Contact" —*A Magazine, Nathaniel West & W.C. Williams, Eds.*

63 "God appears & God is Light
To those poor souls who dwell in Night.
But does a Human Form Display
To those who Dwell in Realms of day." —*W. Blake*

64 "Subject is known by what she sees." —*A.G.*

65 Others can measure their visions by what we see. —*A.G.*

66 Candor ends paranoia. —*A.G.*

67 "Willingness to be Fool." —*Chögyam Trungpa, Rinpoche*

68 "Day & Night / you're all right." —*Gregory Corso*

69 Tyger: "Humility is Beatness." —*Chögyam Trungpa, Rinpoche & A.G.*

70 Lion: "Surprise Mind" —*Chögyam Trungpa, Rinpoche & A.G.*

71 Garuda: "Crazy Wisdom Outrageousness" —*Chögyam Trungpa, Rinpoche*

72 Dragon: "Unborn Inscrutability" —*Chögyam Trungpa, Rinpoche*

73 "To be men not destroyers" —*Ezra Pound*

74 "Speech synchronizes mind & body" —*Chögyam Trungpa, Rinpoche*

75 "The Emperor unites Heaven & Earth" —*Chögyam Trungpa, Rinpoche*

76 "Poets are the unacknowledged legislators of the world" —*Shelley*

77 "Make it new" —*Ezra Pound*

78 "When the mode of music changes, the walls of the city shake" —*Plato*

79 "Every third thought shall be my grave" —*W. Shakespeare, The Tempest*

80 "That in black ink my love may still shine bright"
  —*W. Shakespeare, Sonnets*
81 "Only emotion endures"—*Ezra Pound*
82 "Well while I'm here I'll
            do the work—
and what's the Work?
      To ease the pain of living.
Everything else, drunken
            dumbshow."—*A.G.*
83 ". . . Kindness, sweetest
  of the small notes
  in the world's ache,
  most modest & gentle
  of the elements
  entered man before history
  and became his daily
  connection, let no man
  tell you otherwise."—*Carl Rakosi*

84 "To diminish the mass of human and sentient sufferings."
  —*Gelek Rinpoche*

Naropa Institute, July 1992
New York, 5 March 1993
New York, 27 June 1993

ROCKY FLATS: WARRING GOD CHARNEL GROUND

The word "charnel" derives from "carnal"—*in or of the flesh*. A charnel ground is a place where fleshly bodies are discarded after death, where vultures, jackals, ravens descend to feed upon the juicy raw meat, leaving bloodied severed limbs and bones strewn about. Heaps of bones pile up. The charnel ground is a cemetery, a highly visible bone-yard. It is the ritual spot where Tantric adepts perform the shamanic "chod," or "cutting" practice, that initiates them into the mysteries of death and birth. From a psychological point of view, the charnel ground is the state of mind in which birth and death occur simultaneously. It is a mental process of hope and desperation as well. You can't ignore it. As poet you can't ignore it. The realities of pain, sickness, grasping, death are demonstrated all the time. Hospitals are charnel grounds. The killing fields of Cambodia and Iraq are charnel grounds. Ravaged townships of South Africa are charnel grounds. Urban ghettoes are charnel grounds. The Pentagon is a god realm whose war mentality takes place on the charnel ground of the whole world. The stakes are so high, the weapons so deadly, that no corner of the planet, no form of life is exempt.

Northwest of Denver, Colorado and about eight miles south from Boulder, exists a deadly set-up, occupying a seventeen-mile perimeter of now radioactive land. This specter of death is built upon the neurotic energies of passion, ignorance, aggression, and manifests the fixation of one of the six Tibetan Buddhist realms of existence known as the "warring god realm." Rocky Flats Nuclear Weapons Plant was built on this psychology. Paranoia monitors this condition. Such a mind-set is enviably intelligent in its actions, in its skillful means. It even makes money. It will do anything to maintain its position. It will even create an hallucination of an enemy to maintain itself, perpetuating its aggression through a phantom fear. Rocky Flats remains toxic and perilous, despite the tide shifting towards closing down its nuclear trigger facilities. Nuclear waste will probably outlive our civilization.

ANNE WALDMAN

Rocky Flats was born on March 23, 1951. It was the first and only place for the manufacture of plutonium triggers (called "pits") for hydrogen bombs. Mass production of nuclear weapons was a new concept in 1951. The Los Alamos facility had served the research and production needs of U.S. nuclear development up until that time. In order to concentrate fully on research, the Atomic Energy Commission developed a complex of facilities across the nation to build nuclear weapons. Rocky Flats was chosen over thirty-five other sites. The Atomic Energy Commission originally contracted with Dow Chemical Corporation. This contract passed to Rockwell International in 1975. The Atomic Energy Commission handed the reins to the Energy Research & Development Administration and the Department of Energy replaced them in 1977. They've "managed" or you could say "mismanaged" the plant ever since. Its original cost was upwards of $250 million. U.S. taxpayers now spend $450 million each year to operate the plant. Rockwell International's work force grew to over 5,200 workers in Feb. 1988. Over 100 buildings occupy a site that began with what now seems like a modest 20 structures.

Rocky Flats has been the critical link in the nuclear weapons production chain. Until January 1992, it served two major purposes in the fabrication line: the manufacture of nuclear components for weapons and the reprocessing of obsolete and unreliable nuclear weapons. Rocky Flats imported plutonium, a heavy metallic element that is one of the heaviest known to man. Plutonium does not exist in nature, but is made by bombarding uranium with slow neutrons. Once created, it poses an ongoing threat to the health of many generations because it has a half life of 24,000 years. The DOE's nuclear reactors in Hanford, Washington, and Savannah River, South Carolina produce plutonium. Workers at these plants extracted plutonium from nuclear power plant fuel rods, concentrated it, formed it into ten-pound "buttons" and shipped it to Rocky Flats. Here the raw plutonium was machined into triggers. Rocky Flats workers then shipped the completed triggers by truck to the Pantex nuclear weapons facility in Amarillo, Texas where they were fashioned into finished weapons. Although an extraordinarily complex network, this process, this potential charnel ground of unprecedented rage, was a "smooth" operation for many years, a deadly *fait accompli. But was it really? The subtext was always a terrifying one.*

In spite of serious protests including continual bombardment from the Rocky Flats Truth Force with the likes of Daniel Ellsberg putting pressure on the madness, and occasional stoppages, the process continued functioning and flourishing. The process maintained its hallucination of enemy very well to justify its existence. And now it (we?) must de-activate what it (we? through a dumb complicity, ignorance?) have already created, nuclear weapons too obsolete for the next war. A huge process to de-process, de-possess. Gary Snyder's Zen teacher once said to him, "Become one with the knot itself, til it dissolves away. Sweep the garden. Any size." But what about the next war? The warring god realm mentality isn't easily conquered. It moves on toward next demonic form, knows no national boundaries, has no allegiance (it thinks it does, perhaps), even exists in us if you go deeply enough into your mind. Yet . . . Do I preach to the converted?

We need to meet demon plutonium head-on. Meet and understand the concept, the *words,* terms, implications that describe it. As I speak these words I scare myself. Numerous horrific—yet hidden—scandals over the years occurred at Rocky Flats. A few examples. A major explosion and fire took place on September 11, 1957 when about 40 pounds of plutonium burned in the blaze. No warning to local schools, neighboring cities, county commissioners, health agencies ensued. Seven days after the accident, reactive smoke-stack emissions were 16,000 times the radiation standard. Then an explosion in 1965 resulted in a worker's fingers having to be amputated. Twenty plutonium fires broke out in the late sixties. Radioactive cesium-137 was found in soil samples near the plant up to thirty-one times background levels. A 1969 fire was the most expensive U.S. industrial accident of its time, costing taxpayers $45 million to clean up.

Plutonium emits alpha particles. Skin effectively blocks alpha radiation from plutonium sources outside the body. But when plutonium enters the body by means of inhalation, or ingestion through food or drinking water, or through open wounds, the continuous emission of alpha particles can do extensive harm. Even though alpha particles only penetrate a small amount of tissue they carry enough predator energy to kill the cells they encounter and cause mutations that result in cancer. The amount of radiation given off at Rocky Flats does not remain constant but increases with time, *even after its plutonium trigger operations are shut down.* It is exceedingly difficult for the human system to flush out plutonium. Half of the original mass will remain in the body a century after its entry. "We'll all be glowing for a quarter of a million years" I sang in protest on Rocky Flats premises in 1976, and "mega mega mega mega death bomb—enlighten!" The discovery of high levels of plutonium in the gonads has led to studies of chromosome aberrations. One study shows that plutonium is ten times more effective in causing chromosome aberrations than in causing lung cancer. The tendency of plutonium to concentrate in the gonads means that chromosomal damage can be passed to the next generation. The charnel ground thus perpetuates itself by providing more flesh to feed upon. This is unconscionable. Some plutonium traceable to Rocky Flats by its isotopic composition has already been found in Loveland, thirty miles north of the plant.

Certain operations at Rocky Flats were shut down after the DOE sent nearly a hundred "G" men to investigate mismanagement allegations in 1989. One discovery was that sixty-two pounds of plutonium (enough to manufacture seven nuclear bombs) were lodged in the venting ducts at the plant. Such concentrations threaten a "criticality" or spontaneous nuclear chain reaction which could prove fatal to anyone nearby. To insure against criticality DOE and EG & G (then current owners) said they would remove 20 percent of the total. But is that enough? Hardly a consoling promise.

The U.S. nuclear arsenal today has over 20,000 nuclear weapons, with at least 10,000 of these being long-range strategic weapons designed for maximum accuracy and destructiveness. The Department of Energy plans to produce about 3,500 new nuclear weapons from fiscal year 1991 through fiscal year 1995. And these are proposed even *after* the Gulf crisis slaughter. Now that the Soviet Union has "broken down," every country will want the bomb. The United

States can be the chief seller & broker for this even "braver" new industry. The new catalogue of weapons includes:

B-61 tactical and strategic bombs for planes
B-83 strategic bombs for planes
W-80-1 advanced cruise missiles for bombers
W-80-0 Tomahawk submarine-launched cruise missiles
W-88 Trident II submarine-launched ballistic missiles (long-range)

among other weapons proposed for future production are:

W-61 Interim Earth Penetrator Warhead: to destroy underground command posts and shelters for political and military leaders
B-90 nuclear depth/strike bomb: to blow up submarines, surface warships, and bases anywhere along the coasts of Eastern Europe, the ex–Soviet Union or the Korean Peninsula.

When it looked as if Rocky Flats was set to reopen its plutonium processing operation in Fall of 1991 (although its safety was being fiercely contested at the time, especially after the FBI raid), I attended a town meeting as mother, teacher, poet, citizen. Where I voiced my concerns and quoted from my then-10-year-old son Ambrose's list for ways to guard plutonium, how in fact to *cover it up*. "Get some Indians to come back and make some adobe with ash to cover it up. Let's cover plutonium with all the cigarettes in the world. Let's cover it with linoleum, congoleum. Let's cover plutonium with wood chips that beavers have made." There was something sweet in the boy's innocence, his thinking that there could be a realistic way to bury the monster. I cited cancer statistics, the fact that Boulder has one of the highest incidences of breast cancer in the States, and of prostate cancer in the state of Colorado. I invoked the opinions of reputable surgeons, including my own, who have said the truth about Rocky Flats operations' cancerous effects will *emerge a decade from now*, too late for the health of many local residents. That there is clear documentation of health risks and cancer statistics from former workers and residents in the area. That there are documentations & photographs of mutated animals born on nearby farms. Sheep with three legs and no hair. Just one example. I said all these things.

I was hissed and booed. The meeting was stacked with workers from the plant itself who made speeches justifying the reopening of the plutonium operations wing as a deterrent to war, as an "operation of peace," as needed more than ever after the war in the Middle East. There were testimonies about the plant providing a decent living for Americans who believed in god and their country. That Rocky Flats was a symbol of American democracy and prowess and dignity. That Rocky Flats had helped America "win the Cold War." My mind was spinning. What could I do as person working with words?

I want to be able to crack the code of language that separates us:me from the warmonger. I want to dance in the charnel ground like the nimble-footed *cittipatti* skeletons in the tantric tradition as a warning and a transmutation. This is a practice of attention. For the last five years I have been working on a long poem that proposes to "take on" male energy. I write songs to "call out" the demons. I study lists of tactical weapons. The poems and songs I write live inside images of war and destruction on every level. They attempt to transmute—through language—the warring god realm. They also take me to the town meeting and to the edges of the mandala, which is a ring of fire on the one hand threatening all of space, and on the other burning up false mindviews which threaten annihilation of the relative space—world. I conjure the holy fire, the sacred *chandali* in which one throws in past, all conceptions: god, mother-country, lover, tomahawk cruise missiles, depth/strike bombs. Give up grasping, give up hope, then *wake* to the dangers to our fleshly bodies and body-planet. Shut down Rocky Flats. Shut down all the Rocky Flats the world over. Then guard them well. Don't create more cancerous limbs to be eaten by jackals.

The Department of Energy deems the next years of dismantling Rocky Flats plutonium war-triggers operations a "transition period."

Literally "tons" of plutonium spread throughout several buildings must be consolidated into a smaller area, and then "cleaned up." "Control, management & removal of materials & wastes" is top priority according to the plan submitted July 31, 1992 to Congress from the DOE which describes how the factory will be converted from a weapons-producing complex to an environmental cleanup & economic development project. "Materials" include radioactive substances, classified documents, tools and so on. Under Rockwell's management Rocky Flats had a cottage industry in one of its basements which turned out souvenirs for retiring employees, other mementos extolling nuclear power that were part of glad-handing deals. A purported million dollar a year industry.

Watching & waiting. Articulate the fear, it's a given, it's already happened, Rocky Flats, spurred on by Pentagon directive paranoia has already leashed its havoc on the world. We created this poetics school as an antidote, an antithesis to the going concerns. But then we take them on again, again. Rocky Flats a scant 10 miles away. You can feel the pulse & throb late at night. What poison creeps into your groin, your breast. Turn it around. Guard well. Hundreds of years project, at least.

In the gap of the flames you might find an empty luminous nuclear-free world, humming with beautiful fierce sounds out of which you take your stand, make your poem. *May all beings enjoy profound, brilliant glory.*

JULY 1992, THE JACK KEROUAC SCHOOL OF DISEMBODIED POETICS
With thanks to the Rocky Mountain Peace Center and information provided by Marcia Klotz.

Update:

A memo labelled "Ticking Timebombs" was written by R. J. Ballenger, manager of residue-treatment technology for EG & G Corp., the successor to Rockwell at Rocky Flats (now departing), on September 24, 1992. It describes how substantial amounts of plutonium are still being stored in unstable condition or in potentially unsafe containers and are inadequately protected against fire. This memo comes nearly three years after the plant was shut down for environmental and safety problems. It should be noted here too, that in the spring of 1992, Rockwell International Corp. pleaded guilty to five felonies and five misdemeanor violations of federal environmental law and agreed to pay a fine of $18.5 million, the second largest penalty ever assessed against a U. S. corporation, after the Exxon Valdez oil spill. Members of a special grand jury that heard evidence in the case say now that they had wanted to indict individual employees of Rockwell and the Department of Energy, but were rebuffed by federal prosecutors. They claim that the DOE, its contractors and employees perpetuated an "ongoing criminal enterprise" at the plant, by continuing to violate federal laws. The prosecutors and the lead FBI agent from the 1989 raid, have been subpoenaed by an Investigations Subcommittee of the House Committee on Science, Space and Technology, to review the Justice Department's handling of the case.

Further Update Spring 1994:

Recent information has confirmed the fact that during the two fires at Rocky Flats in 1957 and 1969, most of the plutonium was kept "on site." However, in the late sixties when barrels containing plutonium-laced oil were moved from 903 Pad, an outdoor storage site at the plant's east side, plutonium *did* escape. Most of the air-borne contaminants were blown to the east and southeast of the plant. (Boulder is eight miles north of the plant.) Evidently the problem is decades old, back to the time when the plant first started processing plutonium, using oil to cool and lubricate the machines. Carbon tetrachloride was used to clean the machines. The resulting mixture—oil contaminated with plutonium and mixed with carbon tetrachloride—was stored in thirty- and fifty-five-gallon steel drums on a dirt area outside. No other site would accept the waste for burial.

More than 5,000 barrels contained a total of 250,000 gallons of the poisoned mixture. The mixture, as it turns out, was quite corrosive. After a time the barrels began to leak and the contents poured into the soil. Scientists speculate that two to three ounces of plutonium leaked into the soil. In the late sixties the plant began cleaning up the mess, but moving the barrels generated a lot of disturbance. Some of the people who witnessed the cleanup said the work had to be stopped "because the dust was so intense." Scientists estimate that approximately one ounce of plutonium was suspended by wind and moved off site. This has certainly increased the odds of getting cancer, according to the radiation control division of the Colorado Department of Health.

Additionally, the Defense Nuclear Facilities Safety Board has even more recently warned Energy Secretary Hazel O'Leary that there is a high probability of plutonium fire unless the storage method for plutonium at the site is changed. In a May 26, 1994, letter to the secretary, Board Chairman John T. Conway said plutonium-laden products and other chemical wastes stored together in sealed containers could react, heat up, and cause a fire. There are evidently thousands of containers of plutonium-bearing liquids and solids, as well as plastic, coming in contact with the plutonium in the containers. The safety board is particularly concerned about the button-shaped five-pound ingots whose short-term storage consisted of being wrapped in polyethylene liners and then being placed in containers the size of tuna-fish cans. These were then stored in larger plastic containers. "It is well known that plutonium in contact with plastic can cause formation of hydrogen gas and pyrophoric plutonium compounds leading to a high probability of plutonium fires." Rocky Flats plant officials acknowledge that current plutonium-packaging methods are not suitable for long-term storage, but claim they are in the process of transferring the dread poison to more appropriate containers. They claim, too, that the plutonium is stored in areas with heat detectors and that "the stored plutonium has never set off the detectors." What has mankind wrought? How do we sleep at night? There is currently still no facility in the country capable of storing Rocky Flats plutonium for the estimated 240,000 years it will remain a threat to human health.

Anne Waldman

THE NOMAD TENT

*From the concluding symposium to "The Other North
America," a month-long countercelebration to the
so-called discovery of North America by Christopher
Columbus. The panel took place in July 1992, under
the Jack Kerouac School's summer nomad tent. At the
time of this symposium, coach Bill McCartney of the
University of Colorado's football team was cheerlead-
ing 25,000 young Christian men in an affirmation of
"family values." Their cries of "Jee-sus, Jee-sus," sifting
upwards from Folsom Stadium which sits on the bluff
above Naropa, lifted eerily behind the Kerouac
School's gathering—a gathering which included
anarchists, feminists, pacifists, communists, antinomi-
ans, Blacks, Hispanics, Native Americans, Jews, homosexuals, Buddhists, Sufis, and punk rock singers.*

Welcome—or farewell. To what, or from where? Is the Other North
America a place? a time? a state of mind? Or somehow all three?

Each summer a mirage-like, carnivalesque nomad tent gets
pitched on these lawns, under the great Colorado shade trees—
cottonwood and sycamore—and for a month transfigures the
underlying piece of earth. Two hundred people from across North
America—some from further abroad—approach along the surrounding roadways and gather here to form an *akademi,* an "oak
grove," a literal *grove of trees,* where people wander about talking
to one another, or sit swapping poems and philosophies.

It lasts for four weeks. The *akademi* is temporary, provisional—a
nomad market—a flash of lightning over the mountains or a magic
lantern flicker. Yet it's real, an autonomous zone where we work with
our proudest treasure, Language, to make—not make but *affirm*—
the Other North America. The many "other" north americas.

What's it about? This week Amiri Baraka passed on a few words
Thelonius Monk gave an inquirer about jazz: "It's about freedom,
beyond that it gets complicated."

And it is complicated, maybe *intric*ated is a clearer word. All the complex, intricate weavings of talk; the ideas, conflicts, insights; the humor, anger, frustration, boredom that goes down when several hundred people gather, set up shop, and trade in language for a month. Whatever happens happens in the relationships, in the interstices—that's why I call this a nomad tent. Nomads are people of the interstices, of border crossings and unclaimed territories, of interzones and places in between. That's why we spend a month building things out of speech and writing—our profoundest interstice is language. Language occurs between us, it's always on the hoof.

So, to peer deeply into the words as they pass and discern the stories each comes freighted with. To listen to epics and ballads, battles and conquests that rise like smoke from our mouths. I watch with fear and amusement as on this continent one state government after another attempts to institute as its legal language what they quaintly call *English*—to make it the sole language used in the schools, at the voting polls, in the courtroom. Fear because—but do I need to speak of the painfully outdated agenda that underlies this effort—? something we've seen far too much of in our lifetimes—?

So I'll say why it's amusing. They are trying to legislate a stormcloud. English, or American English, is a windblown document, a swirling nomad tongue. Put your ear close to it and listen: it is a thousand songs of exile, immigration, invasion, abduction, invention. Of curiosity and grief. It is a trail of tears, and the journey continues. What was it Levi said of Robert Duncan's teaching? That he realized, *we were being given maps for further study*. Our language works the same way. This is what brings writers back to it again and again—it gives us *maps* for further study. Maps that lead us to where we are. Have any among us learnt to hear past the words, to sound out the territory? To conjure a real place from vaporous sound?

Where are we then, where is Naropa? What's our *address*?

> ***The:*** old irreducible Anglo-Saxon article
> written with an archaic cipher *thorn*
> now vanished from
> our inscriptions—

the only *English* word
            this address holds
if by English you mean the aboriginal tongue
spoken in England: *Angelond*
            by the old *Angelcynn* the
            'race of Angles'

Naropa: N. Indian scholar, yogin, lineage holder
            in Nyingma-pa Buddhism (Tibet),
former abbot of the great
            Nalanda Buddhist University
ruins can be seen in present-day Bihar State, India.
The name conjures the delicate efflorescence of Buddhism
            throughout Asia—
            as well as present grief
exile and genocide of Tibetan peoples
            scattered across the planet

Institute: Out of Latin by way of Old French—
            to establish, ordain, arrange.
            an enactment of sovereign authority.
            as today in the face
            of unprincipaled governments
                        we collect to affirm our own
                        sovereignty

2130: Arabic numerals
the Moorish expansion into Europe
Oriental sciences
            mathematics
the *zero* a gift of traders from India,
            a nothing the Greeks and Romans
            never had

Arapahoe: Pawnee *Lirapahu*
"traders"
ghost cry of a native peoples
largely

vanished from these grounds
ancestral names return
to our lips each time we recite
        the address we should weep
at their absence
the old ones

Avenue: Latin *ad-venire*
to approach, to come to—
Oh iron and empire!
the forcing of roads
        a literal entry to this land

Boulder: water tumblings
        and glacial erratics,
tectonic plates lifted—
        place-name following eye's perception.
        Old Scandinavian
        akin to modern Swedish *bulderstajn*
stone that causes a
        rumbling noise in water
        boulder: *buller:* rumble
deposited in the language
by Scandinavian invasions
        attack and plunder of the
Anglo peoples—
        conjuring:

Colorado: Spanish, *red color*
noting description of place,
Iberian horseback marauders
        like Scandinavian predecessors
out looking for gold
        themselves now departed
a handful of words
        on the trail—

This is where we are.

The postal address of The Naropa Institute is a collection of old words, a bundle of names and numbers that conjure terrible travels. Today we are here, and in the blink of an eye it will vanish. Monday morning a work crew will arrive, fold up the chairs, dismantle our tent, and cart the whole show away. A brown trodden patch of grass in desperate need of water and sunlight will be all that remains—scar of a wizard's festival. A holy marketplace where thought and counterthought raged.

But are we nomads, endlessly scattered? Does everything depart with the tent? Or are we prepared in some way to belong, to take up residence and inhabit this ground?

Last night several dozen people gathered to consecrate the little clapboard building that houses our Summer Writing Office. For the final years of his life Harry Smith—musicologist, filmmaker, poet, shamanic presence, teacher to many—lived in those rooms, thanks to a Grateful Dead grant. At midnight we held a little ceremony in his honor, about forty people smoking grass, swaying and singing an impromptu blues while Allen played the harmonium. Peter Cole affixed to the building a splendid bronze plaque he'd prepared. Around its borders he'd mounted tendrils, a roach-clip, a lizard. Within—

> *Cosmographer*
> *Harry Smith*
> *Lived Here*
> *Sep '88—Feb '91*

A first step. To make this piece of turf more than a place where nomads mill about before shoving on. To see friends, fellow thinkers and writers, as ancestral presences that make the place sacred. And know they lived out their lives here. *The dead are not dead.* Presences, animating the grounds and the buildings. This year we will be moving a letter-press print shop into Harry's old quarters. To further naturalize ourselves—to bring ourselves home. To this, our speech; and this, our land.

One year will we look back in wonder, and find we've become residents of both?

25 July 1992

CONTRIBUTORS

AMIRI BARAKA'S books of poetry include *The Dead Lecturer, Black Magic Poetry,* and *Reggae or Not;* fiction includes *The System of Dante's Hell* and *Tales.* He has written extensively on Black music and social issues. In 1991, *The Leroi Jones/Amiri Baraka Reader* was published. He has taught at Columbia University, San Francisco State, Yale University, and was director of African Studies at the State University of New York at Stony Brook.

ROBIN BLASER, born in Denver in 1925, was an illuminatus of the San Francisco Renaissance. His major collection of poetry, *The Holy Forest,* which gathers the ongoing work called *Image-Nations,* as well as *Pell Mell* and *Syntax,* was published in 1993 by Coach House Press. Mr. Blaser, professor emeritus at Simon Fraser University in Vancouver, British Columbia, is at work on *Astonishments,* a book of essays.

WILLIAM S BURROUGHS'S numerous books include the now-legendary *Naked Lunch,* which helped pioneer experimental prose based on the cut-up. His recent works include a trilogy— *Cities of the Red Night, The Place of Dead Roads, The Western Lands*—and *The Cat Inside.* Mr. Burroughs, currently living in Lawrence, Kansas, is a member of the American Institute of Arts and Letters and a long-time adjunct faculty member of the Writing and Poetics program at The Naropa Institute.

JACK COLLOM'S collections of poetry include *The Fox, Ice, Little Grand Island,* and *Blue Heron & IBC. Moving Windows,* a book about children's poetry, is based on his "Poetry in the Schools" work from 1974 to the present. He has taught at the Naropa Institute for almost a decade, and was awarded another NEA fellowship in poetry in 1980. His recent books are *Arguing With Something Plato Said* and *8-Ball.*

CLARK COOLIDGE, spelunker, jazz drummer, poet extraordinaire, is a regular visitor to The Naropa Institute. He has performed his work across the U. S. and Europe, and is a contributing editor to *Sulfur.* Books include *Space, American Ones, The Crystal Text,*

At Egypt, Solution Passage, The Maintains and the eroto/porno-graphic novella The Book of During.

RIKKI DUCORNET is a novelist, poet and illustrator. Dalkey Archives is publishing her tetralogy of novels which includes The Fountains of Neptune and The Jade Cabinet, which was nominated for a National Book Critic's Circle Award in 1993. Her short fiction is collected in The Complete Butcher's Tales. She recently received a Lannan Foundation fellowship.

ALLEN GINSBERG is the author of numerous books including Howl, Kaddish, Planet News, The Fall of America, Mind Breaths, and Plutonium Ode: Poems 1977–1980. He is a Guggenheim fellow and a member of both the American Institute of Arts and Letters and the American Academy of Arts and Sciences. Recent books include Collected Poems, White Shroud, Annotated Notes to "Howl" and Cosmopolitan Greetings. He is on the faculty of Brooklyn College, and is co-founder with Anne Waldman of the Jack Kerouac School of Disembodied Poetics where he teaches each summer.

BOBBIE LOUISE HAWKINS has written ten books of fiction, non-fiction, poetry, and performance monologue. These include My Own Alphabet, Frenchy and Cuban Pete, and most recently, The Sanguine Breast of Margaret. She is on the core faculty at The Naropa Institute and oversees the prose fiction track.

LYN HEJINIAN, a resident of Berkeley, teaches on the poetics faculty at New College of California. For eight years she published the seminal Tuumba Press series and is currently co-editor with Barrett Watten of Poetics Journal. Books include Writing is an Aid to Memory, My Life, The Cell, and Oxota: A Short Russian Novel. She has traveled extensively and lectured in the USSR, and in 1990 published Description, a translation of Russian poet Arkadii Dragomoshchenko's verse.

ANSELM HOLLO, a native of Helsinki, Finland, has lived and worked as a poet, translator, editor, journalist, and teacher in many countries. Living since 1967 in the United States, he is the recipient of an NEA fellowship in poetry and two translation prizes from the American-Scandinavian Foundation in New York. Recent books of poetry include Outlying Districts, Near Miss Haiku, and Space

Baltic: the Science Fiction Poems 1962–1987. Translations include works by Swedish novelist Lennart Hagerfors, Austrian biographer Peter Stephen Jungk, and Finland's poet laureate, Paavo Haavikko. Mr. Hollo is an Associate Professor in the Writing & Poetics Program at The Naropa Institute.

SUSAN HOWE is the author of a dozen books of poetry including *The Europe of Trusts, Singularities* and *The Nonconformist's Memorial.* She has written an acclaimed study of American poetics, *My Emily Dickinson,* and Wesleyan University Press has just brought out a book of essays, *BIRTH-MARK: Unsettling the Wilderness in American History.* She is a professor of English at SUNY Buffalo.

NATHANIEL MACKEY teaches literature at the University of California, Santa Cruz, and edits the magazine *Hambone.* He is the author of several books of poetry including *Eroding Witness* and *School of Udra,* and two volumes of prose, *Bedouin Hornbook* and *Dijbot Baghostus's Run,* from the ongoing work *From a Broken Bottle Traces of Perfume Still Emanate.*

BERNADETTE MAYER is the author of many books of poetry and experimental prose including *Memory, Studying Hunger, The Golden Book of Words* and *Utopia.* Her most recent book is *The Bernadette Mayer Reader,* published by New Directions. She is a former Director/Artist-in-Residence of the celebrated Poetry Project at St. Marks Church in New York City. Ms. Mayer works for the New School for Social Research, the St. Mark's Poetry Project, Random House, Praeger Social Sciences, Zone Press, Grove Press, and other non-profit groups.

ALICE NOTLEY is the author of more than fifteen volumes of poetry and prose, including *Margaret & Dusty, At Night the States,* and with Douglas Oliver, *The Scarlet Cabinet.* A playwright, collagist, and teacher, she co-edits the magazine *Scarlet* with Douglas Oliver. Ms. Notley is the recipient of an NEA grant, a Poetry Center Award, and two grants from The Fund for Poetry. She currently lives in Paris.

RANDY ROARK received his M.F.A. in 1991 from the Naropa Institute. From 1982 to 1985 he published and edited the magazine *Friction.* He has lectured at The Naropa Institute and is currently transcribing Allen Ginsberg's lectures and classes from The Kerouac School. He is the author of *Or a Kind of Sophia, History Poems 1990–1994.*

ED SANDERS has a personal history that spans a dozen mini-careers, from classics scholar to mystic-militant peace-and-love activist, from investigative reporter to rock 'n' roll star, from bohemian publisher and bookstore entrepreneur to utopian environmentalist and consumer advocate. He has published fiction, poetry, and non-fiction, including *The Family,* a bestseller about the Charles Manson cult, and *Thirsting for Peace in a Raging Century,* a collection of several decades of poetry. Most recently published is *Murder By Water: A Tale of Great Violence, Organized Crime & Trash.*

LESLIE SCALAPINO received the Before Columbus Foundation's American Book Award, San Francisco State University's Poetry Center Award, and the Lawrence Lipton Prize for her book of poetry, *way. How Phenomena Appear to Unfold* is a collection of essays and poems that are also plays. A trilogy of three "novels," *The Return of Painting, The Pearl,* and *Orion,* was her most recent of three books from North Point Press. Scalapino lives in Oakland, California where she edits and publishes O Books.

ANDREW SCHELLING is Co-Chair of the Jack Kerouac School at The Naropa Institute. Traveler, poet, translator, amateur anthropologist, and scholar of the cultures and poetries of Asia, his translations from classical Sanskrit, *Dropping the Bow: Poems from Ancient India,* won the Academy of American Poets Prize for Translation in 1992. Collections of poetry and translation include *Claw Moraine, Moon is a Piece of Tea,* and *Old Growth.* O Books brought out his collection of essays, *The India Book,* in 1993.

DAVID LEVI STRAUSS writes on art, poetics, and the politics of culture. Since 1982 he has edited *ACTS: A Journal of New Writing.* An ongoing fictive correspondence in word & image, *Odile & Odette,* written in the Yucatan and Chiapas, Berlin, Cuba, and Russia, is being prepared for publication, as is a book on photography, *The Radical Image,* and a book of speculative criticism, *Godard: Beuys: Pasolini: Warhol.*

NATHANIEL TARN was born in Paris and educated at Cambridge, the Sorbonne, and the Universities of Chicago and London. He moved to the U. S. in 1967 where he taught at several universities, retiring from Rutgers as Distinguished Professor of Comparative Literature. His poetry, translations, and essays have been published in some twenty books and booklets. Recent books include a collection of poetry, *Seeing America First,* and a gathering of anthropological and poetic essays, *Views From the Weaving Mountain.*

LORENZO THOMAS, a poet and critic, has published studies on African-American literature and music in *Callaloo, Black Nation, Blues Unlimited, Living Blues,* and elsewhere. Coauthor of *Blues Music in Arkansas,* his collections of poetry include *Chances Are Few* and *The Bathers.* He teaches at the University of Houston, Downtown.

ANNE WALDMAN, poet, teacher, performer, editor, arts administrator, is the author of over thirty books and pamphlets of poetry, including, most recently, *Helping the Dreamer, Not A Male Pseudonym, Iovis* and *Kill or Cure.* She has also edited several anthologies of writing including *Out of this World,* from the St. Mark's Poetry Project which she directed for over a decade, and *Nice to See You: Homage to Ted Berrigan.* She is cofounder with Allen Ginsberg of the Writing and Poetics program at the Naropa Institute, and is the current Director. She serves as an adjunct faculty member at the Institute of American Indian Arts in Santa Fe, and has been a long time student of Buddhism, travelling to India and Nepal since 1970.

PETER WARSHALL earned a B.A. in biology and a Ph.D. in biological anthropology from Harvard University. He studied cultural anthropology under Claude Lévi-Strauss at L'Ecole Pratique des Hautes Etudes in 1966 and 1967. Dr. Warshall has served in public office as a contributor to environmental research, and been a consultant to the U.N. and to USAID on ecology and economic development.

PHILIP WHALEN is Abbot of the Hartford Street Zen Center in San Francisco. Collections of his numerous books of poetry include *On Bear's Head* and *Heavy Breathing.* Books of prose include *The Diamond Noodle, Two Novels,* and *Off the Wall: Interviews with Philip Whalen.*

PETER LAMBORN WILSON lived for 10 years in Iran and India, and has written extensively on Sufism, Persian literature, and Middle Eastern religion. His latest works on these subjects are *Scandal: Essays in Islamic Heresy* (Autonomedia) and *Sacred Drift: Essays on the Margins of Islam* (City Lights). He is an associate editor of *Semiotext(e)* magazine. He also serves as "vice"-president of the Libertarian Book Club, North America's oldest (1949) anarchist (dis)organization.